Reimagining Historic House Museums

AASLH

AMERICAN ASSOCIATION
FOR STATE AND LOCAL HISTORY

ABOUT THE SERIES

The American Association for State and Local History Book Series addresses issues critical to the field of state and local history through interpretive, intellectual, scholarly, and educational texts. To submit a proposal or manuscript to the series, please request proposal guidelines from AASLH headquarters: AASLH Editorial Board, 2021 21st Ave. South, Suite 320, Nashville, Tennessee 37212. Telephone: (615) 320-3203. Website: www.aaslh.org.

ABOUT THE ORGANIZATION

The American Association for State and Local History (AASLH) is a national history membership association headquartered in Nashville, Tennessee, that provides leadership and support for its members who preserve and interpret state and local history in order to make the past more meaningful to all people. AASLH members are leaders in preserving, researching, and interpreting traces of the American past to connect the people, thoughts, and events of yesterday with the creative memories and abiding concerns of people, communities, and our nation today. In addition to sponsorship of this book series, AASLH publishes *History News* magazine, a newsletter, technical leaflets and reports, and other materials; confers prizes and awards in recognition of outstanding achievement in the field; supports a broad education program and other activities designed to help members work more effectively; and advocates on behalf of the discipline of history. To join AASLH, go to www.aaslh.org or contact Membership Services, AASLH, 2021 21st Ave. South, Suite 320, Nashville, TN 37212.

Reimagining Historic House Museums

New Approaches and Proven Solutions

Edited by
Kenneth C. Turino and Max A. van Balgooy

ROWMAN & LITTLEFIELD
Lanham • Boulder • New York • London

Published by Rowman & Littlefield
A wholly owned subsidiary of The Rowman & Littlefield Publishing Group, Inc.
4501 Forbes Boulevard, Suite 200, Lanham, Maryland 20706
www.rowman.com

6 Tinworth Street, London SE11 5AL, United Kingdom

The editors and publishers are grateful to the following people and institutions for photographs:

Will Brown, courtesy of Stenton; Marjory Collins, Library of Congress; Chris Ferenzi Photography; Grant Cottage State Historic Site; Bruce Guthrie; Carol M. Highsmith, Jon B. Lovelace Collection of California Photographs, Library of Congress; Historic New England; Laura Keim, courtesy of Stenton; Robert Kiihne; Daniel Nystedt; Martin Van Buren National Historic Site; Molly Brown House Museum; Old World Wisconsin; Paul Revere Memorial Association; Ron Potvin; Strawbery Banke Museum; Trustees Archives and Research Center; Max A. van Balgooy; and Thomas A. Woods.

British Library Cataloguing in Publication Information Available

Library of Congress Cataloging-in-Publication Data
Names: Turino, Kenneth, editor. | Balgooy, Max van, editor.
Title: Reimagining historic house museums : new approaches and proven
   solutions / edited by Kenneth C. Turino and Max A. van Balgooy.
Description: Lanham : Rowman & Littlefield, 2019. | Series: American
   Association for State and Local History book series | Includes
   bibliographical references and index.
Identifiers: LCCN 2019021241 (print) | LCCN 2019022164 (ebook) | ISBN
   9781442272972 (cloth : alk. paper) | ISBN 9781442272989 (pbk. : alk.
   paper)
Subjects: LCSH: Historic house museums—Interpretive programs—United
   States. | Museum visitors—United States—Services for.
Classification: LCC E159 .R45 2019 (print) | LCC E159 (ebook) | DDC
   907.4—dc23
LC record available at https://lccn.loc.gov/2019021241
LC ebook record available at https://lccn.loc.gov/2019022164

♾️™ The paper used in this publication meets the minimum requirements of American National Standard for Information Sciences—Permanence of Paper for Printed Library Materials, ANSI/NISO Z39.48-1992.

Contents

Introduction

KENNETH C. TURINO AND MAX A. VAN BALGOOY

Are there too many historic house museums, too few, or too many of the same kind?

That's been one of the biggest debates in the museum and historic preservation field for the last seventeen years, sparked by Richard Moe, president of the National Trust for Historic Preservation.[1] In 2002, he observed that house museums all across the United States "are barely getting by" due to chronic underfunding, an extensive backlog of deferred maintenance, and difficulty in attracting or retaining qualified professional staff. To address these issues, the National Trust convened a symposium at Kykuit in partnership with the American Association for State and Local History (AASLH).[2] The gathering questioned common assumptions, traditional approaches, and the consequences of professionalization. The participants concluded that house museums can be emotionally powerful settings that contribute to the stability, pride, and sense of place of their communities but seemed to be stuck in a rut and needed to move beyond the one-size-fits-all approach. Solutions included becoming more relevant to the surrounding community, working collaboratively with nearby museums, recognizing that interpretation should evolve, and taking advantage of modern planning and evaluation tools. They also agreed that converting a historic site into a museum may not be its best use and that more money doesn't necessarily result in a better house museum.

The conversation continued at conferences, in articles, blogs, classes, books, workshops, and within museums. Indeed, this book is a result of the conference *How Are Historic House Museums Adapting for the Future?* sponsored by the Historic House Museum Consortium of Washington, DC, and the Virginia Association of Museums at Gunston Hall Plantation in Virginia on March 15, 2014. We had been invited to give presentations to the 120 participants and saw that historic site practitioners and their boards recognized that the world of historic houses has changed dramatically but weren't sure how to go about reimagining or reinventing themselves.

With the support of AASLH and local funders, we embarked on a series of workshops in subsequent years to lay out a "reinventing process" that has taken us to Missouri, New Hampshire, Vermont, Kansas, Pennsylvania, Wisconsin, and Illinois with more to come. The one-day workshop, *Reinventing the Historic House Museum*, includes an analysis of the most important opportunities and threats facing historic sites in the United States based on the latest social and economic research, with a discussion on how they may relate to the participants' house museum. We share a series of field-tested tools and techniques drawn from such wide-ranging sources as nonprofit management, business strategy, and software development. Drawing from innovative organizations, we profile historic sites that are using new models to engage with their communities to become more relevant, are adopting creative forms of interpretation and programming, and earning income to become more financially sustainable. A key component of the workshop is a facilitated brainstorming session to reinvent an event or program. Working with an actual house museum not only puts theory into practice but demonstrates the value of multiple perspectives for analysis. Indeed, the workshops have been incredibly helpful to the host sites, who serve as the case study for the brainstorming session:

> *Reinventing the Historic House Museum* sparked many great ideas on how we can use our historic homes in dynamic, innovative ways. Since attending the workshop, we have implemented many changes, including a new self-guided tour with interactive elements that have increased our attendance and engaged the public in brand new ways.
>
> —Sarah Bader-King, Director of Public Programming & Events,
> Wornall/Majors House Museums, Kansas City, Missouri

> *Reinventing the Historic House Museum* helped us visualize how the Margaret Mitchell House could connect with the community around us. While the site was very popular with tourists, we were hidden in plain sight from our own community. Our goal was to discuss the challenges we faced and to pursue practical solutions. The workshop allowed us to collaborate with area professionals and hear from colleagues facing similar challenges. We left the workshop with good ideas and a commitment to reimagine our site. As a result of that work, we have increased visibility in the community, created programming relevant to the neighborhood, and are partnering with area organizations to become a community resource and connector.
>
> Jessica Van Landuyt, Director of 20th Century Houses,
> Atlanta History Center, Atlanta, Georgia

The workshop is so packed with information that we quickly run out of time before we've reached the end of the agenda. So many house museums provide excellent examples of reinvigoration and so many useful techniques are available that we can touch on only a few of them in a day. Despite our ongoing efforts to take this workshop across the country, it is often sold-out, and many small sites cannot afford to attend. This book helps fill these gaps.

Consider this book as a combination of a museum conference, a hands-on workshop, and toolbox filled with ideas that tips the scales at more than one hundred thousand words. The book is intended as a guide for house museum boards, directors, and staff seeking a path forward in rapidly changing times. Graduate programs in public history, museum studies, curatorial studies, and historic preservation will discover chapters that will provoke lively discussions about the issues facing the field. We initially planned on a shorter book, but the issues we wanted to explore and number of contributors grew. Max van Balgooy opens by describing a reinventing process adapting techniques from other fields, which is followed by five parts:

1. Fundamentals and Essentials lays out the basic building blocks that provide a stable foundation for success. It's nearly impossible to launch a reinvention process if the board is suffering

from in-fighting, a lack of basic support, or uncertainty about the organization's purpose or goals. This section identifies the basic building blocks that provide a stable foundation for success and provides advice on what museum should know, do, or have ready to begin to reimagine themselves.

2. Audiences are often a major driver of the rethinking process because it causes the organization's focus to shift from its needs to the community's. To avoid a one-size-fits-all approach, programs should be crafted to meet the needs of various audiences. Part 2 discusses some of the major audiences for house museums as well as general advice on engagement. Contributors grapple with such questions as: How should house museums think about their audiences differently? Are the traditional demographic categories still useful? Why do people visit (or avoid) house museums? Who are our core audiences and who do we want to attract?

3. House museums interpret people, furnishings, buildings, and landscapes but are there new ways to look at these familiar topics? The half-dozen chapters in this part 3 examine these topics from various perspectives and help link them to the present by answering questions such as: What topics or subjects can most readily help house museums reimagine their history and significance? How can artifacts, architecture, and landscapes make historic house museums more meaningful and relevant to today's audiences?

4. Tours, exhibitions, and school programs are the bread-and-butter interpretive methods at house museums. Part 4 provides practices that can help reinvigorate house museums and considers how the most popular methods of interpreting house museums can be reimagined.

5. We conclude with two provocative chapters in part 5 to encourage a conversation in the field. Elizabeth Merritt at the Center for the Future of Museums posits some potential futures for house museums, and we welcome you to join the responses of others in the field. Ken C. Turino revisits his 2004 article (with Carol B. Stapp), "Does America Need Another Historic House?," and his 2009 article, "America Doesn't Need Another House Museum," to share how his thinking has evolved.

You may not agree with all the contributors, and indeed, some authors have ideas that differ from others. As a field, house museums are in transition and the story of their reinvention is still being written, so we welcome diverse perspectives. Historic houses are all different: they have different families, different histories, different buildings, and different communities. If you are looking for models of public programs that address social justice issues through Twitter for a late nineteenth-century dude ranch in Montana, you will be disappointed. Instead, we encourage you to step back and focus on the processes described in this book and scale them up or down for your situation. For example, Robert Kiihne's process for creating minds-on exhibitions can also be applied to school programs; many of Mary van Balgooy's approaches for interpreting the history of women are also appropriate for African American history; and Larry Yerdon's holistic analysis of financial sustainability can be adapted for an urban tenement or a country estate.

Indeed, despite the inherent strength in the diversity of house museums, we often merely copy one another, so from the visitor's perspective, they can seem to be all the same. One of the big lessons in reinvention is that the results must be unique and distinctive to your house museum and your community. Copying one another may be a form of flattery, but it's also a recipe for mediocrity. Instead, we should heed the advice of Harvard Business School professor Michael Porter: "At the heart of any strategy is a unique value proposition: a set of needs a company [read: museum] can meet for its chosen customers [read: community] that others cannot meet."[3] Of course developing something new always entails risk, so start small, experiment, and evaluate, using this book as a road map. As Mary Daniel of the Hawks Inn Historical Museum and Delafield History Center in

Wisconsin, a recent host for one of our workshops, noted: "You gave us a blueprint to follow. Thank you for giving us 'courage' to stop churning butter and making candles."

One of the biggest consequences of the under-resourced and overstretched community of house museums is that it is difficult for them to share their successes with others—they just don't have time. The field doesn't learn about them except through publications, blog posts, or conference sessions—that's one of the major reasons we assembled this anthology. There's lots of good work happening in house museums but we're simply not aware of it. Our hope is that this book is a good place to grab ahold of the current thinking about reinventing house museums so that they are more relevant, sustainable, diverse, inclusive, equitable, and accessible, hopefully broadening and deepening the current conversations in the field.

Our thanks to Bill Adair, director of exhibitions and public interpretation at the Pew Center for Arts and Heritage in Philadelphia, and Bob Beatty, formerly vice president of programs at AASLH and now president of the Lyndhurst Group, who were involved in the initial planning of this book. We are grateful to the contributors who made the time to provide the chapters in this book, and we also appreciate the extra behind-the-scenes ideas and support from Melissa Bingham, Gretchen Bulova, Dorothy Clark, Ian Gow, Laura Johnson, Christopher Mathias, David Milne, Mimi Quintanilla, Alexandra Rasic, Nathan Richie, Barbara Silberman, Carol B. Stapp, Sarah Jaworski, Mary van Balgooy, Jay D. Vogt, Larry Yerdon, and Michelle Zupan for reviewing draft chapters and suggesting contributors. We also acknowledge the many colleagues who have explored and discussed the challenges and opportunities facing house museums, many of whom are represented in the extensive reference bibliography included at the end of the book. Michael Maler deserves a big thanks for assembling the bibliography, who gladly undertook this Herculean task during his internship at Historic New England. Finally, much appreciation to the American Association for State and Local History, Atlanta History Center, Campbell House, Freedom's Frontier National Heritage Area, Hawks Inn Historical Society, Historic New England, History Colorado, National Park Service, New England Museum Association, Pew Center for Arts and Heritage, Southeastern Museums Conference, Strawbery Banke, Watson-Brown Foundation, and Wisconsin Historical Society. Their support for the *Reinventing the Historic House Museum* workshops both informed our thinking for this book as well as improved and enhanced the impact and sustainability of historic sites and house museums across the country.

Notes

1. Richard Moe, "Are There Too Many House Museums?" *Forum Journal* 16, no. 3 (Spring 2002): 4–11.
2. Gerald George, "Historic House Malaise: A Conference Considers What's Wrong," *Forum Journal* 16, no. 3 (Spring 2002): 12–19.
3. Michael Porder, *On Competition* (Cambridge, MA: Harvard Business School Publishing, 2008): Kindle edition location 9252.

Part I

Fundamentals and Essentials

Chapter 1

Imagining a Reimagining Process for House Museums

MAX A. VAN BALGOOY

When actress Bette Davis sat down for a photo late in her life, she pulled into her lap one of her prized possessions, a pillow embroidered with the saying, "Old age ain't no place for sissies." I'd say the same is true for old houses.

To avoid becoming irrelevant relics of a bygone era requires the courage to think more broadly and expansively. Leaders in the field must question assumptions, reveal failures, and break traditions. This process will be uncomfortable and demanding. Some museum members and volunteers will complain and quit. It will be much easier to fold your hands and stay the traditional course, leaving problems for the next director or another board, perhaps even another generation. Of course, that might also mean that visitation dwindles, the roof leaks, the garden overgrows, and the organization faces bankruptcy.

If you are sufficiently brave to take up the challenge, allow me to equip you with several tools that can help you analyze complex issues at your house museum and imagine a better future. Every historic site and every community is different, so not all of these tools are necessary for each site. If one doesn't work, try another. The tools in this chapter will help you, as a historic site stakeholder, assess the bigger picture of your organization, review your programmatic successes and weaknesses, address the impact and sustainability of your activities, and see your museum anew from the visitor's perspective.

No matter the situation, your wisest investment for rethinking your site involves listening, observing, and reflecting. No doubt you're facing a challenge that's more difficult than usual, so don't expect an immediate solution. If it was an easy problem, you would have solved it long ago. All solutions require innovation and creativity as well as risk and change. You'll want to think both about the long-term and short-term consequences of an idea before making a final decision. I'm providing a process and tools, but there are no guaranteed results or instant revelations. Whether you're a chef or a surgeon, the same knife can achieve different results.

Assemble the Big Picture

Although you're seeking solutions, to rethink your site you need to start with a close examination of the problem. Historic house museums are incredibly complex enterprises. Don't be deceived: there's usually more happening than anyone expects, so start with an overall inventory of your current programs and activities. Begin by listing everything that your museum produces or distributes to the public that promotes, interprets, or makes your site available to the public, including tours, events, publications, and websites. To be sure nothing is overlooked, I suggest conducting an interpretive activities inventory with a small team of three invested stakeholders, using a checklist for guidance (see Figure 1.1).

Review the list and discuss the results with your team. Often only a few people have a complete picture of their museum's activities and you may be surprised by how much your organization offers. Through this exercise, museum staff may discover they are doing far too much, stretching their resources to the point that rethinking their activities is nearly impossible. In these instances, often there isn't the time or energy to do more, so they have to make the hard decision to cut back in order to move ahead.

The next step in assembling the big picture of the organization involves evaluating each program and activity against the two things that matter to most house museums: impact and sustainability. Impact measures how well you are achieving your goals, maintaining your values and mission, and having an influence. It's the payoff for all of your hard work—your return on investment (ROI). Evaluate every activity and program for impact on a scale of 0 (no impact) to 100 percent (meets all expectations). For example, a school program could be judged as having an impact of 80 percent because it aligns well with the mission and vision, while a fund-raising event such as a golf tournament may have a weaker connection, perhaps 20 percent. Initially, these will be subjective opinions, but the more important aspect is how they relate to each other (e.g., the school program has a much greater impact than the golf tournament).

This will be a relatively simple exercise if you have a clear sense of purpose and direction. For house museums, purpose and direction are typically encapsulated in the site's mission, vision, and values. Together these serve as a well-built highway leading to an important destination or vision, with the mission as the guard rails and the values as the durable paving. If you find yourself hitting too many potholes, drifting off the road, or seem lost, it may be that your mission, vision, or values are vague or incomplete. It's nearly impossible to rethink a house museum without them, so stop to develop these first before proceeding with the remainder of this process.[1]

The second major concern for most museums is sustainability. All museums have limited resources and you need to be sure yours are invested wisely and effectively. Sustainability measures how well your site is surviving and thriving. After all, if the museum doesn't exist next year or next month, your good work will stop. Financial sustainability is perhaps the easiest to measure because you can calculate revenue against expenses to determine if a program is running a surplus or deficit.[2]

Most nonprofits, however, don't have sufficient information to calculate the revenue and expenses for individual programs and activities. Often several programs are combined into a single "education" or "events" account, making it difficult to measure the success of specific programs. Most modern accounting software can easily accommodate this detailed level of bookkeeping by rethinking the account numbering system or creating cost centers. Without this information, making decisions about financial sustainability is nearly impossible because you can't determine

Max A. van Balgooy

Interpretive Activities Inventory

Identify the interpretive activities your museum or historic site has offered in the last three years. Include the title or a short description to provide more details. If there are two or more distinct activities in the same category (e.g., guided tours for the public, connoisseur tours for collectors), identify then separately (e.g., 1A, 1B). Do not include activities that are primarily for promotion or raising funds.

Check all that apply.

☐ 1. Guided tours:
☐ 2. Self-guided tours:
☐ 3. Other tours:
☐ 4. Long-term exhibits:
☐ 5. Short-term exhibits:
☐ 6. Lectures:
☐ 7. Fairs and festivals:
☐ 8. Workshops:
☐ 9. Concerts or performances:
☐ 10. Slide, film, or video presentations:
☐ 11. Other events:
☐ 12. Programs for students:
☐ 13. Programs for teachers:
☐ 14. Programs for children:
☐ 15. Programs for adults or families:
☐ 16. Other programs:
☐ 17. Newsletter:
☐ 18. Books, brochures, or publications:
☐ 19. Store or gift shop:
☐ 20. Website:
☐ 21. Facebook, Twitter, YouTube, or other social media:
☐ 22. Other:

Notes:

Figure 1.1 Use this checklist of common programs and activities at house museums to complete an inventory of what is currently being offered by your organization.

the weaknesses in your financial sustainability. Perhaps your fund-raising garden party is actually losing money while your educational open house brings in significant donations. You may need to stop the rethinking process to collect more detailed financial data, which will better inform your assessment. Otherwise, this might become an exercise in futility.

Evaluating the cost of staff and overhead is a more complex undertaking. It isn't unusual for a museum to remark that a program generated a surplus "if you don't count staff time." It is essential to calculate staff time in the sustainability assessment, even if the program is entirely run by volunteers. The time and energy spent by staff, whether paid or volunteer, could be devoted to other projects, so good managers are always aware of the trade-offs when choosing one activity over another. Overhead or ongoing expenses that occur regardless of the number or type of activities, such as liability insurance, internet fees, bookkeeping services, and mowing the lawn, are usually not considered in the financial sustainability of a program, but they play a critical supporting role. Without them, most programs and activities would cease to exist. An accountant can advise on the best way to distribute expenses for salaries and overhead at your museum.

While ROI is often measured in dollars, there are other important, and more complex, metrics for gauging sustainability. Programmatic sustainability measures the resources that each program attracts, such as volunteers or grant funds, and the support the program gains, such as visitors, members, or community reputation.[3] Most important is understanding the audience. Is the program's audience large enough or willing to pay enough to sustain the program? Does the size or type of the audience justify the resources expended? Is there an opportunity for growth because the potential audience is large or because the program serves as a stepping-stone to other audiences? For example, some museums are weighing the value of their school programs. Could they have the same or a better ROI by pursuing teachers rather than students? Which is more sustainable for the museum: training thirty teachers who each teach classes of thirty students over the course of long careers or assigning staff to conduct thirty field trips for thirty students annually?

Assessing sustainability can become incredibly complex, so at this stage of the process keep it simple by placing your programs and activities on a sustainability scale that runs from negative to positive with 0 in the middle. Programs that generate surplus fall to the right of 0 whereas programs that result in a deficit fall to the left. The distance from 0 represents the size of the surplus or deficit. For example, a $10,000 surplus will be further to the right than a $1,000 surplus. Remember that sustainability is not just about money, but also considers a program's ability to attract resources and build an audience of supporters. At this point, the assessment will be subjective, so more useful measures might be small, medium, large, or break-even effects. Working at a high level will identify broad patterns within your organization.

While you can assess impact and sustainability separately, it is more useful and dynamic to examine them together using the Impact/Sustainability Matrix (see Figure 1.2).[4] As a demonstration, let's imagine a house museum with only three public activities: a school program, a golf tournament, and a garden party. Ideally, each program would fall in the quadrant with the gold star indicating that it is both high impact and sustainable. Unfortunately, it is not typical for all activities to meet both measures. It is likely that the school program advances the mission but is free to visitors, so it's placed in the quadrant with the heart. The golf tournament is a big moneymaker but has very little to do with the mission, so it's in the quadrant with the cash cow. The garden party is supposed to be a fund-raiser, but it loses money and, although it happens on site, it might as well be at the local country club. It's a bunny, a cute pet that doesn't do much for the organization. At a glance, you can see the overall configuration of this museum's activities: although they don't have any stars, it seems that the school program is balanced by the golf

Max A. van Balgooy

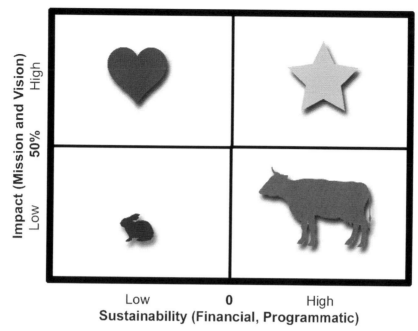

Impact (Mission and Vision)
High
50%
Low

Low   0   High
Sustainability (Financial, Programmatic)

Figure 1.2 The Impact/Sustainability Matrix assesses a house museum's programs against the double-bottom line of mission/vision/values and financial/ programmatic sustainability. Diagram by Max A. van Balgooy.

tournament. The next step is to figure out if either of these programs can be modified to make them into stars.[5] Perhaps a local business would support the school program to make it more financially sustainable? Could the golf tournament transform to advance the mission in some way? Perhaps they could play as teams representing a different preservation project; if they win, that's the project that will be taken up next year. The tough decisions are the bunnies—they're probably someone's favorite activity but should either be discarded or require more investment to move them into one of the other quadrants.

This matrix will be more accurate and useful if your assessments are based on data and criteria rather than anecdote and opinion. For example, sustainability can be measured according to income, grants awarded, or new members enrolled. A set of written goals can help assess how well a program advances the mission. Otherwise, programs can be inadvertently changed, eliminated, or preserved for the wrong reasons. Nevertheless, this assessment will always have a degree of subjectivity and ambiguity, relying ultimately on good judgment. Working as a small group can foster honest dialogue about your museum's areas of ambiguity.

Taken together, this double-bottom line of impact and sustainability should shape and guide decisions at your house museum, suggesting where and how to invest in your programs and determining what programs should be replaced or concluded. When you conduct this exercise with your staff and board, it can provoke crucial conversations about the site's impact and the role each program and activity plays in the organization's success. It helps everyone better understand the big picture and envision how individual changes to an activity can affect the entire organization.

If you establish a consensus on the activities in the star and bunny quadrants, they typically need no further discussion. Congratulate yourself on the programs that are stars and be sure they continue to succeed by integrating them into your long-range plans. Schedule funerals for the bunnies and recognize that by eliminating these programs, you've increased your organization's capacity. Most likely it's the activities in the heart and cash cow quadrants that will generate the most discussion and will require more analysis; after consideration, you may create goals to transform them into stars, or perhaps you will confirm they are actually bunnies. It may also turn out that you need a balance between these activities: the cash cows allow the museum to provide the hearts. To analyze these complex situations, I rely on the Five Forces approach.

Scrutinize Programs Individually

While the museum activities inventory and Impact/Sustainability Matrix provide a sense of your organization's big picture, finding concrete solutions requires an examination of programs and activities on an individual basis. A Five Forces analysis and construction of a Visitor Journey Map are two "rethinking tools" that I often use to design engaging programs.

More than thirty years ago, Harvard Business School economist Michael Porter identified the five greatest influences on competition that have helped businesses navigate to successful positions in the marketplace.[6] While nonprofit leaders may cringe at the word "competition" because they prefer to collaborate and cooperate, Porter uses the term differently.

For Porter, the real point of competition is not to beat your rivals but to find a place in the community that ensures your museum is distinctive, sustainable, and mission-driven. We might equate "rivals" with the high school football team across town that you want to beat in the upcoming game, but Porter reminds us that the origin of the word comes from "river" and that "rivals" are people who are standing in the same river with us. Companies who are in the same business are rivals, whether across the street or across the country. Offering the same product in the same manner as other similar businesses results in a "zero-sum" game in which customers chase after the lowest price.

House museums face a similar situation. They often offer guided tours of period rooms, scholarly lectures, a quarterly special event, a members' newsletter, a fourth-grade school program, and a website. No doubt the staff and board at your house museum view it as a special and unique place, but to outsiders it's pretty much the same as the other house museums around the country, offering the same guided tours of furniture in dining rooms and bedrooms, holding the same demonstrations of butter-churning and candle-dipping, hosting the same lectures on obscure topics, and entertaining students with the same outmoded household technologies, like washboards and wood-burning stoves.

Together, we can break that perception, but that requires thinking beyond our own sites, figuring out how we fit into larger communities, and taking the long view. I encountered this shift at the Homestead Museum in California where we launched "Concerts in the Past" as a unique variant of the common summer concerts in the park that cities offered around us. To fulfill our mission, we hired bands that played popular music from the 1840s to 1920s, such as Dixieland jazz. We kept the event simple so it could be offered free and managed by just two staff members. Our distinctiveness made the event popular—there was nowhere else to experience this type of event—but it was easily copied by other local organizations, who hired the same bands, and our attendance declined. Some might see this simply as the inevitability of competition, but that misses the larger processes at work. Had I known more about the Five Forces at the time, I could have navigated the museum to a better and stronger position, not to beat our rivals but to maintain our distinctiveness.

Max A. van Balgooy

Assessing your house museum's competitive environment using this model will improve and enhance tours, events, and other public programs. To better understand the Five Forces, I've translated them into terms that are appropriate for and applicable to house museums:

1. *Rivalry Among Existing Competitors.* Are other nearby house museums or businesses providing the same program, product, or service? Is the rivalry so intense that you have to lower prices or increase expenses to attract audiences?
2. *Bargaining Power of Buyers.* How many people are willing to buy this product or service or visit your historic site? How much are they willing to pay? What is their interest in your product or programs? Why do they need it? Is it a necessity or luxury? What are the obstacles or stumbling blocks? Would they prefer lower prices or more value?
3. *Bargaining Power of Suppliers.* What resources (money, time, people, materials) do you need to develop and maintain this program or product? Who would be willing to provide these resources? Does the funder, board, members, volunteers, neighborhood, or a government agency have to provide approval or support? How much influence do they have over its implementation or results?
4. *Threat of New Entrants.* Can other historic sites or businesses easily duplicate this program, product, or service? What will encourage or prevent them? How long will it take others to copy your success and diminish your unique position?
5. *Threat of Substitute Products or Services.* How well can the needs or goals met by this product or service be fulfilled in a different way (e.g., docent-led tour vs. brochure vs. smartphone app)?

When conducting a Five Forces analysis, consider one program, product, or service at a time. House museums typically offer tours, exhibitions, events, school programs, memberships, a shop, social media, and a website—too many to be considered together. Although these activities are often related to one another, the analysis proceeds much faster and the results are much clearer if each activity is considered individually.

For nonprofit organizations, the Five Forces analysis has a major weakness: it focuses on sustainability rather than impact. To counter this, start by choosing one of the activities that you previously identified in the heart category (where impact is already high). Work through each force to collect information, at times conducting research to adequately address the questions. You may encounter great ideas and aha! moments as you proceed through the questions but keep going through the entire process. Likewise, keep going even if you generate little or nothing with the first few questions. Each force examines a completely different issue and you may miss an important factor that could be a key to sustainability. Once you have the big picture, your conclusions will be even stronger.

This is difficult work and it is easy to treat it superficially with little or no useful results. If possible, work with a small team of advisors who can provide diverse perspectives and deeper insights into specific programs. Doing it alone often leads to shortsighted or misinformed results. For example, with a school program you might include a teacher among your advisors, whereas an analysis of your guided tours could include a staff member from the local tourism board. With their help, you might discover a new source of support or an unknown obstacle. Although you could meet together as a team to conduct the analysis, it can also be completed through individual interviews. Indeed, it might be more efficient to conduct your research through interviews because you won't have to explain the Five Forces and you can focus on the information provided by one person rather than three at a time. You probably will need to reword the questions so that they make sense to your interviewee, such as "Do you know of any nearby house museums or businesses that are offering programs to local schools?" or "What do you think discourages teachers or schools from participating in our school program?"

Finally, armed with information on each of the Five Forces, consider how your house museum needs to reposition its program, product, or service so that it is distinctive. Only by competing to be unique can your organization achieve sustained, superior performance. Usually, you'll quickly identify some ways to improve but sometimes you won't. In either case, share your results with at least one other person before making any major decisions. Confirming your conclusions with someone else will give you greater confidence and may draw your attention to aspects you overlooked. Finally, be prepared for tough conclusions: a heart activity may need to be paired with a cash cow to be sustainable or what you assumed was a heart is actually a bunny that you need to stop doing.

See Your Museum from the Visitor's Perspective

The second rethinking tool helps you examine an individual program from beginning to end from the visitor's perspective by constructing a journey map. One of the big leaps for those of us rethinking house museums is recognizing that the visitor experience on-site is not an isolated event, but part of a longer journey that starts before the visitor leaves home. When people visit historic sites, they not only take a tour but they probably explore your website, hunt for parking, buy tickets, shop in your store, and use the restroom. While the tour might be outstanding, the entire experience can be spoiled if the visitor couldn't find a parking spot, was greeted by someone surly at the front desk, or encountered a dirty restroom. For most people, a visit to a historic site isn't just about the tour, but the whole experience from beginning to end. If one element goes awry, the entire visit can go bad—even if you had absolutely no control over it (like the weather).

To improve visitor satisfaction and increase attendance and impact, a crucial rethinking tool involves examining the entire visitor experience to be sure every part functions well and works seamlessly from beginning to end. One of the best ways to analyze and improve the experience is through the creation of a journey map, a diagram that lays out every step in the visitor experience from home to museum to back home.[7] It can help organize planning and evaluation, simplify understanding of complex processes, and easily show how different parts of the organization contribute to an excellent visitor experience. In journey mapping, each step represents a touchpoint where a visitor makes a major decision or relies on the site for information (see Figure 1.3). For example, driving to the site is a touchpoint because the visitor is following signs along the street to decide where to go.

To construct a journey map for your site, start by choosing a specific audience (such as walk-in visitors) who have a goal in mind (such as taking the daily tour). Sketching on a notepad or using sticky notes on a wall, identify all of the major steps in the visitors' journey from their home to your site and back to their home. Draw the diagram like a flowchart moving from left to right, stacking elements that are closely related in columns (see Figure 1.4).

Figure 1.3 A visitor journey map lays out each step in the visitor's experience from home to historic site to home again.

Max A. van Balgooy

House Tour: Current Journey for Local Residents

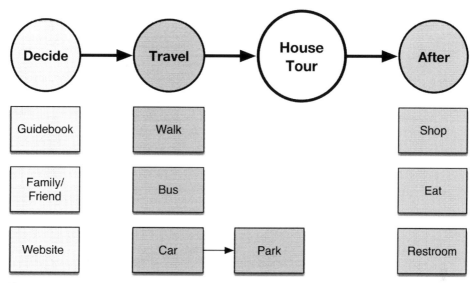

Figure 1.4. Creating a visitor journey map starts by laying out the major visitor actions and decisions. This diagram is for illustration and only shows a portion of a complete journey map. Diagram by Max A. van Balgooy.

As you go through this process, you will quickly discover that you will have to rely on assumptions to fill in gaps and acknowledge that there are several different routes used by visitors. You may also find that the journey is different depending on the audience (such as local residents versus tourists) or program (such as general versus special tours). If you are puzzled by which map to draw, start with the audience or program that is the most popular or has the biggest impact on your site. Later, you can create separate maps for other situations and audiences.

It is crucial to focus on current conditions only; you'll be tempted to add touchpoints that are planned in the future or you'd like to do but don't exist now. Remove superfluous or minor points by including only those that affect at least 10 percent of the current visitors. For example, in today's growing social media environment, it's easy to add Twitter, Instagram, Facebook, YouTube, TripAdvisor, and dozens more, but don't include them if they're not making a significant long-term impact on a visitor's decision to visit.

After you've created your first draft, check your journey map with others to see if you overlooked a step or if it should be organized differently (e.g., someone may notice that tour ticket sales is missing). If your journey map is mostly based on assumptions or anecdotal information, begin to fill it in with more reliable information about your visitors' behavior or characteristics whenever possible (Figure 1.5). For example, if you conducted a visitor survey, you may have identified how frequently visitors were motivated by a guidebook, recommendations from family and friends, or time spent on your website. This phase of rethinking may require analyzing data you already have (such as sales records) or new research (such as a random survey of visitors). Although it may be difficult to obtain data for some touchpoints, if it's important for measuring future performance, you'll want to collect it now to establish useful benchmarks.

House Tour: Participation Rates for Local Residents

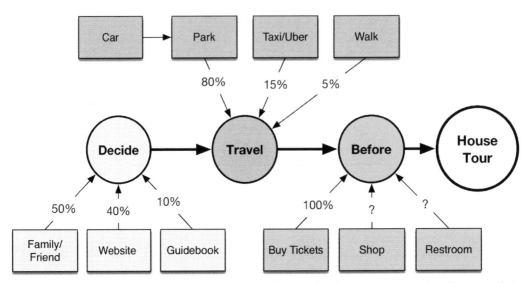

Figure 1.5. Additional data informs participation rates in the visitor journey map and identifies areas that may require further research. Diagram by Max A. van Balgooy.

While constructing this flowchart provides a useful overview of data from your site, journey mapping also involves analysis to identify areas for improvement. Each touchpoint is assessed to determine how much it helps or hinders the visitor experience. For example, are directional signs missing or inaccurate? Are they along the roads most used by visitors? Can they be read at night? Are they lost in a clutter of other signs or leafy tree limbs? Is a directional arrow sufficient or does it need to include distance? What are the ideal locations for signs? Should they have a consistent design so that they are more easily recognized?

Be sure to examine this primarily from the visitor's perspective, not your own. You are probably very familiar with the route to the site and rarely notice signage, but first-time visitors rely heavily on directional signs and may become frustrated if one is missing. Adopt a grading system (such as A–F, 0–10, traffic light colors, smiley face emoticons) and evaluate each touchpoint, noting what helps or hinders the experience (see Figure 1.6).

Check your ratings and rationale with others who can provide useful feedback. If you discover significant disagreements or a heavy reliance on assumptions or anecdotes, conduct visitor research (such as satisfaction surveys or interviews with a random sample of visitors).

The typical result of this process is a long-range plan to achieve as high a rating as possible for each touchpoint. Implementation usually starts with those touchpoints that have the greatest impact on the visitor experience or can be the easiest to improve, but it can also begin with more visitor research to reduce the risk of decisions or to identify the most serious pain points. You may also discover that rather than improving the existing visitor experience, you may want to sharpen and shape it in a new way. For house museums, this can occur if you are attempting to reach a new audience (e.g., local young adults), if you want to introduce new interpretive content (e.g., women, domestic servants, slavery) or techniques (e.g., a self-guided tour on a smartphone), or if a significant new opportunity for your visitors is available in the region (e.g., Uber, a heritage trail).

House Tour: Current Journey for Local Residents

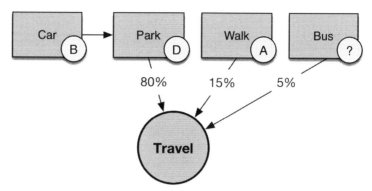

Figure 1.6. A portion of a visitor journey map with touchpoints rated by a letter grade or question mark if unknown. Diagram by Max A. van Balgooy.

You can either revise the current journey map (resulting in "before" and "after" versions) or start fresh by creating a new map, adding or removing touchpoints and including metrics for success (which will help you to create a vision for the future) (see Figure 1.7). While most journey maps are drawn as linear diagrams with a clear start and end point, historic sites may wish to experiment with circular formats to develop a cyclical process for increasing support and building relationships with the local community and maintaining web-based engagement with out-of-town visitors.

House Tour: Future Journey for Local Residents

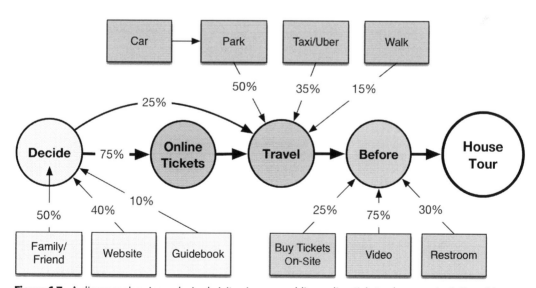

Figure 1.7. A diagram showing a desired visitor journey adding online ticket sales, an orientation video, and travel via Uber or taxi, along with goals for participation rates. Diagram by Max A. van Balgooy.

While journey maps can be a valuable tool for improving visitor satisfaction and providing direction to the organization, it is essential that they are not merely built on assumptions and dreams. Incorporate visitor research before, during, and after this exercise.

Make Rethinking a Strategic and Intentional Process

The overall process of reimaging historic house museums should be strategic, but often staff and boards of house museums are stretched thin by urgent and immediate demands. If the roof leaks, a donor wants an immediate answer, a school group arrives early, and a volunteer fails to show up to lead tours, it's impossible to think about and plan for tomorrow. But tomorrow ultimately arrives while you're facing a similar set of urgencies, and the cycle repeats throughout the entire year while you're left wondering what was accomplished.

As management guru Peter Drucker observes, "Effective executives know where their time goes. They work systematically at managing the little of their time that can be brought under their control." He advises us that "effective executives concentrate on the few major areas where superior performance will produce outstanding results. They force themselves to set priorities and stay with their priority decisions. They know that they have no choice but to do first things first—and second things not at all. The alternative is to get nothing done."[8]

What I've observed is that short-term, daily priorities tend to push away long-term, visionary priorities. We're often victims of the tyranny of the urgent but we can overcome it. We need to spend less time acting and more time evaluating, reflecting, and planning to reimagine our house museums. Armed with the process and tools presented in this chapter and inspiration from others in this book, you will be better prepared to make rethinking a strategic and intentional practice.

Notes

1. To learn more about mission, vision, and values, see the *Encyclopedia of Local History, Third Edition* edited by Amy H. Wilson (Lanham, MD: Rowman and Littlefield, 2017).
2. Learn more in *Financial Fundamentals for Historic House Museums* by Rebekah Beaulieu (Lanham, MD: Rowman and Littlefield, 2017).
3. See also *Nonprofit Sustainability: Making Strategic Decisions for Financial Viability* by Jeanne Bell, Jan Masaoka, and Steve Zimmerman (San Francisco: Jossey-Bass, 2010).
4. In the 1970s, Bruce Henderson at the Boston Consulting Group introduced the "growth-share matrix" to help its clients better manage a portfolio of business units and products. The matrix facilitates management decisions by rating each product according to its share of the market and its potential for growth. I've modified the "growth-share" matrix into an "impact-sustainability" version that's more appropriate for the conditions of nonprofit organizations.
5. For a variety of approaches to assess impact and sustainability, see *Thinkertoys: A Handbook of Creative-Thinking Techniques, Second Edition* by Michael Michalko (Berkeley: Ten Speed Press, 2006).
6. Michael Porter, "The Five Competitive Forces that Shape Strategy," *Harvard Business Review* 86, no. 1 (January 2008): 78-93; Joan Magretta, *Understanding Michael Porter* (Cambridge, MA: Harvard Business Review Press, 2012).
7. David C. Edelman and Marc Singer, "Competing on Customer Journeys," *Harvard Business Review* 93, no. 11 (November 2015): 89-100; James Kalbach, *Mapping Experiences: A Complete Guide to Creating Value Through Journeys, Blueprints, and Diagrams* (Sebastopol, CA: O'Reilly Media, 2016).
8. Peter F. Drucker, *The Effective Executive: The Definitive Guide to Getting the Right Things Done* (New York: HarperCollins, 2017), 24-25.

Max A. van Balgooy

Chapter 2

Enterprising Historic House Museums

LAWRENCE J. YERDON

At a historic house museum somewhere in the United States—midday, midweek in the executive director's office . . .

> The contractor's written estimate for painting the house exterior is 30 percent over the one made in conversation with him earlier in the week—and there isn't enough cash to cover the verbal estimate, much less the written one. Today's mail included a letter from the principal of the local school requesting the historic house's participation in a new educational project. Yes, should be the right answer, but there isn't a staff member who has time for the added assignment. The auditor's bill arrived, and the money set aside to pay her was spent on the water damage caused by a leaking pipe in the carriage house this past winter. The county manager's new budget has a line item for the historic house, but it is 25 percent of last year's budget and 50 percent lower than the previous year.

And so it goes—the financial challenges of running a historic house in a time of restricted resources.

Many, if not most, historic houses derive their operating income from a traditional set of resources: admissions, fees for programs, membership, contributions to an annual fund, campaigns, sponsorships, draws from endowments (if the organization is fortunate enough to have one), local government allocations, and grants (which are generally restricted to specific programming and rarely cover the related management and facility costs).

As has been evident in recent years, these familiar income sources are not dependable and vary widely with the vagaries of the economy, politics, and cultural interests. Seldom are these resources enough to meet the demands of maintaining aging buildings and providing substantive programming.

The challenge is to add new revenue to these traditional resources—revenue that will result in a portfolio of diverse income generators that, in effect, transform liabilities into assets. These new income resources can contribute to the immediate financial situation, but also serve as the foundation for the long-term financial sustainability of historic house museums.

To accomplish a transformation from the traditional to the entrepreneurial, the organization must first begin by reviewing the operation with an eye to the effectiveness and efficiency of current programs while looking for opportunities to reduce expenses and increase existing resources wherever possible.

To effectively transform resources there must be openness to change and new ideas, an active search for new opportunities, development of creative solutions, and taking and managing calculated risks—all requirements to find, develop, and successfully implement new resources of income.[1] Susan Raymond, in *Nonprofit Finance for Hard Times*, makes the point that "revenue strategies that are robust in the face of economic scarcity must be premised on an institutional culture that values new ideas and new approaches. True, innovation must be consistent with, and loyally serve, core mission. But the ability to be flexible to new thinking from outside as well as within the organization . . . is an essential prerequisite to revenue strategy that seeks to seize and execute on creative approaches to resource mobilization."[2] Transformation is not a straightforward process. It is untidy, filled with risk, successes, failures, unanticipated consequences (positive and not), and, frequently, success.

The following case study of the Richard Fitzwilliam House, a fictional historical organization, incorporates many of the problems faced by both volunteer and professional leadership of historic houses. The Fitzwilliam House is a larger and more complex organization than most, but its building stewardship, programming, and fund-raising efforts exemplify the numerous issues and opportunities that singly or in combination face historic houses today.

* * * * *

Opened to the public in 1976, the Richard Fitzwilliam House (RFH) tells the story of Colonel Fitzwilliam and his family, who lived in the house from 1850 to 1973. Fitzwilliam was a decorated colonel in the Civil War, leader in the abolitionist movement, and owner of a major ale and beer brewing company.

The museum was the fortunate beneficiary of two circumstances in the 1970s. The last living direct descendant of the Fitzwilliam family offered the house to a local group of citizens as "a memorial to my forefather and the Fitzwilliam family." At that time, the town's history was on everyone's mind as the bicentennial of the American Revolution approached.

The house, a large Federal-style residence, had been "Victorianized" and expanded following the Civil War when the colonel's fortunes grew subsequent to his purchase and expansion of the Wenham Brewery Company. When the local community group acquired the house, it and its two-story carriage barn were filled with family artifacts and documents dating back to the family's arrival in the town before the American Revolution. The RFH is in the center of town, with ample public parking, and a prominent position on the town green where it shares the landscape with other RFH-owned houses, a popular commercial historic inn, and a high-end restaurant. Several B&B establishments are in the neighborhood as well.

With the surge in interest in history following the bicentennial, the RFH purchased the neighboring Lowd House, a spacious Georgian structure. This acquisition was followed by the gift of the neighboring Sherburne House, a large Colonial Revival house that had been converted to a private girls' boarding school with a rambling multiroom dorm annex at the back of the building. In addition, to the side of the house is a spacious garden shed repurposed currently as a tea room. The tea room serves light refreshments and is a popular lunch spot for locals. It is operated by the museum, and when all direct and indirect costs are considered, it loses money.

Although suffering from decades of deferred maintenance, the Lowd House soon filled with RFH's library and collections storage as the collection grew. And, even though the town has an active historical society and a history room in the public library, RFH found itself the repository of artifacts unrelated to the Fitzwilliam family. The external demands for free storage have grown to the point that much of the Sherburne House's second and third floors and the neighboring Lowd House and its garage contain not only the RFH's collection of furniture, documents, clothing, family papers, and a nineteenth-century Wenham Brewery delivery wagon, but much of the local historical society's collection, and the town's historic fire truck and its first Model T police car. Too much material culture has resulted in too little space and RFH must rent an off-site office for the director and education coordinator at the rate of twenty-two dollars per square foot.

The Sherburne House is in serious need of exterior cosmetic work and major interior infrastructure improvements. The house's two front parlors are operated as a museum store by the Fitzwilliam Guild—a group of volunteers who staff and manage the store. Although popular with local residents and visitors, the store rarely makes a profit when the real costs are factored against revenues. The six remaining first-floor rooms and kitchen in Sherburne have a long tradition of being used for RFH social gatherings and meetings of RFH committees and its board of trustees. The house is frequently offered at no charge as a goodwill good neighbor gesture to other local nonprofits for meetings and fund-raising events. The remainder of the building (six large rooms in addition to multiple bathrooms and former dorm rooms) are filled with collection artifacts, past exhibition materials, and many years of accumulated debris resulting from staff indecision about what should be retained and what should be discarded.

RFH is open for guided tours Tuesday through Sunday afternoons. Tours focus on the domestic life of Colonel Fitzwilliam and his family. Public programming ceases from October through June—the exception is a lecture series offered at the RFH library in Lowd House on occasional afternoons in the winter months. The lectures attract two dozen or more attendees. The library is used by seventy-five researchers annually.

School visitation is strong with nearly one thousand fourth-grade students participating in programs annually. The school program features a participatory experience led by two exceptionally talented actor-educators as Colonel Fitzwilliam and his daughter.

General attendance at RFH began to fall in the 1990s (1,500 paid visitors in 2017), and despite its location in a lovely picturesque town, less than an hour's drive from two major urban areas, RFH has not been able to develop an audience beyond the town's population.

Because of the beauty and reputation of the gardens and properties, the annual fund-raiser, RFH Garden Tea and Tour, sells out with more than nine hundred tickets purchased for the two-day event. As one Trustee pointedly remarked last year, "the Garden Tea and Tour has turned into a sea of gray hair."

RFH's annual financial statements reflect growing annual deficits ($25,000–$50,000) in recent years. The deficits are offset by withdrawals from reserve funds. It is projected that the reserve funds will be depleted within five years.

The staff consists of a full-time director/curator, librarian, and coordinator of education programs—all with lengthy, productive tenures. There are three part-time positions: housekeeper, bookkeeper, and tea room manager. The tour guides and store staff are long-time volunteers. The actor-educators are paid per school group.

RFH is governed by a board of trustees of twenty-one members. Although deeply dedicated to the RFH, the board, as a whole, is wedded to the safe programs of the past and frequently focuses on the implementation of the activity rather than on the outcome.

* * * * *

The first step in finding new financial resources for RFH is a thorough review with the board of trustees and staff members of the current financial situation and efforts to provide resources. Before any changes are made or sources of income augmented, the board must have a thorough understanding of the financial situation as it currently exists. To ensure that the review is thorough and includes a broad and in-depth look at the finances, it would be desirable to have outside professional assistance. Many times, an organization's leadership is so focused on the issues of cash flow and on day-to-day finances that it is difficult for them to see the organization's whole financial position. An outside financial advisor—auditor, CPA, or another nonprofit finance director—may be able to assist with this task. Additionally, data relating to other similar organizations' finances and efforts to increase resources should be gathered from state arts councils and foundations supporting nonprofits.

When a thorough review of the current finances and data is completed, the leadership will be sufficiently informed about the finances to move to a thoughtful examination of the historic house's mission and goals. The leadership must move beyond the predictable "collect, preserve, and exhibit" and design a mission that answers the questions framed by management guru Peter Drucker many years ago, questions that are still relevant today: "What is our business/mission? Who is our customer? What does the customer value?"[3] The result should be a clear and specific statement that is understood and agreed upon by the leadership. The resulting clarity of purpose will allow for specific goals to be developed, implemented, and eventually evaluated.

The question remains: How does the leadership move from the traditional approach to the business of a historic house to a more entrepreneurial viewpoint? The financial review and the exercise of reviewing and clarifying the mission may be enough to spring the leadership into action. Then again, that exercise may not provide enough motivation. For the organization to survive and remain sustainable, the leadership may have to change. That may result in staff members leaving and/or the board needing a significant change in membership. And, at any point in this preliminary activity, a consultant may be the answer to re-educating and inspiring the leadership to acknowledge the financial need and open its collective mind to nontraditional efforts that will be required to grow and diversify its sources of income.

Part of that initial process is an examination of existing successful RFH income-producing efforts and consideration of whether they can be duplicated and tweaked in ways that will appeal to new audiences. For RFH the logical choice would be the successful Garden Tea and Tour fundraiser. The current offering features tea, sweets, and garden tours for an older demographic on Saturday and Sunday afternoons. It is successful and should be retained if attendance remains robust. A new event, patterned on the tea, might appeal to millennials and feature beer rather than tea and be offered in the evening, with music or tours focused on the brewing industry. Here is an opportunity to exhibit the Wenham Brewery truck and tie its history into this social event. A middle-aged audience might respond well to a wine-tasting event in the gardens with paired food contributed by local vendors. The RFH staff and volunteers are already well versed in managing big events like these and more than likely would deliver a new and successful income-producing event. These events may attract new and younger audiences and new volunteers in addition to adding to the bottom line.

Strategy: Adapt existing successful programs for new audiences.

The school program is solid and supported by attendance from local schools, but a sizeable number of schools find they cannot pay for the student program fee and, if they are coming from a distance, the cost of transportation. RFH cannot afford to offer the programs for free. This school program provides an opportunity for RFH to offer sponsorship possibilities to donors who may support an educational scholarship but not otherwise support a historic house. Recent studies demonstrate that the appeal of an opportunity to underwrite a scholarship program covering admission and transportation costs is a very strong motivator for donors.[4] A skillfully developed budget for this program can underwrite many of the management and facility use costs not otherwise funded by fees. One New England historic site underwrites 20 percent of its school offerings with a private donor–sponsored scholarship program. This program structure allows the museum to have a better opportunity to cover management and facility costs.

Strategy: Understand donor motivation and design giving opportunities that respond to donors' needs and interests.

The Sherburne House provides several straightforward and uncomplicated income-producing opportunities. For example, a site rental fee could be gently introduced to the local organizations currently using the space for free. Although this effort may have political pushback, if carefully managed the organizations will understand their responsibility for bearing some of the costs of maintaining this facility for their use. Expanding on the rental strategy, RFH could also go in the direction of many other historic sites and look at income opportunities in the wedding ceremony and reception market. Developing the rental strategy, RFH could add other private events and, because of its location outside two urban areas, potentially provide meeting space for small company retreats. Partnerships with profit-making businesses should always be a consideration— and in this case, site and building rentals could be paired with the restaurant and inn across the green from RFH. This potential relationship could be profitable for both entities.

Strategy: Introduce a fee structure for current non-fee programs. Adapt successful programs from other comparable organizations.

Strategy: Pursue partnerships with profit-making businesses to complement and augment new fund-raising efforts.

The Sherburne House's museum store, popular but not producing a profit, offers another opportunity to upgrade an existing business. The store may be hampered by the volunteer's inexperience in managing a profit-making business and by the staff and volunteer's admirable effort to restrict the product line to items and educational materials closely related to the museum's mission, thereby avoiding unrelated business income tax. An outside vendor not hindered by inventory restrictions may be able to turn a profit and, depending on the business arrangement, be a source of both rental income and a commission as a percentage of sales.

The RFH tea room on the Sherburne House property is another candidate for management from outside. Because the tea room does not appear to be a competitor to the inn and restaurant across the street, the restaurant may consider managing the tea room and capturing the lunch crowd as a good opportunity. This business arrangement could provide steady rent and a commission as a percentage of income while reducing RFH's expenses when the part-time position of tea room manager is eliminated. For RFH, an alternative to the restaurant might be a local caterer or individual interested in managing a small food operation.

The RFH staff has insufficient time and experience to run this operation, so consideration of hiring a part- or full-time staff member or a consultant to manage it is imperative. Expanding on the issue of hiring from outside the nonprofit field, J. Gregory Dees in *Enterprising Nonprofits* cautions that "many nonprofits simply do not have the business-specific organizational skills, managerial capacity, and credibility to succeed in commercial markets. . . . Hiring people with business skills and market focus is not enough. An organization must be receptive to and supportive of the new activities; it also must be able to integrate the skills and values of the new staff."[5]

Strategy: Contract people from the outside with the skills to manage new or altered businesses.

Although not directly an income-producing effort, a well-planned emptying of obsolete and redundant materials on the second and third floors of the Sherburne House would allow the RFH staff to move out of rented space and eliminate an unnecessary expense. An additional positive outcome of an office move to Sherburne House would be a staff more conveniently located in relation to the operation.

Strategy: Adapt the use of existing underutilized property and avoid leasing external properties (see Figures 2.1 and 2.2).

A very big and complicated project, but one that would have enormous impact on the future stability of the RFH, is the management of the collection. Use of valuable space is restricted by the storage of other organizations' materials. In an institution that has increasing financial problems, it is imperative that these storage spaces be put to profitable use. The collections that do not belong to RFH should be returned to the organizations that have stewardship of them. This will have, as we have recognized on earlier projects, the potential for political problems, but can be dealt with if the issues are anticipated ahead of time and a plan is developed to deal with the issues. RFH's purpose is to tell the story of the Fitzwilliam family and its collections policy reflects that. Artifacts that do not fit the collections policy should be deaccessioned in a thoughtful manner and the resulting income, as the collections policy dictates, should be deposited into a restricted fund that supports future acquisitions and direct care of the collection.[6] With the downsizing of the collection having been accomplished, the requirements for RFH storage are fulfilled in the upper stories of the Fitzwilliam's House and two-story carriage house.

With the annex of the Sherburne House no longer doing duty as collections storage and repository of obsolete materials, it offers RFH new opportunities. After first examining the real estate market, RFH can ascertain if there is potential for rental of this space and whether the rental units should be commercial or residential offerings—keeping in mind that office space is the least expensive renovation but generally it is leased at a lower rent than apartments. In most cases the renovation for residential units is more expensive and intrusive in a historic building because of the addition of kitchens and more elaborate bathrooms, but the rental income is higher. Following the conversion of the upper floors and annex, the first floor could remain available for RFH use and for the short-term rental program. For cash-poor organizations, covering capital expenses is difficult, but programs that join historic building preservation with renovations that

Lawrence J. Yerdon

Figure 2.1 The Cotton Tenant House in Portsmouth, New Hampshire, provides an example of adapting and redefining under-performing assets. Built in 1834 as residential rental property, Strawbery Banke used it for storage for more than forty years. Photo courtesy of Strawbery Banke Museum.

Figure 2.2 The Cotton Tenant House after restoration and rehabilitation completed in 2011. The first floor features exhibition space for the horticulture department and the second floor has a residential rental apartment. Photo courtesy of Strawbery Banke Museum.

will create income-producing space are less difficult to fund. In contrast to traditional projects, donors will more readily endorse the idea of preserving historic houses while at the same time providing support for a project that will generate regular dependable income—in some sense, an endowment fund.

Strategy: Redefine under-performing assets and convert them to commercial uses.

The Lowd House, following the improved management of the collections, houses only the library. RFH should consider if the use of this building by the library is in the best interest of the organization and the library. Averaging fewer that two researchers per week, the library consumes a major portion of the RFH annual budget when one considers the salary and benefits of the librarian, building utilities, and short- and long-term maintenance costs. RFH should consider partnering with the history room in the city library and combining RFH's historical collections with those of the city library. RFH would achieve significant savings and researchers will find their work to be easier with local history materials under one roof. Again, attention must be paid to the politics of this radical move.

With the Lowd House empty, RFH has several options. It could expand its rental program based on the Sherburne House model—the result would be continued ownership of this historic building and steady income, some of which could accrue for the future maintenance and preservation of the building. Lowd House could be leased on a short- or long-term basis, or the house could be sold with preservation easements to a private owner.[7] Income from the sale could be applied to a building endowment that would ensure the preservation of RFH's other historic buildings. All these choices have positive and negative aspects. Ultimately, the choice may come down to how radical an action the director and the board of trustees are willing and able to make.

Strategy: Fulfill preservation and mission commitments through other means than direct program use and/or ownership.

The interpretation of the Fitzwilliam House is at the core of the organization's mission. An expansion of the numbers served by the interpretive program would better serve the implementation of the mission and provide additional income. Although RFH's current program serves its audience well, it gives the organization little new to market to the public. The Fitzwilliam's history is rich and should be mined for innovative subject matter and approaches. As an example, the colonel's ownership of a brewery provides an opportunity to take advantage of the latest enthusiasm for locally brewed beers. A strong interpretive presentation and exhibitions would offer RFH new marketing prospects and potential access to those who ordinarily may not have interest in a historic house. Also, the colonel and his family were involved in the abolitionist movement. This connection to an important historical movement may give RFH an opening to partner with other organizations in the area to offer an interpretation of the house, which would give RFH access to other organizations' audiences. RFH's surrounding property and gardens allow for additional income from special educational programs, tours, and interpretation.

Strategy: Offer educational programs that are entertaining, engaging, participatory, and relevant to new audiences. Collaborate with other organizations on programming and share audiences.

* * * * *

The list of strategies offered in this chapter is not exhaustive, nor are the specific solutions suggested for the Richard Fitzwilliam House the only possibilities for introducing new financial resources. The strategies and solutions are intended to suggest what is possible when the profes-

Lawrence J. Yerdon

sional and volunteer leadership of a historic house museum looks beyond traditional approaches to creating income.

As one considers developing any new alternative sources of funding, a business plan is critically important to the success of the project. Although business plans come in many different formats, there are commonalities among them and specific tasks that are required to ensure a successful outcome.[8] These include:

- A definition of the goal—purely income or a combination of mission and income.
- A detailed description of the product or service.
- Assignment of project leadership: a volunteer, existing staff member, or independent contractor. Does this person report to the director or to the board?
- A chart of the personnel required to implement the project.
- A definition of the target market: Who is the potential customer and what is the demand?
- A study of the competition—formal or informal.
- A marketing plan. How will the market be reached?
- A legal review. If the historic house is a nonprofit, can it do this project and not negatively impact its nonprofit status? Does the organization need to create a separate legal entity?
- A checklist for required permits, licenses, and potential ordinance restrictions.
- A list of potential sources of funding to underwrite capital and early operating costs. How will these sources be secured?
- A consideration of the politics: Who needs to know about the project? Who will support it? Is there opposition? If so, what will be the response?
- A calendar of actions.
- A financial plan that includes the following:
  - Income and expense projections
  - Pricing
  - Marketing cost
  - Management costs and fees
  - Costs of facility use
  - Personnel salaries, including benefits and taxes
  - Start-up costs
  - Cash flow

With a business plan in hand, projects are more likely to succeed.

Nontraditional financial resources cannot, nor should they, replace the resources an organization already has in place, but they can add to the income mix. An expanded and diversified portfolio of financial resources (traditional and new) offers the potential for increased income and can mitigate the financial impact on an organization if one of the projects fails. Getting to the place where the culture of the volunteer and professional leadership of historic houses is a continuous, creative, entrepreneurial process is both time-consuming and difficult, but the benefits to long-term sustainability are significant and worth the investment.

Notes

1. Lynne A. Sessions, "Cultural Entrepreneurship: Case Discussion and Conclusions," in *Case Studies in Cultural Entrepreneurship: How to Create Relevant and Sustainable Institutions*, ed. Gretchen Sullivan Sorin and Lynne A. Sessions (New York: Rowman & Littlefield, 2015), 89–97.

2. Susan U. Raymond, *Nonprofit Finance for Hard Times: Leadership Strategies When Economies Falter* (Hoboken: John Wiley & Sons, Inc., 2010), 127.
3. Frances Hesselbein, *Hesselbein on Leadership* (San Francisco: Jossey-Bass, 2002), 55.
4. Raymond, *Nonprofit Finance*, 127.
5. J. Gregory Dees, "Enterprising Nonprofits," *Harvard Business Review* 76, no. 1 (January–February 1998): 8.
6. For a policy statement and guidelines for deaccessioning, refer to the American Association for State and Local History's *Statement of Professional Standards and Ethics (Revised 2016)*, available at http://bit.ly/324Caud.
7. Donna Ann Harris, *New Solutions for House Museums* (New York: AltaMira Press, 2007), 139–203.
8. A search of the internet will provide a wide range of business plan formats with varying degrees of complexity. Choose the least complicated that will work for your project.

Recommended Resources

Beaulieu, Rebecca. *Financial Fundamentals for Historic House Museums*. New York: Rowman & Littlefield, 2017.
Harris, Donna Ann. *New Solutions for House Museums*. New York: Rowman & Littlefield Publishers, Inc., 2007.
Heagney, Joseph. *Fundamentals of Project Management*. New York: AMACOM, 2012.
Hesselbein, Frances. *Hesselbein on Leadership*. San Francisco: Jossey-Bass, 2002.
Lang, Andrew S., and Wayne Berson. *How to Read Nonprofit Financial Statements*. Washington, DC: ASAE & the Center for Association Leadership, 2010.
Russell, Lou. *10 Steps to Successful Project Management*. Alexandria, VA: ASID Press, 2007.
Sorin, Gretchen Sullivan, and Lynne A. Sessions, eds. *Case Studies in Cultural Entrepreneurship: How to Create Relevant Sustainable Institutions*. New York: Rowman & Littlefield, 2015.

Chapter 3

Evaluation Is Not Just Nice, It Is Necessary

CONNY C. GRAFT

Imagine the worst-case scenario: your city council, your foundation, or the county government decides to cut most or all of your funding. How would you respond? Beyond ticket sales, how will you prove that your institution is worth funding in today's economy? Do you have data that proves your historic house museum is making a difference in education and quality of life? Can you present evidence that the funding you are receiving is making history relevant to people's lives today? Are the decisions you are making about your programs and exhibits based on evidence? Evaluation gives you the evidence needed to make a case for supporting your museum even in the worst of times. In addition, evaluation can assist you in determining how to define and measure a successful visitor experience. Evaluation must be a priority.

Evaluation helps you to be very specific about the intended outcomes of the visitor experience. Deciding what you want people to know, feel, and do as a result of an experience in your historic house museum will help your staff, board, and volunteers stay focused on the institutional goals. By using regular evaluation as a driving tool, your work will become more intentional. Feedback from evaluations will assist you in planning what activities to keep doing, what activities to stop doing, and what new experiences to develop.

Evaluation can confirm or surprise you about the preferences of your current and potential audiences. What attracts them to your current exhibitions and programs? Can their experience be improved? What do they know about the time period you are interpreting? Are you boring them with the information they already know or do you need to step back and give them more information? What makes them smile and say "aha!"? Why don't certain segments of your community visit? What aspects of the stories about the people who lived and worked at your site do potential visitors find relevant to their lives today? If you are planning on making some changes to your exhibits and programs, wouldn't it be good to know if the changes you are planning to make are appealing to current and potential visitors before you spend time and money on implementing the changes?

Thorough evaluation to both assess and drive your work assures current and potential funders that their support is making a difference in people's lives. Once you begin to collect meaningful data about the impact of your organization, you can use those studies to approach new funders. And most importantly, evaluation shows current and potential visitors that you care about them.

Before you continue reading this chapter, I want to ask a favor: trust me when I tell you that you can use the following approach to collect data that is meaningful and actionable in historic house museums.

You may be thinking, "This sounds great, but we can't do this here. We don't have the time or the money. I am the only staff member, or we have just two staff members and a few volunteers." You may be thinking that with all the projects you are juggling you can't possibly find time to do an evaluation. No more excuses! While I cannot give you more time or staff, I will provide you with tools and templates you can use to make the time you do spend on evaluation more efficient and valuable. For examples of evaluations conducted in small museums read, "In Lieu of Mind Reading, Visitor Studies, and Evaluation."[1] Remember, evaluation is a planning tool, and that is something you are already doing. Evaluation is not an additional activity; it is a better way to plan for the future.

What Is Evaluation?

Evaluation is the *systematic* collection of information about programs and operations—from the *current and potential user's perspective*—that examines the successes and shortcomings of operations and management *against what you want to achieve*. Let's unpack these terms:

- *Systematic* means that everyone gets the same questions. It also means that you use random sample selection to identify the person to participate in the survey or interview. Before conducting a survey or interview, choose a specific location to invite people to participate in the survey. For example, you might select a bench outside the historic house. Then, select a number between 1 and 3. Let's say you choose 2. Using the specific location and a number, invite every second person who walks by the bench to participate in the survey. If you stick to this process, at the end of the day you should have a sample that is representative of your entire audience. This rule also prevents you from choosing people who look like you or appear to be enjoying the experience.
- *Current and potential user's perspective* should be obvious as this is about finding out what people outside of your board, staff, and volunteers think about your organization, programs, and services.
- *Against what you wanted to achieve* is the most critical part of evaluation. Before you can evaluate the strength or weakness of a program or experience, you must determine what you want people to know, feel, and do as a result of the experience. While it might be nice to find out if people liked or were satisfied with the experience, that information does not help you decide about how to improve the experience.

Evaluation as a Planning Tool

Imagine this typical planning process at a house museum. Someone comes to the staff, volunteer, or board meeting and says, "I just got back from a trip and saw this great program at another historic house and I think we should do something like that here." Then someone else says, "Oh, we could never do something like that here." Then someone else remarks, "I love this idea." The discussion about the program goes on and on. Finally, the board chair interrupts, "We have to get our event calendar out next week, so we need to make a decision. I think we should do it and this is how it will work." Staff and volunteers scramble to do research on the topic, find the objects and materials to do the program, and train the staff and volunteers. The program opens, people come, and at the end of the day everyone celebrates the fact that they pulled it off. The next day the staff and volunteers work on the next program or event.

Is this the best way to plan a new program, exhibition, or event? What is missing from this process? Did the staff decide who the target audience should be for the program before planning the experience? Did the staff decide what they wanted people to know, feel, and do as a result of the experience? Did the staff ask visitors if this is a program they would be interested in attending? For those who came, what ideas do they have for improving the experience? Even though people came to the program, did they learn anything from the experience? Did the program inspire them to learn more about the topic?

Using Evaluation to Plan a Visitor Experience

Evaluation is a planning tool. I will show you how to use evaluation to become more intentional about the work you are doing and involve the visitor in the process of planning the experience (see Figure 3.1). In the center of the visitor experience is impact—the long-term effect of your organization on your members and community. You need to agree on that impact: what people should know, feel, and do as a result of the experience.

Evaluating = Planning
Draft Outcomes and Strategies
Front-end Evaluation
Prototypes
Formative Evaluation
Final Program Exhibit
Summative Evaluation
Impact

Figure 3.1 Impact Diagram

Start with the End in Mind

What impact do you want to have on your audience? What does success look like? If you were to define success for your organization, exhibit, program, or website, how would you do that? If you can't define a successful experience and the impact of that experience, you can't measure it.

For example, while writing this chapter I had to make some tough decisions about what to include and what to leave out. With limited pages, I don't have much space to say everything I want to say (just like in an interpretive program or exhibition). So how do I decide what to include?

I began at the end. I began by imagining what I wanted the reader (you!) to know, think about, feel, or do as a result of this chapter. I wrote some outcomes and they helped me prioritize the information I needed to share. Once I started writing, I returned to the outcomes and revised them several times. It is an organic and evolutionary process. At the end of this chapter, look back at these outcomes and evaluate how well I achieved them.

Chapter Outcomes

As a result of reading this chapter, readers will be able to:

- Articulate why evaluation is essential.
- Describe why articulating your outcomes will ensure you measure what matters.
- Use examples to write outcomes for the projects that you want to evaluate.
- Describe the three different types of evaluation.
- Describe the steps to plan an evaluation.
- Describe the pros and cons of using different methods to collect data.
- Become inspired to make evaluation a priority.

Outcomes are statements that describe a change in what people will know or think about, feel, and do as a result of an experience (see text box "Chapter Outcomes"). Outcomes should be meaningful, measurable, and mission related. Avoid statements such as "Be aware of" or "Understand that" or "Have a sense of." Use action verbs such as describe, articulate, identify, demonstrate, feel, and compare. Action verbs will ensure that the statements are measurable.

The second outcome for the Harriet Beecher Stowe House ("Feel inspired to be a change agent and understand that they can make a difference just as Stowe did") is an excellent example of their intention to connect the past to the present and make the stories they tell relevant to people today (see text box "Examples of Outcomes"). The outcomes also relate to their mission: "The Harriet Beecher Stowe Center preserves and interprets Stowe's Hartford home and the Center's historic collections, promotes vibrant discussion of her life and work and inspires commitment to social justice and positive change."

Writing outcome statements is not easy. When I teach workshops on evaluation, I ask participants to pick one program/exhibition/website and one target audience. I ask them to imagine they have implemented the project and are watching a video interview with their target audience after they have participated in the experience. Imagine you are watching the video and are feeling very happy about what people are saying. Write down what they are saying, thinking about,

Examples of Outcomes

Harriet Beecher Stowe House, Hartford, Connecticut

1. Understand that social justice issues in Stowe's time relate to issues today.
2. Feel inspired to be a change agent and understand that they can make a difference just as Stowe did.
3. Speak up for social justice.
4. Stay connected with the Harriet Beecher Stowe Center.

Dumbarton House, Washington, DC

1. Describe why Washington, DC's, future as the nation's capital was uncertain after the revolution.
2. Describe how women's groups like The National Society of Colonial Dames launched the modern preservation movement despite having limited rights.
3. Feel a connection with the people of the Nourse household.
4. Feel inspired to support local preservation efforts in your community.

Outcomes for teachers, "Remembering Lincoln" website, Ford's Theatre, Washington, DC

1. Use this site as part of Civil War and Reconstruction lesson plans.
2. Use the site to inspire students to learn about the impact of Lincoln's assassination.
3. Use the site to teach students how to research and analyze documents.
4. Recommend the site to other history and social studies teachers.

asking about, and feeling. Include your staff, volunteers, board members, and partners in your community in this exercise. Brainstorm outcomes that describe what you want your target audience to know/think about, feel, and do. Write them on Post-It notes, put them up on a wall and then see where there are similarities and differences. Group those that are similar next to each other. Then ask everyone to pick three outcomes.

It may take you and your planning team several discussions and rewrites before you can feel confident that your outcomes are measurable, meaningful, and related to your specific place and mission. Do not give up. The more time you spend on this part of the process, the less time you will spend on making decisions later about how you design, implement, and evaluate the program. Once you have some agreed upon outcomes, use the Outcome Worksheet (see Table 3.1) to connect your outcomes to your strategies, and to your evaluation plan.

It is very important that you focus on one or two target audiences. Examples of target audiences include families with preschoolers, student groups, or senior citizens who live within fifty miles. Selecting a target audience does not mean that other types of people can't participate in the experience. Focusing on a target audience allows you to design and evaluate the program in a manner that is appropriate for that particular audience. Selecting a target audience will ensure that the methods you use to collect feedback and the types of questions you are asking are appropriate for that one particular audience. Knowing your target audience will also impact the decisions you make about the content of the experience and how you want to engage the audience in the content. Having one target audience in mind will also help you ensure that the outcomes are appropriate for that audience.

Table 3.1 Outcome Worksheet

Target Audience	Know/Feel/Do Outcomes	How to Achieve This Outcome	What We Need to Know	Type of Evaluation	Achievement Indicators
6th–8th grade teachers.	Describe how the book *Uncle Tom's Cabin* galvanized public sentiment and protests about abolition worldwide.	Have students read quotes that illustrate public sentiment and discuss them.	To what degree do teachers say their students can do this.	Formative.	On online surveys, 80 percent of teachers Agree/Strongly Agree that students can do this.

When you fill out this worksheet, you may find yourself changing one of the columns as you think about different outcomes and different ways to achieve them. The worksheet will change again as you begin to collect feedback about your outcomes and strategies.

One way to determine if you have achieved an outcome is to turn the statement into a question. For example:

Table 3.2 Scale

Please rate the following: My students can describe how the book *Uncle Tom's Cabin* galvanized public sentiment and protests about abolitionists worldwide.				
1 Strongly Disagree	2 Disagree	3 Undecided	4 Agree	5 Strongly Agree

In addition to the question above, you should follow it up with open-ended questions such as:

- For those of you who rated this 3 or below, please tell us what we could do differently to make this a 5.
- For those of you who rated this a 4 or above, please tell us what part of the experience contributed to students understanding this idea?

While having a set of clear, measurable, and meaningful outcomes is important, you will discover that the experiences you design will often produce outcomes you did not intend. Sometimes, the unintended outcomes are more meaningful and powerful than the outcomes you intended. For example, evaluations I have conducted revealed these unintended outcomes:

- From a teacher: "This experience helped me understand how to talk to my students about their immigration experiences."
- From a visitor to the Harriet Beecher Stowe House: "This experience inspired me to start writing again."

When to Conduct the Evaluation

After you have drafted your outcomes and strategies, you need to decide when in the planning process you should conduct the evaluation: before, during, or after:

- Front-end evaluation occurs after you have drafted outcomes and a list of potential strategies for achieving them. At this point, you have your ideas on paper, but you have not spent money on training volunteers to do the program or refurnished rooms to achieve the outcomes. Then you conduct a front-end evaluation, where you share the outcomes and strategies with your current or potential target audience. After collecting feedback, you will discover that you need to go back and rewrite your outcomes and strategies.
- Formative evaluation occurs when you have a set of agreed upon outcomes and you have brainstormed some strategies to achieve the outcomes. You may have several different techniques or formats you want to test with your target audience before you build your entire exhibit or implement a new program. You can create prototypes of a section of an exhibition, or you can offer different versions of a program. Once you put up the prototypes or start offering a new program, collect feedback from your target audience. After this step, you may also need to go back a step and rewrite the outcomes and strategies. You will also be able to make more informed decisions about the exhibit or program before finalizing it.
- Summative evaluation is conducted after the exhibition has been built and the final program is up and running. This type of evaluation is often the least valuable because, by the time the evaluation is completed, there may be no money left to make changes. Also, you may be under a looming deadline to create the next new exhibition or program.

Rarely does anyone conduct all three types of evaluation. But even by doing one type of evaluation, it will help you make *informed* decisions about the visitor experience based on evidence. Evaluation is about *learning*, not *accountability*.

Front-end, Formative, or Summative Evaluation: How Do I Decide?

Front-end Evaluation

There is no one perfect answer to this question. Front-end evaluation is conducted before you have written your interpretive or exhibition plan and after you have a draft of your outcomes and strategies. You may want to ask the following questions:

- What images and stories do people bring with them about this topic?
- What questions do they have about the topic?
- How do they want to learn/experience it?
- What do they think about your outcomes and strategies?
- Are there other outcomes and strategies they want for their experience?

One of my favorite examples is a front-end evaluation conducted at Colonial Williamsburg with Randi Korn and Associates. The staff brainstormed some outcomes and strategies and then decided they wanted to find out what people already knew about the events that led up to the revolution.

Randi Korn and I approached visitors entering the visitor center, asked just a few questions, and recorded their responses. I began by saying: If I say the words "American Revolution" what images or words first come to mind? Most respondents said Boston, Philadelphia, the Boston Tea Party, and taxation without representation. Then we asked, "If I say the South and American history, what words come to mind?" As you might expect, they responded with "the Civil War."

Most surprising was when we asked, "If I say the South and the American Revolution, what words or images come to mind?" They looked back at us with blank stares. Even though they knew about George Washington and Thomas Jefferson, they associated these men with Boston and Philadelphia. We continued: "Did everyone in the colonies agree to start a revolution?" Almost everyone stated "yes." How long did it take the colonists to decide to start a revolution? Response: "Overnight." It would be easy to dismiss them as uneducated tourists, but many of the respondents had college educations and some had graduate degrees. While they may not have aced their history classes, they were lifelong learners and were eager to learn.

We discovered that our outcomes were more appropriate for a graduate course on the America Revolution, so we had to revise them for our visitors. We also now knew that when interpreters started to talk about this time period, they needed to start the story differently, using stories visitors recalled about Boston and Philadelphia. Next, interpreters could show visitors the connections to the people and events in Williamsburg, Virginia. The staff also realized we needed to include many stories of those who opposed the revolution and those who sat on the fence. All of the findings also helped us plan interpreter training. This front-end evaluation changed our outcomes and the way in which we designed the program before we invested in training and reproductions.

Formative Evaluation

You should use formative evaluation as people are experiencing prototypes of an exhibition, program, or website. Here you are experimenting with different ways to achieve your outcomes, collecting feedback as you experiment and then making very quick changes to see if the changes improved the results. The type of information you are exploring may include the following:

- Do people know what to do? Are the instructions clear?
- Does the experience inspire them to ask questions?
- Are there ways we can make the experience more relevant?
- Are we achieving our outcomes?

The staff at Colonial Williamsburg used formative evaluation to experiment with "Order in the Court," a thirty-minute program at the courthouse. It was the first time that some visitors were invited to take on roles using a short script along with the interpreters as we reenacted court cases that took place on the site.

We had some disagreements about the best way to set up the program and run the trials. So for a few days we implemented Plan A of the program. Then, the next few days we implemented Plan B. During these two experiments, we conducted surveys and observations before and after the program and compared the results of the two experiments.

As a result of this evaluation, we eliminated several outcomes. Thirty minutes is a short time for a program tackling major topics, and one of the hardest decisions was determining which of the outcomes were the most important. We also shortened the introduction to the program (we observed people leaving the introduction on the very first day) and simplified our role-playing instructions. One of the most important changes came as a result of interviewing visitors after they exited the program. On the first day, when attempting to interview people, I discovered I could not begin to ask my questions because people had so many questions of their own about what they had just experienced. This is, of course, one of the best outcomes you can have for a program.

We also realized we needed a way to help answer their questions. We decided that at the end of the program, an interpreter would announce that he would be standing outside near the maple tree to answer questions people had about the trial. We also learned that by having someone answer their questions in third person, visitors gained a better understanding of what they had just witnessed. Adding a question-and-answer element at the end of the program with a third-person interpreter would not have happened if we had not interviewed people after the program ended.

Summative Evaluation

Use summative evaluation after installing the exhibition and training the interpreters. Choose this method to capture a baseline of how a particular experience is working or not. Use your results to help design a future exhibition or program. At Connor Prairie, an outdoor history park in Fishers, Indiana, the staff used summative evaluation to explore how much—and exactly how—guests were learning during their visit. They asked families to carry a tape recorder and record the first hour of their visit. They transcribed the recordings and analyzed them for clues about how guests and interpreters interacted.

From this evaluation, they learned that interpreters were doing all the talking. Visitors were doing all the listening. It was a one-sided conversation that led to a less-engaged guest, and a less-than-inspiring experience. As a result, they changed their approach to interpretation, making it more guest-focused and interactive. A big part of the change was rethinking the way they trained interpreters. After they had implemented the changes, they did the same study again and found that the conversations were two-way and much more guest-focused.[2]

Steps for Planning an Evaluation

As you work through the ten steps in the process outlined in Figure 3.2, you may find yourself going back and rewriting some steps as you move down the ladder. Step 4 is a very important step because you might find a history, art, or science museum that has done a similar evaluation and you can contact the authors to find out about their study. For step 4, I have included a link to a bibliography on the AASLH website that lists several websites, articles, and books you can review to find examples of evaluations conducted at other museums.[3]

For small museums, you may want to watch AASLH's webinar, "Take the Guesswork Out of Evaluations: How to Measure What Really Matters." This webinar includes a template for a special event survey, a bank of alternative questions you can use, instructions for implementing the survey, and a spreadsheet template you can use to analyze the data.

Notice that the decision about what methods you should use, which you must decide before you craft questions to ask, is step 6 in the process. If you skip right to this step, the data that you collect will not be meaningful or actionable.

There are many different methods you can consider using to gather the information you need to know. When various methods are compared, you will discover that none are perfect or unbiased (see Table 3.3). In the social science research field, triangulation can be very helpful,

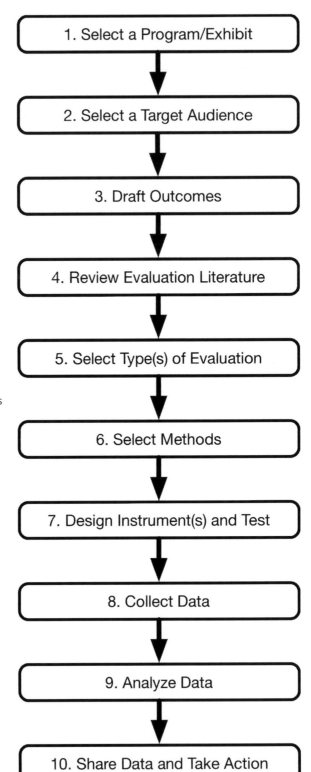

Figure 3.2 Planning Steps

Table 3.3 Evaluation Methods

Methods	Advantages	Disadvantages	Comments
Self-administered Surveys	• Easy to distribute/ manage • Visitor in control	• Don't know what answers mean • Hard to read • Takes people longer to fill out • Not representative • Many wrong ratings • Requires data entry	• Include specific instruction on how to answer each question • Do not put page two on back of page one
Surveys Conducted by Staff/Volunteer	• Representative • Can probe for understanding • Shorter time • All questions answered	• Requires staff/ volunteer • Requires training • Requires data entry	
In-depth Interviews	• Peel the onion • Capture visitor language • Can find out why	• Requires trained interviewer • Takes more time to analyze	• Best when recorded with audio or video
Online Surveys	• Gives visitor time to reflect • Comments more meaningful and articulate • More honest • Inexpensive • No data entry • Automatic charts and tables • Longer-term impact	• Can't probe for understanding • Target audience may not have PC, Internet, or be computer literate	• Can use a paper survey for those who do not have access to PC or the Internet
Focus Groups	• Great for qualitative • Helpful in understanding why people think/feel/do • Video clips very powerful for staff, volunteers, board • Engaging for the participants including community leaders, visitors, potential visitors	• Can be more expensive than other methods • Requires trained facilitator • Requires trained analyst • Requires incentives • Can be done virtually with software like Zoom	• Can be combined with on-site survey or diary • Can be done with cued testing
Observation	• Determines what behaviors you want to see • Determines if certain parts of an exhibition are ignored • Helps interpreters understand behaviors you want them to stimulate in visitors • Tells you how long people spend in exhibition	• Requires training • Requires people who are good observers	• Must be followed up with a survey or interview to find out why people do what they do

especially when you are working with small samples. This practice implies that you are going to collect data in three different ways, from different sources. For example, if you are going to evaluate a tour of a historic house, your three different data sets could include a survey of visitors who toured the house, a focus group of people who toured the house, and observations of the visitors while they are touring.

Evaluation on a Shoestring

There are several things you can do that do not take up a great deal of time or money but can help you with getting started.

- Review evaluations conducted in your organization in the past.
- Contact your chamber of commerce, tourism agencies in your state, and the U.S. Census Bureau to see what data already exists about your audiences.
- Reach out to your local college and/or university. Their departments of education, sociology, and business have professors who are experts in evaluation, and they are always looking for projects for students.
- Reach out to other nonprofits and cultural organizations to see what evaluations they have done.
- To learn about potential audiences in your community, ask the leaders of nonprofits about their audiences and challenges. Invite them for a visit and ask for their feedback.
- Visit websites and associations on the resource list at the end of this chapter.
- Look at the resources at the end of this chapter and share evaluations already conducted at other museums with your staff to discuss the evaluation process and lessons learned.

Tips for Doing Evaluation

- Be sensitive to the feelings your staff, volunteers, and board members might have. They may think about this practice as a type of pass/fail report. You need to help them understand that evaluation, when used correctly, is not a performance review but a way of learning how to improve the visitor experience.
- Involve staff, volunteers, board members, and community partners as you plan an evaluation. You need to build trust from the very beginning so the people who need to make changes trust the data that you collect and understand why change is necessary.
- While you are gathering information from current and potential visitors, also collect information from staff, volunteers, and board members via a survey or interviews. They need to know that their opinion matters. There may not be full agreement between staff and visitors, but it is useful to learn if there is a gap between the two groups so you can address that gap and help staff see your organization through the eyes of your target audience.
- After you decide what questions to ask visitors, ask staff and volunteers to answer the survey as if they are the visitors. When you get the results, share the answers staff thought you would get and compare them to the answers you collected from visitors. Comparing what you and staff think visitors want to data collected from visitors will can be very useful.
- When deciding what questions to include in your survey, write down how you might use that information to make a decision. If the information you are seeking cannot be used to make a decision, do not collect it. Your goal is to ensure that the information you collect is *actionable*.

If you have never done an evaluation, or even if you have just dipped your toe in it, begin with something small such as a special event or a program. Keep it simple. Do not try to collect everything you think you need to know. Consider asking just a few questions for a week or two and then ask different questions the following week. Select one target audience, work on your outcomes and strategies for that small project, and then do a front-end evaluation. Keep in mind that your first goal is to become comfortable in doing an evaluation and getting your staff and volunteers so excited about this practice that they will be hungry for more. Once you begin using evaluation to plan your programs and exhibitions, you will discover new insights and perspectives. Decisions will be made based on evidence. After practicing evaluation on just one or two programs or exhibitions, you will begin to create a culture of evaluation in your institution. Embedding evaluative thinking in your museum will create a lasting impact, internally and externally. Critical thinking and reflection will be valued and reinforced. Evaluation is not just a process; it is a way of thinking about everything that you do. Historic house museums that make evaluative thinking a priority will provide evidence to their community, their visitors, and their stakeholders that their existence is making a difference in peoples' lives.

Notes

1. Conny Graft and Stacy Klingler, "In Lieu of Mind Reading, Visitor Studies and Evaluation," in *The Small Museum Toolkit, Book 4: Reaching and Responding to the Audience*, ed. Cinnamon Catlin-Legutko and Stacy Klingler (Lanham, MD: AltaMira Press, 2012), 37–74.
2. Ken Bubp and Dave Allison, "Opening Doors to Great Guest Experiences," *History News* 62, no. 2 (Spring 2007): 20–23.
3. American Association of State and Local History, "Resource List: Audience Research and Evaluation in History Museums and Related Institutions." Updated January 23, 2017. https://bit.ly/2LYjh59.

Recommended Resources

American Association of State and Local History. "Resource List: Audience Research and Evaluation in History Museums and Related Institutions." Updated January 23, 2017. https://bit.ly/2LYjh59.
American Evaluation Association. http://www.eval.org.
Diamond, Judy, Michael Horn, and David H. Uttal. *Practical Evaluation Guide: Tools for Museums and Other Informal Educational Settings, Third Edition*. Lanham, MD: Rowman & Littlefield Publishers, 2016.
Graft, Conny. "Take the Guesswork Out of Evaluation: How to Measure What Really Matters" (webinar). American Association of State and Local History. February 8, 2017. https://bit.ly/2MlgFet.
Graft, Conny, and Stacy Klingler. "In Lieu of Mind Reading, Visitor Studies and Evaluation." In *The Small Museum Toolkit, Book 4: Reaching and Responding to the Audience*, edited by Cinnamon Catlin-Legutko and Stacy Klingler, 37–74. Lanham, MD: AltaMira Press, 2012.
InformalScience.org. http://informalscience.org.
Visitor Studies Association. http://visitorstudies.org.

Chapter 4

The Essential Role of Boards in Reimagining House Museums

DONNA ANN HARRIS

This chapter is for board members and staff of historic house museums who may be unfamiliar with some basic nonprofit management concepts critical to board service at historic house museums. Most people see board service as honorary or as an acknowledgment of personal achievement. We have found that most board members begin their house museum board service with little understanding of their legal duties as fiduciaries of state-chartered nonprofit organizations: the historic house museum organization itself, its site, and its collections. This chapter explains the board of director's basic legal duties under your state's nonprofit law, ten broader responsibilities of historic house museum board members, and how these responsibilities reinforce good historic house museum stewardship.

Whether your historic house museum is new and managed entirely by volunteers or a long-standing local museum with professional staff, this overview will clarify board members' specific roles. As the governing authority for your historic house museum, the board plays a vital role in setting its future direction, especially as its role is reimagined for the future. We believe that clarifying the board's role will ultimately be helpful for paid staff so that the organization can best use the time and talents of both board and staff most efficiently. All historic house museums, no matter their size and longevity, need a high-functioning and well-performing board of directors to ensure its success.

Legal Duties of Board Members

As legal trustees of a state-chartered nonprofit corporation, your house museum board has certain duties required by your state nonprofit law. Nonprofit board members are fiduciaries who must oversee the assets of the corporation for the benefit of the public.[1] In the case of a historic house museum, the organization's assets are its finances, the buildings and grounds, and the collections. The board is responsible for maintaining and enhancing all the assets of the corporation in their care. These assets are concrete; board members determine how the organization maintains the museum and individual objects over time. Board members can monitor their ongoing

43

stewardship of these assets through inspecting the buildings, grounds, and collection objects regularly to identify preservation issues or collections concerns.

The assets are held by the board of directors on behalf of the public, to whom the board is ultimately accountable. Most states have an agency that provides oversight of nonprofit corporations: forty-five states regulate charitable fund-raising, and forty-one states require nonprofits to register (and, in most cases, to pay a fee).[2] Timely submissions of these reports and fees are a board responsibility often delegated to staff.

In addition to serving as fiduciaries, state-chartered nonprofit corporation board members have three legal duties contained in their state nonprofit law that govern how board members carry out their work. These legal duties are:

1. Duty of care.
2. Duty of loyalty.
3. Duty of obedience to the law.

Duty of Care

Duty of care describes the level of competence and judgment that is expected of a board member. It is commonly expressed as the duty of "care that an ordinarily prudent person would exercise in a like position and under similar circumstances."[3] This means that a board member owes the duty to exercise reasonable care when he or she accepts a nomination to become a steward of the organization.[4] You do not need highly specialized skills to meet the duty of care as a board member; you are expected to provide oversight in the same way you would for your own affairs.

There are many practical ways that historic house museum board members can proactively perform their duty of care at their house museum. Historic house museum board members should regularly attend board meetings; read the minutes, financial statements, and bylaws; and be up to date on all key matters. Most importantly, board members should ask questions about these documents to ensure they understand them. Participating in committee work will also expand your knowledge of the historic house museum and its collections. All board members should participate in the creation of the organization's strategic or long-range plan, since it lays out strategies and future projects. Board members also perform their duty of care by adhering to any restrictions on the use of funds from grant sources, endowments, or individual donors.

The "Statement of Professional Standards and Ethics" from the American Association for State and Local History (AASLH) can help board members be better stewards of their house museum.[5] This document presents clear guidance about the role of the board as the governing authority for a history organization. The AASLH has several samples of ethical guidelines on their website that might be useful if your historic house museum does not have one in place now or plans to update it soon.[6]

The American Alliance of Museum recommends that all museums create the following five core documents.[7] These key documents clarify the board's stewardship responsibilities toward their historic house museum and collections.

1. Mission/vision statement
2. Organizational code of ethics

3. Collections management plan
4. Disaster preparedness plan
5. Strategic or long-range plan

The collections management policy is a critical document for historic sites and is essential to the board's duty of care. This document provides guidance about what the organization collects and why, and how these objects should be displayed, stored, and managed for the benefit of the public.

If your organization is just starting a house museum, you may want to know about the AASLH's "Standards and Excellence Program for History Organizations" (StEPs).[8] StEPs is a self-study program offered by AASLH and designed specifically for small- to mid-sized history organizations, including those managed entirely by volunteers. The StEPs workbook guides organizations in assessing their policies and practices using a Basic, Good, and Better benchmarking system and includes chapters on creating all five core documents mentioned above.

Historic house museums should also follow "The Secretary of the Interior's Standards for Treatment of Historic Properties, with Guidelines for Preserving, Rehabilitating, Restoring and Reconstructing Historic Buildings" for any maintenance, preservation, or conservation activity for the historic buildings that the board owns or manages for others.[9] Whether your property is historically designated or not, these standards provide commonsense guidance for maintenance of your historic house museum.

Duty of Loyalty

Duty of loyalty is a standard of faithfulness; a board member must give undivided allegiance when making decisions affecting the organization. This means that a board member can never use information obtained as a member for personal financial gain and must act in the best interests of the organization.[10]

Historic house museum board members can fulfill their duty of loyalty to the corporation by ensuring that confidential information is not shared with others outside the organization. Every board member should understand and agree to abide by the organization's conflict-of-interest policy and alert the board president if they think that they might have an actual or potential conflict of interest. The AASLH has several sample conflicts of interest policies on their website, free for download.[11] Historic house museum board members should not act on information they receive as part of their board service for personal financial gain, or compete with the organization should the organization be actively collecting objects for the site, for example. The board should deliberate and debate decisions with all board members participating. Once a decision is made— when a quorum is present—the board must act as one body and speak with one voice. Board members can be passionate and disagree, but once the matter has been thoroughly debated and the board decides, it is essential that all board members line up to support the board's decision.[12]

Duty of Obedience

Duty of obedience requires board members to be faithful to the organization's mission. They are not permitted to act in a way that is inconsistent with the central goals of the house museum. A basis for this rule lies in the public's trust that the organization will manage donated funds to fulfill the house museum's mission.[13]

There are many ways that historic house museum boards show their duty of obedience to the law. They should pay payroll taxes on time and adhere to any policies or restrictions on grants, endowments, or donations they receive.

Board members should take care not to endanger the organization's tax status by lobbying inappropriately.[14] The board must make the organization's most recent IRS 990 tax return available to the public immediately upon request. To promote organizational transparency, your board might want to post this document on your website, since it is already available on the web for free at www.guidestar.com. The organization should adhere to state and federal laws, and not discriminate against anyone based on race, color, creed, age, sex, religion, nationality, or sexual orientation.[15] Finally, the house museum should register with the state's charity or nonprofit bureau if it is required, and pay any annual fees.

Both a Working and Governing Board

Historic house museum boards are almost always both working *and* governing boards. Historic house museum board members often *do the work* of the organization because there are few or no staff members. Board members serve as volunteers, and frequently work as docents, run events, maintain collections, and host fund-raisers whether there is staff or not. The historic house museum board also *governs* the organization. The dual role of being a working and governing board can create confusion during a house museum board's transition from being all-volunteer run to having its first professional staff. A good job description for any new staff member can go a long way to help to prevent micromanagement of new staff.

It is a good idea to have written job descriptions for every volunteer officer, board member, and committee chair. These volunteer job descriptions can be short or long, but they should make it clear who does what and the limits of authority for each role.[16] Another reason to have written descriptions for volunteer jobs is to define the chain of reporting and identify the volunteer's supervisor, as this may help prevent misunderstandings about the lines of authority. Volunteer job descriptions may be particularly helpful when paid staff and board members are providing leadership roles for projects and activities, as they should define reporting relationships. Written job descriptions for paid staff should be both routine and realistic for all staff, including part-time positions. Finally, a yearly commitment to training every board member on their roles and responsibilities (see item 7 below) can also help make it clear who does what for the house museum daily.

Ten Duties of Every House Museum Board Member

Board Source™, a national organization whose mission is to inspire and support excellence in nonprofit governance and board and staff leadership, has identified ten duties of all nonprofit board members that advances their organization's mission, vision, and values.[17] We have taken these ten basic responsibilities and expanded upon them in the context of historic house museum management with the hope of making it clear that historic house museum boards have many important tasks.

1. Determine the organization's mission/purpose

The historic house museum board must fulfill the mission of the organization through its actions, resolutions, and fund-raising. Your mission statement explains why the organization exists.

Often, a mission statement is written when the organization is incorporated and may not have been reviewed in decades. Reviewing your mission or purpose statement at least every other year helps ensure that it is still relevant for the current activities or near-term future of your house museum. If the mission statement is old, or parts are not relevant, consider making changes as part of a larger strategic planning effort (see item 6 below).

2. Select the chief executive

If your historic house museum has developed to the point that a paid staff member is needed to serve as executive director, the board should make an offer to the prospective executive director to join the organization after an appropriate personnel search. If the house museum is entirely run by volunteers, the board president often provides day-to-day guidance to other board members and volunteers working on behalf of the museum in much the way an executive director might.

Identifying a paid executive director for your organization is hard work and it takes time, often more than six months, to conduct a proper search. The board may decide to appoint an interim executive director or elevate another staff member to the job as a temporary measure until the personnel search is complete. Use the resources available from your regional or state museum association for your personnel search.[18] These groups can help you create an appropriate job description, give advice about salary ranges, and possibly identify potential candidates.

Historic house museums have increasingly hired local business leaders with no experience in nonprofit management or historic house museums as executive directors. This may be tempting for larger house museums where for-profit management skills might be useful for maintenance of extensive buildings and grounds, or where earned revenue sources are critical. Boards taking this action must understand the limitations of these individuals' breadth of specialized knowledge about historic house museums. If a board chooses the path of hiring someone with a background in for-profit business management as executive director, it is essential that strong nonprofit management, curatorial, maintenance, and grounds staff are in place to compensate for the lack of experience in nonprofits, museums, or preservation. To prevent lapses in museum ethics or standard practices around museum collections, a strong partnership between senior staff and the executive director with a for-profit background is essential.

3. Provide proper financial oversight of budget, establish financial controls

Historic house museum board members are ultimately responsible for keeping their organization well funded. They may delegate some of those fund-raising responsibilities to staff (if there is any), but the board must provide appropriate oversight of the organization's money. Boards do this by having regular financial statements (we recommend monthly), engaging in good accounting practices (such as assigning check-writing and checkbook-balancing duties to different people), and submitting annual tax returns (IRS 990 forms) and any state charities' registration paperwork on time. Even the smallest historic house museum must engage in good financial practices to inspire confidence from outsiders and to attract funding from neighbors and other donors.

4. Ensure adequate resources

Resources are not limited to financial resources. They include human resources in the form of volunteers and staff to run the historic house museum. The board is responsible for ensuring that there are sufficient funds to operate the site, staff to manage the operations, and volunteers to undertake various projects at your museum. Most nonprofit managers assume that the word "adequate," as noted here in Board Source's list, is equal to "enough." We disagree. There is never enough money to manage a house museum. The historic house museum board must be involved in decision-making about the budget and staffing to be certain that your organization has all the assets to maintain the house, landscape, and collections.

5. Ensure legal and ethical integrity/maintain accountability

The historic house museum board must make sure that it adheres to its bylaws and corporate charter, maintains its charitable tax status, and files required reports and taxes on time. These are all part of the board's duty of obedience to the law. Other high-priority policies that historic sites should implement include conflict-of-interest, personnel, whistleblower, and financial accountability/management policies. Adopting an institutional code of ethics for the historic house museum would fall into this last category. The American Association for State and Local History has several code of ethics statements available on their website to use as samples if your organization is writing or revising one.[19]

6. Ensure effective organizational planning

Organizational planning is wide-ranging and includes activities as simple as agendas for each board or executive committee meeting. After the meeting, the board and executive committee meeting minutes need to clearly identify who attended, reports heard, and any actions taken to plan the next steps.

Once your historic house museum is beyond its startup stage, it will need a strategic or long-range plan to help prioritize the goals and projects needed to support its stewardship role of maintaining the buildings, grounds, and collections in the long term. The AASLH has good advice about creating strategic plans.[20] Board members should be actively engaged in formulating any long-term plan and should review it yearly to assure the goals and strategies are being fulfilled by board, staff, and volunteers.

7. Recruit and orient new board members; assess board performance

The historic house museum board is only as good as the nominating committee that identifies, vets, and creates a slate of new board member candidates.[21] The nominating committee is critical for the organization's future, and should not wait to spring into action until just a few weeks before the annual meeting. Rather, this committee should identify the skills that the house museum needs over the coming years so that individuals can be invited to participate on committees in order to ascertain if they would be good potential board members in the future.

We encourage the nominating committee to provide a thorough briefing for any prospective board member in advance of their nomination so that they understand the totality of the house museum's operation. This would include a tour of the house and grounds and a visit to the collections storage area. They should be given any reports about the site, such as the collections care plan and recent reports from the Museum Assessment Program (MAP) or Collections Assessment for Preservation Program (CAP), if completed.[22] We also encourage sharing the museum's most recent financial statement with board member candidates so that they understand the museum's current financial position in advance of being nominated.[23]

Candidates for board service should understand that every board member is expected to make their own gift in addition to their volunteer labor. We recommend that each site create a board contract or agreement that spells out all the board responsibilities and expectations (see section below). This document can help prevent any misunderstanding by board candidates in advance of their nomination.

We recommend that historic house museum boards have specific term limits noted in their by-laws. Term limits permit the organization to benefit from new ideas and perspectives as board members rotate on and off the board each year. Board terms can be two- or three-year terms, and board members should be able to serve for two consecutive terms before being required to rotate off the board for a year. Seasoned board members can be reelected to the board after their one year of "rest."

It is unfortunate that board member performance assessment gets such short shrift in history organizations. Self-assessments of board performance for house museums are not done often enough or with enough rigor to look inward and use these insights to make needed changes. Even if the board started with the most basic of assessments of their activities relative to their volunteer job descriptions, that would be an improvement.[24]

8. Enhance the organization's public standing: be a good ambassador and advocate on behalf of the house museum

All board members should speak positively about your house museum, its staff, volunteers, and other board members in public and private. Being a good advocate for the historic house museum happens at the local grocery store as well as in a foundation's office. Board members are the front line when it comes to public perception about your historic house museum. Make sure board members are up-to-date on current plans and feel comfortable speaking about the historic house museum, its future, and its current activities.

9. Determine, monitor, and strengthen programs and services

Through board member participation in committee work, or as a volunteer working on projects or fund-raising events, board members learn more about the work of the house museum and can make your historic house museum better. Every board member contributes to the future of the historic house museum through their involvement in projects that interest them.

10. Support and evaluate the chief executive

If the board employs an executive director, he or she should be supported in the position by opportunities to attend trainings, speak at conferences, and network with peers. Board members should be supportive of staff through word and deed, whether it is a hearty "well done!" after a difficult board meeting, a birthday card, or a timely raise or bonus. Staff need to know that board members appreciate their work. The board should take time each year to evaluate their executive director and provide bonuses and raises when possible. The American Alliance of Museums has sample staff evaluation plans on their website for download if your organization is a member.[25]

Actions by the Board

The board provides direction for your historic house museum through resolutions and reviews of committee and staff reports when a quorum is present at properly called board meetings. The board, through its bylaws, may give specific authority to an executive committee to take certain actions between board meetings. Those actions should be documented and reported to the rest of the board by circulating minutes of the committee and by reporting at the following meeting. Other committees may be empowered to implement projects or take specific actions by board resolution. It is very rare that individual board members are given authority to make decisions, as decision-making is a collective board responsibility.

Board Role in Fund-raising

Board members certainly contribute their time and talent to the organization, but they also donate money, and are responsible for the organization's finances. They cannot delegate this responsibility entirely to staff. Board members monitor financial statements regularly, adopt the annual budget, put in place appropriate policies (like a gift-acceptance policy), and should have a long-term funding strategy for the organization through a strategic plan. Board members should also make their own yearly gift to the house museum, participate in all fund-raising events, assist the staff in identifying potential donors, sponsors, and members, and identify new board members willing to raise funds.

Individual Board Member Roles

Individual board members should be well informed about the historic house museum's budget, plans, and activities by reading materials circulated to them and by asking questions about any points that may be unclear. Seeking clarification and raising concerns are an individual board member's most important contribution to your house museum. All questions should be answered thoroughly, either at the meeting or in subsequent correspondence with staff or the board president. Adopting a board member agreement (see below) can highlight the specific expectations of individual board members.

We recommend that the board be trained on its roles and responsibilities during a board meeting once a year, because board members come and go each year, if term limits are in place. State museum associations can help you identify consultants or other museum directors that can provide high-quality training.

Board Member Agreement

One way to spell out the expectations for all board members, and for those who might wish to be nominated to the board, is to create a board member agreement. This simple informational document includes key information about board service at your historic house museum. The document should include statements on the following topics:

1. How often the board meets, including the typical date, time, and location. Ideally, the board meeting should be no longer than an hour and a half.
2. Board attendance requirements as noted in the bylaws, term limits noted in the bylaws, and any consequences for not attending the minimum number of board meetings.
3. An expectation that board members will review the minutes, financial statements, IRS 990 informational tax returns, and other documents sent to them in advance of each board meeting and come prepared with questions. Insist that all board members be familiar with the by-

laws, strategic plan, conflict-of-interest statement, collections care policy, and other policies at your museum. A well-prepared board orientation binder should contain all the relevant information and be reviewed with every incoming board member during their orientation.

4. If committee service is expected of all board members, include information about each committee's specific charge, and how often the committee(s) meet.
5. Each board member should help identify new board prospects, sponsors, and potential donors to the museum.
6. Expectations, if any, about board financial support beyond their volunteer participation in events, activities, and projects. State if there is a minimum gift amount expected of each board member. The board president typically contacts board members about their annual gifts and collects the checks.
7. Explain that each board member is an ambassador for the historic house museum and should speak positively about the house museum and its staff in public and private.
8. Identify who is the board spokesperson (usually the executive director or the board president) for any press inquiries. Individual board members should not speak with the press unless authorized to do so in advance. Typical exceptions might be an event committee chairperson who appears on the press release about that event and is encouraged to talk to reporters. Board members should refer any press inquiries they receive to the executive director immediately.

Board President Tasks

The board president has a host of tasks to ensure the progress of the museum. Small, all-volunteer historic house museums without staff often designate the board president as the chief executive officer, spokesperson, and official representative. Once staff is hired, the executive director usually assumes these duties. The board president is usually the executive director's day-to-day supervisor and may sign checks along with the treasurer. It is ideal if the board president reports annually in writing to the house museum's membership about the activities of the museum. The board president's specific duties are often contained in the bylaws and will include chairing board and executive committee meetings, setting the agenda for these meetings, and appointing committee chairs and perhaps committee members. The board president also needs to be an excellent problem solver as he or she is the liaison for issues between board members, between board and staff, or between board members and committee volunteers.

Typical Board Committees

In a quest to broaden the number of workers for the organization, historic house museums often establish committees to undertake the work of the organization. Committees may create efficiencies for the board, but they do not relieve the board of its legal and fund-raising responsibilities. Some committees may be standing committees as identified in the bylaws, or ad hoc or temporary committees designed to take on a specific task for a limited time. Committee members don't all have to be board members. Consider asking other volunteers with subject area expertise to join committees that might interest them.

Typical historic house museum committees include an executive committee, finance/audit, collections, nomination, events, fund-raising, and buildings and grounds. Each committee should have a written purpose or job description and a specific understanding of the limits of its authority.[26]

Board Role in Managing Staff

The board hires, rewards, and terminates the executive director. Other staff are hired or fired by the executive director with board approval and within budget limits. While the executive director is hired by and responsible to the board, executive directors need one day-to-day supervisor, and we recommend the board president for that job. This reporting relationship will prevent board members from thinking they each are "the boss of the staff." Any conflicts between board members and the executive director should be managed by the board president.

Executive Director's Role

The paid executive director carries out the board's vision for the organization and oversees program development, communications, and record keeping. He or she is responsible for fund-raising, managing other staff, working all special events, and acting as a spokesperson. Executive directors coordinate volunteers, attend board meetings, and take care of other duties as assigned. Staff is responsible for the daily and annual work of the organization to fulfill the strategic plan.

Reinventing Your House Museum

Reinvention of any organization is hard work. Historic sites, being traditional local history organizations, may struggle with creating programming that is relevant to their neighbors, members, and the general public. Today's visitors want a different house museum experience than their parents, and thus we must adapt to the interests of these new visitors. The board president and the executive director may be the ones most interested in reinventing the mission and programming for your house museum and must work to persuade other board members of the merits of any new initiative over months or perhaps years. Seeing is believing, and we suggest that board and staff together take field trips to other historic sites that are undertaking transformation activities as a research activity. After the visit the board should hold a candid discussion about any lessons learned from this research. These visits can help convince reluctant board members and help steer your reinvention efforts in a new and better direction.

The Joys of Board Service

Serving on a historic house museum board is both an honor and privilege. As a responsible board member, you are one in a long line of stewards who have worked hard to assure that a tangible piece of American history lives on for future generations of school children, scholars, neighbors, and visitors. Without these history advocates on the board, the visiting public would never know about your museum's special story and how it binds our citizens to the American past. We hope that by being better informed about your role and responsibilities as a board member, you will relish this opportunity and inspire others to take on similar roles at house museums in their hometown. Thank you for your service.

Notes

1. Board Source, *The Nonprofit Board Answer Book, Second Edition* (San Francisco, CA: Jossey-Bass, 2007), 25–26.
2. Suzanne Coffman, "Navigating State Fundraising Regulations," Guidestar.org (May 3, 2016), accessed January 2, 2017, https://trust.guidestar.org/navigating-state-fundraising-regulations.
3. Board Source, *The Nonprofit Board Answer Book*, 25.

4. Ibid.
5. American Association for State and Local History, "Statement of Professional Standards and Ethics" (revised 2016), accessed December 29, 2016, http://bit.ly/324Caud.
6. "Shiloh Museum of Ozark History Ethical Guidelines," accessed December 30, 2016, http://download .aaslh.org/StEPs+Resources/Ethical+Guidelines+Shiloh+Museum.pdf.
7. The American Alliance of Museums has samples of the core museum documents available on their website, accessed January 2, 2017, http://www.aam-us.org/resources/assessment-programs/ core-documents/documents.
8. American Association for State and Local History, "Standards and Excellence Program for History Organizations," accessed January 2, 2017, http://tools.aaslh.org/steps.
9. National Park Service, "The Secretary of the Interior's Standards for Treatment of Historic Properties, with Guidelines for Preserving, Rehabilitating, Restoring and Reconstructing Historic Buildings," accessed January 1, 2017, https://www.nps.gov/tps/standards/four-treatments/standguide/index.htm.
10. Board Source, *The Nonprofit Board Answer Book,* 25.
11. Chester County Historical Society, "Conflict of Interest Policy," http://download.aaslh.org/StEPs+Re sources/Conflict+of+Interest+Policy+Chester+County+Historical+Society.pdf.
12. John Carver, *Boards that Make a Difference: A New Design for Leadership in Nonprofit and Public Organizations, Second Edition* (San Francisco CA: Jossey-Bass Publishers, 1997), 125–29.
13. Board Source, *The Nonprofit Board Answer Book,* 26.
14. Find more information about lobbying in "IRS Publication 4221: Compliance Guide for 501 (c) (3) Public Charities," which describes activities that may jeopardize a charity's tax-exempt status, including political campaign intervention, which is strictly prohibited, accessed December 27, 2016, https://www.irs .gov/pub/irs-pdf/p4221pc.pdf.
15. This statement is Item G under Human Resources in the AASLH "Statement of Professional Standards and Ethics," accessed December 28, 2016, http://bit.ly/324Caud.
16. Generic examples of board and officer job descriptions for a typical nonprofit can be found on the Management Help website, accessed December 28, 2017, http://managementhelp.org/boards/job -descriptions.htm.
17. https://boardsource.org/about-boardsource/. See the complete list of Ten Board Responsibilities in Board Source, *The Nonprofit Board Answer Book,* 3–5.
18. The Field Services Alliance of the AASLH is an affinity group for those working in statewide and regional museum service organizations, accessed January 2, 2017, http://blogs.aaslh.org/ask-fsa-what-is-field -services/.
19. This is one sample of an institutional code of ethics from the AASLH website; there are several for different-size history organizations, accessed December 28, 2016, http://download.aaslh.org/ StEPs+Resources/Code+of+Ethics+Pennsylvania+Historical+and+Museum+Commission.pdf. Independent Sector, a national leadership network for nonprofits, foundations, and corporations committed to advancing the common good, has a Checklist for Accountability to help strengthen board governance and accountability at https://independentsector.org/wp-content/uploads/2018/01/Account ability-Checklist-v2-1-2-18.pdf.
20. Cinnamon Catlin-Legutko, "DIY Strategic Planning for Small Museums," *History News* 63, no. 2 (Spring 2008), http://download.aaslh.org/technical+leaflets/Tech+Leaf+242.pdf.
21. This list of board and committee job descriptions (including the nominating committee) from Board Cafe is generic for all kinds of organizations but is extensive, accessed January 4, 2017, https://www .compasspoint.org/board-committee-job-descriptions.
22. Information about the Museum Assessment Program can be found on the American Alliance of Museums website, accessed January 4, 2017, http://www.aam-us.org/resources/assessment-programs/ MAP. Information about the Collections Assessment for Preservation Program can be found on the Institute of Library and Museum Services website, accessed January 1, 2017, https://www.imls.gov/ grants/available/collections-assessment-preservation-program-cap.
23. A good checklist for board orientation can be found on page 109 of Board Source, *The Nonprofit Board Answer Book.*

24. See the sample of a board self-assessment for a small museum provided on the AASLH website, accessed January 2, 2017, http://download.aaslh.org/StEPs+Resources/Board+Self+Assessment+Shiloh+Museum.pdf.
25. Sample documents available from the American Alliance of Museums, accessed January 3, 2017, http://www.aam-us.org/resources/information-center/sample-documents. Tier 3 members have access to sample documents on the American Alliance of Museums website.
26. There is a good selection of job descriptions for board committees on the Compass Point website, accessed December 29, 2016, https://www.compasspoint.org/board-committee-job-descriptions.

Chapter 5

Reaching New Heights with Volunteers in Historic House Museums

ALEXANDRA RASIC

Volunteering solidified my career path. At fourteen years of age, I joined the volunteer staff at the Homestead Museum in City of Industry, California. I knew I wanted to work in a museum when I grew up, but what kind? The Homestead was my local museum, so when I saw a little blurb in the newspaper aimed at recruiting high school students, I took the bait. I was nervous. I felt way out of my league, but the paid staff was friendly and professional. They put me to work right away, making me feel needed and valued. It was the first time I filled out anything that looked like a job application, and the first time I interviewed for a position. Little did I know that this volunteer opportunity would turn into a temporary position, followed by a part-time position, and then a full-time job. I have worked at the Homestead for more than twenty years, and the volunteer staff is one of the main reasons I find myself motivated and inspired in my current position as director of public programs.

Volunteers bring unique perspectives and skills to our organizations. They are curious, advertise and advocate for us, and share valuable information and observations that the paid staff might not otherwise see or hear. No, I'm not living in a dream world. I also know that volunteers can go rogue, some have a harder time adjusting to change than others, and some might even struggle to remember details such as the name of our organization. Volunteers are not that different from the visitors who walk through our doors every day, so if they can't get our name right, chances are that members of the public can't either.

At many historic house museums, volunteers are the only staff members a visitor will meet. They are a vital extension of the paid staff, and as many of us know and appreciate, sometimes they are the *only* staff. In these cases, volunteers are serving as leaders or trustees of an organization at the same time they are guiding tours, taking care of the collection, assisting with maintenance, and more. So, the question must be asked: If volunteers are playing such an important role in our organizations, why are they such a low priority?

Historic house museums need to commit more resources to the creation, maintenance, and ongoing reassessment of our volunteer programs. For the most part, we have been reactive rather than strategic. We struggle to recruit, train, and communicate with volunteers as our organizations change, becoming increasingly focused on the visitor experience and the expansion of programs. Likewise, we have not been proactive in thinking about how the needs and desires of potential volunteers have changed. Volunteering today is not the same as it was a decade ago. More than ever, volunteers are telling us that they want to do meaningful work—and many of us desperately need their help. With the right training and support, volunteers can help our organizations become more effective and sustainable. It is critical that we begin to address conditions we created, inherited, or neglected, and that we are strategic, innovative, and flexible in the process to help create a culture of ongoing change within our volunteer programs.

Committing Resources

I was lucky to start volunteering at an institution with a well-established volunteer program that included things like a handbook, job descriptions, a recognition program, a newsletter, and a paid staff member whose primary responsibility was to manage the volunteers. This isn't the norm, so when I started volunteering at other museums, I experienced some naïve culture shock. Some museums have a dedicated volunteer coordinator. Others rely on a team of colleagues who work most closely with volunteers and who can comment on things like staffing needs for specific programs, breakdowns in communication, anticipated attrition, and identifying areas where additional training is required. The size of an organization and its volunteer force is often the deciding factor in how it is managed.

Determining the role that volunteers will play within an organization will help paid staff decide how much support the program will need. Institutions with a large paid staff won't rely as heavily on volunteers as a small organization will. In the latter case, volunteer staff might be trained just as much as paid staff on certain aspects of the job, and that investment can help an organization grow and maximize resources in ways that leaders never imagined. Take collections care, for example. That is an area in which many historic houses can provide additional training for volunteers to be able to assist with important, time-consuming tasks like vacuuming textiles, documenting photos, and taking inventory. The institution benefits by saving money and having work completed faster than usual, and volunteers benefit from learning valuable skills and seeing the direct impact of their work.

Once needs are determined, an organization should develop volunteer job descriptions along with a handbook that clearly explains what the organization will provide and what is needed and expected from volunteers. Policies and procedures regarding training, supervision, evaluation, recognition, communication, and discipline must be discussed. There are numerous resources available to help organizations thoughtfully establish their volunteer programs.

The American Association for Museum Volunteers, an affiliated committee of the American Alliance of Museums, offers several prerecorded webinars that address topics such as staffing and managing volunteer programs and transforming the infrastructure of existing programs. The American Association for State and Local History (AASLH) offers an interactive webinar called "Are You Ready for Volunteers?" As its longtime moderator, Bethany Hawkins has found that the most frequently discussed topics revolve around managing change and the benefits of having policies and procedures. She encourages organizations to think about ways to involve volunteers in the creation or restructuring of volunteer programs to give them a better understanding of why things are done the way they are, why things need to change, and how everything an organization does links back to its mission. "Being involved in the planning process adds to the satisfaction of

Alexandra Rasic

many volunteers," she explains. "Often, volunteers are an afterthought, and it's no surprise that there are hurt feelings to deal with as a result of major changes that aren't well communicated."[1]

Explaining why we need to be equitable as our volunteer programs expand is important. An established historic house museum that initially relied on volunteers as guides might have introduced new programs and offerings that require the help of additional volunteers who might not be interested or willing to serve as guides. Sometimes these folks have been integrated seamlessly into a volunteer program, but in other cases, an "us versus them" situation might arise where one group sees itself, or has been treated, as more valuable than another. The amount of time a volunteer has, or is asked to give, can be another point of contention. As volunteer opportunities in our organizations have diversified, a volunteer who gives ten hours a month can be as impactful as one who gives twenty. It depends on the job. In other situations, there may not be a divide in terms of which group is more valuable, but there's a lack of effort to bring groups together to discuss the institution's mission, which everyone is collectively working toward fulfilling. A group that has always functioned and worked productively on its own can continue to do so if there is good communication and sharing of important information.

Ownership Is a Good Thing; Factions Are Not

Organizations with healthy volunteer programs are increasingly considering the establishment of goals for their volunteer programs, further engaging volunteers in the development process. One such goal might be to grow the number of volunteers in roles of program coordination and execution.

In establishing a volunteer program, leaders should also consider how to evaluate volunteers; when to revisit certain documents, procedures, and policies; and how to evaluate things like volunteer satisfaction and recognition. Create a schedule and share it with the volunteer staff. For example, volunteer satisfaction surveys are conducted every March and safety and security training takes place every February, which is also when we ask volunteers to update emergency contact information. Evaluation of guides is an area where many of us struggle to be consistent. Instead of formal evaluations, many organizations are adopting a drop-in approach, letting guides know that paid staff or lead volunteers will periodically join programs to observe both guides and visitors in action and discuss their observations with the volunteer.

Managing Change

Paid staff and volunteer leaders often feel overwhelmed and ill-prepared to manage change. Considering everything on our plates, especially in a small or medium-size organization, reassessing a volunteer program rarely emerges as a top priority. That might be okay for a few years, but not for decades. When structure is suddenly applied to a program that lacked it for years, an organization must be prepared to hear everything from praise to outrage.

The more that management supports change within a volunteer program, the greater the chance of success. If management is not on board, positive change can still take place—but the pace will be slower. Take pride in incremental victories like rewriting job descriptions or adding a new training session. Even small changes to a volunteer program can have a big impact. One that made a big difference at the Homestead was the creation of a Community Service Volunteer (CSV) category and job description. When area schools and businesses started giving incentives to students and employees for volunteer work, we struggled to think of ways to use them because the time we had set aside for training and the time they had to give was limited. My colleague Gennie Truelock came up with a solution: instead of thinking about how these people could fit into our existing program, she created a new category of volunteers with a different set of requirements. The primary role of the CSVs became tied to our two weekend festivals, large events where we desperately need a lot of helping hands. We advertise the opportunity as ideal for people looking for a short-term commitment, and we guarantee them up to ten hours of work per weekend. A great bonus has been that a few people really came to enjoy the time they were spending at the museum and increased their commitment to the organization. We've discovered that the new volunteer category is a great way for people to test the waters, and we are pitching it as such for people who are new to volunteering or unsure about the contribution they can make.

If someone specifically tasked with overhauling a volunteer program is brought into an organization, this should be discussed with volunteers, and the organization must be prepared to address questions and concerns. It helps to be as proactive as possible. Let volunteers know that the museum is dedicating more resources to *them*. Ask volunteers what they feel is needed or lacking. Frame changes in a positive light and consider the best ways to share new information. For example, if an organization creates or updates a volunteer handbook, schedule a meeting with volunteers to review the document. Policies and guidelines addressing things like dress code, dismissal, and training requirements can come across as cold and impersonal when someone hands you something to read and sign versus having a paid staff member or team (that might even include volunteers) present the material and solicit questions and comments. Explaining the changes clearly is important but recognize that not everyone will accept the changes. This might feel very painful at first, especially if you lose volunteers, but it will be better for your institution in the long run as more buy-in is created.

While written policies provide needed structure and information for new members of the paid staff or board, nothing beats on-the-job training and the modeling of ideal behavior. Assessing the comfort level and capability of those who supervise volunteers is especially important and it must be as consistent as possible. Not all of us come into our positions having had volunteer experience, let alone having supervised volunteers. New staff members, in particular, need to understand what is expected of them, how they can be flexible while remaining equitable, and how to address concerns or violations of policy.

When new paid staff members join our team at the Homestead, we make a point of having them shadow colleagues in day-to-day interactions with volunteers. They get to see how we deal with things like check-in (saying hello and letting volunteers know if anything special is happening on site, such as filming or maintenance), the monitoring of tours (to make sure that tours are starting on time, that they are not too large, and that the volunteer is comfortable with the tour group), and addressing concerns (maybe someone is consistently giving long tours or taking visitors into unsafe places). We share details among the paid staff that might otherwise take some time to learn about individual volunteers such as who likes working in the store, who is unable to work weekends, and who needs a phone call reminder the day before their shift.

In this age of technology, many paid staff members are learning that they must be willing to communicate in different ways. While some still might prefer mail by post and phone calls, email and text messages might yield better results for others. Supervisors should regularly communicate with one another and management about what they see, hear, and think might need attention. If disciplinary action is required, problems should be addressed as soon as possible. Disciplining and even letting a volunteer go can be the hardest part of working with volunteers. Having tools in place that define and explain disciplinary measures will be of great benefit to the paid staff and board.

Recruitment, Training, and Recognition

Having volunteers of diverse backgrounds and life stages make our organizations stronger and better informed, yet most of us struggle with how to recruit beyond what our volunteer force already looks like. We want to engage more young people, adults who want to work with children or speak foreign languages, and people with particular skills that our historic sites need. Many of us develop recruitment tools only meant to reach a broad group of people, or we have targeted people like retirees who, historically, have had more time to give. But many seniors are now working longer or engaging in tasks that require more of their time, such as caregiving for friends and family.

As the number of volunteer opportunities has increased in the nonprofit world, there is also much more competition for a shrinking volunteer pool, meaning that organizations need to be more targeted and persuasive in their recruitment efforts. Again, small- and large-scale changes can make a big difference. Thinking about a small-scale change, consider the volunteer application process. Many historic house museums respond to a potential volunteer's interest by handing them a paper application or directing them to a page on a website where they can fill out a form. By the time they get home, the application or piece of paper with the web address could get mixed up with the daily mail or turned into a shopping list. Even worse, they might lose enthusiasm or second-guess their decision to apply. Instead, empower paid and volunteer staff to be more responsive in the moment. Have a short form that a potential volunteer can fill out in your presence and explain what will happen next: "I can't wait to tell our volunteer coordinator about you! Her name is Jane, and you'll hear from her by the end of the week." If your institution uses things like tablets, create a simple electronic form for them to fill out before they leave, similar to the paper version, or ask for their email address and send it to them the same day with a short greeting and invitation to submit their application. A simple personal touch can go a long way. If the timing is right, maybe you can even call to see if the volunteer coordinator (or whoever assists with that role) can come over to say hello or do an on-the-spot interview.

We need to think in terms of current and potential audiences when it comes to visitors *and* volunteers. Look for inspiration and opportunities for creative collaboration in your own backyard. Recently, I met Katie Rispoli Keaotamai, executive director of We Are the Next, a nonprofit organization based in Long Beach, California. Her organization was founded on the idea that they would engage "the next" generation not only with historic places, but with the cultures and cities that surround them. We Are the Next made the leap from wanting to offer programs to youth in local schools to recruiting young volunteers through a community organization to create programs for people their age in surrounding areas. Historic house museums can take inspiration from Katie and her team's strategy:

> We began by approaching local school districts, but quickly realized that our teachers are overwhelmed. They're looking for ways to take on less, not more. While we were discouraged in pursuing programs in schools, we found an ally in after-school program providers. The Boys & Girls Clubs, for instance, are required to have their students participate in community service and different kinds of workshops that build self-esteem and life skills. Club locations were eager to have us provide programs for their students because they fulfilled many of the requirements they needed to meet. In working with youth at the Boys & Girls Clubs and other after-school program providers, we found students with some of the groups were particularly captivated by heritage

conservation. These students were excited to get involved in the field and already were looking for opportunities to perform community service for school and other reasons! We invited some of the more forthcoming students, who directly approached us asking for volunteer opportunities, to join our new Youth Advisory Council. On the council, students help us create curriculum to ensure that the services we provide are engaging and designed from the perspective of those who will be given those services. The students on the council get to gain experience in heritage conservation and build up community service hours, and we get to benefit from having the approach of the next generation guide the work we do.[2]

Katie's initial idea of approaching a local school district is one that many of us have tried with mixed results. While intentions are good, school districts, just like us, have limited time and resources for partnerships. Instead of looking to an entire school district, many of us have better luck finding a teacher or school to partner with. What is so ideal about working with schools and organizations like the Boys & Girls Clubs is that there is a steady stream of "new blood" coming through their doors. So how can we tap into that as we consider what we can do for these organizations and what they can do for us?

One idea is to look at new initiatives in our local school districts such as dual-language immersion programs in elementary schools, which are on the rise across the nation. In these schools, students learn in English at the same time as another language, often one spoken in the community. We can provide opportunities for children and families to develop and put their skills to use, and we benefit by having more bilingual staff to interact with underserved members of our community. If successful, there is great potential for growth and sustainability in a collaboration like this. As students grow, they can learn new skills and assume more responsibility within the organization, serving as mentors to new students coming into the program. Giving young people an active role in our organizations also serves as a way to show that careers in the museum field are valuable and relevant.

Jennifer Chandler, vice president of the National Council of Nonprofits, wrote that young people who volunteer "don't think of working for a nonprofit as a viable career option. By not optimizing the volunteer experience for younger volunteers, nonprofits may be missing an opportunity to cultivate future nonprofit leaders."[3] I couldn't agree more. In addition to the Homestead, I volunteered at three different museums and libraries while I was in college. In the process, I learned about my likes and dislikes (I like working with people more than things), the pros and cons of working in a large versus small institution, and what good management looks like. I often wonder: Had the Homestead not been my first experience as a volunteer in the field, would I have remained as enthusiastic about a career in museums?

Many organizations make a point of talking to new volunteers when they join about the role that paid and volunteer staff play, and for many of us, that's as far as we go. Ideally, reminders of why we're all here and what we're working toward should take place throughout the year in various formats. Newsletters, one-on-one conversations, staff meetings, or training sessions can do the job. And mandatory activities, such as staff training, can reflect the types of engaging programs we offer. This has been on the mind of Anna Altschwager, assistant director overseeing guest experience at Old World Wisconsin, who says, "We're changing up the training process to be as close as possible to the experience we want to provide for our guests. If we want our guests to have a fun, interesting, and engaging day—then our training for *staff* needs to be a fun, interesting, and engaging day."[4] She's experimenting with ways to add games and group work to Old World Wisconsin's training in hopes of creating common ground. The desire to have more fun and engage new staff and volunteers can also be seen in one of Old World Wisconsin's recent

Alexandra Rasic

recruitment ads that features the same kind of engaging graphic design and historic imagery that would be used to entice visitors to the site for a program (see Figure 5.1).

In historic house museums with long-standing guide programs, retraining veteran staff to incorporate new interpretive techniques can prove challenging. Bethany Hawkins at AASLH asserts that it is critical for these organizations to think about ways to include multiple voices and more conversation in things like public tours. For that to be successful, we need to invest in training and supporting guides in learning how to lead tours that are more dialogue-based. "People don't want to be lectured at," she says.[5] Instead, we should teach guides strategies and techniques for

Figure 5.1 Recruitment ad designed by Anna Altschwager. Courtesy of Old World Wisconsin.

facilitating conversations on tours, which can sometimes include controversial or difficult stories. This will be easier for some volunteer staff than others. If there are volunteers who are uncomfortable with the changes or choose not to comply with new policies, then it's time for the paid staff or volunteer leaders to discuss this with them to determine if there are other roles they can play within the organization or if it is time to part ways.

Many of us try to schedule volunteer and guide training to take place at set times throughout the year. While this makes sense for internal planning, it does not enable us to respond quickly when a volunteer with a valuable skill set and limited availability expresses an interest in joining the staff. Instead of waiting for formal training to roll around, paid staff or volunteer leaders can develop flexible training options, including mentoring or shadowing, to bring new volunteers up to speed quickly. Just as we can lose volunteers if we make the application process too tedious, we can lose well-meaning volunteers we bring into our organizations who we fail to train quickly.

Even at social functions such as potlucks and recognition events, paid staff can find fun and engaging ways to share and remind volunteers of the mission of their organization. Slide shows with simple captions or the sharing of thank-you letters or reviews can make the point. We cannot forget that many volunteers join our organizations because they are interested in social opportunities. They are important to build and maintain morale, but they should not be the primary reason why a volunteer program exists. Look for opportunities in your calendar to schedule some of these gatherings before new exhibits, programs, or important seasons so that you can create excitement for what's coming and reinforce other training materials.

Volunteers like to be recognized in a variety of ways. Genuine and specific thanks are most important. Whether face-to-face or by phone, paper note, or email, taking time to acknowledge how your volunteers make a difference at your historic house museum will not only demonstrate your appreciation for, and investment in, the individuals, but add to their overall satisfaction as members of the volunteer staff. Show that you are paying attention. If you saw a volunteer handwrite an itinerary for an overwhelmed guest at a festival, thank them for that specifically. That's going above and beyond the call of duty. If you overhear a visitor giving a volunteer special praise, share that with the volunteer coordinator and director so they can express their appreciation too. If volunteers are comfortable being photographed, share their accomplishments and activities on your website, blog, or social media platforms.

We know that some volunteers are motivated to reach specific milestones such as hours or years of service, and these accomplishments should be acknowledged and celebrated. However, other volunteers, maybe with less time to give, might be more committed to and motivated by the work they do for a particular program or project. Their contributions can be equally valuable. Look at the variety of things that volunteers do within your organization and create recognition policies accordingly. And if you have policies in place, regularly ask the volunteer staff what they think of them and solicit new ideas for recognition.

Maintaining a healthy volunteer program will feel a lot easier if you are strategic about regularly evaluating all the different components involved instead of putting out fires. Just as our institutions are thinking more carefully and critically about the ways we engage with our visitors, we need to do the same with current and potential volunteers. Strong programs require an ongoing investment, and when managed well, they fulfill and often exceed the expectations of both paid and volunteer staff. Volunteers want to do meaningful work, and many historic house museums with limited resources can move to new levels of performance through their volunteers.

Notes

1. Interview with Bethany Hawkins, May 2017.
2. Email message from Katie Rispoli Keaotamai, executive director, We Are the Next, February 28, 2017.
3. Jennifer Chandler, "Volunteer Trends," National Council of Nonprofits, 2015, https://www.councilofnon profits.org/thought-leadership/volunteer-trends.
4. Email message from Anna Altschwager, February 25, 2017.
5. Interview with Bethany Hawkins, May 2017.

Chapter 6

Surviving a Capital Campaign

A Slightly Irreverent Guide to Fund-raising

NINA ZANNIERI

In 2007, the Paul Revere Memorial Association embraced the moment it had long hoped for yet still dreaded: the need to embark on a capital campaign to fund a necessary expansion. The association owns and operates two National Historic Landmark properties in Boston's North End. The Paul Revere House, the 1680 circa home the patriot owned from 1770 until 1800, and the Pierce-Hichborn House, a noteworthy 1711 architectural survival owned for a time by a Revere cousin. The properties also reflect the community's history from Boston's earliest days, through the American Revolution and the rise of the new nation, to its rich nineteenth-century immigrant past.

Over the years, with steady growth in attendance, our modest historic complex had become pot-bound, unable to accommodate the level of programming we wished to do or even welcome visitors with basic amenities or the level of accessibility that one expects at a prominent historic site. For years, we had been looking for a suitable building, which depending on location would provide office and storage space or both along with essential program areas, a museum shop and restrooms. So, we jumped at the chance to acquire a forlorn, but locally significant, 1835 two-family home behind the Revere House on a portion of Paul Revere's original backyard. The building, though in poor shape, still retained enough historic character to complement our other properties and offered enough space (3,500 square feet) to accommodate its transformation into a much-needed education and visitor center. Also, the building's former residents offered access to compelling accounts of the neighborhood's immigrant history, which would enhance our ability to fulfill our mission to tell stories beyond our central Paul Revere focus.

Since the timing of the property acquisition coincided with the one-hundredth anniversary of the association's founding in 1907, initial fund-raising was done under the guise of an anniversary fund. Buoyed by the relative ease of raising $150,000 for a master plan of our entire historic complex, we pushed ahead and officially launched our "New Revere Call to Action" campaign on April 18, 2008, our centennial as a museum. At the time, the association had an operating budget of $850,000, six full-time professionals, twenty part-time staff, annual visitation of more than 250,000, and an endowment of $2.8 million. Yet, despite our accomplishments, including accreditation by the American Alliance of Museums, a good solid base of earned income, highly regarded educational programming, and pretty amazing attendance, the association had no development staff, only a modest fund-raising track record (mostly grants), an almost nonexistent donor base, and had never done an annual appeal. By any definition, we were not "campaign ready." To make matters worse, six months after we launched our campaign, the bottom dropped out of the stock market.

Raising funds can be grueling, even for large organizations with well-oiled development machines. Although we knew we had a lot to learn, we were not prepared for the truly steep learning curve we encountered. Navigating through what we were "told" we had to do or what we "thought" everyone did, led us to question and ultimately challenge some of the prevailing wisdom, as we navigated the journey from launch to completion. It proved to be a long road with detours, unpaved stretches, wrong turns, surprisingly successful shortcuts, and those inevitable backups on the way that cleared as quickly as they developed with no clear explanation. I know, you're still thinking how could the experience of the Paul Revere House be of any use to me at Small Historical Society in Small Town, USA? First, before you waste another moment wondering whether our efforts were successful, the answer is that our results were pretty good or at least good enough! The association exceeded its $4 million capital campaign goal, raising $4.1 million in seven years, and opened its education and visitor center on December 2, 2016. Second, you will likely find that small organizations often succeed specifically because they are less encumbered by large complex organizational structures. Take advantage of the opportunity to break the mold and craft a fund-raising effort that matches your organization.

Since completing our campaign, I have been asked many times, "How did you do it?" My off-handed response is generally, "Don't be afraid to break the rules." What this means is that beyond legal regulations, ethical considerations, and accounting standards, there is no single formula that will guarantee success. The only correct way to do fund-raising or to run a capital campaign is to craft a strategy that is aligned with the idiosyncrasies of your institution and your community. We didn't have some magical plan or even absolute confidence that we would meet our goal. On the other hand, we were confident that we had a compelling, appropriately sized project and that we needed to make the attempt. Ironically, since we began at what was the worst possible moment in 2008, the poor economy gave us a plausible way to justify failing to meet our fund-raising goal. Perhaps acknowledging that failure to achieve some artificially created campaign goal was not the end of the world actually helped us succeed. On numerous occasions when we felt we could not raise another penny or bemoaned how long the fund-raising was taking, colleagues would sympathetically note, "Hey, you've done really well given when you started!" The fact that we met our stated goal, even though we were not ready and launched at a bad time, is what makes our story more compelling and hopefully useful.

While the wealth of readily offered conventional wisdom about how to fund-raise may initially provide the comfort of thinking that there are rules, that if followed, will ensure success; don't be fooled. The only rules that matter are the ones that make sense for your organization. You will have to chart your own course. Give your organization permission to ignore the prevailing wisdom. In the end it matters more what tactics and strategies match your organizational culture and capacity, not what the institution up the street did. Beware the well-intentioned board member, staffer, or donor who says you should do x or y because the Really Good Museum of Great

Nina Zannieri

Stuff raised a ton of money on its combination costume ball and hayride. Know your strengths and play to them and resist the pressure to do otherwise. To provide some guidance, what follows is a look at some ways the association chose to adopt, reject, or embrace the recognized elements of fund-raising and capital campaigns on its way to achieving its goal.

Feasibility Studies

This is a tough one since a thoughtfully conducted feasibility study can be a useful tool. Though they do help some organizations shape their fund-raising effort, you may be able to do this on your own. Rather than spend funds on a formulaic plan to be told what we wanted to hear or, worse, told we had no chance to succeed, we decided to just plunge in. The association hired a seasoned fund-raising consultant to help with campaign staging, strategy, some grant writing, a limited amount of prospect research, and enormous amounts of hand-holding. Her role was like that of a fitness trainer: pushing but not beyond our limits, demanding but sympathetic, and, most of all, realistic. This decision proved to the first of a series of critical steps that helped us craft a campaign that was right for an organization of our size and in our situation.

The Quiet Phase

If, like the association, your organization does not have the capacity to get to half of your goal or more from your leadership and established key donors, then the notion of a quiet phase is essentially moot. You will find that depending on your community and circumstances, either everyone knows you are raising money, or no one knows. It might be argued that smaller organizations in large cities may conduct their entire campaigns under the radar, as their comparatively modest fund-raising is not likely to be considered newsworthy. Not one newspaper covered our campaign. When we did get some stories on our construction, we honestly revealed that we had, at that point, raised less than expected. Still, the article brought us a major donor. We knew from the start we would need to rely to a great extent on new donors. Luckily, we found a few receptive foundations and government sources that were willing to bank on our reputation and recognized that 100 percent giving from our board, though not a large amount, was still a significant accomplishment. We let people know early, and often, that we had a transformative project and the will to make it happen.

Matches and Challenges

It's easy to hate matching grants, particularly ones with hard deadlines. When a foundation or donor offers funds as a challenge or with a required match, it is hard to avoid thinking, "Please, just give us the money." However, matches and challenges do work. They provide a sense of urgency that can be used to get other donors to commit. Savvy donors hate to leave dollars on the table, and really appreciate the fact that their gift is doing double duty by leveraging other dollars. Government grants such as the ultra-competitive National Endowment for the Humanities (NEH) Challenge Grant, as well as several state and local grants, require a match. The association successfully used its NEH Challenge Grant, with its very aggressive deadlines, to drive giving over a three-year period at the front end of our campaign. So, take a deep breath, view it as an opportunity and just do the work to make it happen. In fact, you may even want to ask donors to work with you on creating challenges or matching scenarios at critical moments. Several times during our effort, a challenge or matching opportunity came along when our campaign had stalled with no good prospects left to tap. With a challenge in hand, we suddenly had just enough momentum to summon the energy to turn fence-sitters into donors.

Campaign Materials

From case statements to pledge forms and from videos to descriptions of naming opportunities, small organizations should weigh carefully the cost of campaign materials. Don't be fooled into thinking that you need to spend a lot to raise a lot. However, it is equally important not to use expense as an excuse to forego creating classy materials. Every piece you produce will become the silent face of your fund-raising. You will need a case statement that's both well-designed and well-written (see Figure 6.1). The text you labor over will help you crystallize your message

Figure 6.1 Be sure your campaign materials are well-designed and well-written. The case statement for the capital campaign is the silent face of your fund-raising. Photo courtesy of the Paul Revere Memorial Association.

and become a boilerplate that will be used over and over again for grant narratives, letters, and website campaign pages. The association printed two thousand (more than two print runs) twelve-page case statements that introduced our operation, the project, record of success, needs, challenges, and goals, but not the specifics that were likely to change—campaign budget, funds raised to date, naming opportunities, or schedule. To keep our materials fresh, annual updates were inserted into the original case statements along with a page that provided current campaign status, pledge/donation forms, and any other materials required by the prospect. The updates were loaded with images and conveyed a realistic, sometimes humorous assessment of our progress, challenges, and great appreciation for all those who had given to further our cause. This kept our printing costs down while giving us a polished and always up-to-date case statement to include with grants, individual requests, and corporate appeals.

The other very important piece is your pledge/donation form. Get good advice on what you need to convey to donors and what information they need to supply for you. For example, if you want to encourage pledges but hope to limit the duration, go ahead and suggest that pledges may be one to five years or only one to three years. Ask if you can use their name and the amount given or if they wish to be anonymous or named but not in conjunction with a specific amount. You will be very happy you did when donations come in and you see that you have all the data you need. You will need to create some form of database to manage all this information. We used an Excel spreadsheet and found it served our needs. If you opt for more sophisticated software, be sure you are getting a product that you can support in the long term and are not buying more than you really require.

One final item you may want to consider is a short campaign video. Initially, we rejected this idea due to time and cost concerns, until a younger board member made a compelling argument about the value of video for online applications and with younger donors and offered to pay for it. It turned out to be modestly useful and did introduced some new donors to our museum. Still, if we had felt it was not a good idea or in keeping with our fund-raising strategy, it would have been important for us to say "no," even with an offer of creative direction, time, and funds.

Naming Opportunities

Some of our board members raised valid concerns that naming rights will overwhelm a small building and maybe even send the wrong message to future users of a facility. Yet, if it is done tastefully and is part of the overall signage and interpretive design scheme, it can be a very effective way to raise funds. The association had good success with naming opportunities. Several of our donors, including a few Revere descendants, were very interested in becoming part of the fabric of the building. You might also consider approaching several key donors with the notion of donating to honor a person who has played a significant role in the history of your museum but would never presume to honor him or herself. If you choose this route, let the honoree know that fund-raising is being done on his or her behalf in the event that he or she might not be comfortable with the idea. In our case, the honoree was humbled but very pleased to be able to help us raise additional funds in this manner.

Weigh the Cost but Take Some Risks

While raising funds in a manner that matches your organizational culture is essential, you still should consider opportunities that arise that are somewhat outside your plan such as the use of online giving sites, direct mail, or a donor with a novel idea. Though we had taken direct mail off the table as time-consuming and costly, after a second approach by a firm with a good track record of doing direct mail with a national donor base, we decided to try it. Our decision was ultimately aided by our initial disinterest, which triggered the offer of a no-risk test mailing. This effort did not produce the anticipated level of response either in number of donors or amount given (even the firm was surprised and a bit disappointed), but it did provide us with fifty new solid donors, some of whom now give annually.

While direct mail is an established but old-fashioned method, online fund-raising methods such as GoFundMe and Kickstarter are newer and more attractive, but they are still unproven. There are museums that have used online fund-raising sites with good results. In most cases the "ask" involved an emergency or short deadline that conveyed a sense of urgency that is less easily captured in a capital campaign. The other issue is that these fund-raising websites make no real distinction between causes involving individuals, charities, or entrepreneurs. Some of your best donors may not find this appealing and new donors may be confused about the tax implication for their gifts. Many websites don't transfer the funds unless you reach your goal, so you really need an ace in the hole to make this work.

The association tried this route at the end of the campaign to complete the effort with a bang and meet a time-sensitive match from a donor. Although we had a deal that gave us every penny that was raised, it was a complete bust. Of the thirty donors who responded, two-thirds were either current donors or employees of the firm, who gave to try to prime the pump. We raised $1,800, nowhere near the $35,000 we needed or even the $10,000 the online firm felt we would easily attract. Luckily, we knew our donor would extend her deadline. While she liked the novelty of the online effort, she was as skeptical about its potential as we were. Maybe we failed because we never really believed it would work!

To Gala or Not to Gala

As soon as a capital campaign is announced, people will begin to ask, "So when is the gala?" or "What kind of party are you going to have?" The assumption is that you will, of course, be doing some kind of signature "do": a gala, auction, concert, dance, or quiz show. The association determined early on that we would not attempt any sort of ticketed benefit—our museum had no capacity to sell sufficient tickets to ensure success. Unless your organization has experience with events, avoid this method of raising funds. Well-meaning board members may push back, but unless they step up and sell the tickets and tables, you will not have a positive outcome. Furthermore, large events are labor intensive and may cost more than they raise, so think twice before taking on this fund-raising strategy.

The association did, however, do a few events to raise awareness about our project and fund-raising efforts. In 2008, we staged a party, complete with a huge cake shaped like the Paul Revere House and a reenactment of the April 18, 1908, opening of the museum, to celebrate our one-hundredth anniversary as a museum and to let people know about our plans. We had invited guests but also allowed the general public in at our twenty-five cent 1908 admission price. It was a low-cost, highly successful celebration and awareness-building party. During the long construction phase, we offered hard hat tours. They were quite popular and helped get people excited about the new facility while reminding them that we still had dollars to raise. For many organizations, smaller cultivation gatherings or programs are proving more effective and less costly than major events.

Is It Really a Capital Campaign?

Before you go on record and call a fund-raising effort a capital campaign, make sure that is what you want to do. Does it exceed your organization's regular fund-raising? Is it significant enough? Are you willing to forgo access to funders who explicitly say they do not fund capital campaigns? If the answer is a definite "yes" to all the above, then you have a capital campaign. If you are not sure, hold off and take a moment to rethink whether the campaign designation is a good fit.

Donor Base

Obviously, having an extensive base of individuals, groups, businesses, or foundations that have given is the best way to ensure success. However, if like the association you do not have a robust donor base, make sure you do have a foundation of good will among those closest to your organization or in your community or those who visit or use your services. Even if they have never given, if you are relatively confident you can convert them into donors, you have a very good place to start. Just because you don't have much of a donor base doesn't mean you can't develop a good prospect list. Identify everyone who has shown an interest but has never really been asked to give. Think about all the various connections that might be made to your museum. What companies or organizations have a connection to your community, or the themes covered by your programs, properties, and interpretation? Who supports the other cultural organizations in your community? Who supports other museums that deal with the same content as yours? I know, I know, this begins to sound like poaching donors, but it is fairly routine prospect mining, and we all do it! This is one instance when what others have done may hold some precedent for your efforts. Don't worry, when your campaign is over, they will all return the favor by perusing your donor list.

Crash and Burn

All successful fund-raising involves a fair amount of failure. You may pursue a long-shot donor or try something online as we did and not only come up empty, but perhaps feel some embarrassment for even trying. The association approached one corporate foundation, with the skids appropriately greased by a top corporate officer who was a close colleague of one of our board members who was also a corporate officer at a major Boston corporation. After being assured that the company CEO was very interested in our project, I was invited to meet with the executive director of the foundation. However, from the moment I walked in the door, it was obvious she was just going through the motions, her voice dripping with hostility as I squirmed and thrashed and ultimately burst into flames still trying desperately to make our case. Then there was a glimmer of hope; she invited me to apply and her assistant even gave me a number, $25,000. I dashed back to my office, completed the online application, and pressed submit! Within what seemed like mere moments, actually several hours, our application was denied via a clearly generic email rejection. What had initially seemed like a slam dunk was transformed into a plausible long shot, and ultimately bitter defeat. It was a painful episode, but worth the effort because I learned about the gulf that often exists between the leadership of a corporate foundation and the corporate officers. So be cautious but not too cautious. Weigh the risk both of asking and of passing up an opportunity. There may well be a period when you find you are hearing "no" more often than "yes." Be prepared for at least a few moments of serious doubt along the way.

The Ask

Knowing who to ask, what the ask should be, and how often to ask is tricky. It is hard to know how many times to send proposals or revise letters before calling it a lost cause. Our rule of thumb was, lacking other evidence, three strikes and you're out. There are ways to determine if additional requests might be successful. It isn't unusual for foundations to reject your proposal on the first try and then fund on the second. Perhaps they want to see that you have raised more of your goal or begun your construction. Maybe your first proposal was good, but not great, at making the case. Perhaps your timing is off given other obligations on the donor's plate at the time. If you are applying for grants or foundation support and have been turned down, make the difficult phone call to the program officer or foundation staff and ask them for advice. You may find out something that either provides encouragement to reapply or a clear sense that you will not be successful if you resubmit. You might discover that you asked for the wrong thing and can easily adjust your focus and still accommodate your campaign wish list. Or, you may get confirmation that your time will be better spent pursuing other prospects.

This brings us to a very important tactic: always have a non-campaign request or two ready for donors. We initially thought other asks would dilute our message or be too difficult to manage with a major capital campaign under way, but we were wrong. For example, we raised almost $60,000 in thirty days to acquire an important Revere document within a tight deadline. My initial "Oh no, we can't manage this right now" became, "Actually we do need to do this, it shows who we are and in fact supports our case for expansion." After board members were alerted via email, four carefully selected prospects received a letter and an article we had written about the Revere document. Two of the donors (one in response to the board email and the other to the letter) had only given very small donations to the capital campaign but made large gifts toward the purchase. Two donors who had made significant campaign contributions made additional donations to assist with this effort. One of the donors liked this opportunity so much that they took a second look at our campaign and ultimately made a significant, game-changing gift that put us within $75,000 of our campaign goal. Having other requests ready not only allows you to reach more donors, but it also helps organizations become more strategic about fund-raising. You never know for sure what will appeal to a donor. Some just prefer to help with requests that are immediate and very specific, rather than give to a big, impersonal capital campaign.

Your campaign should also have several layers. You should consider including a portion for a new or existing endowment, appeals for in-kind goods and services, and some discussion of bequests. Though endowment will likely only appeal to a small number of donors, it signals your awareness that all organizations need a financial safety net. The promise of future funds through a bequest or in-kind donations of needed services or materials both offer ways to contribute without writing a check. Making donors aware of these options also increases your potential to strike a chord with a donor who may not be able to give right now. In-kind donations such as the services of a designer for that all-important case statement, architect's fees, or materials for your construction provide great value by reducing costs. Remember to account for bequests and in-kind contributions in your total raised-to-date calculations.

Lessons Learned

Fund-raising is an essential operation for all organizations. It should be viewed as a critical investment of time and money that will pay dividends for years to come. Remember to treat all your donors whether individuals, corporate contacts, foundation personnel, or staff at government agencies with respect and appreciation. Thank them often regardless of the size of their contribution. Also show your appreciation to those who turn you down. Their time meeting with you or reviewing your proposal is valuable. Not only is it the right thing to do but it will serve your organization well in the future. Make sure you have a project that you really believe in, one that has total organizational support. This will involve helping all your staff understand what it means to be in a capital campaign or for that matter any fund-raising effort. All staff members need to be on their toes. They need to view every visitor who comes through the door as either a current donor or a potential donor. They also need to know how to direct a donor who asks for information to the right materials or to the right person.

Whether or not you choose a more traditional approach or opt to break some or all of the rules, it is essential that you develop a campaign that matches your organization's character and comes from an honest internal assessment of your capacity to finish what you have started. If you can't be honest about your organization's strengths and weaknesses, you won't be honest with your donors and you will absolutely set your effort up for failure. On the other hand, if you have done your homework, you will be successful, and even if, gasp, you don't meet your stated goal, you will have set the stage for future fund-raising.

The best part of a capital campaign or any major fund-raising effort is what you will learn about your institution's capacity to thrive and your ability to craft an effective message that appeals to donors and the general public. You will learn who to ask and how to ask. You will come to appreciate all donors, from the anonymous one dollar in the donation box to the major donor whose gift makes you well up with pride and gratitude. Whether the journey is smooth or daunting, it will convince you of the merits of continuing to work with current donors while cultivating new ones. Keep in mind that while it is possible to run a successful capital campaign at an organization that is not by any definition "campaign ready," it will be a much longer and more difficult experience than it needs to be. The most important thing to do is to keep your fund-raising machine, whether modest or magnificent, in good condition and ready for action.

Recommended Resources

Brophy, Sarah. *Is Your Museum Grant-Ready?* Lanham, MD: Rowman & Littlefield, 2005.
Find your local or statewide grant resource, such as Associated Grant Makers in Boston (agm connect.org) or the Foundation Center (foundationcenter.org).

Chapter 7

Success Factors for Small Historic House Museums

MONTA LEE DAKIN AND STEVE FRIESEN

Mark Twain famously said, "The reports of my death have been greatly exaggerated," after a notice of his death appeared in an American newspaper. Like Twain, reports of the death of the historic house museum also appear to have been greatly exaggerated.

In 2002 and again in 2007, two groundbreaking summits explored the future of historic sites, including house museums. Organized by the American Alliance of Museums, American Association for State and Local History (AASLH), and the National Trust for Historic Preservation and held at Kykuit, the Rockefeller estate in Pocantico Hills, New York, the first summit concluded that without significant changes, the future of historic sites, particularly small historic house museums, was dim. Five years later, the second summit was more hopeful, noting the many successful efforts to look at historic sites in new and different ways, including some small house museums. The conclusion from that summit suggested that much had been learned by 2007.

Today, perhaps due in part to the alarm raised during the Kykuit meetings, reports of the death of the small historic house museum do appear to be exaggerated. When many questioned the future of the historic house museum, William Hosley, a consultant and champion of small historic house museums, raised a counterpoint in an article by the *Boston Globe* in 2015: "I feel deeply the opposite. The future of not just tourism but our cultural heritage in general are these thousand points of light, these local communities that have some special thing, that have something deep and meaningful. Not every house museum is great, but I've never seen two alike."[1]

Indeed, there has been a surge in heritage tourism that began even as the first Kykuit summit was held and that continues unabated. As Hosley points out, the small house museum can offer heritage tourists a deep and meaningful experience. That, plus the efforts small historic house museums have made over the past decade, has given them an unexpected lease on life. Scores of small house museums that appeared to have been endangered at one time have continued to survive. More important, there are small house museums that have not merely survived but have thrived. But what has enabled some small historic house museums to thrive? What changes did they have to make to ensure relevancy in these changing times and to entice visitors to their doors? That is what we will explore in this chapter.

Defining the Small Historic House Museum

We first must establish some criteria for what could be considered a small historic house museum. That is a challenge since there is such diversity within the world of historic house museums. There are house museums with small facilities and large collections as well as house museums with small collections in large facilities.

In the essay "Making a Case for the Small Museum" in *The Small Museum Toolkit*, Steve Friesen determines that physical size, collection size, and visitation had too many variables to be used as criteria for the small museum.[2] He arrives at budget and paid staff size as the least subjective ways of determining whether a museum was small. The same applies to the small historic house museum. In 2010, he used $350,000 as the top end for budget and a full-time paid staff of five or fewer. Applying the accumulative rate of inflation between 2010 and 2019, that would mean a comparable budget of just over $404,021 today. Given that many historic house museums do not employ full-time staff, one can still apply a measure of five FTEs (full-time equivalents). Perhaps more critical when it comes to staff would be responsibilities. Unlike larger institutions, small historic house museum staff members frequently have multiple responsibilities ranging from fund-raising to interpretive responsibilities to janitorial duties. We are therefore defining a house museum as small if it has less than a $400,000 budget and fewer than five FTEs with multiple responsibilities dedicated to the site.

While many small house museums are or were independent, more of them have become part of a parent organization. This does not mean their struggles are any less than those museums that continue to operate independently. In fact, most are expected to generate their own revenue and other support regardless of their parent organization's financial condition. For simplicity, however, we will feature only those museums that have a separate budget and a separate staff regardless of whether they have a parent organization or not.

Finally, in some cases our research shows that while a historic house museum might not be considered small anymore by these criteria, it was at one time regarded as a small museum but has now grown beyond that size because of its success. We will include these once-small museums in order to explore how they became successful.

Yet it must also be said that for some historic house museums, small is exactly the size they need to be. To become "bigger" might not always be necessary for a house museum to be considered successful. Growing larger in staff size, budget, or even programs, therefore, should not be a standard for evaluating success. Sometimes small institutions are stronger than larger institutions and this is precisely because of their size. For example, their small size may be more appealing to their community because they have volunteer staff from the community rather than paid professional staff. Or they may be more flexible and even have greater opportunities to be creative because they have a staff that does many things rather than a segmented staff. By not having separate staff members specialized in exhibits, collections, programs, etc., they can avoid compartmentalization, something that can hamper the creative process or impede decision-making. While there are benefits to being small, the question to be asked is this: Are they achieving sustainability and excellence in their operation? In other words, are they successful?

Criteria for Success

How then to determine success? AASLH's Historic House Affinity Group Committee suggests that a small house museum must be financially sustainable, and furthermore, this is the single most critical indicator of its success.[3] But finances do not provide the only path to success. Indeed, there are many criteria that can be used to determine when a small historic house museum has achieved some level of success. For example, satisfaction on the part of paid staff, volunteers, and board members can be a clue. Consistently dissatisfied personnel often indicates that serious problems exist in a museum's operations. Conversely, a happy staff can mean a thriving museum. Another indicator is how visible the leadership is in the local community and beyond. When small historic house leadership plays an active role in the community or with collegial associations, this is a sign that the historic house museum is healthy enough to enable connections outside of its own walls. This can go to yet another level: the more highly successful a house museum is, the broader the scope of its relationships in regional and even national circles.

There are other telling indicators. Reviews by outside sources, including consumer comments on TripAdvisor, Yelp, and other online sites, can reveal much about a small house museum. Physical maintenance is another indicator of success. Not only is deferred maintenance potentially harmful to the historical fabric of the structure, the care or lack of care given to facilities reveals financial and institutional priorities. Finally, attention given to the historical integrity of the museum and its programs speaks volumes about the viability of the site. Indeed, this factor gets to the very soul of the small historic house museum. Museums that are successful and thrive are those that maintain the historical integrity of their historic structure and give careful thought to the manner in which it is interpreted.

Given these standards for success, what is it that distinguishes successful and thriving small historic house museums? What have they done to meet those standards? After surveying a variety of small museums as well as distilling salient points from AASLH's technical leaflet mentioned above, we came up with seven critical institutional behaviors for success, or "success factors," that can be utilized in the small historic house museum. We also determined that while each of these factors can influence the others positively, neglect of any one of them can negatively affect the others. In other words, it is not enough to simply work hard on one or some of the factors, while ignoring the others, and expect a museum to thrive. Those small historic house museums that are successful and thriving pay attention to these success factors.

Success Factors

1. Mission and Vision

Not all opportunities should be taken. Without careful justification, a mid-ninteenth-century house has no more business including a rare collection of Marvel comic books in its parlor than an art deco house has exhibiting butter churns in its kitchen. Polonius' admonishment to his son in Shakespeare's *Hamlet* applies here: "To thine own self be true."

Successful small historic house museums maintain a focus upon mission to make clear the organization's purpose and its overall intention; it is also a standard by which to measure opportunities and initiatives. For example, activities at the Peralta Hacienda Historical Park, located in a community of diverse immigrants in Oakland, California, are related to the home's history as an early immigrant home. Docents at the Molly Brown House Museum in Denver, Colorado, are careful to discern the differences between the real life of Margaret, or Molly, Brown and the way she is portrayed in the musical *The Unsinkable Molly Brown*.

Mission drives interpretation in a historic house, ensuring that it is based upon careful research and communicated with an eye toward accuracy. Mission also provides clarity on what the house is all about. While a successful house museum tries to stay true to its mission, it must be nimble enough to change the mission to align with the discovery of a more accurate history or message. That is exactly what is happening with the new strategic plan for Hunter's Home near Tahlequah, Oklahoma, in the Cherokee Nation, which struggled for years to find an audience. The new plan features what has always been the home's uniqueness—the only plantation-style antebellum home in Indian Territory to survive. But now the thrust of the site has moved beyond interpreting the house to include an agricultural theme based on historical farm records. As the living history site takes shape with gardens, crops, orchards, and livestock, it does so knowing exactly what was grown and the types and breeds of livestock that were raised by the Cherokees. And it hopes this new orientation will increase visitation. The desire to be true to mission (or to find the right mission) and maintain a vision based upon that mission is a common denominator among thriving historic house museums.

As is the case with Hunter's Home, the foundation of a successful mission statement is a historic house's uniqueness. In most cases, historic house museums came about precisely because there was a perception of their uniqueness. It is not, however, enough to just have that perception. With so many historic sites in the United States, that uniqueness must be demonstrated in a way that will draw visitors. This begins with the mission statement and expands to all aspects of operation. There are excellent examples of small house museums capitalizing on their uniqueness. The Lincoln Tallman House in Janesville, Wisconsin, uses a two-day visit by Abraham Lincoln to promote itself. The Molly Brown House Museum capitalizes on both the musical about Margaret's life and the *Titanic* story. The Hearthstone Mansion in Appleton, Wisconsin, prominently notes on its website that it was the "world's first home lit by hydroelectricity." Hunter's Home emphasizes the role it played in the history of the Cherokee Nation. The Haas-Lilienthal House, a San Francisco Gilded Age mansion that survived the 1906 earthquake, is promoted as a National Trust–designated National Treasure. Louisiana's Shadows-on-the-Teche is touted as the National Trust's first house museum in the Gulf South.

2. Leadership

Leadership, incorporating all the dimensions that go into it, is critical to any institution. But nowhere is this truer than for the small historic house museum. Few individuals or institutions would say they are not striving to be successful or striving to be excellent. But simply stating those as goals is not enough. The challenge lies in determining how to be excellent and how to be successful. That is where leadership is critical. So much has been written about the qualities of leadership that we will not spend time talking about them here. But suffice it to say those small historic house museums that are successful have strong leadership. And that leadership must come from the museum's director and the board. In this way, leadership is reflected not only in the programs of the museum but in the relationship between the board and the director. Furthermore, good leadership develops its resources to have the greatest impact for the museum. Successful museums create meaningful ways to engage staff and volunteers because that is the way to move plans forward for the organization.

It was leadership that made a difference in the institutions we looked at, like Shadows-on-the-Teche; Peralta Hacienda Historical Park; Woodlawn Museum, Gardens and Park; and the Molly Brown House Museum. The director at Shadows-on-the-Teche began as assistant director in 1983 and rose to her present position in 1997. She carefully cultivated her role in the community while maintaining connections with the National Trust, the parent organization. Often conducting tours herself in addition to her administrative responsibilities, she still manages to provide leadership within the town of New Iberia and beyond, helping forge a site that is loved by tourists and locals alike. Similarly, the director and board of Peralta Hacienda have developed an institution that has injected itself into local community life while conducting tours for tourists. More to the point, they have managed to leverage their community involvement into financial support from a broad range of local, state, and national funders. Leadership at Woodlawn in Ellsworth, Maine, employs methods that work for this specific site: a top-down leadership style that works well for a small museum, a capable staff that is a result of good hiring practices, a working board that values teamwork, and a long-view approach to projects that includes not looking for one-hit wonders or the latest fad.

Regardless of how a museum is led, strong leadership is critical when a site is confronted with challenges. Those might be either threats or opportunities, depending upon how they are handled. We like the term "opporthreat," which views a threat as an opportunity. As the Kykuit gatherings show, small house museums encounter plenty of threats. The Peralta Hacienda faced major social issues that led to declining visitation, so it decided to deal with them head-on by turning these threats into opporthreats. As they explain it, Peralta Hacienda recognized that it could provide an opportunity for skills training, employment, and empowerment for residents in the low-income, gang, and street violence-prone neighborhoods of East Oakland. The museum placed exhibits within the house that tied it to the local community and hired residents from the surrounding immigrant communities to give tours and tell their stories (see Figure 7.1). They provided afterschool and evening programs as well as providing space for community celebrations.

Figure 7.1 Historic kitchen in the Peralta Hacienda Historical Park, Oakland, California. Foods from the differing cultures in the neighborhood are presented here along with images of local residents that reflect these cultures. Photo by Max A. van Balgooy.

According to the museum's director, "The Peralta Hacienda site is about more than just a historic family that lived in the house from 1820; it's about the community today and what we can learn about history from one another."[4]

Sometimes a museum is faced not with a threat but a great opportunity that demands action. The success of the movie *Titanic* in 1997 gave the Molly Brown House Museum an unexpected and new visibility. The museum took advantage of that visibility, increasing programs and outreach. It had always emphasized the *Titanic* connection but increased its capitalization of that connection. This created precedent for even greater efforts fifteen years later in 2012 during the one-hundredth anniversary of the sinking of the *Titanic*. Similarly, the Haas-Lilienthal House in San Francisco seized on the popularity of the PBS series *Downton Abbey* and was promoted as a nineteenth-century American parallel to the house in the series.

Small museums can capitalize on opportunities offered by anniversaries, national trends, social media, and changes in the community. But the nature of those opportunities does not matter as much as the institutional willingness to seize them. Seizing opportunities requires nimbleness. Because of their smaller size, small house museums can often be nimbler than their larger counterparts. But for the small house museum, flexibility can be an issue. Small museums must avoid becoming so set in their traditional ways of doing business that they do not seize opportunities like those that were presented to the Molly Brown House Museum, or effectively turn threats into opporthreats, as was done by the Peralta Hacienda.

3. Clear Organizational Structure

Small historic house museums come in a variety of organizational structures. Some are part of a larger organization. Many are associated with some sort of parent organization that might be a private nonprofit organization or part of a governmental system. Some may have a powerful friend's group that has a great deal of impact on the operation of the historic house. Still others are stand-alone sites that have no connection or agreement with any governing entity. Regardless of the kind of operating structure a historic house museum may have, successful house museums have found ways to thrive with any of these types.

Denver's Molly Brown House Museum—associated with Historic Denver, Inc., which was founded to save the house museum—is one of the bigger success stories we encountered (see Figure 7.2). Critical to that success is a strong relationship with its nonprofit parent organization. But that relationship did not always benefit the museum. As Historic Denver grew into Denver's most prominent preservation organization, it became involved in major preservation efforts to help save other historic sites in the metro area. Over the years, Historic Denver began to treat the Molly Brown House, which was successful financially, as a cash cow existing mainly to provide income for the organization's other programs. In this situation, the museum survived but couldn't thrive because the resources that could help it do so were being skimmed off. Finally, within the past two decades, Historic Denver formally recognized that the Molly Brown House was its most important resource and had to be treated as such. In the years since, the museum's budget and staff have grown, it has been able to address some deferred maintenance issues, and its more innovative programs have matured, all of which has led the museum to be one of the most successful small historic house museums in the country.

Hunter's Home, a site owned by the Oklahoma Historical Society, has a strong relationship with its parent organization, which has augmented the work done by its small staff of three full-time and

Figure 7.2 Front façade of the Molly Brown House Museum, Denver, Colorado. Image courtesy of the Molly Brown House Museum.

two part-time persons. In cooperation with the society and a friends group, the site recently made a major change. It changed its name from the George M. Murrell Home back to its original name, Hunter's Home, and returned the site to what it had been originally, an 1850s Cherokee farm. With a more suitable mission, it now plays an important part in the history of the Cherokees. The site has begun to receive financial assistance from the Cherokee Nation, and it is this partnership with the Cherokee Nation—unusual in the museum field—that is the driving force behind its current and future expansion plans to create a living history farm and build a visitor's center.

In contrast, Woodlawn Museum, Gardens and Park is a stand-alone site that gets no funding or services from another entity. Despite this, it has successfully operated the historic house known as Black Mansion and the surrounding park that is original to the home. Located in northeastern Maine, Woodlawn draws upon the local community to support its ambitious program of events and tours. These would have been challenging for Woodlawn's small staff. Yet as staff is supplemented by a good-sized volunteer force, strong committees, and an active board, Woodlawn can scale up well enough to carry out the many activities on its calendar.

However a historic house museum operates, the more successful ones have an organizational structure that is a good match for the site, enables healthy partnering, and values the site's mission. Moreover, museum leadership at these sites is always on the lookout for new ways—both traditional and innovative—to leverage a modest budget to achieve goals that work for the site.

4. Internet and Digital Technology

The internet and digital technology represent another opportunity that successful small house museums are using to their benefit. Whether using digital channels, devices, and platforms (regardless of whether they are online or not) to promote the museum's messaging, internet technologies are inexpensive ways to present local history, highlight collections, advertise events, and reach new audiences. The internet levels the playing field for the small museum, allowing it to present a profile online that is as aggressive and dynamic as that of a much larger institution. For example, the Moss Mansion is a small house museum in Billings, Montana, with a budget of $360,000 and one full-time employee. Yet, its internet site is the fourth to show up on a Bing search for the words "historic house museum."

Successful small museums not only maintain active internet sites, they engage in a dynamic use of social media. These days, it is the rare museum that is not actively building community through social media of some type (Twitter, Instagram, Facebook, Reddit). Social media has brought new life to museums, enabling them to create communities in multiple ways never imagined a few years ago. While Facebook is perhaps still the most popular platform and used effectively to build online communities, it is Twitter and Instagram that can provide a glimpse into a museum's daily life that is unmatched by any other platform. Showing pictures of or just mentioning what staff is doing that day—such as dismantling an exhibit case or setting up for the annual gala—provides a glimpse into activities at the site that no one would otherwise see. This confirms to the local community that the staff is not only hard at work but keeping the site in good order.

Successful museums are also keenly aware of the impact of consumer-driven sites like TripAdvisor and Yelp. Monitoring these sites allows a museum to respond to negative entries or other concerns voiced by consumers; moreover, it is a way for sites to demonstrate good will toward people who visit. Additionally, providing an online payment service, whether for an admission ticket or a donation, increases the likelihood that people will attend events or donate to the current cause.

But there is a dark side to technology that museums need to be aware of. With technological advances changing at such a quick rate, museums with limited budgets and small staff need to exercise caution when choosing a format appropriate for its limited resources. It is often best to stick to traditional formats that have proven themselves over time, rather than to invest in the latest fad that may be too expensive or may not stand the test of time. Check out reviews at places like www.cnet.com or ask colleagues what they use. Museums with limited budgets should stay away from the latest tech innovations, like virtual reality, and avoid overpriced online payment services. Some new electronic formats also may not work for a small museum or appeal to the museum's constituents.

5. Creativity and the Art of Adaptation

One of the forces behind successful nonprofits, as recognized by Leslie R. Crutchfield and Heather McLeod Grant in their book, *Forces for Good: The Six Practices of High-Impact Nonprofits*, is mastering the art of adaptation.[5] They points out that successful organizations "are exceptionally adaptive, modifying their tactics as needed to increase their success. Along the way, they've made mistakes, and have even produced some flops. But unlike many nonprofits, they have also mastered the ability to listen, learn, and modify their approach based on external cues—allowing them to sustain their impact and stay relevant."[5] This could also be called creativity, one of the words that has been used repeatedly over the past two decades to define historic house museums. In that time, house museums have worked diligently to become more creative and to adapt to new trends in order to stay relevant. They've had to do this in order to overcome dwindling attendance and income.

Little wonder then that successful small historic house museums place a high value on staff creativity. Guided by mission, research, and opportunity, staff at these museums are encouraged to try out a variety of approaches, both traditional and new, with their programs. Wisconsin's Lincoln Tallman House offers tours that focus on the "cutting-edge" 1872 technologies used in the house in addition to more traditional tours that talk about family and furnishings. Other houses have "dropped the ropes" to allow the public a more intimate encounter with the buildings and their furnishings. The Molly Brown House has objects secured with monofilament, chairs are carefully placed to protect collections, and non-collection items in the kitchen provide a hands-on experience. And where the Moss Mansion once discouraged photography, now it welcomes it. Images showing up on Facebook, Snapchat, and blogs have led to an increase in younger visitors. These imaginative changes have changed the look of historic house museums and inspired an almost evangelistic zeal among staff and volunteers to find what appeals to visitors.

Creativity also shows up in special events, which have been a part of historic house offerings for years and are only getting more creative. Seeking to provide an alternative to gore-infested haunted houses at Halloween, the Molly Brown House introduced a "Victorian Horrors" program twenty-five years ago with actors playing popular authors like Mary Shelley and Edgar Allen Poe and reading selections from their works. It is still the museum's most popular event. In addition, the museum offers special *Titanic* events, Mother's Day teas, and occasional paranormal investigations. Other historic house museums offer ghost tours and some, like the Moss Mansion, offer murder mystery evenings. Another version of this is what the Alexander Ramsey House in St. Paul, Minnesota, calls "Ramsey After Dark." This popular evening program explores the superstitions, customs, and other hidden aspects of Victorian society and is offered throughout the year, not just at Halloween. Equally popular in the community of New Iberia is the plein air painting competition that has evolved into an annual event at Shadows-on-the-Teche. With artists setting up their blank canvases in its gardens and in the nearby downtown, this historic house event has become successful through creative partnering.

Few house museums, however, offer programs in an underserved community like the Peralta Hacienda. The Institute of Museum and Library Services presented the museum with its National Medal in 2017. Yet, while it was recognized for being a catalyst for change in its community with programs such as skills training and Spanish and Mien language tours and labels, taglines on its website reminded the community about its mission as a historic house museum: "History Is a Transformative Agent," "Every Human Being Makes History," and "This House Belongs to All of Us." These are some of the most powerful—and yes, creative—taglines we have ever seen in a house museum.

At one time, it was the rare historic house museum that rented out its facilities. Today, most successful institutions have a rental program, which has become a major source of income. The historic Boettcher Mansion, home to the Colorado Arts & Crafts Society and located near Golden, Colorado, has taken rentals to what some might call an extreme, but it has worked for them. The mansion's main business is rentals for everything from weddings to parties to business meetings. Regular guided tours are provided only by advanced arrangement, but visitors are welcome to wander through the house themselves using a self-guiding brochure. Is it a historic house museum that offers events or an events center that offers a historic house museum experience? Does that even matter? It is one more example of a creative alternative for the small historic house museum.

It doesn't stop with programming. Historic house museums are now dropping the museum part in favor of alternative uses for the historic structure. Historic buildings along the C&O Canal in Washington, DC, and the 1807 Nickels-Sortwell House in the heart of Wiscasset, Maine, are now available for vacation rentals. Indeed, you can book these via VRBO, HomeAway, Airbnb, or TurnKey. Antebellum homes along the Mississippi River are another example; for years, many have offered lodging during the night and guided visits during the day. While few are established as nonprofit museums, these vacation rentals or bed-and-breakfasts nevertheless offer an alternative that can be copied by the small historic house museum. A good example of a bed-and-breakfast following this lead can be found in Butte, Montana. The Copper King Mansion was and still is the most elegant house in Butte, built by copper baron William A. Clark in the 1880s. Tours are offered throughout the year. Although the mansion is not a nonprofit, income from tours and overnight stays goes toward the upkeep of the building, which is lavishly furnished to mirror the Victorian period of the house. The mansion has become a critical part of Butte's appeal to visitors and genealogists seeking their mining roots.

At their core, small house museums that are successful look for innovative solutions to adapt to a changing environment and to overcome difficulties. And they are not afraid to do this with reflection and evaluation until they get it right. As noted by Max van Balgooy, president of Engaging Places and coeditor of this book, "The trick is being creative while still focused on mission, sustainability, and preservation. As we all know, just because it's a new idea doesn't mean it's a good idea."

6. Evaluation

Since some ideas are not always good ones, an organization that has a willingness to try and even fail at new programs and ventures must engage in self-examination to discover what works and what does not. That makes evaluation an important component to a house museum's success. There are a variety of ways evaluation can be done. Among the best are offered through AAM's Museum Assessment Program and AASLH's Standards and Excellence Program. We have found that most successful historic house museums have had one of these evaluations done at some point in their history.

Visitor evaluation is also useful. Indeed, determining visitor reaction to a museum's programs, exhibits, and services can show what works and what does not. Small, medium-sized, and large museums have come together in the Denver metro area to create the Denver Evaluation Network, which has helped member organizations, including historic house museums, do visitor studies. While these various methods of evaluation can be time-consuming, they ultimately pay off.

One important area where visitor evaluation has paid off is in audience assessment. By understanding its audience, museum staff can more easily size up visitor patterns so that resources can be deployed more effectively. Staff at the Molly Brown House Museum determined that it had two audiences: residents and a global audience familiar with movies that featured Molly Brown. The Moss Mansion realized that it also had two audiences but saw these differently from the Molly Brown House. It characterizes its audiences as seasonal: spring/summer when the tourist and wedding season is in full force; fall/winter when fund-raisers and local events like Halloween occur. Understanding their audiences has helped these two museums direct staff time and resources in a more financially productive and focused way.

7. Collaboration and Collegiality

Closely related to community engagement is collaboration and collegiality. And let's be frank here: there is always some degree of competition between museums, whether it be for donor support, admissions, or community recognition. Yet collaboration is usually good for all participants, whether they compete or not. Collaborative efforts include joint marketing and programs, mutual workshops, and even shared resources. Some collaborative efforts are limited to specific projects, while in other cases, historic houses of varying sizes have joined together in associations with collaborative goals in mind. In Washington, DC, there are forty members of the Historic House Museum Consortium, the "At Home in Chicago" group has twenty members, and the Bay Area Historic House Museums has members in seven counties in the San Francisco area. Shadows-on-the-Teche is promoted as part of Cajun Country along with the Tabasco® pepper sauce factory, the oldest rice mill in New Iberia, and other sites that make up the area's cultural heritage. For museums that are involved with tourism, such collaboration is critical.

Collegial networks offer collaboration and more. They provide professional support and services to each other, ranging from monthly meetings to discuss issues or listen to guest speakers to large annual conferences. Collegial groups can be vital to small historic house museums in relatively isolated communities and come in varying sizes and scope. For example, a small historic house museum on Colorado's eastern plains can belong to, in ascending order of scope, the Association of Northern Front Range Museums, the Colorado-Wyoming Association of Museums, the Mountain-Plains Museums Association, the American Alliance of Museums, the American Association of State and Local History, and the National Trust for Historic Preservation. Any and all of these organizations provide vital support for members in the form of publications, meetings, and, most important, access to a network of colleagues who are willing to provide advice and other support. In our years in the museum business, we have found that those museums taking advantage of these collegial networks thrive and those that do not often struggle.

These then are the factors, presented in various degrees, that can be found in small historic house museums that are successful. Mission and vision, leadership, organizational structure, creativity and adaptation, internet and digital technology, evaluation, and collaboration are all critical to thriving as a small historic house museum. Despite dire forecasts, the large number of historic house museums present in the United States at the dawn of the new millennium have not passed away in any large numbers. There are doubtless many that are still struggling. But there are also many that are not only surviving but are thriving. And like Mark Twain, they will live on to make major contributions to American culture.

Notes

1. William Hosley quoted in "The Great Historic House Museum Debate," *Boston Globe*, November 16, 2015.
2. Steve Friesen, "Making a Case for the Small Museum," in *The Small Museum Toolkit, Volume I*, ed. Cinnamon Catlin-Legutko and Stacy Klingler (Lanham, MD: Altamira Press, 2012), 41–59.
3. Historic House Affinity Group Committee, "How Sustainable Is Your Historic House Museum?" (Technical Leaflet 244), *History News* 63, no. 4 (Autumn 2008).
4. Holly Alonzo quoted in Institute of Museum and Library Services, "Using History to Transform a Community: Peralta Hacienda Historical Park," March 13, 2014, https://www.imls.gov/news-events/project-profiles/using-history-transform-community-peralta-hacienda-historical-park.
5. Leslie R. Crutchfield and Heather McLeod Grant, *Forces for Good: The Six Practices of High-Impact Nonprofits, Second Edition* (San Francisco: Jossey-Bass Publisher, 2012).

Chapter 8

Reimagine House Museums

Loosen Up but Don't Let Go!

THOMAS A. WOODS

Constructivist theory has emerged as a critique of the usual historic house tour and as an approach some believe can cure the historic house malaise. The core meaning of constructivism is that people "construct" their own meanings in the classroom or at a museum based on their prior knowledge, past experiences, and social situation. Constructivist educational theory is related to ideas about the interpretive nature of history that accepts the validity of multiple perspectives about the past, and research that shows people make their own personal meaning of the past. The theory and these concepts about the nature of history and how people make meaning are intertwined and evolved at about the same time.

Constructivist theory sprang from the initial ideas of John Dewey and then developed and blended with several other educational theories. George Hein and other learning theorists and museum educators have advocated a constructivist approach to museum exhibitions and interpretation for some time.[1]

How visitors make meaning in a museum or historic house is a key concept within constructivism. As director of the Center on History-Making in America, Lois Silverman was one of the earliest proponents of the idea that visitors make their own personal meaning from their experience of museums and historic sites. She worked with historians like David Thelen, then editor of the *Journal of American History*, and she echoed the concerns and participated in discussions that were taking place in the field of academic history. According to Silverman, the concept of meaning-making "emerged as a response to and means for dealing with the country's changing cultural landscape and the fact that multiple and often conflicting points of view indeed exist and clash in our society." Silverman and others argue that history is an interpretation of the past, and "communication does not occur in a linear fashion, with one active party conveying information to a passive other, but that communication is a process in which meaning is jointly and actively constructed through interaction."[2]

But while Silverman emphasizes the importance of making space for visitors to make their own meaning, she acknowledges that "like historians, museum educators do not need to abandon the role of purveyors of excellent interpretation. The paradigm of meaning-making simply opens the door for museology, as well as history, to consider some desperately needed expansion."[3]

George Hein argues that constructivism is more than multiple perspectives and how to make meaning. Hein's *Learning in the Museum*, published in 1998, was a manifesto for creating a "Constructivist Museum." In concluding his argument, Hein writes, "Visitors make meaning in the museum, they learn by constructing their own understandings. The issue for museums, if they recognize this principle, is to determine what meanings visitors do make from their experience, and then to shape the experience to the extent possible by the manipulation of the environment."[4]

Since constructivist learning theory first emerged from schools for teachers, and its first application was in schools, it is there where we should begin to explore the origins and implications of the theory and its application before we consider its application to museums. David H. Jonassen, a professor of educational psychology and educational reformer, was arguably the first to popularize the concept.[5] The constructivist idea emphasizes the role of the learner in learning, or meaning-making, and deemphasizes the act of teaching:

> Knowledge for constructivism cannot be imposed or transferred intact from the mind of one knower to the mind of another. Therefore, learning and teaching cannot be synonymous: we can teach, even well, without having students learn.
> A core notion of constructivism is that individuals live in the world of their own personal and subjective experiences. It is the individual who imposes meaning on the world, rather than meaning being imposed on the individual. . . . The notion of "truth" and "certainty" are replaced by the term "viability"; any knowledge to be constructed has to be viable for its agent under the particular conditions of the case.[6]

Advocates contrast the constructivist approach with the "didactic" or "transmission" approach, in which teachers determine learning objectives and seek to transfer knowledge to students through direct instruction and lectures, among other strategies. Constructivist instructional planners "do not adopt learning and performance objectives that are internal to the content domain." Instead they "search for authentic tasks and let specific objectives emerge and be realized. The goal, for instance, is not to teach a particular version of history but to teach someone how to think like a historian."[7]

Despite the emphasis here on the role of individually driven learning, in a constructivist model teachers provide "scaffolding," "multiple perspectives," and "authentic tasks" to help support audience-directed experiences. Scaffolding guides the "learner from what is presently known to what is to be known."[8] Remember, as I noted earlier, that Lois Silverman also emphasizes that her suggested approach to meaning-making did not eliminate the role of the historic site interpreter. Both constructivist teaching theory and Silverman's meaning-making approach suggest that these new methods complement teachers and interpreters, and do not supplant them.

There has been criticism of the constructivist approach from within the teaching profession. Critics have pointed out that constructivist theory is one of learning, or meaning-making, without a clear teaching theory or instructional strategies: "In contrast to instructional-design theories that describe specific events outside of the learner that facilitate learning, learning theories describe what goes on inside a learner's head when learning occurs and are, therefore, less directly applied

Thomas A. Woods

to educational problems. . . . In the light of this, constructivists and instructional designers are often on opposite camps."[9]

Instructional designers further complain that since constructionists view learning as a personal interpretation of the world, "they show little concern for the learners' entry level skills." In addition, it is difficult for teachers (or interpreters) to assist with learning:

> [C]onstructivists contest that learning objectives are not possible and that all understanding is negotiated. The conundrum that constructivism poses for instructional designers is that if each individual is responsible for knowledge construction, then designers can not [sic] determine and ensure a common set of outcomes for learning. Besides, the instructional designer's access to individual learners' cognitions is extremely indirect and limited. The evident autonomy of learners in knowledge construction makes it difficult, if not impossible, to predict how learners will learn or how to plan instructional activities. Hence constructivist instruction is from a theoretical perspective at least, an oxymoron.[10]

As a result, using a strictly constructivist approach, how do teachers or historic house interpreters provide the constructivist "scaffolding" that helps move visitors as learners from one level to another?

Furthermore, since constructivists allow learners unlimited discretion to select what is studied and how it is studied, it "creates problems of accountability that students will learn. Learners might construct the wrong knowledge, skills and abilities."[11] Drawing on a host of educational research and publications, Yiasemina Karagiorgi and Loizos Symeou quote another critic of constructivism and suggest that having students construct their own learning strategies in poorly designed environments is "not a great virtue but abdication of our responsibility as teachers and instructors. . . . [S]tudents do not know or understand their own learning mechanisms."[12] Partly because of these barriers, constructivist teachers have struggled with the requirement to achieve state- or federal-mandated learner outcomes.

One additional striking criticism from another source is that like all knowledge, constructivism is itself a perspectivist product of a time, place, and group of people, in this case a "privileged," "western, liberal, and individualistic" group, and does not serve other racial and social groups well.[13]

One of the major challenges in applying constructivist theory to historic houses or museums, as it has been in schools, is the central idea that there is no point in developing themes or desired outcomes, or even expecting to communicate content. According to George Hein, many assessments find that visitors learn little of the content of exhibitions, therefore, "if learning of this type is so difficult to accomplish, maybe it's the wrong outcome to expect from a museum visit."[14]

Two recent books, *Letting Go? Sharing Historical Authority in a User-Generated World* and *Anarchist's Guide to Historic House Museums*, have aligned with a constructivist critique of museums and historic houses. The editors of *Letting Go?* explore the concept and methodology of "de-centering" authority from the museum to the audience. The editors argue that there is a crisis in history museums because they continue to use their own curatorial expertise and programmatic design to transfer their information and views to their audiences. They suggest that museum audiences had changed, now expecting to be active participants in museum programs, not simply passive recipients of curatorial authority. The editors' primary question seems to be "do the changes that our culture is experiencing fundamentally challenge museums' traditional relationships to their constituencies?"[15] A major related question is: "If one shifts away from declarative take-away messages and invites visitors to contribute new ideas and fresh conversations, how does one measure success?"[16] These are the same basic questions we saw teachers struggling with to use constructivist theory in the classroom.

Various authors in the volume address these questions in different ways and advocate different levels of "de-centering" authority. The implication of the "de-centering" authority concept is that museums need to abandon the thematic and learning objectives structure undergirding interpretive plans for exhibitions and historic houses. According to some of the contributors, preconceived themes and learning objectives are too centered on the intention of the historic house or museum and knowledge transfer, rather than on the audience's own knowledge and their experience and meaning-making in the exhibition.

In the interesting conversation between John Kuo Wei Tchen and Liz Ševčenko, Liz describes her time at the Tenement Museum and how they organized their thematic program around "questions" rather than "themes," which she defines as "a series of factual statements, or learning objectives."[17] I applaud the inquiry approach as an effective "scaffold," a wonderful minds-on, interactive strategy and, if done with open-ended questions and in a nonthreatening manner, one of the best ways to achieve some level of interaction.[18]

But as anyone who has ever visited the wonderful Tenement Museum or who has led an interpretive tour themselves knows, visitors are often at a loss about what questions to ask and frequently fall back on "Is it real?" or "Is it a reproduction?" Without some introductory information and guidance, the exhibition, tour, or program often goes nowhere. Reminiscing is often the fallback for many visitors. Nostalgia is not necessarily bad. It does create a connection and entry point to the exhibition, and offers an opportunity to build on preexisting knowledge and understandings—all part of a constructivist approach—but that may be the end point for many visitors, a criticism we see from teachers critical of constructivism. But historic houses and museums are fully able to build on this initial connection, rather than having it end, by providing scaffolding and making further historical connections, possibly generating Mihaly Csikszentmihalyi's "flow" experience characterized, in this case, by complete absorption in the historic house or museum encounter.[19] We should aim high, not low.

In a second example from *Letting Go?*, Benjamin Filene writes about the "Open House" exhibition at the Minnesota Historical Society, which is clearly conceived as a constructivist exhibition that attempts to "write out" the curator and educator. In this exhibition, rooms from a particular house were re-created, and aided by contextual panels, first-person immigrant voices representing those who have lived there bring the spaces to life with particular activities or memories. Filene's essay suggests that the museum had no preconceived theme for the exhibition and wanted to invite visitors to interact with it, finding their own histories within the re-creations, making their own meanings. At the same time, though, the museum clearly "selected" the primary sources and memories for visitors to hear, and underlying the exhibition is the theme "not only do ordinary people make history; they can be *historians*."[20] Our "constructions" of exhibitions are themselves thematic in what we include and exclude, whether we acknowledge or speak the themes, just as perspective informs our historical interpretation, whether acknowledged or not.

As historians and program developers, we select the objects and the information that we convey to the audience. It is hard to envision any program or exhibition that would eliminate curatorial intentionality. How far should we go to eliminate intentionality? It is not only statements or words

Thomas A. Woods

alone that constitute intentional transmission of information. Whenever we design a space or select objects, themes, learning objectives, and interpretive "hooks," we place ourselves at the center of meaning-making.

How far should we go as we seek to avoid information transfer or the museum or historic house perspective? Should we simply scatter objects and word salad around, like modern abstract painters, and then title our productions "Untitled" to avoid suggesting content, and invite the audience to speculate among themselves what it all means?

Enter Franklin Vagnone, who has recently emerged as a major critic and gadfly for historic houses. Vagnone has created a stir with his self-designated "historic house anarchist" brand in his blog and recent book.[21] The historic house anarchist arguments largely align with constructivist learning theory, but they go further in gleefully criticizing historic houses and propose to abandon all present approaches. In their book *Anarchist's Guide to Historic House Museums*, Vagnone and coauthor Deborah Ryan itemize their "fundamental critiques" of historic house museums:

1. "Historic House Museums reflect political and social propaganda, often telling only partial truths to the communities that surround them";
2. "Historic House Museums have nothing relevant to contribute to conversations";
3. "Historic House Museums are boring"; and
4. "Historic House Museums have been narrowly curated and do not reflect real life use."[22]

Vagnone and Ryan offer many suggestions they believe would break the mold of historic houses. They argue that guests want to experience a historic house much like they do their own homes. Not unlike George Hein, they suggest that historic house interpretive planners should abandon the practice of creating "predetermined messages" because "guests create their own meanings through their individual experiences."[23] They believe they should be allowed to "experience" a house by wandering through the house at their own pace, moving through it as they want to, as if it were their own "typical path," and discover meaning on their own. Guests want the ability to "touch, experiment, and learn about the House and its history through immersive tactile interaction," so there should be objects they can handle and "usable objects could be placed in each room that could be sat on, opened, and engaged."[24] Visitors should be able to "touch it, smell it, taste it." There should be sound and tactile experiences, engaging all five senses. "Guests should have access to almost everything."[25]

In fact, living history sites, which include many historic houses, have been fulfilling these suggestions since the 1970s. Visitors move through most living history sites at their own pace, often without ropes to limit their movement, encountering stationed interpreters who provide opportunities for interaction. Often, when safety and law permit, visitors are invited to participate in whatever activity is ongoing at that station. At living history farms (most of which include historic houses), for instance, that could include cooking, gardening, making hay, or feeding—even butchering animals—or any number of seasonal activities. All senses and emotions are engaged, and many objects are either reproductions, analogous objects, or part of a tiered collections policy in which some original objects without provenance can be used. You can sit down in a chair when you are tired. This experience would seem to fulfill Vagnone and Ryan's requirements.

But Vagnone and Ryan only briefly discuss living history programming at historic houses, and, ironically, they largely dismiss it. They disapprove of first-person living history in which period-clothed interpreters take the character of someone from the past and interact with visitors. They describe these "re-enactors" as "off-putting": "There is awkwardness in the pretense of the pretend, especially if we are forced to participate in an imaginary world that is not of our own making. . . . While history lovers may enjoy the make believe, less seasoned visitors may find the pretense to be off-putting because it places them in the role of an other, confused and unwelcome." The authors also believe that "period dress" creates a theatrical "fourth wall" between visitors and the experience of the historic house.[26] The authors offer a slightly more nuanced perception of third-person living history interpreters, where the interpreters do not pretend to be a person from the past, but only demonstrate the tasks of the past. "[T]he conceptual disconnect does not seem to carry through when the costumed docents are undertaking the actual tasks for which they are dressed. We have often experienced costumed docents cooking in HHM kitchens using historically accurate methods and tools, and found their conversation while at their work to be somehow comforting. Maybe it is the familiar smells or the shared food that makes these moments memorable. We suspect it is the authenticity of a shared experience that reaches across the eras."[27]

But finally, the authors have a larger problem with living history. They believe that living history projects a "disconnect" between what is "real and what is theatre" and that "guests often see us as mildly kooky adults playing make-believe, pretending that the long dead owners of the House just left the room."

Instead, they propose that it would be much more effective to "invite guests to conjure up a world of their own and imagine how they would maneuver through it, than it is to create a fully rendered, but homogeneously experienced pretend place."[28] They conclude that "costumed characterizations" simply don't work at historic houses, because the "obfuscation leaves guests questioning whether their roles are as unwilling participants or exposed voyeurs." They dismiss a living history approach by concluding that historic house museums should "[a]cknowledge that the pretend romance of Historic House Museums is not necessarily the best way to frame public communications or programming."[29]

Vagnone and Ryan also discount special events as an effective approach to improving historic house programming. The authors say that it is common for the historic house staff to do the "easier task" of creating "one-off events" while leaving the "house experience unaltered, traditional, and boring." This leads to the staff seeing the house as a "place for special events rather than as a cultural asset." For some reason, they assert that "trust is lost when HMHs facilitate interesting events, but fail to reinvigorate the basic tour experience."

Hein and the "historic house anarchist" critiques do part ways in several significant areas. Hein believes museums have a story to tell[30] and that history theater is effective at museums. He writes, "Drama and theatre are gripping, powerful media to draw visitors into a scene, make the human connection to objects apparent to some, and allow visitors' imaginations to expand and associate rich meanings with the objects displayed."[31] He includes living history interpretation in this assessment too:

> Both theatre and drama represent ways to extend modalities for visitor learning in the museum. Drama, the use of theatre techniques that engage the learner actively (through interaction with a first-person interpreter or by being drawn into a theatrical process), and theatre, usually a more formal situation involving a script and a production that engage the visitor emotionally and intellectually but not necessarily physically, can help to expand the visitors' access to the content of the museum.[32]

In Hein's estimation, then, historic house narratives, history theater, and living history can be effective strategies that allow visitors to create their own meaning while historic sites' actors/interpreters create "scaffolding" stories, scripts, and performances.

In spite of the constructivist admonition against programs or exhibitions with themes and learning objectives, most experts on interpretive program design have recommended, and continue to recommend, developing programs based on themes and learning objectives or desired outcomes.[33] Based on his definition of interpretation—that interpretation aims "to reveal meanings and relationships" not to communicate "factual information"—and his first and fourth principles of interpretation—that emphasize relating to visitors' "personality or experience" and provoking rather than instructing them—it could be argued that even interpretation pioneer Freeman Tilden recommended "visitor-centered" interpretation in 1957.[34] Recent interpretive planning guides, which incorporate the idea of a visitor-centric museum and the idea of multiple perspectives, continue to recommend themes and desired outcomes. One of the best such examples is *Interpretive Planning for Museums: Integrating Visitor Perspectives in Decision Making*. The authors develop a fully formed and articulated approach to interpretive planning, but it is not unlike the process followed by many interpretive planners for years. In a nod to constructivist theory, they note, "As the perceived role of the museum visitor has moved from one of information consumer to one of knowledge constructor based on active engagement, museums have increasingly become visitor-centric."[35] Yet the authors describe a well-developed approach to theme and outcome-based interpretation in their book.[36]

In *The Participatory Museum*, Nina Simon describes five stages of interface between the visitor and the institution beginning with the individual consuming content, and the fifth stage concludes with individuals engaging each other in social interaction.[37] She acknowledges that all stages rest on the foundation of content. She advocates for audience-centered design, but that does not mean "throwing out the things the staff think are important . . . it means framing them in the context of what visitors want or need."[38] For example, in a historic house, she acknowledges the importance of interpretive staff who can "provide the most consistent kinds of social experiences, and staff can be an important bridge to support and enhance even the most social exhibit design."[39]

Although discouraged by both constructivists and historic house anarchists, providing content and creating themes and desired learner outcomes or objectives at historic houses are central to creating scaffolds that allow dialogue to emerge and encourage growth in understanding to occur in both visitors and museum professionals as they interact.

I have spent much of the past twenty-five years working with historic sites in Hawai'i. Some projects there can demonstrate how interpretive plans can provide rich visitor experiences, and how important it is to develop strong themes and for interpreters to provide scaffolding for visitors to gain more understanding about the historic places they are visiting. The Kona Coffee Living History Farm, owned and operated by the Kona Historical Society (KHS), is a good example of how a project can enlist local communities in developing a historic site to help them feel an enduring connection to it. Opened to the public in 1999, this seven-acre coffee farm contains a modest 1925 Japanese-style coffee farmhouse and outbuildings. After the property became available to the KHS, they immediately formed a local Kona Coffee Farm Advisory Committee. Kona coffee farmers themselves played a significant role in guiding the development of the project. In addition to the advisory committee, a Friends of the Uchida Coffee Farm was created. The friends provided volunteer labor and played an important fund-raising role. Both groups were multiethnic, reflecting the historic nature of coffee farming and the present community.

Under the supervision of a restoration architect, volunteers from the local community assisted in restoring the buildings and property, using methods commonly used to repair their own coffee farms. Older coffee farmers even made coffee farm and household tools, like the ones used in the 1920s to 1940s. In addition to extensive research in secondary sources and primary documents, including Mr. Uchida's diary, extensive oral history interviews were conducted with older coffee farmers. Fusae Uchida Takahara, one of the last members of the Uchida family to live on the farm in the early 1990s, assisted the curators of the farm in identifying, assembling, and creating a furnishing plan to reflect the items the family had in the house and other buildings and, through her oral history, fleshing out the story of the site. She provided lists of meals and family recipes.

The interpretive approach at the Kona Coffee Living History Farm is a mix of guided tour and third-person living history. Much of the tour compares the attitudes, objects, and activities of the *issei* (first-generation immigrant) with the *nissei* (second generation), demonstrating the pervasive tension between generations over a desire to retain ethnic identity and the pressures of Americanization, a contentious dynamic displayed in nearly every facet of life. Third-person living history interpreters stationed in the house demonstrate the foodways of the Uchidas and other coffee farmers, and the guides become third-person living history interpreters in the fields and at the *hoshidana*, demonstrating the activities of the period.

Most visitors to this place know very little about the history associated with it and the house is quite different from any they have ever experienced. How do you move visitors beyond their original assumptions, few as they might be, about what it might have been like for a Japanese immigrant family to live on an isolated Kona coffee farm in the 1920s–1945 era? There is clearly a need for some "transfer" of information from interpreter to visitor at this site to enable the visitor to make any sense of the place at all.

The site has an extensive interpretive manual that provides information for the interpretive guides. The manual is divided into two main sections: a methodology section that includes learning theory and a station-by-station organization that includes a "big idea" and content summaries, station themes, and desired learner outcomes that identify potential cognitive, affective, and psychomotor outcomes, with suggested objects, stories, and activities to achieve the outcomes. Each station section begins with a suggested "hook" to begin the interpretation of each station, but interpreters are free to develop their own hooks too. Hooks are nearly always open-ended questions and are meant to engage the attention and interest of visitors, not to elicit correct answers. In addition, each station includes questioning strategies to get visitors to think about different points of view, particularly those of the first- and second-generation family members. These are the scaffolds that help visitors emotionally connect and empathize with the original residents and to move to new, more complete understandings of Kona coffee farmers. Without guidance from a tour guide, visitors would have virtually no way to make sense out of the Uchida house, the farm itself, or the intergenerational pressures and conflicts they encountered.

Affective learning opportunities are planned and offered throughout the historic site experience. As visitors enter the home, they are asked to remove their shoes, just as guests to the house did during the period of interpretation. Those who are able to do so are then invited to sit cross-legged on the floor on a Japanese *zabuton* (cushion), near where Mr. Uchida used to sit in the same way to read his paper at night after tending to his coffee trees.

Thomas A. Woods

As they later move into the kitchen, they encounter interpreters who make meals each day that the historic site is open to the public, following simple recipes provided by Fusae Uchida Takahara. The smell of coffee stick fires and food cooking pervade the house and the surroundings. The *kudo* is a typical masonry Japanese open-fire, grate-type stove designed specifically for cooking rice and other Japanese food. A special opening in the concrete base is sized for the *hagama* (rice pot). Sheet metal covering another hole provides a place for tea kettles and frying pans and all other cooking containers. There is no chimney, and smoke exists through a slatted wall. There was no oven in the kudo, in the American sense, in which one could bake bread or other similar foods, but the children later added a small kerosene oven the size of a microwave, across from the kudo to bake bread, part of their efforts to become American.

Visitors experience the outbuildings and fields in much the same way as they experience the house. As part of a guided tour, they meet a donkey, the animal power on the farm, and they become physically involved in activities wherever it is safe and appropriate to do so in the coffee mill and hoshidana drying platform.

Another example from the KHS is also useful in understanding how interpretive "scaffolding" is essential to generating a positive, interactive visitor experience. KHS opened the H. N. Greenwell Store in 2007. Although a general store, the same interpretive principles can be applied to a historic house. The store has been restored to the 1890s era, just before Greenwell died, and stocked with reproduction merchandise of that era.

At this site, an interpreter orients visitors before they enter the store. They are provided a general historical background for Kona history and general stores along Kona's Mamalahoa Highway, and then are oriented to their impending experience in the H. N. Greenwell Store. Visitors are asked to choose one of three characters: Manual Golarte, a Portuguese *mauka* (up-mountain) dairy farmer; Louisa Catherina Todd, a young French woman married to a local rancher who ran a small hotel in their large house; and Kekoanui, a Hawaiian *paniolo* (cowboy) who managed H. N. Greenwell's Hawaiian-related businesses of the period: fish ponds, goat skins, and wholesale coffee purchases from Hawaiian coffee farmers. Each of these characters have a bartering and shopping list that is linked to their gender, personal job, ethnicity, and elevation of occupancy on the island, all significant variables in Kona.

When visitors enter the store, the storekeeper welcomes them in third-person (referring to we, he, her, they) as a living history interpreter. Visitors become a second-person (you) living history participant with their designated character who has a defined barter and/or purchasing list that connects with their gender, job, ethnicity, and elevation on the island. One of the visitors is designated as the character shopper, though they are encouraged to share the designation so anyone who wants to can participate with the shopping list. For larger, mixed groups, two or all three characters can be selected by different individuals. As visitors request an item, the shopkeeper retrieves it and explains to the "shopper" why they might like it due to their gender, ethnicity, job, and elevation on the island. Visitors become engaged, enjoy the presentation, pose many questions as they interact with the period-dressed interpreter/shopkeeper, and talk with each other about the purchases, creating that social link between visitors. There are no first-person living history barriers that might make the visitor feel uninformed or uncomfortable about the process. Some version of this approach could easily be adopted at a historic house with an imaginative interpretive planner.

Finally, let's not dismiss special events as the historic house anarchist did so readily. They can play a very important role in making your historic house an important asset for the community.

They have made Hawaiian Mission Houses Historic Site and Archives (HMH), for instance, a meaningful part of the Honolulu community again. Most HMH events are not "one-off," but a series of events that repeat each year.

Theater and music are ways for a historic house or site to connect emotionally to a community and helps audience members connect to each other through shared experience. Music is an important part of the themes at HMH because missionaries associated with the site introduced hymns—multiple voices with harmony—into Hawai'i and initially trained young chiefs to appreciate Western music, which they modified and adapted to create their own unique Hawaiian music. To focus on music, HMH built an outdoor performance mound with community volunteers, and created a four-part series of Saturday performances of Hawaiian music and hula, accompanied with conversations about the music. Leading Hawaiian musicians and chant and hula teachers are part of a Hawaiian *mele* (chants, songs, or poems) advisory *hui* (group) that plans the Hawaiian music programs with staff. The hui selects the annual theme, divides it across four performances, recruits performers, and identifies appropriate mele and hula. It is one of the most authentic Hawaiian performances on the island of O'ahu and has become a favorite among locals.

Theater is another major interpretive methodology at HMH because of its emotive quality. HMH stages a three-weekend summer Shakespearean play on the outdoor stage, commemorating the fact that the first public program there was a play in 1907 (see Figure 8.1). The focus is Shakespeare because some missionaries to Hawai'i were fans of Shakespeare. HMH won two Po'okela Awards in 2016, given by the Hawaii State Theater Council, for excellence in several categories for statewide theater performances.

Figure 8.1 "The Tempest," performed on the outdoor stage at Hawaiian Mission Houses' annual Shakespeare performance, 2015; in 2016, HMH won two Po'okela Awards for excellence in several categories from the Hawaii State Theater Council. Photo by Thomas A. Woods.

Thomas A. Woods

There is no need to feel confined to your historic house or site. Sometimes you can fulfill your mission at another location. In addition to on-site Shakespearen performances, HMH staff take theater programs off-site to a nearby cemetery to perform regularly sold-out performances of the Cemetery Pupu (in this case with heavy, local-style hors d'oeuvres) Theater. Staff select a theme, then five people buried in the cemetery are chosen who reflect that theme; staff members do extensive research and contract with a script writer and a director, and performers are hired for five long-form monologues. Actors stand next to the cemetery memorial for the person whose stories they tell (see Figure 8.2). After the performance, there is a talk-back to discuss the history and performances with those involved. These performances have become so popular, the site is selling complete contract performances to corporations, organizations, and family groups, and HMH recently received a substantial grant to bring the program into the schools in a slightly different format.

None of these exceptional KHS or HMH visitor experiences are possible without the "scaffolding" of an interpretive guide, musician, or actor. They don't tell visitors how to think or feel, but they allow visitors to generate their own meaning from their experiences and the scaffolding created through careful research, community input, and expert interpretation.

Historic houses can accommodate many of the important new understandings about how people learn, how they make meaning, and the perspectivist nature of history without giving up on the role of careful interpretive planning, including themes and desired learner outcomes. While there are many viable historical interpretations of events or people in the past, history is not simply whatever someone wants it to be, a purely relativistic production without convincing evidence or persuasive argumentation. History is perspectivist, but not relativistic. Pure constructivism is an

Figure 8.2 Actor Zachary Thomas Woods during a performance of Dr. Joseph C. F. Rock at Cemetery Pupu Theater, O'ahu Cemetery, in 2015. Photo by Thomas A. Woods.

almost impossible path for historic houses or other museums to follow and remain meaningful to visitors, but we can adopt some of its insights. Historic houses and other historic sites will best be served by providing carefully considered programming with strong and meaningful themes, desired learner outcomes that include cognitive, affective, and psychomotor programmatic guidelines, and liberal use of open-ended inquiry. Interpreters, or "scaffolders," are essential to help visitors go beyond their initial assumptions and to make meaning on their own. The scaffolders can provide content expertise and emotionally impactful experiences while acknowledging and highlighting differing perspectives. They can encourage visitors to connect personally from their own background and with each other. Be creative, use a variety of interpretive methods, not just a guided tour. But, done well, even that much-maligned approach can be successful. Let's not void the value of thorough research and high-quality interpretive planning and programming. Let's not "let go," but let's loosen up.

Notes

1. George Hein, *Learning in the Museum* (London: Routledge, 1998); George Hein and Mary Alexander, *Museums: Places of Learning* (Washington, DC: American Association of Museums, 1998); George Hein, "The Challenge and Significance of Constructivism," keynote address at Hands-On! Europe Conference, London, November 15, 2001, http://george-hein.com/papers_online/hoe_2001.html; George Hein, "John Dewey and Museum Education," *Curator* 47, no. 4 (October 2004); Kodi R. Jeffery-Clay, "Constructivism in Museums: How Museums Create Meaningful Learning Environments," *The Journal of Museum Education* 23, no. 1 (1998): 3–7, http://www.jstor.org/stable/40479108.
2. Lois Silverman, "Making Meaning Together: Lessons from the Field of American History," *Journal of Museum Education* 18, no. 3 (Fall 1993): 7.
3. Ibid., 8.
4. Hein, *Learning in the Museum*, 179; George E. Hein, "Is Meaning Making Constructivism? Is Constructivism Meaning Making?" *Exhibitionist* 18, no. 2 (Fall 1999), http://www.george-hein.com/downloads/Hein_isMeaningMaking.pdf.
5. See David H. Jonassen's more than 37 books, 180 journal articles, and 64 book chapters. For specific guidelines from Jonassen, see "Thinking Technology: Toward a Constructivist Design Model," *Educational Technology* 34, no. 4, (1994): 34–37.
6. Yiasemina Karagiorgi and Loizos Symeou, "Translating Constructivism into Instructional Design: Potential and Limitations," *Educational Technology and Society* 8, no. 1 (January 2005): 17.
7. Hein, *Learning in the Museum*, 25–40; Karagiorgi and Symeou, 19.
8. Karagiorgi and Symeou, 20.
9. Ibid., 22; also see Virginia Richardson, "Constructive Pedagogy," *Teachers College Record* 105, no. 9 (December 2003): 1629.
10. Karagiorgi and Symeou, 20.
11. Ibid., 22
12. M. D. Merrill, "Constructivism and Instructional Design," *Educational Technology* 31, no. 5: 45–53, as quoted in Karagiorgi and Symeou, 22.
13. Richardson, 1633; note that Hein was aware that constructivism was a perspective, *Learning in the Museum*, 98.
14. Hein, *Learning in the Museum*, 93.
15. Bill Adair, Benjamin Filene, and Laura Koloski, eds., *Letting Go? Sharing Historical Authority in a User-Generated World* (Philadelphia: The Pew Center for Arts & Heritage, 2011), 11.
16. Ibid., 14.
17. John Kuo Wei Tchen and Liz Ševčenko, "The 'Dialogic Museum' Revisited: A Collaborative Reflection, in ibid., 93.
18. See Thomas A. Woods, "Teaching Sense of Place at Historic Sites in Hawaii," *Journal of the West* 46, no. 2 (Spring 2007): 41–42.
19. Mihaly Csikszentmihalyi, *Flow: The Psychology of Optimal Experience* (New York: Harper Perennial, 2008).

Thomas A. Woods

20. Benjamin Filene, "Make Yourself at Home—Welcoming Voices in Open House: If These Walls Could Talk," in Adair, Filene, and Koloski, 150.
21. Franklin D. Vagnone and Deborah E. Ryan, *Anarchist's Guide to Historic House Museums* (New York: Routledge, 2016).
22. Ibid., 52.
23. Ibid., 138.
24. Ibid., 140-41.
25. Ibid., 155.
26. Ibid., 103.
27. Ibid.
28. Ibid., 104.
29. Ibid., 105-6; see Scott Magelssen for his withering constructivist criticism of living history museums and thematizing at living history museums. Scott Magelssen, *Living History Museums: Undoing History Through Performance* (Lanham, MD: Scarecrow Press, 2007), especially 39.
30. Hein, *Learning in the Museum*, 151.
31. Ibid., 169.
32. Ibid., 168.
33. Sam H. Ham, *Environmental Interpretation: A Practical Guide for People with Big Ideas and Small Budgets*, (Golden, CO: Fulcrum Publishing: 1992), 33-44; Larry Beck and Ted Cable, *Interpretation for the 21st Century: Fifteen Guiding Principles for Interpreting Nature and Culture* (Champaign, IL: Sagamore Publishing, 1998), 59-63; John A. Veverka, *Interpretive Master Planning: The Essential Planning Guide for Interpretive Centers, Parks, Self-Guided Trails, Historic Sites, Zoos, Exhibits and Programs* (Tustin, CA: Acorn Naturalists, 1994), 40-43, 45-51, 90-91; Lisa Brochu and Tim Merriman, *Personal Interpretation: Connecting Your Audience to Heritage Resources* (Fort Collins, CO: Heartfelt Publications, 2012), 14, 34; Lisa Brochu, *Interpretive Planning: The 5-M Model for Successful Projects* (Fort Collins, CO: National Association for Interpretation, 2003), 100-5; Marcella Wells, Barbara Butler, and Judith Koke, *Interpretive Planning for Museums: Integrating Visitor Perspectives in Decision Making* (Walnut Creek, CA: Left Coast Press, 2013), 49, 89-92, 114-18; Jessica Foy Donnelly, ed., *Interpreting Historic House Museums* (Walnut Creek, CA: AltaMira Press, 2002), 51-54, 210-28.
34. Tilden, 9.
35. Wells, Butler, and Koke, 30.
36. Ibid., 49, 89-92, 114-18.
37. Nina Simon, *The Participatory Museum* (Santa Cruz: Museum 2.0, 2010), 26.
38. Ibid., 34.
39. Ibid., 28-29.

Recommended Resources

Becker, Carl. "Everyman His Own Historian." *American Historical Review* 37, no. 2 (January 1932): 221-36.
Karagiorgi, Yiasemina, and Loizos Symeou. "Translating Constructivism into Instructional Design: Potential and Limitations." *Educational Technology and Society* 8, no. 1 (2005): 17-27.
Novick, Karagiorgi. *That Noble Dream: The Objectivity Question and the American Historical Profession*. Cambridge, England: Cambridge University Press, 1988.
Roberts, Lisa C. *From Knowledge to Narrative: Educators and the Changing Museum*. Washington, DC: Smithsonian Institution Press, 1997.
Wells, Marcella, Barbara Butler, and Judith Koke. *Interpretive Planning for Museums: Integrating Visitor Perspectives in Decision Making*. Walnut Creek, CA: Left Coast Press, 2013.
Woods, Thomas A. "Perspectivistic Interpretation: A New Direction for Historic Sites and Museums." *History News* 44 (January/February 1989): 14, 27-28.

Chapter 9

Value of History Statement

HISTORY RELEVANCE

Version April 2018

History Relevance promotes shared language, tools, and strategies to mobilize history organizations in the United States around the relevance and value of history. We support history organizations that encourage the public to use historical-thinking skills to actively engage with and address contemporary issues and to value history for its relevance to modern life.

We call on organizations to endorse, share, and use the statement on the value of history in contemporary life. With common agreement, commitment, and open conversation about why history is important, we believe the historical community can change the common perception that history is nice, but not essential. To date, more than 250 organizations have endorsed the statement.

To Ourselves

Identity: History nurtures personal and collective identity in a diverse world. People discover their place in time through stories of their families, communities, and nation. These stories of freedom and equality, injustice and struggle, loss and achievement, and courage and triumph shape people's personal values that guide them through life.

Critical Thinking: History teaches vital skills. Historical thinking requires critical approaches to evidence and argument and develops contextual understanding and historical perspective, encouraging meaningful engagement with concepts like continuity, change, and causation, and the ability to interpret and communicate complex ideas clearly and coherently.

To Our Communities

Vibrant Communities: History is the foundation for strong, vibrant communities. A place becomes a community when wrapped in human memory as told through family stories, tribal traditions, and civic commemorations as well as discussions about our roles and responsibilities to each other and the places we call home.

Economic Development: History is a catalyst for economic growth. Communities with cultural heritage institutions and a strong sense of historical character attract talent, increase tourism revenues, enhance business development, and fortify local economies.

To Our Future

Engaged Citizens: History helps people envision a better future. Democracy thrives when individuals convene to express opinions, listen to others, and take action. Weaving history into discussions about contemporary issues clarifies differing perspectives and misperceptions, reveals complexities, grounds competing views in evidence, and introduces new ideas; all can lead to greater understanding and viable community solutions.

Leadership: History inspires leaders. History provides today's leaders with role models as they navigate through the complexities of modern life. The stories of persons from the past can offer direction to contemporary leaders and help clarify their values and ideals.

Legacy: History, saved and preserved, is the foundation for future generations. Historical knowledge is crucial to protecting democracy. By preserving authentic and meaningful documents, artifacts, images, stories, and places, future generations have a foundation on which to build and know what it means to be a member of the civic community.

★ ★ ★ ★ ★

Endorsing this statement in principle is an initial step. We encourage you to adapt and incorporate these ideas into projects, training materials, mission statements, websites, marketing materials, and other institutional outlets. The seven core values are not new, but we believe that their articulation with the intent to make real, measurable change across the profession and into public realms represents a fresh start for our discipline. For more details, visit HistoryRelevance.com.

Part II

Audiences

Chapter 10

Using Historic House Museum Audiences to Drive Change

KATHERINE KANE

There are more history museums in the United States than any other kind of museum. And there are more historic houses and sites than other types of history museums.[1] Historic houses are a dime a dozen, scattered through every community and county. Most of them are using a business model developed one hundred years ago.

But change is underway. Museums are asking how current audiences—and potential audiences—can help historic houses rethink how they should work.

This chapter has reflections from a long career in museums, and what those reflections mean for historic houses generally, and for the Harriet Beecher Stowe Center specifically, as the Stowe Center built a new identity and public life.

Importance of the Public's Trust in What We Do

Many historic house museums were once the homes of prominent individuals or families, buildings that stand out in their town or neighborhood, and which people couldn't bear to tear down. People get fired up about preserving a building because it has always been there, or represents the nostalgic past, or because they don't like change, or the building is the last one left or is architecturally significant, or because the owner was rich or famous. A nonprofit is organized, or the local or state historical society is convinced to take it on.

Nonprofit incorporation brings legal and ethical responsibilities. The museum must act to the public's benefit: as a nonprofit, the public measure of impact and performance is less financial than mission based. In exchange for a mission benefiting the public and public relief from the expectation of financial profit, the organization is relieved of paying various federal, state, and local taxes, and the donors who "invest" in the nonprofit receive a tax benefit for their financial gift. This important bargain is at the center of all nonprofit public responsibilities, including historic house museums, and, in exchange, brings obligations of transparency, ethical behavior, and acting in the public good.

But the public's trust can be ephemeral. It takes time to build trust and it can be gone in an instant. Once gone, it is difficult to rebuild. As a group, the public still trusts museums.[2] Retaining this trust is the responsibility of every historic house museum. Every museum must act in the public trust; each museum that doesn't threatens all museums.

Do Historic House Museums Matter to the Public?

The public cares about historic house museums, or there wouldn't be so many of them. These museums are gathering places, bringing people together, giving historical perspective and a glimpse of the past. They demonstrate the power of place, physically illustrating that historical information and context is important for understanding. The public trusts historic house museums to be authentic and truthful. And if you ask visitors what they think, and why historic house museums are (or aren't) important to them, they'll tell you.

Who Are the Audiences and What Do They Want to Do at Your Historic House Museum?

People visit historic house museums because they like the acceptable voyeurism of visiting domestic environments: they want to peek into other lives, see how people lived, be in their intimate spaces, and look at their furniture and household goods. What is more human than the place where people cooked, slept, and tucked in their children (or had them tucked in)?

Visitors are curious; they want to go to the place where something happened, someplace that's different, or is beautiful, or odd. They want to see the new place that's been getting lots of word of mouth, or they are fans of the historic figure and are making a pilgrimage. Or, it's just there, and they are there too, and they'll give it a try. And they come because they trust historic house museums to be authentic, honest, and truthful.

Segment them as we will, audiences are complex creatures. As individuals, they are making a purchase and a decision about how to spend their time. As members or donors, they are deciding how much, if any, financial support they want to give the museum. Their decisions are affected by the museum's reputation, by how much time they have, the ticket cost, their expectations of what will happen, and by their previous experiences at similar sites.

Most people visit historic house museums with at least one other person, a family member or friend. It is a relatively casual social experience with friends or family (unlike for the museum itself, for whom it is a serious business). They are locals or from another country. They are tourists; teachers and their students; neighbors, volunteers, or shoppers. They are funders, members, and community leaders. They are on vacation, visiting friends (or taking visiting friends around to see the local sites), part of a bus tour, and just passing by.

Historic house museum visitors tend to be educated, white, and female. After all, women make most of the purchasing decisions and plan family time. They tend not to be people of color, less prosperous people, or people who didn't grow up going to historic house museums. They are not the people who think historic house museums are boring. And they are NOT those who never visit (obviously). What do these visitors and non-visitors tell us about visiting historic house museums and what they expect from their experience versus what happens?

Even though visitors are educated people, they are not particularly knowledgeable about the historic house museums themselves, the relevant history, or about how historic house museums work. After all, museums, historic sites, and historic preservation have codified professional approaches to the business of preserving and operating historic house museums, an approach with its own language, best practices, and worldview. These shape what historic house museums do and how it is done.[3]

Why Do Audiences Matter to Historic House Museums?

It seems a simple question, but it's at the heart of historic house museums' challenges and failures. Some answers are obvious. Audiences matter because the public—whether they are attendees or not—*keeps historic houses alive and sustains them* for the future by participating and engaging, donating and talking about them. They matter because the lack of public interaction means the resource stream isn't present and the site fails financially. They are the revenue and attendance numbers, and the word of mouth that makes the museum succeed or not. Historic house museum audiences are voters and taxpayers. Without them, there is no general popular support, or nonprofit status. They visit, attend programs, buy memberships, and support the sites financially. They are the people who asked that these places be preserved.

Audiences matter because, after all, *it's the museum's job*. Legally and ethically, historic houses are responsible to the public that granted them tax-exempt nonprofit status. The bottom line is not the almighty dollar, it is a satisfied public. Historic house museums are obligated to the public.

Historic house museums are responsible to the public whether people visit or not. They are responsible when the public drives by on the way to work, and when they use the lawn to play with their children or have a picnic. I don't mean this in a direct, private-property legal sense; I mean it in the ethical and moral sense. Historic house museums can be like the anchor stores in the mall: they make the rest of the neighborhood look good when they take care of their buildings.

Audiences matter to historic house museums because—well, *it's nice to get attention*. You've preserved an amazing building at great expense of finance and effort. Surely everyone will be interested. You've expended energy and thought on a site experience and it's a pleasure to be appreciated. Just as in *Field of Dreams*, you feel like if you build it (or restore it) they will come. (And maybe they will and maybe they won't.)

Audiences matter because they *bring the humanity into the human space*. Visitors populate the rooms and bring their intellect and emotional reactions, making the houses living spaces again. Audiences matter because these spaces are theirs. And because historic houses are so human, the experience of visiting can evoke empathy and build emotional and human connection between the visitor and the site.

Audiences Matter Because They Can Motivate Change

By listening to what the public wants and incorporating their thoughts and ideas, there can be a mutually exciting loop engaging the public and building an extended support system, which drives the change that will help the museum change and thrive. Public interaction with historic house museums changes both. Members of the public bring their observations and ideas, their experience of the world, and their varied perspectives. If historic houses are paying attention by observing and listening, systematically gathering formal and informal feedback, watching, and asking, there's a lot to learn. When this information is combined with published research on public opinions and behavior in museums, the historic house museum can build a mission-based programmatic framework that will make it stand out among its peers. In turn, this knowledge can fuel programmatic and creative strength, improve performance and impact, and drive change, transformation, and success.

And Yet, Historic House Museums Are Not Meeting Public Responsibilities

As organizations, historic house museums are static and inert, and fixed in their ways. They're not demonstrating innovation, engagement, movement, and energy. Programming is predictable and inadequate. Most are telling essentially the same story (prosperous family builds beautiful home, look at all their great stuff) in the same way. The museums have trained visitors to expect the same thing everywhere, to be passive. House tours are famously boring, presented as a lecture, with no effort to engage participants.[4]

Historic house museums—like most museums—aren't operated for the convenience of the visitor, but for their own convenience, with open hours during the workday, rather than times when more people are free to visit. Listening to audiences can change this.

Historic house museums only tell part of their site's story. For example, the interpretation may discuss the wealth associated with the house, but not the source of that wealth. It's uncomfortable to talk about slavery, robber barons, or money. And visitor demographics don't reflect the community or the country, so these museums are fulfilling only a small portion of their public responsibilities.[5]

Historic house museum audiences don't reflect their communities, focusing on elite and middle-class men, but not the poor, the female, the young, those of color, or forgotten or unimportant people. Visitors see only one angle or point of view, and people outside the mainstream don't see themselves, so why would the historic house museum have meaning for them? The stories of people from marginalized groups are missing. The other people who lived or worked in the house, like the children and the people who cared for them, the staff, servants, or enslaved people, are also missing from the story. And those are just the people inside the house.

Telling the whole story is particularly important at the homes of national figures or famous people. Historic house museums ignore the human imperfections of these individuals, yet these imperfections make them more interesting. Just like the rest of us, they weren't perfect, they made mistakes, and they acted to the values of their day rather than ours.

Historic house museums have names that make it impossible to know what they are and misrepresent the site. They should reflect the site's mission, story, or activities, perhaps the "John and Jane Doe Family Farm Home." What does "The John Smith House" tell a potential visitor? It could be something like "Revolutionary War Hero's Amazing Home, the Colonel John Smith House." If he was married, it could be the "John and Jane Smith House," so that the other half of the population is included. (Those earlier married women don't have their names on the land title because they were not able under law to legally own the house; does that mean they had no interest or role in the design or operation of their home?)

Historic house museums take themselves way too seriously and are blind to how they present themselves. If the museum is the most prominent house in the neighborhood, surrounded by a fence or wall, why would local people feel they are welcome? Museums have a secret language, a specialized jargon even board members and non-museum-trained staff and volunteers don't understand: "accession," "deaccession," "reinterpretation," the differences between conservation and preservation. Consider the acronyms: AAM, AASLH, NEMA, CHS, NEH, IMLS.

Given all of this, why are we surprised that attendance and engagement is dropping? If we care—and who cares more than those of us associated with historic house museums—this is a matter of survival.

What Can We Do?

The answer to "What can we do?" is up to every site. Each site must evaluate its history and his-toric characters, its location, physical plant, and competing organizations, and programmatically connect all of that with content that the public wants.

Historic houses aren't just about the past. No one walking in the door can time travel, but every visitor carries their personal experiences into these spaces. Museums can listen to their public, asking them what they want and why.

1. Invite the public to be part of imagining what the historic house museum can be and take advantage of perspectives from outside the museum. These external voices can have a big impact and help the museum inspire, provoke, and engage.
2. Find ways to reach people outside the usual visitors and build content that appeals to those who don't participate in the museum: non-visitors, people who don't look like your usual visitors, people of lower socioeconomic classes, people who think they've already visited. This means working differently by bringing outside voices into the museum, treating them with respect, and listening.
3. Leverage what you have. Uncomfortable history should not be ignored but incorporated into the interpretation. Come to terms with it; help people understand.
4. Be brave and take risks: try things out; make mistakes.
5. Make hard and thoughtful choices about what not to do as well as what you will do. There isn't enough time or money to do everything, so make choices.
6. Harness technology, connecting with people who will never be able to visit.
7. Recognize and promote all the things the museum does, not just the details of programs. Historic houses preserve the built environment, make the city/countryside look good, act as education centers and places of informal learning, give people a chance to get out of them-selves and use their imaginations, leverage the power of place, and make the past present.

Working this way brings a competitive edge; sells more tickets; attracts new visitors, members, and donors; gets attention; and is exciting and stimulating.

Deciding What You Are: The Harriet Beecher Stowe Center as an Example

The Harriet Beecher Stowe Center in the early 2000s was an introverted, invisible, and un-known organization. Over three decades, the organization rethought itself and transformed into a new kind of historic house museum. Doing so meant struggling with many of the issues we just reviewed.

In 1994, the Stowe Center board had changed the organization's name from the Stowe-Day Foun-dation to the Harriet Beecher Stowe Center, deciding that the center was more than a collection of historic buildings but a center for thought and conversation. However, describing the vision is one thing, carrying it out is another. It took ten more years to bear fruit, as the center made major decisions about itself and gathered the staff and board needed to drive the new concept.

The center tightened the mission, deciding to be a museum, program center, and research library. The new mission connected Stowe's work as a writer and the issues she wrote about: *The Stowe Center preserves and interprets Stowe's Hartford home and the Center's historic collections* (a traditional museum mission element, based on the center's 1941 founding documents and in that sense, irrevocable), *promotes vibrant discussion of her life and work* (language directly from the museum founder's will), *and inspires commitment to social justice and positive change.* Given that Stowe's best-known work is *Uncle Tom's Cabin*, an internationally best-selling antislavery novel whose title character became an insulting racial slur, the center cannot ignore the nineteenth-century social issues Stowe wrote about, and which continue as issues today. *This mission works to live up to the public trust*, from following the instructions of the museum's founder, to recognizing the legacies of past practices. And with this mission, the Stowe Center began to overcome inertia, expanding the story, incorporating multiple viewpoints, and humanizing the historic figure of Harriet Beecher Stowe.

Building programmatic content around such a mission was easier said than done. How do you conduct a house tour that inspires commitment to positive change? How do you present programs with vibrant discussion? How do you know if it's working?

Stowe was a white woman, raised in financial poverty but rich in intellectual stimulation by her charismatic father, Reverend Lyman Beecher, among her eleven siblings, in an atmosphere where each was expected to be able to argue opinions. She was well-educated for a girl of her day (her older sister Catharine Beecher founded four schools and was one of her teachers), and when her father moved the family to Cincinnati, Ohio, in 1836 (on the Ohio River, across from slave-holding Kentucky), she met and married Calvin Stowe, professor, theologian, and her intellectual equal, and they began their family.

Raised in Connecticut when slavery was still legal (as it was until 1848), Stowe's experiences in Cincinnati shaped her antislavery sentiments. She visited a friend in Kentucky, in a household with enslaved servants, and she reported witnessing the auction sale of human beings. In Cincinnati, she lived near a community of free people of color, among whom were formerly enslaved people. She learned that her cook, a woman of African descent, was self- emancipated when the woman's owner came looking. Stowe and her husband and brother Henry Ward Beecher helped fugitives along the informal Underground Railroad.

In Cincinnati, she became a published writer, leveraging her skill and her famous Beecher name, and learning quickly that she could help support the family with articles and stories. So as the U.S. national debate on slavery grew, with abolitionists becoming more radical, legislation more restrictive, and the country's fragmentation more apparent, the Beechers argued about what to do. Stowe had six children when, in the summer of 1849, as her husband was away, her youngest, eighteeth-month-old Charlie, died of cholera. We know the details of this death from letters she wrote to Calvin. The emotion of this grief, and her anger at the latest proslavery federal legislation, the Fugitive Slave Law, all went into *Uncle Tom's Cabin* (1852).

The book's impact is difficult to overstate. It was an international best seller, a financial success, and controversial from the beginning. It was banned in some southern states and prompted a mini-industry of proslavery "anti-Tom" novels. (Stowe wrote *A Key to Uncle Tom's Cabin* [1853] in response to critics who challenged her portrayal of slavery.) It helped take abolition from the fringe to the mainstream. The novel infiltrated popular culture. It was so popular, everyone stole it, most particularly the theater. It was adapted immediately for the stage and has been called America's most performed play because it ran, in big shows and small, in theaters and opera houses across the country for ninety years. Everyone saw it, a troupe visited town at least once a year. But adapting it for the stage transformed *Uncle Tom's Cabin* into something other than an antislavery story. The abolition content was stripped out; black characters were performed by whites in blackface; key characters were played for humor rather than tragedy; and brave, young, strong, religious Tom became a passive old man.

In a career of fifty years, as author of thirty books including four antislavery books, Stowe was one of the nineteenth century's most widely read authors. The controversial issues she wrote about from slavery to incest, the misrepresentation of *Uncle Tom's Cabin* on stage, the associated development of the racial slur "Uncle Tom," and Stowe's gender make her the most-important, least-known American woman. *Uncle Tom's Cabin* made her an international celebrity.

At the Harriet Beecher Stowe Center, when we began planning reinterpretation for the 1871 Stowe House, Stowe's home for almost twenty-five years, a National Historic Landmark that opened to the public in 1968, we convened informal conversations with visitors, members, donors, and non-visitors and asked them what the house tour should be like and what they wanted to do in the house. These were not social science–based formal focus groups, they were informal conversations, and, combined with more formal research, they yielded critical perspectives that shaped the house's reinterpretation. We wanted to know if and how the Stowe Center mattered to the public.

The home of the most-important, least-known American woman, with a strong supporting collection, had a lot of opportunity. We knew both that people were interested in Stowe once they knew a little about her, and that "Uncle Tom" was a barrier. When I joined the Stowe Center, I asked history colleagues around the country who was doing interesting work at historic house museums. The answers were not many: the Tenement Museum, Drayton Hall, maybe a few others.

At the Stowe Center, we noticed that visitors personally identified with the tragedies of Stowe's life and connected the headlines of their day with the issues of Stowe's. It was clear that visitors wanted to talk during the tour, share their own thoughts and experiences, rather than passively listen to a lecture from the tour guide. And it was clear that the old historic house interpretive model was not working for the Stowe House: Stowe's story and impact was not carried by the decorative arts and furniture in the house and by a lecture-based guided tour. The public wanted something else.

The center's award-winning, conversation-based issue discussions, salons at Stowe, were inspired by the salons of the eighteenth century and the twenty-first-century adaptation by the Providence (Rhode Island) Athenaeum, where they picked a topic for an informal Friday evening discussion, with wine and snacks. The Stowe Center adapted these in 2008 as facilitated parlor conversations around a current issue connected to Stowe's work. The salons were a big hit. They are deceptively simple: conduct an open public conversation with a facilitator and experts on the topic as resources. Soon, all the center's public programs were conversation- rather than lecture-based. The next step was to adapt the house tour. The opportunity for reinterpreting the Stowe House came with a collections-preservation-driven systems upgrade, which meant deinstalling the house.

Open to the public in 1968 with a guided tour through period rooms featuring Stowe's family, domestic life, and writing career, the house tour was little changed in fifty years. And changing historic house tours is notoriously difficult. Tour guides get set in their routine and breaking the mold is challenging. With the Stowe House deinstallation, we asked: Will everything go back just the way it was? The answer, of course, was no. Deinstalling the house would change the tour.

Public Input to the Stowe House Transformation

Staff began with research on the Stowe House, Stowe's life, Stowe and her visitors' correspondence about it, publications about the house from her day, an evaluation of the collection, most of which is from the Stowe and Beecher families, published research on visitor attitudes and preferences, informal focus groups, and input from scholar advisors.

The center participated in AASLH's "Visitors Count!" surveying house tour visitor satisfaction and opinions, benchmarked with other historic houses nationally. The 2008 Connecticut Cultural Consumer study conducted by Reach Advisors, a research and predictive analytics firm, focused on emerging shifts in the external landscape, and brought valuable information about the museum-going audience which aligns with HBSC research, showing that visitors want action, activity, immersion experiences, authenticity, and inclusive and difficult history. Results of the center's audience research, public expectation, and the headline issues of the day made it clear it was past time to completely change the standard house tour and replace it with a dynamic, responsive visitor experience.

We wanted to know who the Stowe Center audiences are and what they want to do at the museum. We thought that if we listened to them, we'd have to change our methods. People said they wanted to understand how Stowe's work fits into American history and how she found the courage to accomplish what she did at a time when women had fewer rights. They wanted to know how Stowe found the motivation to "go against the grain . . . [and] keep going." They wanted to hear Stowe's words, and they wanted a place for conversation and discussion about Stowe and issues she cared about, including the abolition of slavery and racial and gender equity. They wanted a sense of connection with Stowe. They wanted to sit down in her parlor. They said media was okay but didn't want to see screens in the period rooms. They wanted an interactive, tactile, and varied experience. They wanted opportunities for reflection and self-exploration. And they insisted they wanted to wrangle difficult content.

In developing the story line and themes, staff, working with consultants, made important decisions:

- Focus on *Uncle Tom's Cabin*, Stowe's best-known book, and its huge impact on the United States, and deemphasize her other writing.
- Democracy demands constructive citizen involvement. Stowe is an example of a person with impact and can inspire others to act on issues they care about.
- Many of today's issues are rooted in the past. Visiting Stowe's home can get people to learn and think about them.
- The tour isn't about the decorative arts or architecture; plenty of other historic house museums do that. The house is a stage, a setting, for the tour experience.
- Some rooms are period rooms; those that do not further the story (a pantry, a dressing room, the guest bedroom) are gallery and media spaces.
- The new Stowe House experience is with a tour guide (or, as we call them, interpreters). Fifty percent of visitors say they want a guided tour, 50 percent don't. We chose to use guides for content delivery and security reasons. This is a situation where there is no right answer and the one you make will not be satisfactory.

- The experience uses facilitated discussion rather than lecture. This means tour guides must be comfortable with silence, waiting for response, able to manage some discomfort or conflict (after all, *Uncle Tom's Cabin* is about race and slavery), and able to share the stage.
- The tour uses dual chronologies. The Stowe House in Hartford is her retirement home, so the perspective is retrospective. The tour describes Stowe's life chronologically, using the spaces and collections in this retirement home. In the dining room, interpreters discuss both the Stowe family's use of the room and Harriet Beecher's childhood meals where her parents expected family members to conduct lively, well-argued discussion about the issues of their day. These two chronologies are possible because modern audiences are used to complicated chronologies in their media; movies and television routinely use flashbacks and flash forwards and confusing timelines.
- The public sits down in Stowe's parlor (on reproduction chairs) for a facilitated activity using copies of documents from the collection.
- The tour experience ends with a call to action.
- Except for one dedicated room, media is present but not visible.

There were lessons along the way. Most of the tour, even the media, was prototyped, or tried out, before the house was deinstalled. This meant that the visiting audience was integral to the change process as their feedback helped build a stronger tour. The staff changed, as some were not comfortable with new ways. Interpreter recruitment and training has changed considerably, adding facilitation and listening skills to historical knowledge and the ability to tell a good story.

The Stowe Center Audience

The Stowe Center's house tour audience is the standard house museum audience: women of a certain age, education, and resource level, the traditional historic house visitor. The center's program audience, which used to be demographically like the house tour visitor, has changed completely and now represents the diverse population of Greater Hartford. Over more than a decade, with salons and other programs, the center has built a reputation (a trust) as a safe place to talk about difficult topics, a place where we bring people together to talk across racial, class, and ethnic lines. With the new Stowe House experience, the goal is to expand to reach a more varied audience. Early indications are that this is happening.

Public Reactions to the Stowe Center Interpretation

The Stowe House reopened in the summer of 2017 with the new interpretation. Public reaction has been strong and largely positive. Visitors are surprised they get to talk during the tour; one said, "The tour is set up as an open dialogue between guests and guide and prompts thought-provoking discussion which we are in dire need of in this country." Others said, "It wasn't necessarily about the house, it was more about Harriet, her writing, her family and the impact that she made on a social level as it relates to slavery in America" and "Best tour of a home I ever had, she brought Harriet Beecher Stowe to life for me."

The country's fragmentation is also clear from visitor comments and conversation; talking about the past is one thing but talking about the present is another. Visitors may be reluctant to listen, or they may leap to conclusions. One woman said, "I was not expecting to have a political discussion while on vacation." Since tours are partly driven by the individuals who are on the tour, interpreter skill in handling such feedback is critical. Challenging questions and comments are an opportunity for a learning exchange.

With this kind of interpretation, the staff conducting the tour is even more critical. We recruit for different skills and train new interpreters differently. Training sessions happen often, including daily discussions in the half hour before opening, where staff shares various techniques and help one another.

Final Thoughts

After this experience at the Stowe Center, it's clear to me that in reaching out to the public, there are questions that can prompt useful discussion and decision-making.

Questions to Ask the Public

Use these questions with the board, key donors and stakeholders, members and visitors, and especially with those who don't attend or engage with the museum. These conversations can be in small invited groups, or at open house days, or after a tour or program. The facilitator should be experienced, and follow up on answers, probing for more information. It may be uncomfortable for staff, therefore, keep staff presence to a minimum. Have a note taker capture the feedback to share with staff and board.

- What is this house about? What COULD it be about?
- What is being ignored that is at the center of the story? What is the elephant in the room?
- What do you want to DO here?
- If you are not visiting the museum, why not? What would make it interesting?

Additional questions to ask yourselves:

- What does the public want? How do you know?
- How is this site different from other sites? What opportunities does that give us?
- What are our colleague competitors doing at other nearby sites? How can we complement or differ from them? How can we avoid doing the same thing they do?
- Who visits the museum? Who avoids visiting and why? What can you do about it? Have you gotten their input?
- What are you going to leave out?

I believe that successful change and transformation should be organic, created as much as possible from the community, staff, and board. By taking this approach, the change is slower, but it is more likely to be successful and to last. All of us associated with historic house museums must help our sites find their own special niche. There are innumerable stories to tell about the American experience. Audiences are critical to accomplishing that goal.

Notes

1. Institute for Museum and Library Services, "Distribution of Museums by Discipline, FY 2014," https://www.imls.gov/assets/1/AssetManager/MUDF_TypeDist_2014q3.pdf.
2. Reach Advisors, "Museums and Trust," *Museums R+D Monthly Memo* 1, no. 8 (June 2015).
3. For a discussion, see Franklin D. Vagnone and Deborah E. Ryan, *Anarchists Guide to Historic House Museums* (Walnut Creek, CA: Left Coast Press, 2016).
4. Michelle Zupan, "The SCARY Truth Facing Historic House Museums," *Views from the Porch* (blog), October 28, 2015, http://blogs.aaslh.org/the-scary-truth-facing-historic-houses/.
5. Betty Farrell and Maria Medvedeva, *Demographic Transformation and the Future of Museums* (Washington, DC: AAM Press, 2010).

Chapter 11

Cultural Heritage Travelers and Historic House Museums

AMY JORDAN WEBB

The inspiration to reimagine experiences at historic sites can be driven by a desire to create more meaningful experiences for visitors but can also be driven by the desire to find new sources of earned income in a time when contributed revenues may be shrinking. Museums and historic sites across the country are looking for creative ways to increase their appeal for today's audience, generating additional earned income to offset operating expenses while still respecting the historic integrity of their sites.

As historic house managers look for creative ways to rethink visitation and create new sources of income, cultural heritage travelers are a logical target audience. Unfortunately, managers of many historic house museums do not always fully understand which travelers in their area might be interested in visiting historic houses, nor do they know how to reach them. Developing an understanding of the current trends in cultural heritage tourism is a key to tapping into this lucrative target market that offers intriguing opportunities for visitation growth and visitor engagement.

* * * * *

What is cultural heritage tourism? Why is it a desirable target market for historic houses?

So what exactly is cultural heritage tourism? The National Trust for Historic Preservation defines cultural heritage tourism as "traveling to experience the places and activities that authentically represent the stories and people of the past and present." Cultural heritage travelers are an especially attractive target market as multiple studies completed over the past several decades have shown that these travelers stay longer and spend more money than other kinds of travelers.

The first national study on cultural and heritage tourism was completed in the late 1990s, and the most recent study was completed by Mandala Research in 2013.[1] According to the 2013 study, 76 percent of all leisure travelers in the United States participate in cultural and/or heritage activities while traveling, translating to 129.6 million adults each year.[2] This percentage has remained relatively consistent across the different local, regional, and national studies on cultural and heritage travelers. The 2013 report divides cultural heritage travelers overall into five segments based on the extent to which cultural heritage attractions influenced their travel choices. These leisure travel segments include:

- "Passionate" travelers for whom cultural or heritage activities are the primary driver in their decision.
- "Keeping it Light" travelers who might include a cultural or heritage activity if it looks like it will be fun.
- Other segments include "Well-Rounded/Active" travelers who enjoy a broad range of activities including historic sites, "Aspirational" travelers who express a desire to visit historic sites but may not follow through, and "Self-Guided/Accidental" travelers who may not express an intention to visit historic sites, but might visit if they came across them while exploring other areas of interest.[3]

Even for the passionate cultural heritage travelers for whom culture and history are their primary motivation, offering itineraries with a balance of leisure activities will have the strongest appeal. The variety of cultural heritage traveler segments helps to emphasize the importance of offering visitor experiences that can be customized to meet the interests and time frame of different visitors.

* * * * *

Work with a tourism agency such as a convention and visitor bureau or a state tourism office to better understand visitors traveling in your area. Understanding the demographics of visitors in your area and identifying areas of overlap with cultural heritage travelers will provide guidance as new visitor experiences are developed for target audiences.

Virtually every study completed on cultural heritage travelers has shown that they spend more than other kinds of travelers. The most recent 2013 Mandala study found that cultural heritage travelers spend an average of $1,319 per trip as compared to $820 per trip for all other U.S. travelers. Spending by cultural heritage travelers increased to $994 per trip in 2009, an impressive 33 percent increase.[4] These spending characteristics make cultural heritage travelers a very attractive target market, leading to the creation of partnerships between cultural and heritage attractions and the tourism industry.

Cultural Heritage Tourism and Historic House Museums

Ironically, while cultural heritage tourism has been growing in popularity over the past few decades, managers at many historic house museums have seen visitation over this same time period stagnate or even decline. In part, these visitation trends for historic house museums can be attributed to increasing competition from the growing number of historic house museums across the country. In addition, competition is also coming from other cultural and heritage attractions that have been developed and promoted to this target audience as well as other competition for a shrinking amount of leisure time.

Cultural heritage travelers may stay in a historic inn or bed-and-breakfast, take a walking tour of a historic neighborhood, drive along a historic byway, explore a heritage area, or shop or dine in a historic building that has been adaptively reused as a store or restaurant. Savvy business owners for historic lodging, dining, or shopping establishments are finding ways to share the story of their locale as part of the experience at their site, allowing visitors to soak in the history of the region in many different ways. While complementary activities focused on the heritage of an area can increase the overall appeal for potential cultural heritage travelers, it also creates competition for the visitor's time. Some of these experiences offer opportunities to engage more of the visitor's senses (smell, touch, taste, sound, and sight), offering interactive experiences that may have greater appeal for today's travelers than a traditional "velvet rope" tour.

Other cultural heritage attractions are not the only activities competing for the cultural heritage traveler's time. Leisure time is increasingly becoming a scarce commodity. Juliet Schor's *The Overworked American: The Unexpected Decline of American Leisure* found that "since 1973 free time has fallen nearly 40 percent—from a median figure of 26 hours a week to slightly under 17."[5] Shor's research further indicates that "the average employed person is now on the job an additional 164 hours, or the equivalent of an extra month a year."[6]

There is increasing competition for leisure time in general between hectic and demanding work schedules, family commitments, children's activities, new technologies, and other personal interests. With smartphones, laptops, tablets, and smart TVs, the vast majority of people in the United States have immediate access to movies, video games, and television on demand, and social media sites available at their fingertips.

Historic site managers are often at a disadvantage in today's competitive environment as they often do not have access to current tourism research about cultural heritage travelers. Additionally, the tourism industry is a fast-paced, pay-to-play industry, and all too often historic sites have limited financial and human resources to invest in building marketing partnerships with tourism entities. While social media can help even the playing field, staff at historic sites often lack online media skills to take full advantage of this opportunity.

Recognizing that leisure time has become a scarce commodity, it is even more important for historic house managers to make information about their sites easy to find, and to offer a variety of tour experiences tailored to different interests and time constraints. New technologies for cell phone or audio tours offer opportunities for visitors to tailor the content and timing of a tour experience to match up with their areas of interest and schedules. At the same time, offering a variety of guided and self-guided tour options along with other program opportunities can provide appealing ways for visitors with different interests to engage with a site. Packages, itineraries, advance-purchase tickets, and combination tickets are other ways site managers can streamline trip planning for time-strapped travelers.

Principles for Successful and Sustainable Cultural Heritage Tourism

Over a twenty-year period (1989–2009), the National Trust for Historic Preservation's heritage tourism program focused on learning from cultural heritage tourism efforts across the country. The National Trust's involvement with heritage tourism began in 1989 when the National Trust for Historic Preservation received a three-year challenge grant from the National Endowment for the Arts to work in sixteen pilot regions in four states (Indiana, Tennessee, Texas, and Wisconsin). Over a three-year period from late 1989 to early 1993, the National Trust's Heritage Tourism Initiative tracked the results in all sixteen pilot regions to determine what it took to create successful and sustainable heritage tourism programs. This work was continued through the National Trust's Heritage Tourism Program (1993–2009). While these experiences demonstrated that every individual site or program faces different challenges and opportunities that require different solutions, five guiding principles emerged from the pilot regions that continue to be important components for success for cultural heritage tourism efforts today.

Five Principles for Successful and Sustainable Cultural Heritage Tourism

1. Collaborate

By its very nature, cultural heritage tourism requires effective partnerships. Much more can be accomplished by working together than by working alone. Collaborations and partnerships can be formal or informal and can be formed around common themes or around a shared geography such as a community, county, corridor, or region. Connecting the stories at your historic site to other visitor attractions increases the overall appeal of a destination for cultural heritage travelers. Tourism entities are most frequently set up using political boundaries, such as a city or county-wide convention and visitor bureau or a statewide tourism office.

Preservation organizations, state historical societies, museum associations, or other regional efforts such as heritage areas can also provide an umbrella for joint marketing and programming. For example, historic house museums in Knoxville, Tennessee, have partnered on a joint admission or "combo" ticket to seven historic homes, along with creating a website at www.hhknoxville. org to market all seven sites. Their coalition, called "Historic Homes of Knoxville," is also exploring ways to develop a pool of shared funds to support capital improvements.

Thematic as well as geographic connections can provide a basis for collaboration. For example, in 1999 the National Trust for Historic Preservation helped to create the Historic Artist Homes & Studios (HAHS) through an initiative that included several of the National Trust's historic sites. Thanks in part to dedicated support from the director of Chesterwood, the home and studio of prominent sculptor Daniel Chester French and a National Trust Historic Site, the HAHS has grown to become an independent coalition of thirty museums representing the homes and working studios of American artists. The networks' shared connection to American artists offers opportunities to compare experiences and challenges formally or informally. In 2013, HAHS sponsored a three-day workshop in Santa Fe, New Mexico. In 2014, HAHS launched a shared HAHS website.

As thematic clusters can often cross these political boundaries, regional efforts such as a heritage area, cultural corridor, or historic byway can be used to link sites across political boundaries. While federal funding for National Scenic Byways has been eliminated in recent years, federal funding is still available for other regional efforts such as National Heritage Areas and National Historic Trails. Other regions are finding alternatives to federal funding through private philanthropy or other state or local government funding. Even without external funding, local or regional partnerships can provide mutually beneficial opportunities to achieve shared goals.

2. Find the Fit Between the Community and Tourism

Cultural heritage tourism should make a community a better place to live as well as a better place to visit. In the last half century, the demographics of the American family have changed with more dual-income families and an expanding number of hours spent at work. This, combined with increasing family commitments for children's activities, has meant that travel patterns have been shifting from longer, multi-week summer vacations to a greater number of shorter getaway trips closer to home. As shorter trips are more likely to include repeat visits to the same destination, it has become more important for historic sites to offer a variety of experiences to attract repeat visitors and for sites to ensure they are also relevant for local residents within their community.

During recent economic downturns, travel industry research cited an increasing number of "staycations" (vacations spent at home rather than traveling to another destination). Although the economy has improved, a January 2016 report from Destination Analysts indicates that 22 percent of trips for all leisure travelers in the previous year were staycations, indicating that this kind of vacation may be here to stay.[7]

Historic sites do not always need to fully abandon their original purpose. For example, the Touro Synagogue in Newport, Rhode Island, is both a historic site open to visitors and an active synagogue. As the oldest synagogue in the United States, it has an active tour program while simultaneously serving an active Jewish congregation of 125 families. The National Trust notes that "each year, over 30,000 visitors cross the synagogue threshold to pray, see its magnificent interior, and hear its remarkable story."[8] As visitation patterns change, other historic sites may realize that they can also provide a valued service for their local community as well as functioning as an attraction for out-of-town visitors. These services may be connected to the site's original use or may be an entirely new community use based on the current needs and interests of local residents. By responding to changing needs in the community, historic sites can remain a relevant and valued part of the community.

3. Make Sites and Programs Come Alive

Look for ways to make visitor experiences exciting and interactive by engaging as many of the five senses as possible. The National Trust's Farnsworth House in Plano, Illinois, worked with Luftwerk in 2014 to create an art exhibition that used light and sound to transform the house into the backdrop for a post-sunset visual and auditory experience that celebrates the clean modern lines of the home.

With the growing popularity of culinary tourism, historic sites and museums are finding creative ways to incorporate food into programming. In at least on instance, a new business has been created focusing on the connection between museums and food. The Los Angeles–based "Art Bites" program offers unique classes for all ages that combine cooking lessons with art history. Classes typically involve a guided tour of an exhibition followed by a cooking lesson in a nearby commercial kitchen using recipes based on the period and focus of the exhibition. The class culminates in a shared meal where participants socialize and taste the results of their cooking efforts.

There has been much debate about the merits of a live guided tour versus the use of technology to provide a recorded tour. A live guide may have the opportunity to chat with tour-goers before the tour begins to find out more about their specific interests and the amount of time they have available, and well-trained guides are able to customize their tour presentation in response to the interests of their group. On the other hand, technology can also provide memorable experiences. Many years ago, on a trip to Chicago, I took an unforgettable audio tour of Oak Park, which incorporated the voice of Frank Lloyd Wright explaining how he came up with the design for a home featured on the tour. The tour concluded in Unity Temple where audio-tour listeners could remain as long as they wished while listening to a concert previously recorded there. The key is to take full advantage of the opportunities provided by any interpretive technique used to tell the story of your site.

Hands-on experiences have been proven to be among the most memorable for visitors. Interpretive research has shown that visitors will remember 10 percent of what they hear, 30 percent of what they read, 50 percent of what they see, and a whopping 90 percent of what they do.[9] As part of an interpretive visitor experience in a church in Lancaster County, Pennsylvania, that was part of the Underground Railroad, families were separated and invited to role-play. After learning about the "conductor's" cues to let "passengers" on the Underground Railroad know when it was safe to travel, participants used that information to try to bring other family members to safety. By making visitors *part* of the story rather than simply telling or showing them the story, this experience becomes much more meaningful. Finding ways to connect visitors to your site through role-playing, hands-on experiences, or even volunteer work can create lasting connections.

4. Focus on Quality and Authenticity

Today's cultural heritage traveler is more sophisticated and will expect a high level of quality and an authentic experience. For example, in addition to their regular guided tours, the Gamble House in Pasadena, California, offers a variety of special tours including a "Behind the Velvet Ropes" tour where visitors are invited to explore inside the rooms where docents open up drawers and doors to reveal intricate craftsmen details. True craftsmen aficionados can take the "Details & Joinery" tour offered by craftsmen contractors and woodworkers to learn more about the home's details including wood inlay, metal work, and art glass. These tours are offered at a premium price point that makes them profitable for the Gamble House. At the same time, they offer a more in-depth experience that allows visitors to have a more meaningful connection with the site.

5. Preserve and Protect Resources

Many cultural, historic, and natural resources—including historic sites and many objects in their collections—are irreplaceable. Once they are gone, they are lost forever. As new interactive and hands-on activities are contemplated for historic sites, it is important not to lose sight of the fragile nature of historic sites and their collections. An activity or program that works well at one site may not be appropriate for another. Every historic house museum has different resources, stories, audiences, and community, and to be successful, it is critical to focus on what makes a particular site unique and different to set it apart from every other place. Historic site managers need to balance the preservation and conservation of their site with appropriate opportunities for programming that can keep their site relevant and appealing to visitors—as well as contributing to the financial sustainability of the site.

Developing cultural heritage tourism programs is an incremental process that does not produce changes overnight. While many people equate tourism with marketing, responsible cultural heritage tourism programs include a comprehensive effort that encompasses tourism development, marketing, and management. While the guiding principles still ring true for both strong and weak economic climates, in tough times historic house museums need to place an increased emphasis on tracking results and being prepared to make their case with key decision makers. Many attractions are finding that technology and social networking are not only good ways to reach out to new audiences, they also offer cost-effective alternatives to other approaches.

Creative Ways to Reimagine Historic Sites

As historic houses look for ways to reinvent visitor experiences to draw more visitors and to become more financially sustainable, managers are taking a new look at all areas of earned income.

Historic houses are looking at ways to increase revenues from their gift shops, cafes, special events, facility rentals, and even overnight accommodations as strategies to generate new or increased sources of earned income.

The profitability of museum gift shops depends on a variety of factors and often requires specialized expertise in merchandising and inventory control. The Hotel de Paris, a National Trust for Historic Preservation historic site in Georgetown, Colorado, has added a "Dames Delights" section to their gift shop. As members of the Colonial Dames downsize, they can donate items to the Hotel de Paris for the museum's gift shop. Sales are a 100 percent profit for the museum, and donors can write off their donations on their taxes.

Special events can bring new audiences to historic sites. Several L.A. museums have teamed up to offer an annual "Museums of the Arroyo Day" with free admission to multiple historic homes and heritage attractions in East Los Angeles as well as free transportation between all participating sites. While this event is geared more toward raising the awareness of local residents about attractions in their backyard, this increased awareness can translate to expanded visitation as local residents become ambassadors for area attractions, especially as they suggest things to do and see to visiting friends and relatives.

Many historic sites offer facility rentals to offset expenses. Weddings, corporate events, private parties, and film shoot locations are just some of the ways that historic sites have capitalized on the unique appeal of their locations as rental venues. Rental income can provide a valuable source of earned income to offset operating expenses, although rental income comes with some risk. The potential financial benefits of facility rentals must be carefully weighed against the potential for damage to the building or collections as well as the demands that facility rentals can place on overburdened staff. Several of the National Trust's historic sites, including Drayton Hall and Cliveden, have discontinued facility rentals because of damage to the site and staff burnout.

While less commonly found, some historic house museums are offering overnight accommodations to generate revenue. Colonial Williamsburg is perhaps the best-known example of offering overnight accommodations for visitors within the historic district. Smaller historic sites have also embraced overnight accommodations. At Fort Garland State Historic Site in Fort Garland, Colorado, an early adobe fort once commanded by the legendary Kit Carson, visitors can pay fifteen dollars to spend the night in the bunkhouse as part of certain special events. At the Nevada Northern Railway National Historic Landmark in Ely, Nevada, visitors can choose between overnight accommodations in a 1906 bunkhouse or a working caboose. In Vermont, the Landmark Trust USA offers Naulakha, the home of author Rudyard Kipling, as a vacation rental. Amenities for guests include a private museum tour relating to Kipling's years in Vermont.

Shared use is another strategy to help achieve financial sustainability. The City of Harrisonburg (Virginia) purchased and renovated the historic Hardesty-Higgins House (constructed 1848–1853) in the early 2000s as a multiuse facility. Today, this historic building on Main Street houses the Valley Turnpike Museum, Harrisonburg-Rockingham Civil War Orientation Center, a visitor center for the local tourism office, a gift shop, a bakery/cafe, and offices for several local community organizations.

Marketing for Success

Many historic house museums rely more heavily on public relations strategies such as news releases rather than on paid advertising due to the limitations of their marketing budgets. Regardless of the marketing methods used, it is important to understand how cultural heritage travelers are getting information about potential travel destinations.

Just like leisure travelers overall, cultural heritage travelers are planning many of their trips on short notice. According to the 2013 Mandala Research study, 20 percent of cultural heritage travelers book their trips less than fourteen days in advance, and the number of travelers booking more than three months in advance dropped from 23 percent in 2009 to 10 percent in 2013.[10] Travelers may also defer some decisions until they arrive at their destination, making it important that information about visitor attractions and services are readily available in locations where visitors can find them. This includes visitor centers as well as lodging facilities, restaurants, and other major attractions in the area.

Increased use of the internet for travel planning is making it easier to plan a trip on short notice, and cultural heritage travelers are three times more likely to use mobile devices such as smart phones or tablets to research events, travel deals, or get recommendations on things to do or places to stay than other kinds of travelers. Facebook is the most popular social media site for cultural heritage travelers with more than 75 percent reading and posting on a regular basis. Quick Response (QR) codes continue to be popular, with more than 25 percent of cultural heritage travelers using a QR code to visit a website using their smart phones.[11]

While younger travelers (millennials and Gen X) are more comfortable making travel plans using mobile devises and social media, this gap continues to close as older travelers such as baby boomers become more comfortable with mobile planning. Nearly 70 percent of millennials and 60 percent of Gen X travelers used a mobile phone to plan travel in 2015, as compared to only 34 percent of baby boomers. However, usage of mobile phones to plan travel increased from 25 percent to 35 percent between 2014 and 2015.[12]

While the tourism industry has labelled travelers with an interest in history and historic places as "heritage" or "cultural heritage" travelers, it is important to note that the majority of these travelers do not self-identify as "cultural heritage travelers." Marketing materials for this target audience should include compelling descriptions of the visitor experiences offered but should not necessarily describe them as "cultural heritage tourism" experiences.

Lack of funding has forced many historic house museums to reevaluate their offerings, allowing them to identify audiences with the greatest potential and focusing programs and marketing efforts to reach that target audience. Recognizing that in tough economic times visitors are also feeling the economic pinch, some attractions emphasize value during economic downturns in order to attract audiences that may have less disposable income than they did previously. Taking advantage of anniversaries and celebrations is another way that historic house museums have found to enhance their visibility. Historic house museums are also reaching out to the local community in new ways, working to establish a deeper connection with locals who may have the ability and interest to do more than just a one-time visit or tour.

In reimagining historic house experiences for today's cultural heritage travelers, it is important to understand the factors these travelers consider when choosing leisure trip activities. In creating their travel itineraries, cultural heritage travelers want to combine cultural experiences with a variety of other activities including shopping, dining, getting out into nature, and exercising. While historic house museums have traditionally focused on providing a cultural experience, the broader interests of cultural heritage travelers offer opportunities for historic house museums to expand their offerings with an increased focus on their gift shop, restaurants or eateries, gardens, and other recreational activities. Offering a wider range of activities and experiences appeals to the broader interests of cultural heritage travelers, providing an incentive for them to stay longer and spend more money at your site. In addition, diversifying the experiences and offerings at your site can also attract new audiences.

Balancing Roles as Curator, Interpreter, and Financial Steward of a Historic House

In finding the balance between caring for collections and providing meaningful and interactive visitor experiences, historic house museums have traditionally tended to emphasize collections care. While collections are indisputably important, it is time for the pendulum to swing toward a stronger focus on the visitor experience and a secure financial operating budget. Today's visitor experiences can range from specialized or customized tours to match up with the interests or availability of your visitors, to other kinds of activities such as behind-the-scenes tours, hands-on learning activities, or interactive opportunities to experience a site in a new way—a cooking class, a unique dining experience, yoga or dance classes, gardening, or, in some cases, perhaps even the opportunity to spend the night at the site.

For historic site managers, finding the balance between the sometimes competing goals of preserving the site and conserving the site's collection with offering interactive visitor experiences that go beyond the "velvet rope" tour is further complicated by the challenge of increasing earned revenue to make the site financially sustainable. While it may seem safer to prohibit new uses that introduce new risks to your site and collection, sites that reject opportunities to attract new audiences risk becoming slowly obsolete as their visitation and budgets shrink, leaving them without adequate resources to maintain the site and limiting the site's potential to impact the lives of visitors. Historic site managers may embrace some activities for their potential to generate revenue to sustain the site, such as event or wedding rentals. In other cases, sites may have the opportunity to provide events or activities that help to make the site come alive by allowing visitors to not only see and hear, but also to feel, smell, touch, and taste as they experience the site in a more intimate and memorable way.

Making smart and strategic choices about balancing the needs of the site with the interests of visitors is one of the most difficult yet important challenges facing today's historic site directors. The decision that is right for one historic site may be the wrong one for another, as every historic site faces different preservation, conservation, interpretive, and financial challenges. As more historic sites experiment with new ways to provide experiences to appeal to today's cultural heritage travelers, there are opportunities to learn from the experiences of your peers. All too often, the visitor experience at historic house museums remains static while the interests of cultural heritage travelers are constantly evolving. To remain relevant, the managers of historic house museums must build partnerships not just with their peers but with the tourism industry to develop new visitor experiences and marketing strategies that align with the current interests and habits of cultural heritage travelers.

Notes

1. Travel Industry Association of America, *Profile of Travelers Who Engage in Cultural & Historic Activities* (Washington, DC: Travel Industry Association, 1997).
2. Laura Mandala, *Cultural and Heritage Traveler Study* (Alexandria, VA: Mandala Research, 2013), 11.
3. Ibid., 16.

4. Ibid., 11.
5. Juliet Schor, *The Overworked American: The Unexpected Decline of American Leisure* (New York: Basic Books, 1991), 22
6. Ibid., 29.
7. "The State of the American Traveler: Destinations Edition," *Destination Analysts* 19, no. 3 (January 2016): 3.
8. National Trust for Historic Preservation, "Touro Synagogue," accessed April 15, 2018, https://saving places.org/places/touro-synagogue.
9. John A. Ververka, *Interpretive Master Planning* (Helena, MT: Falcon Press Publishing, 1994), 10.
10. Mandala, *Cultural and Heritage Traveler Study*, 12.
11. Ibid., 14–15.
12. "The State of the American Traveler," *Destination Analysts* 18, no. 4 (July 2015).

Recommended Resources

Mandala, Laura. *Cultural and Heritage Traveler Study*. Alexandria, VA: Mandala Research, 2013.
Hargrove, Cheryl M. *Cultural Heritage Tourism: Five Steps for Success and Sustainability*. Lanham, MD: Rowman & Littlefield, 2017.
Cultural Heritage Tourism (website). www.culturalheritagetourism.org.

Chapter 12

Finding Numen at Historic Sites

RON M. POTVIN

As early as the seventeenth century, Irish bishop Jeremy Taylor (1613-1667), the "Shakespeare of Divines," recognized the special power that places hold. "The Divine presence hath made all places holy," he wrote, "and every place hath a Numen in it."[1] Derived from Latin, numen originally meant divine will or power. In the twentieth century, religious scholars associated numen with the "magical" power of holy objects. Ethnologists identified it as a quality contained in some objects and places that facilitated connection with the "lives, feelings, and hardships" of people in the past.[2] Material culture historians defined numinous objects as those "endowed with special sociocultural magic," through association with a person, place, or event.[3] The idea of numen has crept into other forms of culture. In *Memory and Dream*, fantasy novelist Charles De Lint identifies numen as "a spiritual force, an influence one might feel around a certain thing or place."[4]

Numen provides meaning to objects and places that transcend common museological ideas like aesthetics, materials, and connoisseurship. The value of numen falls outside the work of most appraisers and is less tangible than money. It is emotional, spiritual, and individualized, drawing upon each person's own educational and cultural associations and belief systems. Numen facilitates mental "time travel," allowing people to feel a closer connection to the past. Numen is conveyed through an object's or place's unique story and is experienced most strongly through imagination and touch or the engagement of multiple senses. Within these "remembered" stories about a sacred past, there exist opportunities for museums to facilitate numinous experiences.[5]

Advocates of some of the first house museums recognized the powerful numen present in these special places, even if they lacked precise vocabulary to describe these feelings. Instead, they used the language of religion, commonly referring to historic sites as "shrines" and visitors as "pilgrims." In the rousing finish to his popular speech "The Character of Washington," orator Edward Everett predicted "the grateful children of America will make their pilgrimage" to Mount Vernon "as to a shrine."[6] Supporters of Monticello urged Americans to preserve Jefferson's home "as a patriotic shrine for the children of America."[7] The religious meanings of these words became intertwined with other emotion-laden cultural concepts like patriotism and with the jingoism that drove the rapid growth of house museums in the early twentieth century. This connection between spiritual and secular beliefs engaged supporters in campaigns to preserve historic homes and resonated with people who sought emotional engagement with the past.

The historic house museum movement in the United States was born during a cultural moment, a confluence of trends and beliefs that provided momentum to the creation of secular shrines. That moment has passed, and house museums have struggled to regain momentum. The ascendance of academic history within professionalized house museums, the commercialism of the post–World War II era, and postmodern suspicion of patriotism and religious faith gradually eroded the emotional and spiritual content and meaning of historic places. The vocabulary of the early historic house museum movement was effective because it spoke to the culture of that period. The efforts of modern house museums to build and engage audiences are hampered by their inability to tap into the numen that was exploited by the founders of early historic sites. History museums and historic sites often neglect the needs of people who seek emotive connections with the past. Powerfully numinous objects remain in storage, disparagingly referred to as memorabilia or curiosities, and many historic house museums erect literal barriers to keep visitors at a mandated safe distance from collections and interior finishes.

However, the "turn of mind or aspect of one's personality" that compels some people to visit historic sites in an effort to transcend time, feel empathy, and experience awe remains part of the human condition.[8] In 2003 and 2004, ethnographers Catherine M. Cameron and John B. Gatewood used surveys to study the reasons that people visited Gettysburg National Historic Park and steel industry heritage sites at Bethlehem, Pennsylvania. They wondered why Americans are "such avid consumers of the past, especially when it comes to trips to museums and heritage sites," even though their passion for history "does not parallel knowledge of it." Cameron and Gatewood wanted to know, "What is the draw of history?"[9] They concluded that, "Some people make a personal connection with a site that may be manifest as a deep engagement, empathy, or spiritual communion with the people or events of the past." Cameron and Gatewood called these people "numen-seekers."[10] In Bethlehem, 63 out of 313 survey responses, or about 20 percent, revealed numen-seeking qualities such as a desire to escape in time, experience authenticity, and identify personally with the past.[11] The results were similar at Gettysburg, where 19.5 percent of visitors cited "personal connection" as a reason for visiting the site.[12] Accepting a baseline of about 20 percent of visitors to historic sites as numen-seekers provides guidance to shape programming and interpretation for a sizable portion of the audience.

Cameron and Gatewood note that some sites, especially those that focus on human tragedy, might be more effective than others at eliciting a numinous response.[13] Battlefields, memorials, sites of tragedy, and other emotionally charged places are often powerfully numinous. Many visitors to the Vietnam Veteran's Memorial in Washington, DC, seek emotional and spiritual connection to that period and to comrades, friends, and family who served and died during the war. Many visitors leave "offerings at the wall," profound and ordinary objects associated with particular events and people that possess their own powerful numen.[14] The Oklahoma City National Memorial, which commemorates the site of the 1995 bombing of the Alfred P. Murrah Federal Building, and the 9/11 Memorial at Ground Zero in New York are also places of numen that attract memorial offerings.[15] An impromptu memorial appeared at the finish line of the Boston Marathon within a few hours after the bombing in 2013, attracting thousands of numinous objects including running shoes, race bibs, and photographs. This led to the creation of a digital repository of pictures, videos, stories, and social media that allow the public to explore how the event was experienced by Bostonians and by people who were "far away but deeply engaged in the unfolding events."[16]

Numen may also explain the contested nature of Civil War monuments in the aftermath of the violent 2017 white supremacist rally in Virginia. Public sculptures commemorating the Confederacy provoke intense emotional responses and hold opposing meanings depending on the belief systems of people engaged in the debate. The importance of these monuments lies beyond historical facts. For some people the existence of Civil War memorials is a painful reminder of oppression, while for others their removal symbolizes the passing of the dominant culture with which they identify. There seems little chance of reconciliation between these divergent points of view, and several cities have removed, destroyed, and covered Civil War monuments.[17]

The numen of historic sites is also connected with public memory, a collective, sometimes mythologized, understanding of the past. Numen-seekers at the Betsy Ross House, for instance, may be attracted to the site by the apocryphal story of the creation of the original American flag. The desire to promote historic sites through association with the first U.S. president led to countless claims of "Washington slept here," many, if not most of them, unsupported by anything but tradition.[18] Henry James wrote of the "Gluttony of the public for false facts" at historic house museums in his story, "The Birthplace."[19] Efforts by professional staff to "demythologize" the past and to provide "factual" history risks casting aside the emotional and spiritual impact—the numen—of historic sites. As Patricia West points out, "The tension between popular myth and 'objective' research in house museums" is almost as old as the historic house museum genre. In the early twentieth century, West writes that "a dynamic conflict between scientized professionalism and voluntarist romance became a hallmark of the American historic house museum."[20]

Although "professionalism" won the battle, there remains a demand for a mythologized and sacred past, perhaps more so among visitors to historic sites. There are myriad reasons for this including the continued desire to find comfort within a "simpler" past that contains pleasant associations of heroic figures and clearly defined principles and motivations. In fact, it seems the more that our historic sites dispute the existence of an idealized past, the more urgent the demand for the older "traditional" stories becomes for some visitors.[21] Historical myths motivate some people to seek their confirmation at house museums. Outright rejection of a sacred and mythologized past by historic house museums might create a "backfire effect" among visitors and harden their preexisting biases, particularly when facts challenge their worldviews and sense of cultural identity. This phenomenon is of special interest to science communicators who have developed techniques to debunk myths about climate change and vaccines, for instance.[22]

Numen-seekers desire stories that appeal to their emotions and to their urge to connect spiritually with places and objects that inspire awe and reverence. They seek this at historic sites because they are tangible links to the past, where visitors can stand within the same places "of warmth where real people lived and breathed."[23] Authenticity is important, but people gauge what is "real" in different ways—intellectually, tactilely, and emotionally—and historic sites should avoid approaches that disregard the importance of a sacred past. Museums might acknowledge benign mythology and utilize it as a point of access to good history. If mythology must be entirely discarded—as is the case with stories that marginalize enslaved people, American Indians, and women—historic sites should replace these narratives with stories that are dramatic, stirring, and true, rather than delivering authoritative history to audiences that are culturally suspicious of authority and intellectually resistant to opposing facts. As Patricia West notes, "This approach rejects a dry search for debunking facts in favor of an explicit search for meaning," allowing sites to "align with our audiences in a shared journey toward connection with the past through physical experience of its material remains, a task less scientific than spiritual."[24] Within true stories about a sacred past, historic sites can provide authenticity and facilitate numinous experiences.

The desire of some people to find numen in places and objects may be less an idiosyncrasy than an elemental part of human nature. In his self-described "Elvis book," *From the Holy Land to*

Graceland: Sacred People, Places and Things in Our Lives, Gary Vikan identifies the key elements of sacredness at historic house museums. Vikan demonstrates that Graceland is "much more than a popular tourist destination," and Presley "much more than the King of Rock 'n' Roll." He argues that Graceland is a *Locus Sanctus* ("holy place"), Elvis its resident saint, and "the hordes of fans standing in the heat on Elvis Presley Boulevard" its "pilgrims."[25] Vikan identifies seven characteristics sought by visitors to historic sites like Graceland and by fifth-century pilgrims travelling to the *Loca Sancta* of early Christian mystics and saints: sacred time, sacred itinerary, communitas, mimesis, rituals, sacred souvenirs, and votives. These qualities repeat and build one upon the other with "elegant simplicity" no matter the period, and the behaviors of visitors seeking these qualities vary based only upon the nature of the shrine. These characteristics are sometimes evident at historic sites, but rarely simultaneously and seldom with planning or even awareness on the part of the museum that something meaningful is occurring. It is possible to facilitate interactions between visitors and historic sites as a way to fulfill the desires of numen-seekers.

First, *sacred time* is the notion that orienting visitation to sites based upon specific dates on the calendar will "compound the intensity of the spiritual encounter."[26] These special dates include biblical holy days, birth and death anniversaries, or the commemoration of notable achievements. For instance, Christian pilgrims flock to Bethlehem on December 25, mourners visit Ground Zero on September 11, and tourists observe "Washington's birthday weekend" at Mount Vernon every February.[27] Second, pilgrims follow a *sacred itinerary*, a particular route of travel that includes other "secondary but complementary" sites related to the primary *Locus Sanctus*. Elvis fans visit his birthplace in Tupelo, Mississippi, and travel to the recording studio where his career began in Memphis, Tennessee. The effectiveness of a sacred itinerary as an "organizing criterion" for pilgrims, especially in its ability to broaden the economic impact of tourism, is evident in the popularity of heritage travel.[28] For instance, one for-profit company offers itineraries for customers to "capture the deep, rich, Christian heritage of our country and the people who founded it."[29] For numen-seekers, visiting secondary sites increases the strength of feeling about the primary *Locus Sanctus*. Many historic sites offer their own versions of sacred itineraries with walking tours, combination and package ticketing, and even mobile applications that permit numen-seekers to "curate" their own self-guided heritage tour.

The third quality is *communitas*, a "commonness of feeling" among pilgrims expressed through the sharing of experiences and the retelling of stories about the subject of their interest or adulation. Communitas may occur spontaneously during a gathering of people at a historic site, and perhaps more powerfully at sites that serve as focal points of local communities. In their article "A Golden Age for Historic Properties," John Durel and Anita Nowery Durel recognize the importance of "affinity groups" as a means to participate in the activities of historic house museums and to "appreciate the meaning and spirit of the place." According to the authors, this quality sets historic sites apart and attracts "people who value beauty, nature, heritage, a connection to place, and a deeper meaning in life."[30]

The fourth quality sought by pilgrims to historic sites is *mimesis*, or imitation. Mimesis may include obvious mimicry of actions or appearance of people from a particular period, or "a more subtle, ongoing identification with a particularly appropriate sacred figure whose story was believed to provide a model outcome from which the pilgrim might benefit."[31] Mimesis is an especially rich area for historic sites, and it occurs in several ways. For instance, some historic sites provide interpretation through role-playing. The "Follow the North Star" program at Conner Prairie in Indiana is a participatory experience that encourages visitors to assume the roles of fugitive slaves. This immersive program encourages empathy with the plight of people seeking freedom under extreme

Figure 12.1 A sixth grader practices mimesis as part of an innovative participatory history project at a middle school in Rhode Island. Photo by Ron M. Potvin.

duress.[32] On a larger scale, hundreds of people might experience mimesis simultaneously through military reenactment. As Tony Horwitz has observed in *Confederates in the Attic*, mimesis among Civil War reenactors ranges from casual participation to "hardcore" reenactors who meticulously research and reproduce minute elements of the experience.[33] Less extreme imitative gestures include preparing food by using period recipes, often from cookbooks sold at historic sites. Interpreters sometimes practice mimesis, most commonly by wearing period clothing.

Rituals, the fifth characteristic, are actions intended to evoke or reinforce the memory of a historical person or event. Rituals may be simple in nature, such as placing flowers on the grave of a deceased "saint" or signing a guest book. Other rituals are complex and require devotion on the part of the person performing the action. During Elvis Week, Graceland pilgrims participate in a variety of rituals including gravesite vigils, decorating contests, and Elvis impersonations. As with the latter example, some rituals facilitate mimesis, such as dressing in meticulously researched period costume or participating in historically appropriate military drills. Similar to religious observances, rituals are public acts of devotion that demonstrate common fealty and connect the performer emotionally and spiritually with a person or event from the past.[34]

Finally, *sacred souvenirs* are objects that are removed by visitors from a special site, and *votives* are things that are left behind, like the "offerings" at the Vietnam memorial. Sacred souvenirs are unlike items typically sold in gift stores, and are closer in nature to holy relics collected by early Christians who believed the bones of saints and bits of material touched by Christ carried powers of healing and protection that passed from object to object and from object to person through contact. Holy relics are "part of a chain of objectified charisma, whose links are held together by contagion, seemingly without limit."[35] Since the average pilgrim did not have access to true relics, a "contact relic," or sacred souvenir, sufficed.[36] In the early years of the American republic, locks of hair from the founders were highly treasured, and some of them are now in the collections of museums. The State Museum of Pennsylvania, for instance, has a lock of Washington's hair collected in 1797 by a barber who preserved it as "a precious relic."[37]

Possessing such an object provides physical form to veneration and a tactile connection to a distant shrine. Vikan describes "the almost overpowering desire to touch among Elvis pilgrims," which is "evident in the frequency with which those at graveside lean forward to touch the brass marker" and by sheets of protective plastic throughout Graceland.[38] The desire for relics and sacred souvenirs has sometimes led people to apply numen to ordinary objects, either intentionally or through fanciful attribution.[39] This urge is also evident in the proliferation of "treasure hunters" with metal detectors, antiques "pickers," and in the theft or damage of collections at historic sites. Pecuniary motivations are often secondary to the opportunity to touch or possess sacred objects.

Museums typically use restrictive methods to separate visitors from the objects of their desires. However, historic sites would better serve audiences by offering controlled opportunities for numen-seekers to interact with numinous objects, rather than simply "roping off" collections from the public. Touching, smelling, manipulating, and other tactile experiences that violate the so-called Rembrandt rule can evoke powerful memories, open new worlds for sight-impaired people, and permit visitors to form their own meanings and connections to an object.[40] Historic sites should also ease restrictions on other types of interactions such as the taking of photographs and "selfies." As Nina Simon points out, these are primarily social activities, undertaken to share personally meaningful places and objects with friends and family using social media, a form of communitas.[41] As these images become "viral," their meaning changes relative to the viewer, representing a modern form of the "contagion" spread by sacred relics. At Graceland, Vikan observed that for most tourists "the most valued souvenirs of their visit have always been their own photographs."[42] Historic sites might also discover a surprisingly brisk market for ordinary things that find their way by the dozens or hundreds into museum basements and informal storage spaces. A renovation or restoration might produce countless hand-forged nails, bits of early clapboard, and intact chimney bricks. Appropriately framed, mounted, and packaged, this useless detritus may find new life by providing a legitimate means for numen-seekers to acquire sacred souvenirs.

Votives also serve several purposes, according to Vikan, "as a record of the pilgrim's visit, as a "perpetuation of his devotional contact," and as "a thank-you for a blessing received or anticipated."[43] At religious sites, these offerings often include the crutches of people healed by their contact with the shrine. Sacred souvenirs and votives both allow for contact with a shrine in absentia, using objects as a medium. Votives are most impactful if encountered by others who act as witnesses to the devotion of the person who left it behind, and people often choose to leave votives in highly visible locations and at meaningful places. At the No Name Pub in the Florida Keys and at other bars and restaurants, patrons staple to the walls dollar bills with decorations or messages for others to read. Graceland permits "magic marker votives," hand-scrawled messages written by fans, but only on the side of a long fieldstone wall facing the street.[44] Historic house museum director and "anarchist" Frank Vagnone calls the practice of leaving votives "fingerprinting," the idea that "we want to leave a bit of ourselves behind (when we visit) an historic site." Although sites seldom allow it, Vagnone believes that fingerprinting is vital to historic house museums.[45] Fingerprinting may also include spiritual offerings facilitated by museums through opportunities and places for quiet contemplation and reflection. In addition, the opportunity to leave their labor behind as an offering to a house museum might motivate some volunteers.

Ron M. Potvin

Figure 12.2 Patrons staple dollar bills with decorations or messages to the walls at the No Name Pub in the Florida Keys. Photo by Ron M. Potvin.

Whether we call them pilgrims or numen-seekers, a significant portion of visitors are looking for experiences that historic sites do not typically provide. They are seeking liminality—the ability to stand at the threshold between the present and the past and gaze in both directions. We might also call this quality "deep relevance," the linking of events in the past with opportunities for visitors to create their own meaningful numinous experiences. This process is more than intellectual. It requires spiritual, emotional, and tactile connections with a historic site. During the anniversary of Washington's birthday at Mount Vernon, the site encourages visitors to imitate Washington through "Pose with the President" selfies, take part in a wreath-laying ritual, and leave a birthday card for Washington, among other numen-affirming activities. When sites do not provide opportunities like these, numen-seekers may create them for themselves, in ways that fall outside the boundaries of museum etiquette. Or, they might leave frustrated and unsatisfied, and the numen of your historic house museum, for these visitors, will be forever negative.

Notes

1. Reginald Heber, ed., *The Whole Works of the Right Reverend Jeremy Taylor* (London: Longman, Brown, Green and Longmans, 1850), 224.
2. John B. Gatewood and Catherine M. Cameron, "Battlefield Pilgrims at Gettysburg National Military Park, *Ethnology* 43, no. 3 (Summer 2004): 208.
3. Rachel P. Maines and James T. Glynn, "Numinous Objects," *The Public Historian* 15, no. 1 (Winter 1993): 10.
4. Charles De Lint, *Memory and Dream* (New York: Tom Doherty Associates, 1994), 231.

5. Research by neuroscientists at MIT suggests a closer connection between areas of the brain that are involved with memory recall and emotion than previously understood. The authors of the study did not specifically suggest this, but their findings suggest that the ways in which the past is remembered is connected to a person's emotional response at the time the memory was created. For instance, a person's emotions upon learning of the Kennedy assassination are an important component of future experiences with objects and places associated with the assassination. The ways in which people remember the more distant past may be related to their emotional response or the emotional setting when they learned about an event. See Anne Trafton, "Neuroscientists Reverse Memories' Emotional Associations," *MIT News*, August 27, 2014, http://news.mit.edu/2014/brain-circuit-links-emotion-memory-0827.
6. Edward Everett, "Character of Washington," in Robert Irving Fulton and Thomas Clarkson Trueblood, *British and American Eloquence* (New York: Ginn and Company, 1912), 281.
7. As quoted in Patricia West, *Domesticating History: The Political Origins of America's House Museums* (Washington, DC: Smithsonian Institution Press, 1999), 115.
8. Catherine M. Cameron and John B. Gatewood, "Seeking Numinous Experiences in the Unremembered Past," *Ethnology* 42, no. 1 (Winter 2003): 65.
9. Ibid., 55.
10. Ibid., 57.
11. Cameron and Gatewood used a slightly different method of calculating this percentage. They grouped the sixty-three responses identified as evidence of numen-seeking with seven responses identified as evidence of visitors seeking to create memories under a single heading they termed "personal experience" to produce a total of seventy-four responses in this category. Using the number of respondents (64) who produced responses in this category and the total number of respondents (185), they concluded that 27 percent of respondents were seeking personal experiences. See Cameron and Gatewood, "Seeking Numinous Experiences," 60–62.
12. Gatewood and Cameron, "Battlefield Pilgrims," 204.
13. Cameron and Gatewood, "Seeking Numinous Experiences," 67.
14. Thomas B. Allen, *Offerings at the Wall: Artifacts from the Vietnam Veterans Memorial Collection* (Nashville: Turner Publishing, 1995).
15. See, for example, Edward T. Linenthal, *The Unfinished Bombing: Oklahoma City in American Memory* (Oxford, UK: Oxford University Press, 2001).
16. *Our Marathon: The Boston Bombing Digital Archive*, http://www.northeastern.edu/nulab/our-marathon-the-boston-bombing-digital-archive-2/.
17. See, for example, David A. Graham, "Local Officials Want to Remove Confederate Monuments—but States Won't Let Them," *The Atlantic* (website), August 25, 2017, https://www.theatlantic.com/politics/archive/2017/08/when-local-officials-want-to-tear-down-confederate-monuments-but-cant/537351/.
18. See, for example, Ron M. Potvin, "Washington Slept Here? Reinterpreting the Stephen Hopkins House," *History News* 66, no. 2 (Spring 2011): 2, 17–20, and "George Washington Slept Here," Smithsonian.com, December 1999, http://www.smithsonianmag.com/history/george-washington-slept-here-128209448/.
19. Henry James, "The Birthplace," in *The Short Stories of Henry James* (New York: Modern Library, 1948), 486–547.
20. Patricia West, "Of Babies and Bathwater—Birthplace 'Shrines' and the Future of the Historic House Museum," in Seth C. Bruggeman, ed., *Born in the U.S.A.: Birth, Commemoration, and American Public Memory* (Amherst: University of Massachusetts Press, 2012), 261–62.
21. See, for example, Suzanne Sherman, "Will History Only Remember the Founders as Slaveowners?" *The American Conservative*, April 18, 2016, http://www.theamericanconservative.com/articles/will-history-only-remember-the-founders-as-slaveowners/.
22. John Cook and Stephan Lewandowsky, *The Debunking Handbook* (Australia: University of Queensland, 2011), https://www.skepticalscience.com/docs/Debunking_Handbook.pdf.
23. Ron M. Potvin, "House or Home? Rethinking the House Museum Paradigm," *History News* 65, no. 2 (Spring 2010): 9-10.
24. West, "Of Babies and Bathwater," 263–64.

25. Gary Vikan, *From the Holy Land to Graceland: Sacred People, Places, and Things in Our Lives* (Washington, DC: AAM Press, 2012), 2.
26. Ibid., 114.
27. See Seth C. Bruggeman, ed., *Born in the USA: Birth, Commemoration, and American Public Memory* (Amherst: University of Massachusetts Press, 2012).
28. Vikan, *From the Holy Land*, 116–17.
29. See the website of Spiritual Heritage Tours, http://spiritualheritagetours.com/.
30. John Durel and Anita Nowery Durel, "A Golden Age for Historic Properties," *History News* 52, no. 3 (Summer 2007): 7–16.
31. Vikan, *From the Holy Land*, 139.
32. "Follow the North Star," Connor Prairie website, http://www.connerprairie.org/things-to-do/events/follow-the-north-star.
33. Tony Horwitz, *Confederates in the Attic: Dispatched from the Unfinished Civil War* (New York: Vintage Books, 1999).
34. Vikan, *From the Holy Land*, 147–58.
35. Ibid., 29.
36. Ibid., 74.
37. "Locks of George Washington's Hair," State Museum of Pennsylvania website, http://statemuseumpa.org/locks-george-washington-hair/.
38. Vikan, *From the Holy Land*, 151.
39. See, for instance, Laurel Thatcher Ulrich, "An Indian Basket," in *The Age of Homespun* (New York: Alfred A. Knopf, 2001), 42–74.
40. Ron M. Potvin, "Chasing the White Whale? Flexible Use of Museum Collections," *History News* 69, no. 4 (Autumn 2014): 15.
41. Nina Simon, *The Participatory Museum* (Santa Clara, CA: Museum 2.0, 2000).
42. Vikan, *From the Holy Land*, 163.
43. Ibid., 167.
44. Ibid., 169.
45. Frank Vagnone, "Fingerprinting: A Defense of Leaving Your Mark," on the blog *Twisted Preservation*, https://twistedpreservation.com/2014/09/21/fingerprinting-a-defense-of-leaving-your-mark/.

Chapter 13

Community Engagement

Radical Renewal for Historic House Museums

DAWN DIPRINCE

"I never knew museums could be for me," explains a Latina elected official. In two busy years, at El Pueblo History Museum in Pueblo, Colorado, we doubled our visitation and nearly doubled our revenue because we convinced more people that, indeed, our museum was *for* them and *about* them. We did this work through community engagement—not bigger budgets or more staff. We leapfrogged over meager budgets and no marketing funds by building relationships with the people in our community.

As a director of history museums, I am always intrigued by solutions that are based on historic practices. Community engagement seems like a fancy new term in museum work, but it really is based on the practices that your grandmother would have used to organize around an issue, an event, or a need in the community. Community engagement is human-to-human network building. It flourishes on face-to-face meetings, lots of hot coffee, and telephone calls. It is perfect for smaller museums because it does not require cutting-edge technology. Instead, it thrives on time, patience, and good listening.

When we set about to grow our museum, we pledged to open our arms wider than before and not just include but invite more people in. In *The Participatory Museum*, Nina Simon outlines five reasons that people don't visit museums and we focused our work on two of these challenges: museums are not relevant to my life and museums don't include my story or my voice.[1] Many museum professionals express frustration that more people don't visit exhibitions or attend programs. They insist that the public just doesn't get it or that they don't have the right priorities. I would argue that the opposite is true. When museums have low visitation, it is generally that the museum doesn't get it and/or doesn't have the right priorities. No business—cultural or otherwise—can succeed if they blame or critique the public for not visiting. The museum is not the point of our existence. It is the interaction between audience, public, and museum that is the point.

Thus, community engagement succeeds when we learn to build relationships with people who do not visit museums. For a lot of demographic and economic reasons, traditional history museum audiences are shrinking. According to the American Academy of the Arts, visitation among adults had declined 13 percent over a thirty-year period. In addition, each new generation is less likely to be interested in visiting historic sites, but as people aged, they were also less likely to visit a historic site.[2] If you wish to grow visitation, revenue, and community engagement, your museum must open its arms wider and encompass the very people who do not visit your museum. Part of this process can be painful because as history museums we must come to terms with the ways in which we have collectively as an industry and individually as museums excluded voices and stories from the broader historical narrative. House museums tend to preserve the beautiful spaces of wealthy and/or powerful individuals and, as a result, often perpetuate a historic narrative of power and wealth, which generally overemphasizes hegemonic voices of white men. Community engagement and building relationships with new audiences often also means that we have to revise our museums and the content we exhibit. Working with these new and hopeful audiences to revise your museum's narrative is the perfect way to build a relationship with them.

Rethink Audience

Community First

History and house museums often consider tourists to be their primary audience. We imagine that our museums help outsiders understand more about our town or city. We argue that we are good for our communities because we fuel our local tourist economy. While these things are true, they are not generally enough to sustain a museum. At the 2007 Kykuit summit on the sustainability of historic sites, museum industry leaders determined that "the long-accepted tourism business model is not a sustainable business model for most historic sites; and serving the needs of the local community (not the tourist audience) is the most valuable and most sustainable goal for most historic sites."[3] When tourists are our primary audience, this usually also means they are our sole revenue source. A museum business plan that focuses on tourism includes a never-changing museum experience and hefty marketing costs to adequately connect with traveling audiences. This model rarely attracts local visitors unless they are bringing someone who is visiting from out of town.

But, let's imagine a museum whose primary audience is the community. A museum business plan that focuses on engaging the community creates dynamic museum experiences, enjoys a diversified revenue stream, and can do more with fewer marketing dollars. Our experience has shown us that a dynamic museum that serves its community also attracts tourists, but the inverse isn't true. In my role with History Colorado, I oversee seven history and house museums around the state. We originally had a passive business approach geared toward tourists. We witnessed immediate positive change any time we actively engaged and served the local community. Moreover, many of our sites transformed from seasonal operations to year-round, and our tourist-based traffic has remained steady.

Form Audiences—Don't Wait for Them

Museums often fail when they try to replicate or preserve the same experience to reach the same seemingly loyal audience. This is why: our audiences don't stay the same. Their interests don't stay the same, they may move, their life might get more complicated, and the world is ever changing. It is tempting to try to devote all experiences and programs to your core group of devoted museum goers. Yet, audiences are dynamic organisms and museums should match that dynamism to continue to attract audiences. We often think about audience in the wrong way. When we speak of audience, we visualize a group of people who preexist and our goal is to find the key to connect with this group. Audiences do not preexist. Rather, as Michael Warner writes in his "Publics and Counterpublics," a public (in our case, a museum audience) is formed around the text (in our case, a museum experience).[4] Imagine the Sunday afternoon when Beyoncé released her blockbuster album *Lemonade*. A variety of people across the country—perhaps even the world—downloaded all the necessary apps and collectively listened to it and in that moment they (mostly complete strangers) formed an audience. When that hour of listening ended, the same audience dispersed and collected into other audiences. It is helpful to remember that our audiences are dynamic, self-organizing, and ever changing.

Understanding how audiences form means that we can actively build them. Audience development is not a passive guessing game. Community-engagement practices empower museums to proactively gather audiences in the development and implementation of your programs and experiences. If you wish to target a new demographic, meet with representatives from that group and build appealing experiences together. The audience will form itself along the way.

Rethink Purpose

Community engagement at museums is successful when it serves as a philosophy and not just a practice. I often witness museums that dabble in community engagement for small, specific projects (usually when working on token projects with underrepresented audiences). To be successful and authentic, community engagement must infiltrate the museum mission. It is about creating a human-centered museum instead of an object-centered museum. Objects and artifacts at museums are always important but they should be framed within human stories and with a human audience in mind.

The shortcut for building a community-engaged museum is to focus on museums as educational institutions—a nod to the ideal that we must perpetuate history as a product *and* a process. When you refocus a history museum or house museum into an institution whose primary purpose is to educate its local community, you will discover more opportunities to engage with audiences, grow revenue, and to fund-raise. For example, within the community museum network of History Colorado, education has enabled us to grow our audience and our revenue with programs like summer camps, History Take Out programs, oral history training, memory-writing workshops, modern homesteading workshops, preservation education programs, and after-school programs.[5] At El Pueblo History Museum, our educational revenue grew by ten times in two years because we refocused our energy on engaging local kids and adults with programs that resonated with our mission and our story.

Philosophy Matters

Community engagement can feel untethered and unproductive without a strong philosophical foundation. Our community-engagement work is grounded in a deliberate pedagogical approach based heavily on the work of Paolo Freire, a Brazilian educator who has written extensively about his theories of popular education. He describes traditional education processes as the banking method of education, where "knowledge is a gift bestowed by those who consider themselves knowledgeable upon those whom they consider to know nothing."[6] This statement, which is relevant to many classrooms, also resonates in many museum practices. We often operate from the belief that we as institutions possess the knowledge and our guests are empty vessels where we deposit information. Freire describes that "education thus becomes an act of depositing, in which the students are the depositories and the teacher is the depositor."[7] This likely looks familiar to us. It is a guided house tour, where the guide might answer a few questions but mostly dominates the discussion. It is a school tour where kids are sitting with their legs crossed while an expert volunteer lectures and the kids are shushed and reminded to be quiet. It is also a museum experience where guests quietly glide from text panel to text panel, or object to object, passively reading about history.

A humanizing educational model, which is the root of community engagement, recognizes that we all have something to teach and all have something to learn. For museums, it reminds us that our institutional knowledge is not more important than the personal knowledge and history of our visitors and our community. At El Pueblo History Museum, we recognize that the people who enter our doors are bearers of history and culture, and we look for ways to learn and share their histories. We acknowledge that we co-create and co-author our history. Moreover, as a museum of our state historical society, we also acknowledge that the objects on display are co-owned by our Colorado guests. Humanizing museum pedagogy, for example, is a school tour where kids are engaged in a hands-on activity—tortilla making, weaving, costumed reenacting—that enables them to build their own knowledge and fuel their own creativity. This pedagogy is reflected in an oral history program where community members are given the tools to capture and collect the histories of their fellow community members. Museums practice this pedagogy when they invite community members to advise on exhibition development or offer museum experiences for guests to share their own stories. Here are several examples:

- Hands-On History at Trinidad History Museum. Trinidad History Museum is a campus that includes three house museums. They have implemented a hands-on Friday education program for local elementary students who do not have school on Fridays. Students can bake bread in the outdoor adobe oven. They get to make adobe to learn about the construction behind the two-story Baca House. They plant and harvest vegetables in the site's heritage gardens, just to name a few examples.
- At El Pueblo History Museum we have created neighborhood memory-writing projects where we guide residents in writing, recording, and sharing their collective personal histories of where they live. For example, the Salt Creek Memory Project was a collaboration between the museum and the past and present residents of Salt Creek to co-author the rich history of their community. The project included several layers of collection, preservation, and interpretation. The museum worked with both professional and community historians to collect more than thirty oral histories, training community members to collect oral histories and to use its audio equipment. These newly trained community historians had a big impact on the project, enabling the museum to more than double the oral histories collected and to collect Spanish-speaking oral histories. The community stories became the basis for an arts-based interpretation of Salt Creek's history, including a mural painted on portable sheets of metal that will eventually be placed in the neighborhood and fine arts photography documenting the resident storytellers in specific corners of Salt Creek that were most meaningful to them. We hosted an exhibition of the program, and the oral histories were immediately available to the public on SoundCloud.
- At Byers-Evans House Museum, we recently transformed the house museum into the Center for Colorado Women's History. This expanded mission of the museum still honors the historic inhabitants and belongings within the house, while it also broadens ways for the community to connect to the museum. In addition to the traditional house museum tours,

the Center for Colorado Women's History also has an active community/scholar advisory committee, a new changing gallery in the museum's carriage house that is focused on Colorado women's history, plus an annual fellowship that works with three scholars, artists, or activists in building new knowledge and understanding around women's history and Colorado. The Center for Colorado Women's History has generated significant new interest and energy in the museum, which has led to new partnerships and opportunities including leading the statewide effort around the 2020 Women's Suffrage Centennial.

What Does Community Engagement Look Like?

Free Tickets

There is a lot of museum industry debate about the role of free tickets and community engagement. Free admission can be a powerful tool for community engagement. However, it fails when it is the only strategy used to engage new audiences. Moreover, it never works if museums simply assume that cost is the sole barrier to coming to a museum. Families with limited resources scrimp and save to attend amusement parks or other places they think are worth the time and money. Non-museum goers do not visit museums because they think they are not worth their time and money—regardless of their income levels. Free admission is a great strategy if it also accompanies museum narratives, programs, and practices that are more inclusive and relevant to people's lives.

For example, at El Pueblo History Museum, we worked with a committee of forty local people to develop an exhibition, *El Movimiento*, about the Colorado Chicano movement, a civil rights movement in the 1960s and 1970s focused on Mexican American rights. We worked weekly for six months with the local committee to add local Chicano movement stories to the exhibition.

Figure 13.1 The community chair of *El Movimiento* committee speaking at the exhibition opening. Photo courtesy of El Pueblo History Museum.

When we opened the exhibition, we had more than one thousand people in attendance—the most people ever for a History Colorado exhibition opening at any property. In gratitude, we gave committee members a year's worth of free membership so that they could easily bring others to visit the exhibition that they helped to create. One committee member brought a group of teenage boys who were at-risk for gang recruitment. He thought the exhibition would help them by understanding their legacy. We happily gave them all free admission to the museum. This is how free admission can work as part of a larger community-engagement strategy—not in place of it.

Phone Calls

Like many history museums and house museums, our community museums have little to no marketing funds. We have found that our best marketing tool is the telephone. When we work with the community, we collect contact information every chance we get. Personal phone calls to recruit people for programs or share information about an event or program are more effective than social media, newspaper ads, email newsletters, postcards, etc. Phone calls cost nothing but a bit of time. A human voice is a powerful tool—even if we must leave a message on voicemail. We find that this is a great job for volunteers, as many of our older volunteers live alone and are eager for opportunities to chat with other people. We give them an easy script and a phone list, and we are rewarded with a marked difference in attendance.

Human Meetings

Community engagement works best when you can host meetings with hot coffee and real people. Collaborating online is a possible tool for those who have geographic limitations, but grassroots organizing generally needs to happen in person—especially if you are targeting any audience where technology may be a burden. Human meetings are the most successful when they are well organized, so people feel like they are not wasting their time, but that they are also flexible to the needs of your community members. For example, when El Pueblo History Museum worked with a community advisory committee for our exhibition *El Movimiento*, our very first meeting took more than three hours and only included introductions. Each committee member, nearly forty in all, introduced themselves by answering the question: Where were you in 1974? While this took much longer than anticipated, we learned so much history, we learned about the diversity of experiences on the committee, and we honored people's lives and contributions.

Community engagement requires the ability to accommodate your community's style, time frame, and culture. Human meetings, when done in the right spirit, allow you to build trust with your community group. It is important to remember that community engagement is a gift that your community gives to you—not the other way around. Patient and attentive body language (including no use of your cell phone during the meeting), good listening, and willingness to meet when your community can—sometimes outside of normal working hours—are key ingredients to create trust and authentic community partnerships. For example, at El Pueblo History Museum, we developed memory trunks designed to be used by people who have loved ones with memory loss. The trunks provide artifacts and music from decades past that can jumpstart meaningful conversation based on longer-lasting long-term memory. In an effort to better understand this audience, we collaborated with the Alzheimer's Association to engage a group of people diagnosed with Alzheimer's. The association gave us training before our first collaboration meeting. We scheduled the meetings early in the day, for limited amounts of time, and we offered space for the spouses to meet while we were collaborating with our team. We also had to moderate our meeting style and expectations. The human insight from this advisory group was much more helpful than any other research that we used for the project. (As a bonus, we were told by the association and the spouses that the meaningful work was beneficial to our advisors too.)

IRL Social Networks

We often think of social networks as something Mark Zuckerberg invented, but social networks have existed long before computers. These are what I jokingly call IRL (text speak for In Real Life) social networks. These are the social networks that can be organized (remember phone trees?) or informal (like all the parents you know from your kid's soccer team, your neighbors, or the people you see at Mass every Sunday). When you successfully engage community members, you also receive the gift of their social networks. These IRL social networks bring you the kind of communication, marketing, and promotion that money cannot buy. When we opened an exhibition on the Salt Creek Memory Project, we printed five hundred postcards for people to hand out. Within two hours, our community group walked door to door in their neighborhood and handed out the postcards in person. We had to create special flyers on the spot so that they could keep sharing the exhibition information. We have one incredible community volunteer, Rita, who has an amazing text-messaging network. When she is on board with a project, she sends out text messages to this large group of people who know her personally. She can sometimes quadruple the turnout for an event with the use of this text message network.

Grassroots versus Grasstops

I have a good friend who is a community organizer. She differentiates between grassroots and grasstops community engagement. Grasstops organizing is when you connect with local elected officials and others in official leadership roles. Grassroots organizing is when you connect with the everyday people of your community. Most organizations and cultural institutions think that they are engaging the community when they connect with grasstops. However, the most authentic and successful community engagement comes from grassroots organizing, which is certainly trickier to accomplish because it often involves going to different spaces than you might be accustomed.

For example, we had an exhibition called *Children of Ludlow* that focused on the tragic labor battle in southern Colorado that ended in the deaths of twelve children. For grasstops organizing, I would have presented a PowerPoint to Rotary, Lions, and Kiwanis Clubs, which I did. However, our most successful engagement came from presenting to local labor unions. Presenting to local labor unions was much more complicated because their meetings are private. You have to build trust to earn a spot on their meeting agenda; you only get a few minutes, and you are often speaking to working men and women who just finished a long work shift and aren't immediately interested in hearing about a local museum when they really just want to go home. We took all of these extra steps to connect with this community, and we discovered a treasure of people who had never been to our museum (or any museum) but were very interested in learning more about the Ludlow Massacre. Many of these visitors brought their children and grandchildren to the exhibition so they could pass on this relevant history to their descendants. The added bonus: the museum is still invited to speak at labor events—four years after the exhibition first opened.

How Can We Engage Our Community?

Human-Centered Design

Human-centered design uses empathy and creativity to solve problems. The process starts by understanding the needs of people and community then developing innovative solutions to address those needs. In a *Harvard Business Review* article, authors Robert I. Sutton and David Hoyt define human-centered design as "a hands-on approach that focuses on developing empathy for others, generating ideas quickly, testing rough 'prototypes' that, although incomplete or impractical, fuel rapid learning for teams and organizations."[8] Designing programs and solutions from the community's perspective is a double win, as it leads to unexpected ideas that also have lots of community support. In practical terms, this is the difference in a museum exhibition that takes years to develop and thousands of dollars versus a quickly changing museum exhibition that costs very little and adapts to audience feedback.

Like many museums, History Colorado's community museums have small budgets. The human-centered design has enabled us to do more, change quickly, and keep fresh with few resources. Designing with our community in mind and/or at the table empowers us to take more risks, share the labor, and expands what seems possible. For example, when a small child pulled the fire alarm during an evening lecture, we started to offer donation-based childcare during lectures instead of discouraging people from bringing children.

Rhetorical Triangle

We often focus on what we want guests to gain or learn from our museums. While this might be an acceptable place to start, it ignores what the guests might want to gain or learn from their visit to our museums. As passionate experts, we can become obsessed with sharing our specific knowledge to our audiences. We think that if we preach at length about our expertise that people will get it, but we forget to ask ourselves if they even want to get it.

Aristotle, if still alive today, would remind us of the rhetorical triangle. The word "rhetoric" certainly has a bad reputation in modern times, but for Aristotle it was about persuasion. If we really are museum experts who are passionate about sharing our love and knowledge, we need to find ways that persuade our guests to care about what we have to share. The rhetorical triangle is a simple concept that connects us (the speaker/writer/museum) with our audience and the topic or the message. We are successful when we keep these three things in balance: what we really want visitors to learn; what audiences want to experience; and the message, information, experience that bridges the museum with audience. For example, school kids come to our museums hoping to have a fun day outside of the classroom and we hope they learn some history. So, instead of forcing them to sit on the floor with their legs crossed while we lecture them about history, we help them build their own knowledge of history by making tortillas over an open flame, forming adobe bricks, dying wool with natural plants, making their own protest posters, wearing costumes and reenacting historic figures. The message succeeds and the museum and the kids both achieve our goals.

The Medium is the Message

Marshall McLuhan is the theorist behind this well-known phrase: "the medium is the message." He theorized that the medium used to convey a message is more important than the content of the message. For example, consider a president who uses Twitter to communicate with the public; the use of Twitter is part of the message—it's a short, quick, direct media that doesn't require perfect prose. Marshall would argue that the president's use of Twitter is more essential to his message than the content of his tweets.

So, what does this have to do with museums? It is a reminder that how we tell a story is as important as the what, why, and who of the story we tell. Let's apply this logic to the mainstay of house museums: the guided house tour. The guided house tour is the medium used to share the history of the house with visitors. The choice to use a guided house tour, arguably, expresses more to visitors than the content of the tour. It says that visitors cannot be trusted in the museum without supervision, that the visitor's experiences and knowledge are not important to the experience, and that the visitor must be passive consumers of the expert content. One of our museum volunteers used to require our young school visitors to put their hands in their pockets while in the house museum. A hands-off, hands-in-pocket tour conveys a message that your body is not welcome in this space and ultimately that this museum is not for you. We can interpret uplifting stories about human empowerment in our house museums, but if we do it in a disempowering way, that becomes the message that we share with visitors.

The Baca House is a two-story adobe house museum in Trinidad, Colorado. Like many house museums, it was full of roped-off historic objects that related to the era of the house and only four of these objects were directly related to the house's historic occupants. The house tour of this museum has experienced declining attendance despite that fact that people enjoy the history of the Baca family who once lived in the home. Our media of hands-off period rooms and guided tours conveyed the house's history as unrelatable and uninspiring, so we are in the process of replacing the roped off objects in several rooms with the Wool Studio. The Baca family was sheep ranchers who purchased the two-story adobe home with twenty-one thousand pounds of wool. Both indigenous and Hispano women of the region used wool in their daily and creative practices. Many of the community's residents are descendants of this tradition. The Wool Studio offers hands-on space that interprets this story and cultural history in a way that resonates with guests and honors the community's cultural practices. It also demonstrates how the right museum medium is part of community engagement.

At El Pueblo History Museum, we replaced several lengthy text labels with Legos. The text labels discussed how historians thought the original El Pueblo, an adobe trading post established in 1842, might have looked even though the building likely evolved over the years and we have a limited record of its structure. We minimized the text, included a primary document description of the site, and added a much later romanticized painting of the trading post. Then we invited museum visitors to use the building blocks to create their own theories of what El Pueblo might have looked like 175 years ago. Visitors of all ages have spent hours designing elaborate trading posts. The use of building blocks—combined with a few primary documents—as an interpretive medium instead of "expert" text conveys that our guests are historians who are welcome to theorize about the look and shape of our community history.

Coauthorship

Part of human-centered design is embracing coauthorship. Museums are well respected for the information that we share with visitors. According to the American Alliance of Museums, history museums are the number one most trustworthy source of information in America. We have many experts, curators, and scholars who can assist in developing the knowledge shared through museums. While it is important to be seen as trustworthy experts, it is equally important for history museums to recognize that our visitors are also experts.

At El Pueblo History Museum, we acknowledge that the people who walk through our doors also possess knowledge of history. We have designed programs, exhibitions, and workshops that encourage visitors and the community to share their knowledge and history with the museum. As a community museum, it is important to create space and methods that empower the community to coauthor our collective history. We have to surrender some authority (notice how "author" is the root of the word "authority"), but it also means that more people feel an ownership of the museum and its programs.

For example, the "Museum of Memory" is a public history initiative at El Pueblo History Museum designed specifically to garner history and stories from the community and museum visitors. We have a gallery space where visitors can add memories to a map of Pueblo County, add a chip to a jar to indicate the neighborhood where they grew up, use chalk to fill in the blank "Pueblo Is . . . ," or use a vintage typewriter to share a story about a first kiss, first communion, or other firsts. This space is completely cocreated by our visitors, which means it is always changing, always exciting, and encourages repeat customers.

Meeting Practical Needs

While our mission inspires museum staff, we realize that the preservation of history isn't as important to everyone else—especially when they have real-world, everyday problems to solve. Several of our community museums host afterschool programs that teach history in fun, hands-on ways. But families sign up for the program because it solves a childcare problem for them. For working families, our afterschool program's commitment to fostering a greater understanding of history in youth is just a bonus. Our Hands-On History After School program continues to exceed our expectations in numbers and fosters a happy love of history in local children. This is exactly the kind of museum magic that can happen when we find ways to intersect our mission with the practical needs of our communities.

Hands-On Authenticity

We live in a world that is seemingly obsessed with technology. Thus, many museums look for technological pathways to be relevant and get noticed. A museum blog recently declared it had discovered the secret to making eighteenth-century art appealing to teens. The answer involved memes and SnapChat. Using technology to appear modern and hip can backfire because technology can often be expensive, frequently breaks, and is generally outside the skill set of a small museum staff. The good news, however, is that we do not need to meme-ify our museums. We have found the opposite to be true. Audiences—including teens—are searching for different and authentic experiences. They already have easy access to virtual worlds simply by pulling a phone out of their pocket. History museums can and should provide a vastly different experience, including opportunities to interact with real humans or get one's hands dirty. Our visitors find deeper satisfaction in cooking their own tortilla over a fire or making an adobe brick. Even our teen volunteer program has taught us that young people would rather stack firewood with their friends than post to our Instagram account. People are searching for authentic, hands-on experiences, which is something history museums already know how to do.

Think Outside Your Walls

When I started working in the museum field, the actual museum space had a sacredness to museum staff. We didn't want to bring the museum out into the community; we wanted people to walk through the doors of the museum. We were museum people and loved museums, and we were convinced that if people just crossed our threshold that they, too, would love museums. But, in all honesty, we were obsessed with the bricks and mortar and not the mission. The museum—even the grandest house museum—is really just a conduit for a grander mission.

Dawn DiPrince

Community engagement means that you meet people where they are—not where you are. You might meet people in their neighborhood or at someone's kitchen table. In all honesty, we make accommodations like this for donors all the time. Being able to engage with your community is also a gift, and we should strive to make similar arrangements to make those connections. At the same time, please be cognizant that people feel welcome to meet at your museum. When you engage your community, it is best to let them decide if they would rather meet at the museum or someplace that might be more convenient.

Finally, programming and interpretative opportunities also exist outside of the museum walls. As mentioned earlier, El Pueblo History Museum hosted the Salt Creek Memory Project where a local artist created a large mural of the neighborhood history based on the oral histories collected by the community. The mural was painted on sheet metal attached to the walls at the museum as part of a temporary exhibit and will eventually be moved into Salt Creek. It will remain an artifact of the neighborhood, sharing the history with residents and visitors. It will also symbolize a wall of the museum that is extended into our community—growing our interpretative surface area and our reach.

* * * * *

Community engagement is a great business practice that can grow revenue and visitation at history and historic house museums. It is also a powerful tool for making meaning and developing resonance within your community. It requires a commitment to the philosophy and practices of community engagement, which acknowledges that museums have much to learn from their communities and audiences. Community engagement is human based, which means that it doesn't require a lot of technology, fancy exhibition design, or money. Most of all, our museums can become electric and lovable when we invite more people in to share, build, and create with us.

Notes

1. Nina Simon, *The Participatory Museum* (Santa Cruz, CA: Museum 2.0, 2010), iii.
2. American Academy of the Arts, "Humanities Indicators: Historic Sites," last modified February 2016, https://humanitiesindicators.org/content/indicatordoc.aspx?i=101.
3. Jay Vogt, "The Kykuit II Summit: The Sustainability of Historic Sites," *History News* 62, no. 4 (Autumn 2007): 17–21.
4. Michael Warner, "Publics and Counterpublics," *Quarterly Journal of Speech* 88, no. 4 (November 2002): 413–25.
5. Community museums of History Colorado include seven museum sites across the state, including Byers-Evans House Museum, El Pueblo History Museum, Fort Garland Museum, Fort Vasquez, Healy House and Dexter Cabin, Trinidad History Museum, and Ute Indian Museum.
6. Paolo Freire, *Pedagogy of the Oppressed* (New York: Continuum Books, 1993), 77.
7. Ibid., 72.
8. Robert I. Sutton and David Hoyt, "Better Service, Faster: A Design Thinking Case Study," *Harvard Business Review* (blog), January 6, 2016, https://hbr.org/2016/01/better-service-faster-a-design-thinking-case-study.

Recommended Resources

DiPrince, Dawn. "Hands-On History: Museum of Memory + Participatory History." Community Memory (blog). https://communitymemory.wordpress.com.
Freire, Paolo. *Pedagogy of the Oppressed*. New York: Continuum Books, 1993.
Simon, Nina. *The Participatory Museum*. Santa Cruz, CA: Museum 2.0, 2010.

Part III

Different Approaches to Familiar Topics

Chapter 14

"Do Something Transformative"

CALLIE HAWKINS AND ERIN CARLSON MAST

Debates. Protests. Elections. Immigration. Slavery. Facts and lies. These are just a few of the issues that have dominated the headlines in recent years. While it may be simpler to process these issues as specific to our moment in time, they have been reignited time and again throughout our history. As discouraging as that may be, there is also ample room for comfort, power, inspiration, and even hope that we have dealt with these issues before as a nation and have blueprints for potential solutions. With relative ease, we can identify original, historical evidence of times when the United States fell far short of its ideals, allowing racist, sexist, and/or xenophobic propaganda to influence law, engaging in censorship, and turning a blind eye to injustices. Likewise, evidence abounds of how people have worked to counteract those injustices by legislating, voting, marching, and boldly sharing their stories.

This back-and-forth throughout U.S. history provides a roadmap to us as citizens. In some ways, this roadmap leads us to reflect on what not to do—how not to react—but at other times, it provides us with a clear path forward. What is imperative is that we know our history, and that historic sites—specifically historic houses—serve a foundational role in this endeavor. In his 1981 book, *Mickey Mouse History*, Michael Wallace urges museums and historic sites to "press ahead beyond social history to become places that deal with politics as well as culture; that reconstruct processes as well as events; that explain the social relations as well as the forces of production at work in the societies whose stories they seek to tell." Similarly, Morris Vogel, president of the Lower East Side Tenement Museum, wrote in 2014 that "surviving structures and spaces are gifts; they allow us, in our own time, to summon up the struggles and choices, the truths and values that past generations confronted and drew on in building lives, families and communities."[1] As stewards, we have the power to reveal—or obscure—these gifts, the stories contained within them, and their significance to our communities today. If we obscure stories about violence, about inequality, about hate, because they are difficult topics and raw, because they might cast a shadow on an otherwise beautiful place, or because they induce a fear that the staff or the audience cannot handle, we are holding our communities back from the "good history," meaning evidence-based history with appropriate context, that they should expect from us.

Do something transformative. That was the charge given to the capital project team tasked with restoring and opening President Lincoln's Cottage to the public in the early 2000s. By definition, the challenge was that interpretation at the Cottage should cause a marked change in someone or something. While that charge has been interpreted in different ways over the years—what change is being sought and how is it being done and measured—it has always guided how the Cottage team approaches its work and has set the standard for how the organization has evolved. In short, by changing someone's perspective, you can change how they see themselves in relation to history and how they view their own civic involvement today. For example, the tour's goal is not to change minds, but rather to offer new perspectives and opportunities for engaging on contemporary issues. Every visitor likes to think they would have been an abolitionist in the nineteenth century, when in fact very few people in the United States identified as abolitionists on the eve of Civil War. By offering visitors ways to become civically engaged in contemporary issues around race, slavery, and immigration, the Cottage is essentially challenging visitors to become more engaged civically today in order to shape history. Thus, the Cottage has earned a reputation from day one for pushing the boundaries of historic house interpretation.

President Lincoln's Cottage and the adjacent Robert H. Smith Visitor Education Center, which houses exhibits, a museum store, and staff offices, opened to the public for the first time in 2008, after an eight-year capital restoration project. The Cottage, which is the only national monument in the country that receives no government operating support, sits on the campus of the Armed Forces Retirement Home, known as the Soldiers' Home in Lincoln's time, and still serving as a home for approximately five hundred veterans today. The Cottage was saved and opened to the public primarily because of what Lincoln accomplished there during his presidency. While in residence at the Cottage, Abraham Lincoln visited with wounded soldiers, spent time with self-emancipated men, women, and children, led the nation through war, weathered a reelection campaign, and developed the Emancipation Proclamation (see Figure 14.1). The human cost of the Civil War surrounded him every summer he and his family were in residence, undoubtedly impacted his thinking, and strengthened his resolve to challenge the status quo. The Cottage served as a home for Lincoln to develop his brave ideas. We believe the world still needs a home for brave ideas and are committed to being that place. Today, our mission is to reveal the true Lincoln and continue his fight for freedom.

Individuals unfamiliar with our organizational history sometimes incorrectly assume our work pivoted dramatically at some point—that we intentionally changed from a traditional historic house museum to a place that hosts conversations on challenges facing veterans or exhibitions

Figure 14.1 President Lincoln's Cottage in Washington, DC. Photo by Bruce Guthrie.

Callie Hawkins and Erin Carlson Mast

on modern slavery, for example. In reality, doing something transformative started up front and with the basics. It began with rigorous scholarship to support the interpretation and a commitment to have the core experience itself—the guided tour—be a vehicle for transformation and a wellspring for programmatic innovation. It is through the tour, first and foremost, that we interact most intimately with the public in conversations on historical issues that Lincoln wrestled with during his presidency and how they impact our lives today.

Early research about Lincoln's time at the Cottage yields new perspectives on a crucial period of our national history that remains hotly contested to this day. It would be tempting to think of the Cottage as a pastoral retreat, a refuge or sanctuary from the chaos of war, but the evidence suggests it was an embattled sanctuary at best, a place that forced Lincoln to confront reality even while giving him the space and perspective to develop solutions. The research reveals recollections of Lincoln's development of the Emancipation Proclamation while living at the site, as well as recollections of conversations Lincoln had with colleagues, friends, and visitors about the meaning and course of the war and emancipation. The richness of these newly discovered primary sources and the power embodied by the authentic Cottage led staff and advisors to the conclusion that they should explore new approaches to interpretation that would highlight what made this place important to Lincoln—that it was a space to gain new perspectives and to reflect upon, develop, and shape ideas.[2] The decision to "furnish" the Cottage with ideas rather than things was further influenced by data that indicated the traditional "velvet ropes" historic house tour model had been in a steady decline. The team was simply playing to the site's strengths, Lincoln's ideas versus objects, but this approach was rare enough that many early conversations contemplated whether the method would succeed or fail.

Fortunately, the method has succeeded, and the Cottage has incorporated this model into all aspects of site management. As described in *Museums of Ideas*:

> By breaking with the traditional model, President Lincoln's Cottage reveals to visitors from the start that they are about to experience something different. Establishing place and time is crucial to helping visitors understand the influences on President Lincoln and the situations he had to navigate. But rather than merely representing a bygone era, the Cottage experience adds context to the struggle humanity has long faced with ideas of liberty, justice, and equality. Whereas spaces filled with furnishings create a connection with peoples' own daily living, spaces filled with ideas cause people to reflect on their own views, politics, ideas, and decisions. The tour was the first expression of the Cottage's efforts to be a transformative place of ideas, but the emphasis on ideas has since permeated all aspects of the site operation, from educational programs to the museum store. The result is that President Lincoln's Cottage is a starting point for discourse on ideas that transcend time, can prompt real action to improve conditions today, and give the visitor experience lasting relevance.[3]

The Cottage is far from the only historic house museum considering how to engage audiences in conversations that connect the past and present. In a 2014 issue of *Forum Journal*, leadership at the Lower East Side Tenement Museum, Jane Addams Hull-House, and President Lincoln's Cottage discussed how their sites defined their period of significance as "now." Some sites might seek to identify an issue with current significance, perhaps choosing to focus on a local, national, or international issue based on the audience they most closely serve, as is the case with Hildene, the home of Abraham Lincoln's son, Robert. Hildene's programming focuses on local issues that reflect the local civic involvement of its last resident. Sites might also look at an issue of historic importance to the site, such as women's rights, or one of contemporary importance threatening the existence of that site, such as how many coastal towns like Annapolis,

Maryland, and Newport, Rhode Island, are tackling the issue of climate change. It may be an external issue, such as an influx of refugees from a war-torn country, that ties to an adjacent historical issue of local concern, including war and immigration. The issue might be ongoing, as with racism in the United States, or cyclical, as is the case with election season influencing visitors' questions at presidential sites.

The Cottage did not set out with the goal of taking on a current issue or issues and then methodically determining which issues it would champion. It came organically. The site was already heavily invested in interpreting slavery and emancipation, as well as other issues Lincoln had to address during his time in residence such as veterans' affairs, immigration, war, and refugees. Academic historians had encouraged the telling of "good history" at the site, using multiple perspectives to outline the progress and limitations inherent in the Emancipation Proclamation as well as to offer interpretation on the Thirteenth Amendment, which legally abolished slavery. Staff were careful not to suggest the Thirteenth Amendment was the silver bullet, and yet it became clear that visitors were drawing that mistaken conclusion on their own. Abraham Lincoln himself hoped and predicted that the Thirteenth Amendment would be the "King's Cure to end all ills." In this case, the president's prophecy was all wrong. Not only did black Americans continue to suffer near-slavery in many forms, actual slavery, as it is legally defined, continues to this day, around the world, affecting more individuals than at the height of the transatlantic slave trade. Thus, for the Cottage, interpreting the modern iteration of slavery and other current issues was deemed necessary to telling "good history." That modern slavery, or human trafficking as it is sometimes called, is also a local, national, and international issue meant that it allowed the Cottage to continue to serve audiences from down the street to around the world.

When commemorating the 150th anniversary of the Emancipation Proclamation in 2012, the Cottage chose not only to focus on the historical resources and the context of slavery and emancipation in Lincoln's time, but to also look at the issue and context of slavery in the United States 150 years later. The goal of this decision was to understand how actions of the past shaped present-day circumstances, and to take both that history and modern context into account when advocating for change for the future.

To that end, in February 2012 we opened *Can You Walk Away? Modern Slavery: Human Trafficking in the United States*, an exhibition that won national and international recognition (see Figure 14.2). The exhibition acknowledged up front that no straight line can be drawn from historical slavery to modern slavery. Slavery was still legal in several states and constitutionally protected on the eve of the Civil War. And there is no shortage of people who argued that slavery was a necessary evil, or even a moral good. Yet many states—and countries—had abolished slavery, and views about slavery being a moral good were held by a minority of people in this country, many of them actively benefiting from the oppression of millions of people who no doubt felt differently about slavery. Today, the issue is different. Slavery is illegal everywhere and its victims are not confined to any one race—though there are groups at greater risk, and in some countries race, religion, and ethnicity are very much a factor in exploitation. While the "shackles" of legal slavery were abolished in Lincoln's time, modern and virulent forms of slavery persist. At a fundamental level, human rights abuse is one and the same. Until 2000, when the Trafficking Victims Protection Act passed through Congress, prosecutors used language rooted in the Thirteenth Amendment when prosecuting modern-slavery cases—there wasn't a different law available. Further recognizing the connection between slavery past and present, President Barack Obama advocated for a change in the language used to describe human trafficking. In a 2012 speech at the Clinton Global Initiative, Obama urged, "I'm talking about the

Figure 14.2 Guide staff at President Lincoln's Cottage use a dialogic approach to orient visitors to the site and the unique tour experience. Photo courtesy of Chris Ferenzi Photography.

injustice, the outrage, of human trafficking, which must be called by its true name—modern slavery." Invoking Lincoln in the modern struggle to combat slavery was not only reserved for activists. We also recognized that perpetrators of the crime of human trafficking itself referred to him, too, as former pimp Iceberg Slim exclaimed, "I've got to con them [girls in his control] that Lincoln never freed the slaves."[4] This approach gave visitors an entirely new perspective on Lincoln's legacy and transformed their understanding of history. As David McIntire, a teacher from Wichita, Kansas, posted on our Facebook page, "This exhibit changed me. I am substantively different as a result." Feedback from visitors confirmed that the exhibition helped them link present efforts to combat human trafficking to past struggles for freedom and called visitors to action against human trafficking in their own communities.

The historic importance of President Lincoln's Cottage as the "Cradle of the Emancipation Proclamation," and its record of providing high-quality youth education programs, led content advisors for *Can You Walk Away?* such as Polaris, a leading non-governmental organization fighting modern slavery in the United States, to recognize the Cottage as the institution best positioned to launch a program aimed at educating and engaging young people on the issue of modern slavery. Through Polaris, we met and began working with a group of four local high school juniors who were dedicated to raising awareness and acting against human trafficking and modern slavery in their school. These students, who named their group Students Opposing Slavery (SOS), sought out the Cottage to provide guidance and expertise to formalize and further develop their movement. We leveraged our expertise on historical slavery and as a museum dedicated to providing education as a public service to create a school-wide assembly on the issue, and along with the students, developed classroom lessons for middle and high school teachers connecting slavery, past and present.

As SOS took shape, Cottage staff and student leaders envisioned the project as an anti-human-trafficking, youth-engagement program with global reach. This vision was possible thanks to international relationships fostered by supporters and partners we had developed in the brief years prior to taking on the SOS program. We realized that we needed a cornerstone event that would bring together youth abolitionists from around the world to the "cradle of the Emancipation Proclamation." Bringing students together would allow for personal connections, generation of creative ideas, and an exchange of information that would keep SOS chapters engaged in the modern abolitionist network. It would also allow us to bring people to the site to tackle the issue of slavery, just as Lincoln did while living at the Cottage.

In developing the SOS program, the Cottage worked with the founding students to create the annual Students Opposing Slavery International Summit, a week-long program each summer that convenes youth (internationally defined as ages fifteen to twenty-four) from around the world to raise awareness of human trafficking and modern slavery (see Figure 14.3). During the summit, youth participants develop big ideas around ending modern slavery and emerge from the experience with the tools they need to continue Lincoln's fight for freedom in their own communities. As a historic site, the Cottage also wanted to follow the arc of history of the site; develop and expand the learning opportunities the site provided; and become the go-to place for youth education on a crucial human rights issue with direct ties to the site's history. By convening the SOS International Summit at the Cottage each summer and supporting students year-round as they take on leadership roles in their communities to raise awareness about the more than 20.9

Figure 14.3 Youth from around the world gathered at the Students Opposing Slavery International Summit at President Lincoln's Cottage in 2017. Photo copyright President Lincoln's Cottage.

Callie Hawkins and Erin Carlson Mast

million people currently enslaved worldwide, we meet the mandate to do something transformational and fulfill our mission." The SOS International Summit has been recognized as a groundbreaking youth educational program and model for the field. Yet it is important to remember the SOS program is one feature in a continuing journey and was possible in large part because of an ongoing commitment to having tough conversations about our nation's past and present with visitors each and every day on our tours. Indeed, the tour itself sets the stage for a transformative week. As an SOS International Summit participant wrote in 2015, "When I went inside Lincoln's Cottage, I felt as if Lincoln . . . he talked about his unfinished work. He understood that slavery hadn't completely ended. I feel that he was passing the torch on to us."[5]

While our programs are a recognizable, external effort of bridging past and present in transformational ways, internal decision-making has also been continually impacted and modified in response to new scholarship. For example, as our understanding of human trafficking deepened, we made deliberate changes to museum store merchandising, focusing on survivor-made and fair-trade items and requiring all vendors to sign forms stating that their supply chains are slavery free. Similarly, when the cocoa matting in the first floor of the Cottage needed to be replaced, we prioritized ethical labor practices over historical accuracy. While our original carpet had been selected for nineteenth-century period appropriateness, we determined that a new certified slavery-free carpeting was a powerful demonstration of preservation and interpretation of President Lincoln's brave ideas for our world today and, therefore, even more historically accurate.

These decisions were opportunities to establish clear ethical standards as an organization and received support from the board of directors. For us, it was not good enough to instruct others on their power as consumers or on the benefits of purchasing survivor-made and fair-trade items, we wanted to "walk the walk" when it came to practices in potential conflict with our organizational values. Making preservation and merchandising decisions that fully reflect our mission also gave us additional opportunities to communicate both our mission and ways that the public can support the organization. Not only do these efforts offer unique interpretive opportunities for staff from tour to store, but visitors also are moved by our commitment to this issue and motivated by this call to action.

We also take fair labor practices very seriously with our own staff—for example, being compliant with overtime rules long before they were mandated—recognizing that our integrity as an organization is as important as our credibility as public historians to our ability to continue to do transformative things.

Opening the dialogue of the past to include the present changes the dynamic. Rather than offering a story at a remove, we give visitors context and resources that empower them to take action in their own communities. We know that understanding matters to our visitors and we remain committed to sharing new scholarship and perspectives on all our tours and programs. But we have also learned—as have colleagues in the historic house museum community—that interpreting issues with contemporary significance requires a committed governing board, strong mission alignment, community trust, robust partnerships, and staff training. This does not mean there will be a consensus, but there has to be considerable trust by all players involved.

In discussing our programming, colleagues often express doubt that their own board would be similarly supportive. It can be easy to place blame on a board but bringing the board around in support of such changes falls as much on the shoulders of the staff leadership as on the board itself. Indeed, several Cottage board members expressed skepticism about creating an exhibit that looked at modern slavery versus one with a purely historical focus but noted their trust in the staff and its track record. Within a year or two, those same board members expressed to all assembled at a regular meeting that despite their previous reservations, they were glad they had supported the change because they were now convinced it had been the right direction for the organization.

Not all boards are created or developed equally, of course, and some can prove downright risk averse and resistant to change. This may happen when a historic site retains very strong connections to descendants of original occupants and/or to organizational founders, but it does not have to. On the one hand, there is the experience of a site in the Southeast that, despite working with communities, partners, and the board on major proposed changes to the interpretation, was faced with several board members—descendants of the founder—who were offended by and resistant to the proposed changes. The changes proposed to create a more inclusive, holistic story of the place and organization. Although those efforts fulfilled the organization's progressive past, the board was not as supportive as the team had hoped. On the other hand, the Belmont Paul Women's Equality National Monument, which has long retained connections to women in politics through its board, events, and community outreach, had full support to be a place of pilgrimage and meeting point as part of the Women's March on Washington, DC, in January 2017.

Transformative results require transparency and continual self-assessment. At President Lincoln's Cottage that includes year-round formal surveys, regular review of third-party feedback such as TripAdvisor, and regular strategic-planning efforts. If a strategic plan is most useful when it serves as a guide to determine whether a new action should be taken, then our mission and vision had to reflect what was unique and uniquely appropriate to President Lincoln's Cottage. This alignment is not always evident at historic house museums. As a litmus test, if simply changing the organizational name results in your mission and vision statement being interchangeable with that of any historic house in your region, it may not be specific enough to provide the kind of guidance your team needs and transparency for your community to understand what you're truly about. And if your stated mission is limited to the past, your community may be surprised when you act on contemporary issues.

There are historic house museums that actively demonstrate the importance of this type of transparency in mission and vision. The Harriet Beecher Stowe Center in Hartford, Connecticut, interprets the author of *Uncle Tom's Cabin* through tours, programs, and events. At first glance, some of their offerings may not seem particularly relevant to Stowe, such as a panel discussion on mass incarceration in twenty-first-century America. However, their mission illuminates the connection clearly: it's not only to preserve and interpret Stowe's home, but to "inspire commitment to social justice and positive change."[6] Their mission provides them a clear rationale for hosting thought-provoking events on contemporary issues, in turn establishing trust with their community.

Instilling this trust can only happen if a historic site knows and understands its community. At President Lincoln's Cottage, we actively share authority with our visitors and partners by paying attention to the way they are impacted by contemporary issues, and to what we can do to respond to their needs. By the same token, we are not here only to reinforce what people know, but to encourage them to think more deeply about the past and to apply the lessons of the past to contemporary issues. Failing to establish this community dialogue can lead to mixed reactions regarding contemporary issues. Take the case of a well-meaning site in the Northeast with a history tied to the Underground Railroad. In response to the black lives matter movement, they erected signs in solidarity across the property. The staff saw this as a natural connection and did not consider it provocative. By all accounts, the local community responded in anger. Some found the decision glaringly inappropriate, if not an affront to the local community, and called the staff to let them know. Members of the community removed signs, only to be put back by the site staff, who clearly viewed themselves as advocates for a cause not dissimilar to the site's former inhabitants. One by one, the signs disappeared until the site ran out of them and did not buy more. The conversation was over before it could even begin.[7]

It is crucial to understand perceptions of your organization by the community you serve and be transparent about your purpose in your mission, particularly when it deviates from the well-recognized norm of historic sites that focus exclusively on a single family or period of significance isolated in the past. Unlike purpose-built museums, historic sites must contend with charges that they are putting words in the mouths of people from the past. If you are not meeting your community where they are, the chasm between their perspective and that of your organization may prove too wide to allow for mind-opening dialogue and transformative change.

At the Cottage, our community has come to see us as a resource, and in many ways looks to us in times of political uncertainty to understand what the historical parallels are to our current situation. In the summer of 2016, we held a three-part comedy series inside the cottage with DC Improv, appreciating the tensions surrounding the presidential campaign season and a collectively expressed need for laughter. The move was tied directly to Lincoln's well-documented consumption of satire and appreciation of the medium as both a pressure release and source of searing commentary. The series was not without criticisms, in spite of all appropriate warnings and disclaimers about offensive language. And yet, some of the most critical guests came back for the very next installment in the series. Overall, the move was well received and viewed as wholly appropriate while still being innovative, responded to a community need, and built upon an existing partnership with DC Improv. A few months later, we recognized the community needed something else entirely. We stayed open late the night after the 2016 presidential election, sensing our community needed a secular place of reflection to gather peacefully. More than one hundred people attended, with same-day notice, on a day of pouring rain, and we received universal appreciation for the event itself. Our language was specifically informed by Lincoln's own language about being a house divided and striving for unity. Because we have built trust with the community over our nine years of operation, keeping the site open late the day after the election was viewed as a natural outlet for reflection not just a political statement that came out of nowhere. Our efforts were grounded in years of community building and public outreach and gave us the ability to sense when our community needed to laugh, needed to cry, or just needed a moment.

The Jane Addams Hull-House Museum—historically a site of social justice in Chicago—has also found unique ways to build on the trust they have established in their community. In the past few years, their exhibitions have focused on exploring "new forms of advocacy and action by positioning the museum as an ally in social movements" and have highlighted "contemporary community organizers such as the Chicago Coalition for Household Workers, which is fighting for minimum wage laws to be extended to domestic workers in Illinois." The Hull-House Museum has also developed several calls to action for visitors that bring attention to a host of contemporary issues, including empowering visitors to advocate on behalf of human rights for prisoners in solitary confinement. Similarly, through their work with restorative justice groups in Chicago, the Hull-House Museum believes their site "can play a role in decreasing the violence in our city."[8] By incorporating contemporary issues in their exhibits, programs, and tours, the Hull-House

Museum has established themselves in their community as an appropriate center for conversations on social justice, a core component of the house's original purpose.

In addition to a strong mission and vision, and sharing authority with the local community, finding the right partnerships is crucial to interpreting contemporary issues in historic house museums. When the idea for a new exhibit in the Visitor Education Center on Lincoln and immigration started to develop, we followed a similar path to the one we followed when creating *Can You Walk Away?* First, we recognized the need to leverage existing relationships with scholars and the immigration community. Then we recognized a need to develop additional partnerships and programming around the issue of immigration today. By working with the American Immigration Council, U.S. Citizenship and Immigration Services, and our colleagues at the Lower East Side Tenement Museum, we gained access to the most current information on this rapidly evolving issue and drew in audiences that had heretofore not connected Lincoln's presidency with this issue—despite Lincoln signing "An Act to Encourage Immigration" on July 4, 1864, the day he moved to the Cottage for his final season in residence. That act, coupled with Lincoln's experience with immigrant veterans while living at the Cottage, made it a natural mile marker to connect the modern debate surrounding immigration to the historical debate in Lincoln's own time.

Similarly, the Hull-House Museum recognized that partnerships could help return the site to its historical roots of peace-building in Chicago. As Lisa Lopez, former associate director at the museum, said, "Though our staff may not be the ones working on the ground, we can amplify the voices of those workers and of the youth of color who are bearing the brunt of this violence. The museum staff has long desired for our site to again be at the center of social justice activism in Chicago. The site has always been used by historians interested in movement-building, but the shift to engage artists, activists and policymakers brought new energy to our work."[9] For the Hull-House Museum, they sought to both build on previous partnerships, and also to branch out into new areas of expertise. Partnerships require considerable work and mutual commitment, but the payoffs can be significant, especially for organizations that would not otherwise have the capacity to carry out the work on their own. Likewise, engaging on contemporary, political issues with your audience can lead to staff burnout and disaffection, unless adequate investment is made in staff support and resources, such as trainings and listening sessions.

Hand in hand with knowing your external stakeholders, empowering your internal constituents, that is, staff, to do "good history" is critical before your site can tackle contemporary issues. When we present on the success of the SOS program, we often are asked by our colleagues in the field how they can replicate the program. The short answer is that first staff must be trained in the proper historical context and a site's audiences must be prepared to receive it. If historic house museums are not well versed in how to interpret slavery in a historical context, then efforts to interpret slavery in a modern context will seem disingenuous. If the public senses a disconnect, it will be harder to engage them on the modern significance. At the Cottage, the history is inherent in everything we do, and has been since we opened. We laid a foundation for dealing with these issues through our interpretation and team training prior to opening in 2008. Given that our history is politically charged and still a source of profound misunderstanding and disagreement, we knew interpretation and training would have to be rigorous and data driven. We do not have a mandate to change minds—but we do feel a responsibility to open all minds to new perspectives. This started as practice in interpretation and training, but has since permeated all aspects of our operation, including merchandising, our interactions with partners, and our employee handbook.

Interpreting contemporary issues at historic sites can be scary because of the feelings and personal experiences that audiences bring to the conversation. But this is nothing new for sites that deal with the recent past. There are different sets of opportunities and challenges depending on how many people in your audience experienced the history of your historic site firsthand. In either case, staff training is very important to alleviate those fears and apprehensions. Routine communications are important (such as at regularly scheduled staff meetings, or by alerting the team that the site is responding to calls-to-action), but not enough.

At President Lincoln's Cottage, we treat training on contemporary issues the same way we treat training on historical content—by consulting experts and scholarship, providing staff with resources to deepen their understanding, and offering ample opportunities for dialogue on how to best incorporate this into tours. It is a habit of our practice to seek out content advisors for exhibits on contemporary issues. As part of our work with them, advisors agree to host a training for our full-time and part-time staff. We record the training and use videos in training new frontline staff. These trainings have yielded great results as they equip staff with the tools and language they need to understand and interpret contemporary issues and can create buy-in from staff who may have otherwise felt hesitant to do so. We have also developed ad hoc forums for staff discussions, sometimes when we see a need, sometimes when the team requests it. One recent type of this training was an open forum specifically for frontline staff and their supervisors to discuss strategies for relating historical problems that Lincoln faced in a divided nation to our own contentious political climate. Frontline staff shared their concerns, ideas, and requests in a way that created a conversation with immediate utility for their work.

The Lower East Side Tenement Museum in New York City has faced this issue in even starker terms. For nearly thirty years, the museum has interpreted the immigrant stories of the 97 Orchard Street tenement house, with the mission of enhancing "the public's appreciation for the role immigration plays in shaping the United States' national identity."[10] In the wake of the 2016 presidential election, the site experienced a steep increase in the number of negative comments related to immigration, as appreciation for immigrants and refugees declined. As a result, the team at the museum has enhanced their procedures for dealing with difficult contemporary connections. As Miriam Bader, the museum's director of education, said in November 2016, "The political climate has created a need for new skills or superpowers to facilitate the conversation." Fortunately, the museum has experience with this. "We've always been a dialogue-oriented museum that invites visitors into the conversation and engages them in co-constructing the story," Bader said. Well versed in providing historical context to contemporary issues, the Tenement Museum has invested in training its staff to respond to potentially awkward or negative comments that question the site's mission.[11]

When historic sites become interchangeable, they lose what makes them special. Every historic site has something unique to contribute to the conversation on our national past, present, and future, which means there are infinite threads one might choose to follow. Getting to that authentic place and providing resources for citizens to use the past to understand the present and guide their future requires a lot: continual reflection on the value of your site's stories to the communities you serve; building trust with your board, colleagues, partners, and audience; and transparency with your mission and vision. Being part of the present requires the courage to reveal the historical truth, the evidence your site offers about the past, before offering yourself as a resource for where that past has led us. Together we can provide the historical context and resources for each citizen to help create a more perfect union.

Notes

1. Erin Carlson Mast, Morris J. Vogel, and Lisa Lopez, "The Period of Significance Is Now," *Forum Journal* 28, no. 4 (Summer 2014): 45.
2. Erin Carlson Mast, "Furnished with Ideas: A New Model of Historic House Interpretation," in *Museums of Ideas: Commitment and Conflict* (Edinburgh: Museums Etc., 2011), 203–4.
3. Ibid., 214–16.
4. Iceberg Slim, *Pimp: The Story of My Life* (New York: Simon and Schuster, 2011), 87.
5. Abhishek Basu, "Schoolboy in Lincoln's Footsteps," *The Telegraph* (Calcutta, India), July 20, 2014.
6. "About Us," Harriet Beecher Stowe Center, accessed August 30, 2017, https://www.harrietbeecher stowecenter.org/about/.
7. Nicole Higgins De Smet, "Museum's Black Lives Matter Signs Stir Tense Discussion," *Burlington Free Press*, July 11, 2016, http://www.burlingtonfreepress.com/story/news/2016/07/11/museums -black-lives-matter-signs-stir-tense-discussion/86938224/; Judy Simpson, "Black Lives Matter Signs Stolen from Underground Railroad Museum," WCAX-TV, October 14, 2016, http://www.wcax.com/ story/33394643/black-lives-matter-signs-stolen-from-underground-railroad-museum.
8. Mast, Vogel, and Lopez, "Period of Significance," 48–49.
9. Ibid., 49.
10. "About Us," Lower East Side Tenement Museum, accessed August 30, 2017, http://www.tenement.org/ about.html.
11. Sebastien Malo, "At New York Immigration Museum, Guides Cope with Hostile Remarks," *Reuters*, November 21, 2016, http://www.reuters.com/article/us-usa-immigration-museum-idUSKBN13G2BI.

Recommended Resources

Erin Carlson Mast, Morris J. Vogel, and Lisa Lopez. "The Period of Significance Is Now," *Forum Journal* 28, no. 4 (Summer 2014): 43–51.

Erin Carlson Mast. "Furnished with Ideas: A New Model of Historic House Interpretation," in *Museums of Ideas: Commitment and Conflict* (Edinburgh: Museums Etc., 2011): 203–4.

Robert Newhouse. "These Teens Are Working to End Modern Slavery," *Teen Vogue*, July 20, 2017. http://www.teenvogue.com/story/these-teens-are-working-to-end-modern-slavery.

Chapter 15

Listening for the Silences

Stories of Enslaved and Free Domestic Workers

JENNIFER PUSTZ

In January 2011, a new British import took the United States by storm. The Public Broadcasting Service (PBS) debuted a new series as part of its program *Masterpiece Classic*: *Downton Abbey*. Each January for the next five years, U.S. audiences welcomed the aristocratic Crawley family and their staff of domestic servants into their homes and became enthusiastic consumers of all things "Downton." The program's popularity and historical setting in early twentieth-century England made it a natural inspiration for programs at historical societies, libraries, and house museums that share a similar audience. On several occasions, house museums also welcomed *Downton Abbey* into their hallowed halls. A touring exhibition of costumes from the program has visited several historic house museums, including Biltmore, the Richard H. Driehaus Museum, and the Paine Art Center and Gardens. The Winterthur Museum, Gardens, and Library hosted their own one-venue-only exhibition of *Downton Abbey* costumes.[1]

At the time, I was the museum historian for Historic New England. In 2009, I had launched a lecture about the history of domestic servants in New England, which I presented at several Historic New England properties and occasionally at libraries and historical societies in the region. Once *Downton Abbey* emerged as a phenomenon, speaking invitations increased significantly, with some inquiries about my "*Downton Abbey* lecture." While I was always careful to remind audiences of the many differences between the reality as we understand the mistress-servant relationship in the United States and this fictional dramatization of English country estate life, I often found it a useful reference point. There is little doubt in my mind that the popularity of the program raised public consciousness and curiosity about what took place in the kitchens, laundries, and servants' halls in the homes of the fictional Crawley family's American peers.

However, as I indicated in *Voices from the Back Stairs: Interpreting Servants' Lives at Historic House Museums*, visitor interest in domestic servants was keen long before *Downton Abbey*'s run.[2] House museum professionals were also eager to present a more balanced story, although they often found themselves frustrated by the lack of documentation and artifacts upon which to hang the interpretation, and limited budgets and staff time to dedicate to the necessary detective work required to tell these stories well. Despite these challenges, several house museums have made significant progress in telling a more inclusive story of domestic life in the years since I completed the primary research for *Voices from the Back Stairs*. I suspect many others hope to join them given what *Downton Abbey* has taught us about our potential visitors' interest in the subject matter.

Downton Abbey's early twentieth-century setting represents the peak and slow decline of the country estate era in the United States and likely reinforces a specific idea of the glamour of Gilded Age life for the wealthy and the drudgery their lifestyle imposed on domestics who served them. Visitors may not realize that this bifurcated domestic world existed long before the Gilded Age and could be found at times in middle-class homes. Regardless of when a house was built or who lived in it, all homes have something in common: a need for labor to maintain the lifestyles of those who live within. Meals did not cook and serve themselves and clean clothing did not emerge magically from laundry tubs and clotheslines. Families who could afford to hire other people to take care of dirty, demanding, and onerous chores reliably did so. Each historical period presents challenges when it comes to researching and documenting domestic workers, but all offer the reward of telling a more complex and relevant story.

Why Interpreting Domestic Servants Matters

By embracing the interpretation of the full spectrum of activities of resident site staff, historic house museums demonstrate that everyone's history is important. Of the many joys I experience in the process of talking to the public about domestic servants, one of the greatest is hearing audience members share their own stories. Some recall nurses, maids, and cooks who worked in their homes many years ago. Others share the stories of their grandmothers, mothers, and aunts who worked at some of the elaborate estates that once existed along Boston's North Shore. Some memories are fond, some more critical. But all are valuable because they allow visitors to see their own history in places that may initially seem very distant.

Servants' stories also matter because they require historic house museum staff to see their sites in new ways. This fact may be valuable simply in the ability to market a new tour or experience to existing audiences or to appeal to new ones. However, I like to think that the re-examination required by researching and interpreting the stories of a site's servants leads to richer and more engaging stories. In the late 1980s and 1990s, many house museums started introducing servants as a way to better represent the racial and ethnic diversity present in these households and to highlight the labor of women (who made up the majority of domestic workers as a labor force). Incorporating the realities of race, ethnicity, and gender are great starting points and site staff are doing well with depicting more diverse households. The more challenging issues related to class differences, social stigma, and complex relationships between the servers and served are still difficult for many site staff but have the potential to generate the most rewarding opportunities for civic engagement.

In this chapter, I share some recent experiences related to interpreting enslaved and free domestic workers at house museums where I have worked or have been otherwise involved since moving to New England. I make this choice not because these are necessarily all the *best* examples, but because they are the ones about which I can offer the most insight. The servant population of any locality is likely to be quite different because domestic workers and wage laborers in general are more likely to be African American or foreign born. My hope is that readers can

Jennifer Pustz

see glimpses of similar situations at their own properties in which a new approach to old stories might be warranted.

What's in a Name? Servants, Domestics, Staff, Free, and Enslaved

The interpretation of domestic labor is fraught with issues related to language. At the Royall House and Slave Quarters, volunteers and staff have consciously adopted the terminology "enslaved men and women" instead of "slaves," a recognition of the personhood of men and women who had the condition of slavery forced upon them. Former plantations in the South have grappled with the issue of retraining guides to use "enslaved" over the long-used term of "servant" to refer to the men and women held in bondage on their sites.[3] Sensitivity through language is one of the easiest and least expensive things historic site staff can offer their audiences; therefore, it is a conversation worth having with guides in the context of training related to interpreting domestic work, regardless of the period being interpreted.

Domestic servants, in the context of this chapter, is the general term I use to refer to men and women who worked within the household and, in most cases discussed here, also lived in the home of their employer. These individuals may have specific duties or job titles, including butler, housekeeper, chamber or parlor maid, waitress, laundress, cook, or children's nurse, and in census records from 1860 forward, they are usually identified as servants in relation to the head of household. A second sphere of labor was located outside of the main house in more well-to-do families. This circle might include a coachman, chauffeur, houseman or handyman, and garden and grounds staff; they were more often men, and although they might also live at their worksite, they typically lived in outbuildings where they had more freedom to come and go than those whose work and residence was closer to the family. These men are sometimes identified as "servants" in the census, but this terminology seems less appropriate. Therefore, as a whole I tend to describe the labor force present during an interpretive period as domestic staff, domestic workers, or domestic labor, retaining "domestic" to indicate that they are associated with a private dwelling as opposed to a hotel or boardinghouse.

However a house museum staff chooses to refer to domestic laborers, when possible, I and others who advocate for their stories prefer to use personal names when they are known. Saying their names makes them more present in the story, and giving them agency by using the active voice is a powerful tool to remind visitors that these workers were more than hidden machinery that ensured a functional household.

Free and Enslaved Labor in the Eighteenth-Century Home

Finding the people who worked at historic house museums, whether their names are ultimately uncovered or not, presents the first major hurdle in the effort to reinterpret a site's story. After moving to New England, I quickly learned that the earliest censuses in the United States (1790, 1800, and 1810) could only provide aggregate data. Only if I knew *exactly* which family members resided in the home at the time of the census would I be able to estimate how many servants might have lived there, but even that information would be limited to gender and, in some cases, a range of ages (although African Americans were typically identified as "negro," "slave," or "other free person," and drew attention to their presence). Gathering information about households before the first national census of 1790 was even more challenging. Although some towns and colonies did conduct their own censuses, one can't always rely on the existence of such records. In addition to a paucity of documentary evidence, I also encountered the challenges of interpreting slavery in northern colonial households. In such cases, documentation continued to be elusive but I was most concerned about how these stories could be shared in an authentic and sensitive way. Two sites in particular offer examples of ways to manage limited documentation and to interpret potentially difficult narratives from the eighteenth century: the Sayward-Wheeler House in York Harbor, Maine, and the Royall House and Slave Quarters in Medford, Massachusetts.

The Sayward-Wheeler House (c. 1718), which is owned and operated by Historic New England, provides an example of the types of documentary resources that are available to uncover stories of enslaved men and women, primarily in eighteenth-century coastal cities and towns. Documentary sources are often scarce for properties of this period, unless family papers were saved and deposited in archival collections. For example, a small but rich collection of documents written by Jonathan Sayward provides the background for the story that follows, while a nearby eighteenth-century Historic New England property, Hamilton House (c. 1785), is more challenged by a lack of family papers. Documentation-poor sites must work harder to create a story based on those told around the edges in period newspapers, town and church records, and legal documents. I have often suggested to colleagues that we "listen for the silences" and think critically about why documentation might not exist (absences sometimes speak louder than presences) and how we can creatively engage visitors in conversations around gaps in knowledge. Even when an extraordinary source like a personal diary is available, however, one still must scour the records and be creative to fill in the inevitable blanks.

York, Maine, is small compared to the ports of Portland to its north and Boston to its south, but its history includes families who engaged in the slave trade or held men and women in bondage. The Sayward-Wheeler House was the home of Jonathan Sayward, a Loyalist who remained in the American colonies during the Revolutionary War despite considerable threat to his safety. It was also home to at least two enslaved men, Prince and Cato, whom Sayward mentions in his diaries.[4] Sayward records that both left his service to fight on the side of the patriots. Although he doesn't record his feelings about their decisions, the documentation of their presence brings them out of the shadows of the site's history.

The story of Prince is further enhanced by documents in the pension application by his wife, Dinah Prince, part of the National Archives collection of Revolutionary War Pension and Bounty-Land Warrant Application Files, which has been digitized and made available by Ancestry.com.[5] The file includes several statements by York residents that support Dinah's claim for a widow's pension by providing information about the couple's marriage, memories related to Prince's service during the war, his death, and Dinah's widowhood. Sayward's diary and the pension file provided enough information to construct an interpretation of the site that better represents the diverse makeup of the household, elaborates on the political tension that existed within during the war with an example related to race, and highlights a source of information that provided a surprising amount of detail about Prince's life.

The home of another Loyalist has provided the venue for a deeper investigation of northern colonial slavery. The Royall House and Slave Quarters is a small historic house museum located in a densely populated neighborhood in Medford, Massachusetts, less than ten miles north of Boston. During the period in which it was home to Isaac Royall, his family, and some sixty enslaved men, women, and children, the house was the focal point of a five-hundred-acre gentleman's estate. Today, only a fragment of the property survives to surround the high-style Georgian mansion (built 1732–1737) and the slave quarters that stands thirty-five feet away. For one hundred years,

Figure 15.1 Interpreting the two-story slave quarters at the Royall House opened new stories and perspectives on slavery in New England. *Source:* Max A. van Balgooy.

the Royall House interpretation centered on the Royall family, an extraordinarily wealthy family of Loyalists who made their money in all branches of the triangular trade.

Between 1999 and 2001, an archaeological excavation on the property resulted in the recovery of thousands of fragments representing objects from all realms of everyday life on the estate. China teacups, wine bottles with the family crest, and crystal wine glasses reflect the lifestyles of the wealthy, while redware milk pans and cream pots document the life and work of the enslaved labor force, and clay marbles and broken tile refashioned into gaming pieces suggest the resilience and humanity of the enslaved population. The dig offered the board of directors an opportunity to reflect upon the organization's mission and provided them with a sound body of research created by Alexandra Chan, one of the archaeologists, whose dissertation and subsequent book focused on the two sides of life at the estate.[6] After a strategic-planning process, the board adopted a new mission that placed equal weight on the family of wealthy Loyalists and the enslaved Africans.

In 2008, the board took the first step toward providing a more equal interpretation by reinterpreting the physical spaces in the main house. The first step was deinstalling a bedroom located above the kitchen that had been decorated in the Colonial Revival style, and interpreting it empty with a copy of the probate inventory taken following Isaac Royall Sr.'s death in 1739, which lists "negro beds and bedding" among the contents. A grant received from the

1772 Foundation in 2009 expanded the scope of the reinterpretation to include a reinstalled period kitchen, kitchen chamber, and connecting staircase that opened to the public in 2011. As the transformation continued, the board of directors decided to change the name of the organization from the Royall House Association to the Royall House and Slave Quarters to more accurately reflect the story it wishes to tell. The next stage of progress shifted toward building a new, on-site school program, "Parallel Lives," and an outreach lesson, "Belinda's Footsteps," both of which feature the story of Belinda Sutton, a woman enslaved by the Royalls who successfully sued for a pension from Royall's estate.

All of these accomplishments have been achieved due to careful management of limited funds and a passionate group of volunteer board members. Like many small historic house museums, the Royall House and Slave Quarters has an annual budget of under $100,000, small paid staff (two part-time employees), and a largely volunteer workforce. The strength of the mission and importance of the story have led to growth in visitation (although total numbers are still small compared to larger sites) and recognition from peers.

Despite the success on the interpretation front, the board faces challenges to increase the size of its endowment and the site's capacity to meet the needs of a growing reputation, and to ensure that the interpretation visitors come to hear is delivered by the volunteer guides. Grant funds have supported the board's efforts to tell a more balanced story, but they have not yet led to permanent funds that would sustain and grow these projects and the staff to support them. The board continues to work with volunteer guides to offer a quality and consistent tour experience to visitors, with the understanding that some of the deeper nuances of the relationships between the two halves of the household may not always be sufficiently interpreted. Like most house museums, changes to the interpretation roll out slowly, with the hope that as more people are exposed to the site's mission and story, more will come forward to actively participate. Although the Royall House and Slave Quarters has a distance to travel to reach the capacity the board of directors envisions, it has successfully transformed itself from just another Georgian house museum to one that encourages visitors to see the house and the adjacent slave quarters as the settings for a complex narrative about relationships between wealthy families and the men and women they enslaved.

As some of the country's oldest architectural resources, eighteenth-century house museums can be rich deposits of historical memory as well as shells waiting to be filled with material that revives their past through contemporary relevance. They are often most in need of a fresh approach because they are likely to have been among the properties with the longest history as museums. Embracing the perspectives of the enslaved or free African American men and women whose labor was necessary for the household's survival can be one way to present these sites in a new light.

Nineteenth-Century Industrialization and the Domestic Service Boom

Researching domestic labor in nineteenth-century homes can be like night and day depending on which end of the century is under investigation. Gathering material on domestic workers at the beginning of the century requires many of the same skills and strategies required to do so for the eighteenth century. Family papers, full-text newspaper databases, and town records are the best options for understanding the composition of these households. However, by the middle of the century, the amount of resources increases significantly thanks to more detailed census records, growth in the number of newspapers and magazines, and an increase in publication of domestic and household manuals. These changes occurred alongside an increasing percentage of families who employed at least one domestic servant. The ability to relieve the lady of the house of dirty and distasteful household labor by hiring another woman to do them became a sign of middle-class status. Industrialization created more white-collar jobs and, as a result, more middle-class families. The increase in the population of women working in domestic service is documented by statistics as well as an increasing presence of livery-wearing servants in advertising and other popular media.[7]

During my decade at Historic New England, I was repeatedly struck by the ability of the organization to interpret one theme across space and time through the lens of its collection of historic properties. Domestic service was a perfect subject for this approach given the many properties that had been home to domestic workers, although some sites were better documented than others. One of the challenges of interpreting a single historic site is to give visitors a greater sense of its place in historical context. How does one help tour visitors understand that the servants' rooms they see are but one example of a very complex and individualized realm of work? The solution I found emerged over time through the creation and presentation of the public lecture to which I refer earlier, which highlights three Historic New England properties, all of which interpret the lives of late nineteenth-century families, but with very different domestic situations.

Of the three sites, the most recognizable to general audiences is the household of the Codman Estate in Lincoln, Massachusetts. The main block of the Codman house was built circa 1740, but the service wing was substantially enlarged in the 1860s and 1880s. This long string of connected rooms includes all those one would expect to see in a country house from this period: butler's pantry, servants' hall, kitchen, and laundry, with two sets of back stairs that lead to small bedrooms above (currently used for storage). The work rooms are unfurnished but contain the remnants of domestic technology employed by a staff of seven or more house servants: annunciators, a massive cast-iron range, and laundry stove. The spaces themselves are the most revealing because they suggest the presence of the sizable and specialized group of domestic workers typical of this time and place.

The Codman family left behind about one hundred linear feet of family papers, which have been studied by a variety of scholars, including one graduate student who specifically researched the domestic servants who lived and worked at the Codman Estate. Despite the richness of the archival record, however, documentation of the servants is relatively limited. One story that does emerge is that the Codman family faced the challenge of the often-discussed "servant problem," particularly when it came to engaging and retaining a suitable cook. The family scrapbooks also include a series of snapshots taken of five members of the domestic staff posing for a photograph on a snowy day. Three of the women wear typical servant attire (a simple work dress and morning and afternoon livery); the children's nurse, Marie Reine Lucas, and coachman Watson Tyler wear dark suits of clothes that reflect their higher standing among those employed by the Codmans. Information from the census fills in some of the remaining blanks in terms of the servants' ages and ethnic backgrounds. One goal of the lecture is to begin by presenting the type of servant staff audience members are likely to have in mind based on their exposure to programs like *Downton Abbey*. A second is to suggest that relationships between mistresses and servants varied greatly. The Codmans may have had many cooks, but the children's nurse and coachman worked for the family for decades, therefore, relationships between upstairs and down are difficult to generalize even within one household.

Roseland Cottage, the home of Henry and Lucy Bowen and their family, in Woodstock, Connecticut, offers a similar view of domestic life at a remote country retreat, although on a slightly smaller scale. Site-specific information about the Bowen servants is somewhat sparse as well, but the family and house servants are reliably documented in the census, although in many cases they were at their home in Brooklyn Heights when the census taker visited. The constantly changing list of servants is recorded in the census, with the exception of Jane Stuart, whose presence spanned five decades, further emphasizing the transient nature of most domestic labor.

The final property, Castle Tucker, in Wiscasset, Maine, allows audiences to see a dramatic difference between the multiple-servant households of the Codmans and Bowens and the more typical one-servant households of middle-class families. Although Richard and Mollie Tucker were relatively well-to-do when they moved into this imposing Federal-style home in 1868, over time they experienced a slow decline in their income that ultimately led to taking in boarders in the 1890s. Soon after their purchase of the home, Mollie Tucker begins to write about what would become an ongoing frustration with finding and keeping domestic help. The Tucker family papers contain voluminous correspondence between Mollie and her husband (who was often away tending to business ventures) and eventually her grown children, who left home to pursue a variety of careers. Mollie's correspondence regularly documents the hiring and subsequent departure of many servants, suspicions of theft, and other frustrations, which echo those expressed by many women who complained of the "servant problem" in magazines and other popular literature. The challenges of this remote, one-servant household brilliantly demonstrate how different the life of a single maid-of-all-work might be compared to a chamber or parlor maid at the grand Codman Estate in Lincoln.

The three households described in this lecture provide valuable context when presented at other house museums interpreting the same period. Historic New England partnered on occasion with Stonehurst, the Robert Treat Paine estate in Waltham, Massachusetts, for a special program, "Exploring the Back Stairs," that took advantage of the documentary resources of the lecture and several well-preserved and -restored servants' rooms at Stonehurst. The program began with the "Voices from the Back Stairs" lecture described above, followed by a presentation by Stonehurst's curator that introduced the history of the H. H. Richardson–designed mansion, the Paine family, and the known information about domestic servants and hired men who worked on the grounds. Robert Treat Paine was a passionate and well-known supporter of social welfare programs in Boston during the 1880s and 1890s. He founded workingmen's clubs, industrial education programs for young boys and girls, and cooperative banks to help families move out of tenements and into their own homes. This context was kept in mind during the subsequent tour of the servants' spaces in the house, which seem to reflect Paine's interest in providing healthy environments for his own workers. While one half of the group toured the servants' spaces, the second viewed the family bedroom wing, where they learned about the duties of chambermaids, ladies' maids, and valets. The program was offered seasonally, in spring and fall, in conjunction with the timing of the Paine family's move to or from their winter home in Boston. This theme allowed an opportunity to discuss the enormous efforts required to clean the house top to bottom, to cover (or uncover) furnishings with specially made dustcovers, and pack or unpack the family's trunks. The program's success was measured by the fact that it routinely sold out before any additional publicity was required and that participants seemed to enjoy the opportunity to see the property in a new light or, in many cases, for the first time. These examples demonstrate the power that nineteenth-century homes reveal in the relationships created around domestic labor in a variety of settings.

Jennifer Pustz

The End of Domestic Service in the Twentieth Century

By the end of the first quarter of the twentieth century, domestic service had declined significantly as a major category of employment for American women. Factories and department stores selling mass-produced goods provided opportunities for unskilled women and secretarial training offered a path to "pink collar" jobs in offices. Many middle-class families replaced their maids-of-all-work with new electric appliances, such as washing machines, refrigerators, and vacuum cleaners, which promised to remove the drudgery from household work.[8] Wealthy families continued to employ domestics to care for large estates and to support lavish entertaining, but even they downsized over the course of the century.

From a research perspective, twentieth-century records continue to improve in terms of the amount of information collected in census records, which are now available through 1940. Depending on the period under consideration, there may still be descendants of the family who owned the estate or who were employed there to share memories and family photographs or documents. Collections of product packaging and domestic equipment may be acquired through resources like antiques shops or online auction sites. The number of public domain archival materials (produced prior to 1923) digitized and freely available online continues to grow on a daily basis. Therefore, reconstructing the domestic world of the twentieth century can be a more straightforward affair.

Historic New England's Phillips House in Salem, Massachusetts, interprets the life of the Phillips family and their domestic staff circa 1919 and is a veritable treasure trove of domestic machinery. Although members of the Phillips family lived in the house well into the second half of the twentieth century, the kitchen still features its massive cooking range, a soapstone sink, annunciator, and a wall of glass-enclosed shelves filled with all manner of gadgets and gizmos, now long obsolete yet carefully preserved. The basement laundry room is anchored by a long row of sinks, a set kettle for boiling clothes, and a laundry stove to heat multiple irons at once. Finally, a long, steep staircase connects the kitchen to the hallway on the third floor that includes three bedrooms and a bathroom for those who worked in the house. Unlike many house museums, even those with an interpretive focus on the twentieth century, Phillips House retains a remarkable level of authenticity within its service wing.

Staff at the site have also been able to recover the stories of several members of the domestic staff, many of whom worked for the Phillips family for extraordinarily long tenures. Three live-in domestics, a cook, first-floor maid, and nursemaid, lived in the third-floor servants' quarters, which included a modern private bathroom for their use. Catherine Shaughnessy was a long-time employee who started as young Stephen Phillips's nursemaid and later took on other duties in the household. Delia Cawley and Bridget Durgin are known to have served as waitress and cook during the 1919 interpretive period. Due to the fact that Phillips House presents relatively "recent" history, site staff were able to conduct oral histories with relatives of the Phillips's domestic staff.

The stories of these women, as well as the two men who lived off-site and were charged with care of the grounds, carriages, and automobiles, are the foundation for a popular program at the site, "The Irish Experience," offered each year around St. Patrick's Day. The all-Irish domestic staff at Phillips House is something of an anachronism for the twentieth century. Irish servants were prevalent in Massachusetts homes in the mid- to late nineteenth century, but by the twentieth, Irish Americans had established themselves in the state, particularly in local politics. "The Irish Experience" provides a window not only into the domestic world of the Phillips House but also into the international context of their time. The interpretation of domestic service at Phillips House is part of what makes the property unique, especially in a city with an extraordinarily rich collection of historic architecture.

The Salem example seems a fitting case upon which to conclude because of the sheer abundance of options a visitor has if they are interested in history. It is a microcosm of sorts with its wide range of authentic or theatrical experiences that represent the Great Age of Sail, the Salem Witch Trials, house museums of various vintage, and the impressive and diverse collection of the Peabody Essex Museum. The traditional house museum has a lot of competition in an environment with so much to choose from. I have often referred to historic house museums as the original "immersive experience." There is no need for virtual reality when once can walk into and experience spaces in which real people lived, loved, and worked. Servant interpretation matters because it provides a relatable access point for any visitor who has washed a dish, swept a floor, or made a bed. However, once the visitor is in the door, it is up to us to make sure those dirty dishes, flyspecked floors, and unkempt beds have meaningful stories behind them.

Notes

1. "Dressing Downton: Changing Fashion for Changing Times," http://www.dressingdownton.com; "Costumes of Downton Abbey," http://www.winterthur.org/Downtonabbey.
2. Jennifer Pustz, *Voices from the Back Stairs: Interpreting Servants' Lives at Historic House Museums* (DeKalb: Northern Illinois University Press, 2010).
3. Jennifer L. Eichstedt and Stephen Small, *Representations of Slavery: Race and Ideology in Southern Plantation Museums* (Washington, DC: Smithsonian Institution Press, 2002).
4. Jonathan Sayward Diaries, 1760–1799, Manuscripts octavo volume S, American Antiquarian Society, Worcester, Massachusetts.
5. Ancestry.com, "U.S., Revolutionary War Pension and Bounty-Land Warrant Application Files, 1800–1900 [Database on-Line]" (Provo, UT: Ancestry.com Operations, Inc., 2010).
6. Alexandra A. Chan, *Slavery in the Age of Reason: Archaeology at a New England Farm* (Knoxville: University of Tennessee Press, 2007).
7. Faye E. Dudden, *Serving Women: Household Service in Nineteenth-Century America, Volume 1* (Middletown, CT: Wesleyan University Press, 1983); David M. Katzman, *Seven Days a Week: Women and Domestic Service in Industrializing America* (New York: Oxford University Press, 1978); Daniel E. Sutherland, *Americans and Their Servants: Domestic Service in the United States from 1800 to 1920* (Baton Rouge: Louisana State University Press, 1981).
8. Ruth Schwartz Cowan, *More Work for Mother: The Ironies of Household Technology from the Open Hearth to the Microwave* (New York: Basic Books, 1983).

Chapter 16

Interpreting Women's Lives at Historic House Museums

MARY A. VAN BALGOOY

> The historical invisibility of women is often due to the fact that we look for them in exactly the same activities as are pursued by men, and thus we cannot find them.
>
> —Gerda Lerner, *The Majority Finds Its Past: Placing Women in History*

> It is learning how to take our differences and make them strengths. For the master's tools will never dismantle the master's house. They may allow us temporarily to beat him at his own game, but they will never enable us to bring about genuine change.
>
> —Audre Lorde, "The Master's Tools Will Never Dismantle the Master's House"

Everyone knows you need the right tools to ensure success in your job. So it is when interpreting women at historic house museums. Many sites have tried by adding women to the story, but in the end the prominent man takes the lead and changes history while the woman follows. Is this an accurate representation? No. Historians use many tools in interpreting history, and the tools used by present-day historians give the impression that men make history. However, by using a different set of tools to interpret women, a new narrative arises where women are just as active as men, participating in all facets of society and redefining history as we know it.

When the historic house movement started in the mid-nineteenth century, especially with the establishment of the Mount Vernon Ladies' Association to save George Washington's home, it defined the preservation movement as well as the interpretation for others to follow: saving homes of white male leaders of political, economic, military, and artistic stature and presenting their homes as shrines to the public. Consequently, this placed women's lives and experiences on the periphery, giving visitors a very distorted and limited view of the past.[1]

The field of history reinforced the idea that only elite men made history. At the end of the nineteenth century, history was professionalized in colleges and universities. It became a social science that stressed scientific methods and objectivity. As the new academic scholars conducted research for their accounts, they came to favor certain sources over others for historical facts, specifically those collected from documents believed official and unbiased: government records, court accounts, and legal papers.[2] Generally, these documents did not include much information about women as they were not allowed to fully participate in activities of the government. Therefore it seemed that, from the sources historians referenced for their research, men initiated change and the course of history.

This approach to history remained relatively unaltered until various factors came together in the late 1960s and 1970s to spur the growth and creation of women's history as a separate field, namely the civil rights and women's movements as well as the rise of social history that concentrated on the lives of ordinary people. Historians, especially women, began actively asking questions about the traditional narrative of history and why it did not include women's involvement. As these scholars taught, researched, and wrote about women, they discarded the old methods, developed new tools, and began to rewrite history. Moreover, their scholarship transformed history by demonstrating women's agency, contributions, and centrality to everyday life big and small.

Historic house museums tried to follow suit. Sometimes it worked; most often it did not. Many museums added women into the existing interpretation using traditional methods to research and portray women's lives and experiences. In other words, sites looked for women in the same activities pursued by men and, of course, found little. Accordingly, women's stories remained in the background and were included only when they contributed to the main story line. While he went off to fight in the Revolutionary War, she managed the household and contributed to the war effort by making musket balls for the army. While he led families on the overland trail to settle the West, she bravely joined him and quietly endured the hardships along the way. While he worked in industry, she stayed home and took care of the children.

Another way historic sites incorporated women into their interpretation was by placing them in the home applying the Victorian ideal of a woman—a white, middle-class domestic caregiver with sole responsibility for the home and children. This approach also had its pitfalls. It overlooked the changing image and perception of a housewife over the centuries; it limited women to the home and family; it idealized domesticity and depicted it as the universal feminine norm; and it treated household technology as improving women's lives.[3]

Analyzing Women and Where to Find Them

How then can historic house museums successfully incorporate women into the story of a site? By starting with the right tools. The best tools to use are those developed in women's history. Most people believe women's history focuses only on women as subjects. It is more than that. Women's history is also about the research, approaches, and methods used to uncover women and their significance in the historical narrative. Indeed, historians in other fields have borrowed the tools used by historians of women due to their findings and methodologies. Five of the most significant innovations that have come out of women's history as it has developed and that historic sites can take advantage of are (1) recognizing differences between women and men and among women; (2) applying new approaches and methods toward sources; (3) rethinking and challenging the traditional periodization of history; (4) understanding gender as a social construct; and (5) perceiving the fluidity between the public and private realms of human affairs.[4]

1. Differences

As the field of women's history developed, historians realized they needed to move beyond traditional research and practices and construct new criteria and concepts to interpret women's lives

Mary A. van Balgooy

and experiences. One direction led historians to rewrite history by comparing experiences between men and women in settlement, slavery, wars, work, and technology. Historians also compared women of different classes, races, ethnicities, regions, and religions.[5] Consequently, the "difference" between women and men and among women became one of the most significant organizing concepts for women's history and opened a whole new avenue for historians to explore, learn about women's involvement in all realms of society, and recognize the range of women's activities.

How might difference uncover a new story about women at a historic site? What might be revealed? The answers may be surprising and show how women took risks, faced challenges, and played a pivotal role in history. The Betsy Ross House takes this approach and as a result provides a richer and more compelling story of Ross during the American Revolution and independence (see Figure 16.1).[6]

Figure 16.1 At Betsy Ross House in Philadelphia, Carol Spacht portrays Betsy Ross in her upholstery shop to present a richer and more compelling interpretation of women during the American Revolution. *Source:* Max A. van Balgooy.

How did Ross, a woman, experience war and freedom? More specifically, how did Ross, a crafts-woman living in the city of Philadelphia, react to the revolution? How did she face boycotts once she committed herself to the revolution? How did British occupation of Philadelphia affect her? What did it mean to be a single mother in the eighteenth century? By asking these questions, Ross becomes a real person and not just a woman who contributed to the war by making musket balls and the first American flag.

Ross and her first husband, John, had recently established their upholstery business in Philadel-phia when the call to boycott European goods went into effect. Having sided with the colonists, Betsy turned to making flags, tents, and bedding for the Continental Army using domestic prod-ucts. This change in their business was certainly not as profitable as making accoutrements for the elite class, and they strived to make a living. To make matters worse, John died in January 1776, leaving Ross a widow. Less than a year later, she married again. As a mariner turned pri-vateer for the army, her second husband was away at sea for long periods of time, leaving Ross on her own. When it looked like the British were about to capture Philadelphia, Ross had to ask herself: Do I flee and risk losing everything? Or stay in the house to protect it from looting and risk exposure to the enemy? What if the British accuse me of treason? In the end, she decided to stay and endured eight months of British occupation without her husband even though occupation caused her greater problems—a scarcity of goods. Before the occupation, prices were already high for staples like flour. Now they threatened to skyrocket. And with scarcity came crime as men and women fought to survive. During this time, Betsy probably gave up her shop and worked for another upholsterer.

Although the British would leave in 1778, it did not mean life would become better. In 1778–1780, the city experienced severe economic hardship that caused riots and more crime during which Ross' first daughter was born and died. She bore another daughter in 1781, the same year the British caught her husband and threw him into prison, where he died the following year. When the war was over, Ross would marry a third time, but with the war's end, independence did not bring her stability or fame. Well into her aging years, Betsy struggled to keep her family financially afloat. War and independence for Ross brought a decrease in status that she was never able to improve.[7] As visitors learn, the legendary story of Betsy Ross making the first American flag that elevated her in history would come well after her death.

Instead of discovering how Ross *contributed* to the Revolutionary War and independence and focusing on how she *experienced* this time period as a woman, visitors witness her in several overlapping dramatic stories and make connections to contemporary issues facing women today.

2. Sources

Betsy Ross and her descendants did not preserve any of her personal papers or shop accounts. Much of the research conducted by staff and historians consisted of applying new ideas and approaches toward sources, thereby developing a fuller account of Ross and women of her class. How might a historic site use this approach to research women? There are several ways.

Susan Ware, who wrote a biography of Amelia Earhart, states that she had not discovered any new documents about the aviator. Instead, she made use of the same research materials but asked different questions about them. For example, what did Earhart's actions say about how women were supposed to behave in the 1920s and 1930s? How did it compare to expectations of men? What happened when Earhart stepped out of the perceived role of a woman? How might her actions differ from women of another class, race, or ethnicity? Overall, what can Earhart's life tell us about women during this time? By asking these questions, Ware reveals the battles Earhart faced to fly, gain acceptance as an aviator, and promote the ability of women to enter any and all professions.[8] Her book expose another side of Earhart's life that was missing in previous biographies and that the Ninety-Nines, who preserve and interpret Amelia Earhart's birthplace, have incorporated into their interpretation, providing a fuller and more meaningful account of Earhart to the public.[9]

Other women historians realized that traditional archival sources were inadequate to unearth women's contributions and activities, so they turned to what were considered unconventional resources: newspapers, census and statistical data, organizational and employment records, photographs, oral histories, and material culture. Although historic sites already used many of these sources in their interpretation, women historians elevated them to that of "creditable" documents. In *Families and Farmhouses in Nineteenth-Century America,* historian Sally McMurry combines historical analysis of written documents with the analysis of house plans, illustrations, architecture, and the landscape, treating them all as equally important. By doing so, she discovered that women as well as men sent architectural plans to agricultural journals between 1830 and 1900. Some women contributed plans independently and under their own name, while others influenced designs submitted by their husbands. In fact, McMurry found that agricultural journals encouraged women to participate because they believed their views were just as important as men's.[10] Her research method and findings made a significant contribution to the field of architectural history. As one reviewer of her book states, "its discussion of women's contributions to house form and design is a badly needed corrective in a field dominated by research on men's roles as architects, builders and artisans."[11]

The Herbert Hoover National Historic Site relied on similar resources to interpret Herbert Hoover. Hoover left the area as a young child after both parents died. Rather than concentrating on the man and his later accomplishments at his birthplace, the National Park Service (NPS) chose a different approach and placed Hoover and his family in a broad context focusing on nineteenth-century Iowa farm families.[12] Middle school students analyze a schematic plan of Hoover's two-room birthplace and how a family of five lived in a fourteen-by-twenty-foot house. How did the family use space? How did their house compare to others in the town? Curriculum materials also include a portion of the 1880s census. Who lived in West Branch? What work did people do? And by researching the community, NPS uncovered not only that more women than men populated the town but that the houses owned and headed by women differed widely in class and status. Using these sources to research and understand Herbert Hoover's life, historians found that women were present everywhere, participating and affecting the community in myriad ways. The research carried out by NPS broadens our understanding of women in late nineteenth-century life in the Midwest.[13]

Finally, historians learned that in collecting materials on history, most archives and special collections in libraries had accumulated papers that were heavily biased toward men's endeavors. When archives saved women's documents, they catalogued them in such a way as to make their records difficult to locate. In conducting research for her book, historian Linda Kerber found, "Libraries have often catalogued women's papers as 'family miscellany' or 'Letters from Ladies'" that writers drew upon as a charming anecdote to a story rather than real history.[14] To find women in the archives, historic house museums must use search terms and subject headings in a creative way. However, this is not always easy unless one has an advanced degree in library or archival science. Where possible, historic sites should take advantage of the expertise of specialists, librarians, and archivists at academic libraries, historical societies, and state archives and historic preservation commissions to find primary sources on women. These institutions may be able to find new information related to a historic site or surrounding area and provide greater insight into the context of the day.

In conducting research on women for Peerless Rockville, a Maryland historic preservation organization, archivists and professionals helped me to locate documents that I would never have found on my own or know about, including divorce proceedings, maps, shop accounts and ledgers, cemetery records, town and city directories, and arrest warrants for escaped slaves. They proved invaluable and opened a whole new avenue of inquiry for me in interpreting women in my hometown.

3. Periodization—The Need for a New Timeline?

The use of traditional sources was not the only area women historians questioned. They also challenged the standard timeline of history. Most commonly, historians make use of wars (the American Revolution, the Civil War, World Wars I and II), the economy (farming, industrialization, technology), and settlement (colonization, westward expansion) to divide history into periods. But what historians may have regarded as turning points in history may apply to some people but not others, as women scholars point out. Joan Kelly's influential article "Did Women Have a Renaissance?" confirmed that women did not experience an increase in status during the Renaissance in Europe, rather, developments adversely affected them. In her study, Kelly establishes criteria for gauging the relative contraction or expansion of powers of Renaissance women and for determining the quality of their historical experience—the regulation of female sexuality compared to men's, women's economic and political power compared to men's, roles of women and access to education, and ideology about women.[15] Historic sites can take this approach, too, to see if women's lives improved or declined from events on a standard timeline or judge whether different events changed their lives, thereby creating a need for a new timeline.

When writing a guide to historic houses and places about women for Peerless Rockville, I decided to develop a new timeline to gain a new perspective about women as diverse as Ann Maria Weems and Frieda Fromm-Reichmann. I decided on a timeline about women's rights.[16] My timeline detailed what women lacked as rights in the nineteenth century: the right to vote, participate in government, own property, retain earned wages, access higher education, and keep custody of children in the case of separation or divorce. My timeline also included when women attained new rights. Using this timeline revealed much more about how women in the community sacrificed, navigated, and participated in community life—large and small. Two families of the same time period are a good example. They are the families of Rebecca Veirs and the Beall women.

Born on a farm in Maryland in 1833, Rebecca Veirs married at age twenty into a local prominent family. In 1880, she filed for divorce. As Veirs claimed in court, her husband was a habitual drunkard incapable of taking care of himself and supporting his family. She also claimed he was abusive and violent toward her and their children. Veirs asked the judge not only for a divorce but also for possession of the family farm, custody of their minor children, alimony, and money to pay the attorney's fees—rights she could not claim for herself in the 1840s but could by the 1880s. Although the court granted only a separation, not a divorce, the judge did grant Veirs everything else, including that her husband paid her attorney's fees.[17] But that is not the end of the story. Veirs took advantage of her new status and rights. She purchased, developed, and sold land in

Mary A. van Balgooy

her hometown and kept her earnings as a married woman. And she founded and led a woman's association to manage the town's long-neglected cemetery into a successful business.[18]

As I continued to research women in my town, I found the Beall women living across the street from Rebecca Veirs also a striking example of women living through this period and exercising their rights. The Beall-Dawson House interprets the lives of the Beall and Dawson families using a traditional timeline of family and U.S. events. They concentrate on the marriage of Upton and Jane Beall, birth of their children, construction of their home, Upton's business activities including slaveholding, visits from important political and military men (John Quincy Adams, Marquis de Lafayette, General George McClellan), Upton's early death, and how his wife, daughters, and extended family lived. In this narrative, the Beall women are portrayed as wealthy females entertaining elite society in a domestic setting.

However, applying a women's rights timeline to the family, a different picture emerges that is much more striking, relevant, and engaging where the women are not passive but active players who took advantage of opportunities and risks during the nineteenth century. When Upton died in 1827, he left Jane, age thirty-four, one-third of the estate and the rest to his three surviving young daughters (in accordance with the law at the time). Jane did not remarry, thereby retaining her property for herself, and ran the family estate until she died in 1849. What is significant is that she was a single mother with limited rights in a growing town and perhaps more successful than her husband in business. Her daughters, who also never married, inherited the full estate and more. The middle daughter managed the property, declaring herself in the 1860 census as a farmer. In 1863, the youngest daughter, Margaret, manumitted their slaves by compensation and later sold land to them. By 1870, only Margaret Beall was still living. When the railroad came through, she was the first to take the opportunity and go into development. She sold her land, building the town into a larger community. And she realized all that she had done: in the 1900 census, the eighty-three-year-old Margaret listed herself as a capitalist. By using the timeline I developed, a new image of these women emerges, good and bad, with many topics to discuss and linked with visitors' own lives.

It is very easy to get caught up in the particulars of a woman or man's lifespan and/or traditional timelines, leading sites to miss the overarching story of people's lives. By creating a different timeline, historic sites may discover a new story that is much more intriguing and important in understanding the men and women who lived and worked at a site.

4. Gender as a Social Construct

As women historians put into practice the concept of difference, the differences between the sexes and how people construct meaning became a powerful analytical tool. In 1986, Joan Wallach Scott wrote an article entitled "Gender: A Useful Category of Historical Analysis." It demonstrates how gender was a social construction itself, how the very meaning of the categories "man" and "woman" varied according to time, context, and place; how these categories developed into roles and identities for men and women to fulfill and became perceived as natural; how issues of power and rights played into these definitions of masculinity and femininity; and how these social structures affected the lives and experiences of ordinary people.[19]

So how does one use gender as an analytical tool? By asking historical questions about a woman's era, experiences, and place whether it pertains to status or location. What were the expected roles of women at the time? Did it constrain a woman in her pursuit of an education, a skill, or a job? How did it vary by region, class, and/or race and ethnicity? Or turning the question around: It is not that women could participate in the war, but could they participate like men? Could women conduct business like men? Earn an education like men? What might have prevented them? What might have been the barriers? How did women overcome them? The answers to these questions give a much greater understanding of women's perceived and actual roles in society at a particular time. Rosie the Riveter/WWII Homefront National Historical Park in Richmond, California, takes on gender as one of its primary interpretive themes and successfully illustrates how ideas and beliefs about women, men, and race were formed, supported, and transformed during World War II and after.[20]

Through temporary and permanent interactive exhibits in the restored Ford Motor Company Assembly Plant, visitors confront how the government mounted a campaign with Rosie the Riveter as a national heroine embracing her patriotic duty to work in the military industry but not giving up her femininity as a woman and housewife. The exhibit shows how women responded but under different circumstances from men (e.g., dealing with childcare, housing, and unemployment after the war). As one visitor summed up her visit: "The history covered here leaves you reeling. Would the country have recovered as quickly from the Great Depression without the war? Where would women (and women's equality) be today without the chance we had during the war to work outside the home? How did they expect women and other minority groups to just go back to their menial positions after they had had a taste of meaningful work, greater respect, etc.?"[21]

Using gender as a key tool changes how we think about women, including the stories of Betsy Ross, Amelia Earhart, farm women, enslaved women, female workers, and even men such as Herbert Hoover. It is a tool that makes us "see" all the actors playing their equally significant parts in the story. More important, it allows visitors to relate their own experiences to those in the past, giving them examples of how they might respond and bring about change in their lives and communities.

5. Public vs. Private Realms

The last accomplishment of women's history has been wiping out or blurring the lines between what historians call public and private spheres. In 1966, Barbara Welter wrote the pioneering work "The Cult of True Womanhood: 1820–1860," laying out the concept of "separate spheres" in mid-nineteenth-century America, where men and women occupied two very different worlds.[22] Women occupied the private sphere of family and home, while men inhabited the wider world of politics, work, and public life. Welter's essay serves as a foundation for later important works, but the limits of the separate spheres model soon became apparent. African American, working-class, and immigrant women as well as southern and western women did not manifest this pattern. And it seemed that the white, northern, middle-class women that Welter focuses on had more in common with the men of their own economic and social class. As more research and studies came out, women scholars began to dismiss the idea of separate spheres and started to demonstrate that the line between public and private was much more fluid and complex than believed.

Even though historians broke away from this theory, many historic sites, including those that interpret a different time period and region, continued to portray women in the private sphere of the home. But what is the better story to connect visitors to a site? The stereotypical angel

Mary A. van Balgooy

managing her home and children, or a wife and mother such as Elizabeth Cady Stanton fighting for women's rights? Or Harriet Beecher Stowe writing *Uncle Tom's Cabin*? Or Frances Seward, a woman in poor health, supporting the women's rights movement as well as hiding runaway slaves in her basement?[23] Women may have been restricted in what they could do, but they were active and did contribute to the public realms of society whether it may be religion, philanthropy, politics, or business.

The Molly Brown House Museum in Denver, Colorado, had to contend with such a characterization of Margaret Brown, famous to most of the American public as a survivor of the *Titanic* disaster. Not only did museum staff have to deal with this mythic role, but they also had to deal with stereotypes about western women—in this case, an uneducated woman who became wealthy and worked to create the perfect domestic sphere in the Wild West. All of which obscured her real life and contributions to society and the historical significance of women in the West. In the 2000s, the Molly Brown House tackled these myths to reveal the actual Margaret Brown in its tour and exhibits—"an educated, well-traveled social activist who influenced national and even international politics."[24] Through research, historians and staff discovered how Brown used her wealth and influence on issues such as women's suffrage, workers' rights, and the juvenile justice system. They also learned about her continual pursuit of education. In the end, her life showed she was not an ostentatious lady in the private sphere of the home entertaining the upper classes but a woman, wife, and mother who actively took part in society to enhance and enrich people's lives.[25]

* * * * *

Many historic house museums have interpreted women at a superficial level because of the tools at hand. By incorporating these five tools of women's history—difference, new sources, different timelines, gender, and looking at women outside the home—into research and interpretation, sites can delve deeper into women's lives, expand their knowledge about their experiences and contributions, and tell the important role they played in history, perhaps offering an even a richer story than that of the principal character of the house.

The Bradford House in Duxbury, Massachusetts, did just that. Faced with low attendance and a house in need of major restoration, staff looked for new stories to engage visitors, donors, and the community. Digging into their collections, they found the women of Bradford House even more extraordinary than Captain Gershom, the main subject of the tour. Revealing this new information about the women of Bradford House, bringing their stories to the forefront, the organization raised the money needed to restore the house and reinterpret the site (see Figure 16.2). Not only have they seen an increase in attendance, but it has been well received with local schools because the new interpretation clearly aligns with their lessons in topics such as abolition, civic involvement, and slavery.[26] And their peers have taken notice of this exemplary project. In 2018, they won an American Association for State and Local History Award of Merit (Leadership in History Awards).[27] They are a model for other historic houses to follow.

The reinterpretation of the Betsy Ross House, Molly Brown House Museum, and Bradford House demonstrate how women were visible in all sorts of activities and major events and that their stories are just as powerful as men's. What differs were the tools to find them. And when you have the right tools, historic sites can offer a new narrative that is more relevant, striking, and transformative to a visitor.

Figure 16.2 By shifting the focus of exhibitions to the women who lived in the house, the Bradford House in Massachusetts has increased engagement with visitors, donors, and the community. *Source:* Max A. van Balgooy.

Notes

1. One approach that historic house museums have taken to women's history is to research and interpret the preservation of a site where women have been involved. Their stories have proved to be just as important and compelling as that of the site's main character. See Bonnie Hurd Smith, "Women's Voices: Reinterpreting Historic House Museums," in *Her Past Around Us: Interpreting Sites for Women's History*, Polly Welts Kaufman and Katharine T. Corbett, eds. (Malabar, FL: Krieger Publishing Company, 2003). See also Patricia West, *Domesticating History: The Political Origins of America's House Museums* (Washington, DC: Smithsonian Institution, 1999).
2. Patricia Mooney-Melvin, "Professional Historians and the Challenges of Redefinition," in *Public History: Essays from the Field,* James B. Gardner and Peter S. LaPaglia, eds. (Malabar, FL: Krieger Publishing Company, 1999), 7-9; Julie Des Jardins, *Women and the Historical Enterprise in America: Gender, Race, and the Politics of Memory, 1880-1945* (Chapel Hill: The University of North Carolina Press, 2003), 20-22.
3. See *More Work for Mother: The Ironies of Household Technology from the Open Hearth to the Microwave* by Ruth Schwartz Cowan (New York: Basic Books, 1983).
4. Gerda Lerner, *Living with History/Making Social Change* (Chapel Hill: The University of North Carolina Press, 2009), 166-68. For the current state of the field, please refer to Cornelia H. Dayton and Lisa Levenstein, "The Big Tent of U.S. Women's and Gender History: A State of the Field," *Journal of American History* 99, no. 3 (December 2012): 793-817.
5. For examples, see *Westering Women and the Frontier Experience: 1800-1915* by Sandra L. Myres (Alburquerque: University of New Mexico Press, 1982); *Unequal Sisters: A Multi-Cultural Reader in U.S. Women's History* edited by Vicki L. Ruiz and Ellen Carol Dubois (New York: Routledge, 1999); *Within the Plantation*

Household: Black and White Women of the Old South by Elizabeth Fox-Genovese (Chapel Hill: The University of North Carolina Press, 1988); *Ar'n't I a Woman?: Female Slaves in the Plantation South* by Deborah Gray White (New York: W. W. Norton & Company, 1999); *Out to Work: A History of Wage-Earning Women in the United States* by Alice Kessler-Harris (New York: Oxford University Press, 2003).

6. Throughout this chapter, I am using the last names of women rather than their first names to put them on equal standing with men.

7. Marla R. Miller, *Betsy Ross and the Making of America* (New York: Henry Holt and Company, 2010).

8. Susan Ware, *Still Missing: Amelia Earhart and the Search for Modern Feminism* (New York: W. W. Norton & Co., 1993); Susan Ware, "Writing Women's Lives: One Historian's Perspective," *Journal of Interdisciplinary History,* 40, no. 3 (2010): 428–30.

9. See www.AmeliaEarhartMuseum.org.

10. Sally McMurry, *Families and Farmhouses in Nineteenth-Century America: Vernacular Design and Social Change* (Knoxville: The University of Tennessee Press, 1997).

11. J. Ritchie Garrison, review of *Families and Farmhouses in Nineteenth-Century America: Vernacular Design and Social Change* by Sally McMurry, *Journal of the Society of Architectural Historians* 49, no. 3 (September 1990): 354.

12. National Park Service and the Organization of American Historians, *Exploring a Common Past: Interpreting Women's History in the National Park Service* (Washington, DC: National Park Service, 1996), 9. This booklet has been updated twice and is available online at http://www.npshistory.com/agency_history.htm.

13. Visit https://www.nps.gov/heho/learn/historyculture/herbert-hoover.htm for more information.

14. Linda K. Kerber, *Women of the Republic: Intellect and Ideology in Revolutionary America* (New York: W. W. Norton & Co., 1980), xi.

15. Joan Kelly, *Women, History, and Theory: The Essays of Joan Kelly* (Chicago: University of Chicago Press, 1984), 19–50.

16. In developing a timeline for women, consult reference books such as *The Routledge Historical Atlas of Women in America* by Sandra Opdycke (New York: Routledge, 2000); *The State of Women in the World Atlas* by Joni Seager (New York: Penguin Books, 1997); and *Where Women Stand: An International Report on the Status of Women in 140 Countries* by Naomi Neft and Ann D. Levine (New York: Random House, 1997). These references connect women to particular places and also place women in an international context for a comparison of women's lives, rights, and experiences. Other books to refer to include *Born for Liberty: A History of Women in America* by Sara M. Evans (New York: The Free Press, 1989) and *Women and the American Experience: A Concise History* by Nancy Woloch (New York: McGraw-Hill, Inc., 2001).

17. Montgomery County [Maryland] Equity Papers, MSA-T415, Box 65.

18. Mary A. van Balgooy, *Women Who Dared: A Guide to the Places in Rockville Where Women Dared to Challenge Expectations Both in Society and in Themselves* (Rockville, MD: Peerless Rockville Historic Preservation, Ltd., 2010), 8–9.

19. Race and class also play into gender relationships. For more information, see Joan W. Scott, "Gender: A Useful Category of Historical Analysis," *The American Historical Review* 91, no. 5 (December 1986): 1053–75, and Dayton and Levensten, "The Big Tent of U.S. Women's and Gender History," 795–97.

20. Rosie the Riveter/World War II Home Front National Historical Park, "General Management Plan/Environmental Assessment, Chapter 1: Background" (Washington, DC: National Park Service, 2009), 12. Founders called the National Historic Park "Rosie the Riveter" even though it interprets the experiences of women and men during this time. Naming or renaming a site that includes a woman's name or names can make a powerful statement in itself and convey to visitors the significant part women played in history.

21. Bfarly, Review, TripAdvisor.com. Accessed Aug. 25, 2017, https://www.tripadvisor.com/ShowUserReviews-g32964-d734959-r462488340-Rosie_the_Riveter_World_War_II_Home_Front_National_Historical_Park-Richmond_Califo.html#REVIEWS.

22. Barbara Welter, "The Cult of True Womanhood: 1820-1860," *American Quarterly* 18, no. 2 (July 1966): 151–74.

23. In the interpretation of these houses, their husbands are present but not necessarily the main character in the story because of their wives' powerful presence. Refer to the Elizabeth Cady Stanton House in Seneca Falls, New York; the Harriet Beecher Stowe House in Hartford, Connecticut; and the Seward House Museum in Auburn, New York.

24. Laura Harbold, "Beyond Unsinkable: The Real Molly Brown," in *Humanities* (May/June 2007), https://www.neh.gov/humanities/2007/mayjune/feature/beyond-unsinkable.
25. Kristen Iversen, *Molly Brown: Unraveling the Myth* (Boulder, CO: Johnson Books, 2010).
26. DRHS Receives Award for Bradford Project, 2018, http://duxburyhistory.org/news/drhs-receives-award-for-bradford-project/.
27. Telephone conversation with Executive Director Erin McGough on Sept. 1, 2017; email with McGough on May 30, 2018.

Resources

There are too many books and articles to recommend, but here's a start that I hope will lead you to others:

Dayton, Cornelia H., and Lisa Levensten. "The Big Tent of U.S. Women's and Gender History: A State of the Field." *The Journal of American History* 99, no. 3 (2012): 793–817.
Kaufman, Polly Welts, and Katharine T. Corbett, eds. *Her Past Around Us: Interpreting Sites for Women's History.* Malabar, FL: Krieger Publishing Company, 2003.
West, Patricia. *Domesticating History: The Political Origins of America's House Museums.* Washington, DC: Smithsonian Institution Press, 1999.

Mary A. van Balgooy

Chapter 17

Where the Magic Happened

Historic Homes as Sites of Intimacy

SUSAN FERENTINOS

All museums are sex museums. So claims cultural scholar Jennifer Tyburczy, and I have to agree with her. Wittingly or not, museums play a role in enforcing or challenging existing assumptions about sex, gender, and societal power. Yet, while a few museums in the United States (and still more elsewhere) have boldly embraced this role and explicitly focus on sexuality (the Museum of Sex in New York City, the World Erotic Art Museum in Miami Beach, and the Leather Museum in Chicago, for instance), historic house museums have been far more reticent in exploring the "sexual architectures" that structure domestic space. I suggest that it is high time to change this situation.[1]

Now, to be clear, when I refer to sexuality, I am talking about far more than simply sexual intercourse between a man and a woman. Instead, I take a broad approach that encompasses a gamut of topics from biological urges and private desire to cultural customs, moral instruction, and power relations. This chapter maps out my ideas for incorporating the history of sexuality into historic house interpretation. I begin with an introduction to the historical study of sexuality—why it is a valid area of inquiry and what, exactly, we mean when we use the word "sexuality." I then present some of the ways historic house museums are currently interpreting sexuality-related topics. From there, I discuss how museum staff might go about learning more about the history of sexuality, and finally, I offer suggestions on how to incorporate this information into interpretive programming at historic house museums.

Why Consider the History of Sexuality?

Historic house museums have both practical and intellectual reasons for incorporating the history of sexuality into their interpretation. To begin with the most obvious, what *better* place to explore physical intimacy than in that most private of settings, the home. Domestic space is a common site of sexual expression, and it is where most children in the past were conceived, born, and taught the morals and manners of the culture to which they belonged. In truth, historic house museums already reference sexuality in various forms. If the situation seems otherwise, as Alison Oram points out, it is simply because the house is presenting a conventional, uninterrogated story that relies on cultural tropes of heterosexual love and marriage. Yet, quite often, houses have much richer and complex tales to tell.[2]

In addition, sexuality is a topic that most people can relate to on some level. It provides a captivating window onto the past, familiar enough that visitors can see the commonality between themselves and previous generations, while also conveying enough historical difference to reveal the culturally contingent nature of something that may seem to the average person to be a biological force, unaffected by change over time or by cultural assumptions. In her memoir of serving ten years as the curator at the Museum of Sex in New York City, Sarah Forbes writes, "Every exhibition should be filled with a few sticky moments, displays so engaging, shocking, beautiful, or inciting that they force a patron to stop, read, and absorb."[3] Sexuality can serve as that sticky moment in a house museum.

In a more academic vein, the history of sexuality is an established subfield within historical scholarship, having developed over the last fifty years. Its growth was related to the profession's increased focus on the ways race, class, and gender shape all facets of society. With these new approaches, historians began to see sexuality as integral to our understandings of difference in the United States. As Elizabeth Reis succinctly puts it, "Attitudes toward sex play a significant role in setting and maintaining the frontiers of gender, ethnicity, race, class, and religion, even the threshold that separates childhood from adulthood."[4]

John D'Emilio and Estelle Freedman concur, stating that "the history of sexuality in the United States has been, and no doubt will continue to be, characterized by a tangle of power relations that constantly reconstruct sexual norms." And this is perhaps the most compelling reason to consider the history of sexuality. Sexuality is all about power, and studying it can offer a stunningly clear vision of who has power in a given situation and who does not. By analyzing sexual mores over time—and considering whom they benefitted—we get closer to understanding where we as a society have come from and the ways that many of our own contemporary cultural assumptions are grounded in exercises of power.[5]

Relevant Sexuality Topics

Within the realm of sexuality, we encounter a wide array of topics, ranging from the explicit (oral sex, incest) to the prosaic (marriage, pregnancy, adolescence). Admittedly, some subjects are better suited to public tours than others, although I urge readers to push themselves a bit in their assumptions about what is possible within the structure of a house museum. Ten years ago, hardly any history museums were discussing lesbian, gay, bisexual, transgender, queer (LGBTQ) history; yet now, a museum that has *not* explored this topic may well give the impression of being behind the times. Below, I outline some topics within the history of sexuality that are likely to be relevant in historic house interpretation.

1. Sexual Behavior

Obviously, the concept of sexuality includes sexual behavior, be it heterosexual or homosexual, intercourse or other types of pleasuring, a solo or a group activity. However, behavior is only one aspect of sexuality—and a difficult one to interpret at that. Historical sources seldom discuss the sexual activities specific people engaged in, and so finding historical information about past residents of a specific house is unlikely to be a fruitful effort. As such, staff at house museums may find it easier to begin interpreting sexuality with topics other than sex acts.

2. Courtship and Marriage

Sexuality also includes courtship and marriage, both common topics on historic house tours. Yet, although house museums frequently mention these topics, they often do so without providing any historical analysis, as if these institutions were timeless and a familiarity with these customs in the twenty-first century is sufficient to understand the nuances of courtship and marriage in a different historical era (see Figure 17.1).

In reality, however, people have understood the purpose of marriage differently at different points in history and among different subcultures, such as those based on race, class, or religion.

Figure 17.1 Commonplace activities, such as marriage, can serve as a jumping-off point for discussions of sexual norms and moral values in different eras. This image pictures a World War II–era wedding at St. Andrew's Church photographed by the Matson Photo Service. The original photograph is labeled simply, "Lang Wedding." Photo courtesy of G. Eric and Edith Matson Photograph Collection, Library of Congress.

Eighteenth-century yeomen may have understood marriage primarily as the creation of a household economy involving two people joining economic forces and creating additional laborers in the form of children. Urban tradespeople in the Early Republic may have seen marriage as a patriotic exercise aimed at creating future thoughtful citizens of the democratic experiment. Elite families of the Old South may have approached marriage as the joining of dynasties and fortunes, and middle-class professionals in the late twentieth century probably saw love and affinity as the most important requirements to a successful marriage. Changing understandings of marriage shed important light into the larger contours of a given era.[6]

In addition, the perceived purpose of marriage influenced the ways people went about finding potential spouses. A potential mate's work ethic is revealed in environments that may not be conducive to romance. Religious devotion may be nonnegotiable if one sees marriage as preparation for God's kingdom, whereas an affectionate nature becomes more important when love is seen as an essential component to a happy marriage. Furthermore, courting tended to take place within the family home when compatible family status was deemed a requirement for a successful marriage. Courting became "dating" and moved to commercial entertainment venues around World War I, at the same time that engagement with consumer culture, like marriage, became a mark of entry into adult status. Not incidentally, the shift "from front porch to back seat" also coincided with a rise in premarital sexual activity in the United States.[7]

And even amid these changing standards and expectations, some individuals within U.S. society have always chosen to forego marriage, sometimes even courtship. What can these alternative choices reveal?[8]

3. Pregnancy, Childbirth, and Child Rearing

Changing ideas about sexuality also influence pregnancy, childbirth, and child rearing. While pregnancy is a common result of heterosexual intercourse, birth rates have changed over time and thus reveal insight into changing expectations and lived realities. Birth rates were higher when children were an accepted source of labor within the household economy. Birth rates declined in the mid- to late nineteenth century, in conjunction with an increasingly romanticized idea of children as precious creatures whose innocence should be protected and indulged. The means of birth control available at a given time—herbs, breastfeeding, rhythm, condoms, diaphragms, the pill—is also relevant and touches on the history of medicine, law, and the cultural importance placed on motherhood.[9]

Once children arrived, they needed to be reared, and this included being schooled in acceptable manners and comportment, as well as the skills and knowledge they would need to be adult members of society. The messages children received about their bodies and their desires, the degree to which they were exposed to sex (in the barnyard or in communal sleeping quarters, for example), and what they were taught about the relationship between sexual expression and sin indicate cultural anxieties and foretell a future generation's comfort or discomfort with their sexual impulses.[10]

4. Race, Class, and Gender

As mentioned earlier, sexuality is a necessary component of understanding race, class, and gender in U.S. history. Different groups have operated under different rules of propriety, and plotting out the many subtle (and not-so-subtle) parameters of sexual access illuminates the structures of power. In a similar vein, the myriad strictures governing who can do what with whom and which activities are considered "normal" for a given group provide a clear illustration of the concept of intersectionality. In the words of Megan Springate: "intersectionality is the recognition that categories of difference . . . including—but not limited to—race, ethnicity, gender, religion/ creed, generation, geographic location, sexuality, age, ability/disability, and class intersect to shape the experiences of individuals; that identity is multidimensional. These identities are not mutually exclusive but interdependent."[11]

We can see intersectionality at work when we consider the different approaches to the sexuality of various groups. For example, generally speaking, women's sexuality has been a source of cultural anxiety throughout much of U.S. history—marked by various efforts to control female sexual expression through cultural attitudes, laws, patriarchal family structures, the chaperone tradition, the importance given to reputation, and the threat of rape, to name but a few. However, this control played out quite differently for women of different races and classes. For example, slaveholding men of the Old South exercised control over the sexuality of white women (their wives and daughters) quite differently than over the sexuality of the African American women they enslaved. Similarly, several historians have demonstrated the many ways medical understandings of sexual deviance carried heavy connotations of racial and class difference, and Jennifer Tyburczy has explored the ways museums have reinforced these associations as well.[12]

Richmond National Battlefield, in an effort to introduce a gendered analysis into its interpretation, hosted a Bread Riot walking tour (outside park boundaries) considering this historical event through the lens of gender. As part of the tour, guides noted that "male observers tried to strip the women [protesters] entirely of any semblance of female respectability (and thus prevent the rioters from attaining one of their prize goals) by referring to the mob as 'a handful of prostitutes.'" This is a clear example of the ways that stepping outside of proper gender roles (by engaging in public protest, for instance) is often construed as a violation of the sexual and social order, illustrated here by the way that the women's demand for food was conflated with lower-class sexual deviance.[13]

Likewise, the sexual components of the history of race in the United States cannot be ignored, and yet they too often *are* ignored by those entrusted to share the past with a wide audience. Of particular note in this regard is the history of slavery. I contend that it is impossible to get a full sense of the system of racial slavery in the United States unless sexual violence is a substantial part of that story. Without a consideration of the implications of enslavers' complete access to the bodies and reproductive systems of those they enslaved—no matter what age—we cannot fully grasp the psychological and spiritual damage slavery inflicted upon this country. Nor can we understand the fuzziness of the historical (and contemporary) concept of racial "purity" or the utter irony of the late nineteenth-century Jim Crow laws designed to maintain it.[14]

While this discussion of the topics encompassed within the history of sexuality is by no means exhaustive, I hope it has demonstrated that the field is much broader than simply what people do when the lights are low. Instead, the larger topic of sexuality reminds us to consider questions of power within a given historical moment. In many ways, the intimate setting of a historic home provides the perfect site in which to explore attitudes, assumptions, and behaviors related to sexuality. To do so, however, requires some on-the-ground adjustments to the stories we tell within historic house museums, a task that occupies the remainder of this chapter.

Current State of Interpretation in the History of Sexuality

When visiting historic sites, I have seen many exciting opportunities to introduce the history of sexuality into interpretation, but overall, I am surprised by how few sites are employing substantive historical analysis of this topic. Too often, interpretation seems to rely on a tacit assumption that sex, marriage, and the meanings of parenthood are historical constants, carrying the same significance and connotations regardless of historical moment. In contrast, historians of sexuality approach sexuality largely as a social construction. Even though much of sex and reproduction are biologically determined, the choices, meanings, and emotions surrounding these areas of life are influenced—and to some extent, determined—by the time, place, and culture in which they occur. Thus, these concepts need to be interrogated when we find them in the past. We cannot assume—or let our visitors assume—that we know without investigation why people in the past chose to get married (or not), who their primary emotional and physical intimates were, or why they had children.

Furthermore, in the cases when change over time *is* acknowledged, many historic house museums give the impression that sexual mores have steadily relaxed over the course of U.S. history. Yet, the evidence does not support this conclusion. A topic as nuanced as sexuality has not followed a linear historical path. Strict moral codes can coexist with accepted behavior that may seem shocking to a modern eye. For example, late nineteenth-century middle-class courtship carried a relatively strict code of conduct. Chaperones governed the degree of intimacy (both physical and emotional) that an unmarried couple could engage in; a dizzying array of cultural norms governed the behavior of men and women when meeting new people; and young people, particularly women, often entered their marriage bed without the slightest bit of information to guide their first sexual encounters. Yet, during the same historical period, prostitution was a thriving trade in most urban areas and (not coincidentally) the rate of sexually transmitted diseases was alarmingly high. This evidence suggests that many middle-class men were active in two competing moral systems, treating prospective wives in a manner that emphasized their "higher virtues," while at the same time engaging in a bawdy subculture marked by male-oriented amusements, interclass socializing, and prostitution.[15]

Clearly, understanding the history of sexuality is more complicated than a simple march toward permissiveness. In addition to the contradictions of any given time, the very idea that we can say what behavior is or is not more permissive is problematic. One of the main points of studying the history of sexuality is to see that what might be considered shocking in one era is another era's norm. To build on the previous example, most middle-class visitors in our own era would probably find it more acceptable for two people in a romantic relationship to have sex before marriage than for a man to visit a brothel. Yet, during that earlier era, it would probably have been more shocking for a middle-class man to make sexual advances to a "respectable" woman of his own class to whom he was not engaged.

As a means of moving beyond our assumptions about sexuality in the past, below I describe some statements I have heard presented at historic house museums in passing, without substantive historical discussion. I have coupled these statements with some questions that might serve as starting points for deeper discussion in the future.

She never married.

- Do we have any evidence why she made this choice?
- How common was it during this era for women to remain unmarried? (In the aftermath of war, for example, simple demographics could mean there was a shortage of men of marrying age.)

- What were the implications of a woman remaining unattached to a man during this era?
- How did she survive economically outside the system of marriage?
- What parts of the world did she gain access to by not marrying? What parts of the world were closed to her as an unmarried woman?

She died in childbirth.

- Why did women die in childbirth so much more often in the past than they do now?
- What were some common ways that women died while giving birth?
- In a medical emergency, when a decision needed to be made between saving the mother or the infant, was there a cultural assumption of whose life would receive priority? What does this illustrate about the larger cultural assumptions of the era?
- How did the connection of marriage to sex and childbirth—and thus, possible death—affect young women's feelings about reaching adulthood and about their husbands?

He was an early European "settler" and took a Native American wife.

- What culture did the woman belong to? What were the marriage customs of this culture?
- Did this couple abide by the marriage traditions of the wife's culture, or by European understandings of marriage? Or is this relationship more accurately described as conquest of war than as a "marriage"?
- How were marriages between Europeans/European Americans and Native Americans understood during this period of colonization? Were these relationships understood differently by colonizers and by the relevant Native communities? Were such unions common?
- What role did this couple's children (and children of mixed Native/European ancestry generally) play in their respective communities?

By thinking more deeply about what stories may lie behind basic facts, we can begin to see the potential of placing such information within its historical context and sharing that context with visitors. Such an effort will both illustrate that people in earlier generations grappled with a similar degree of complexity as we do in our own times; it will also provide a more fleshed-out impression of your house's former occupants, increasing the likelihood that visitors will find something with which to relate to in the past.

Where to Find Sources on the History of Sexuality

Those of us who find the detective work involved in historical research to be part of its charm are in luck; researching the history of sexuality requires perseverance, creativity, and a love of sleuthing. Unlike many other aspects of history, sexual thoughts, desires, and actions—being both deeply personal and potentially scandalous—are sparsely documented in primary sources. References to sexuality do exist, however, and historians have managed to piece together an admirable body of secondary work by drawing on those materials.

Indeed, scholarship on the history of sexuality is a good place to start when exploring your site's connections to this topic. Secondary literature can offer a clearer sense of the type of information that can be revealed by considering questions related to sexuality. It can also provide a context for the particular period your site interprets. This context can be indispensable, as it will allow you to address questions that are not directly dealt with in the primary sources related to your site. For example, "We do not know, specifically, why she chose not to marry, but we do know that many educated women of her generation who had professional ambitions opted to remain single, out of concern that the demands of caring for a house, husband, and children would interfere with their ability to pursue employment outside the home."

In many situations, providing a larger historical context will have to suffice. If no personal writings related to sex, love, marriage, crushes, jealousies, infidelities, romantic friendships, pregnancy, childbirth, or moral instruction exist for your house's residents (and they may well not), providing the cultural context for such topics will still relay relevant information. In the happy event that specific evidence does survive (an adolescent diary, perhaps, or letters describing the emotional ups and downs of a pregnancy experienced far from one's female network of support), secondary literature can still ground individual anecdotes within larger historical trends.[16]

In addition to personal writings, other types of documents can also be useful sources of information. Laws criminalizing certain activities illustrate the parameters of acceptable sexual behavior in a given time and place. Arrest records and newspaper reports detailing arrests provide a glimpse of what people were actually doing, as well as a public commentary (in the case of newspaper accounts). Court records allow sexual criminals (as well as community members who witnessed the events) a chance to speak for themselves, to a certain extent, though researchers should also keep in mind the circumstances surrounding such testimony that may render it less than a reliable account. Like legal records, religious writing and sermons can be a source for uncovering sexual anxieties of a given time, as well as the parameters of what was considered moral behavior.

Sex and moral education materials aimed at children portray an idealized version of a given time, with which people's actual experiences might be compared. In a similar vein, romance novels, songs, and (in the twentieth century) movies can also be read as artifacts of cultural aspiration and anxiety. Medical writings and case studies offer additional information, although they often reveal more about the attitudes and assumptions of those in the medical profession than about their research subjects. Finally, oral history can be an invaluable source of study in the history of sexuality, particularly when trying to access the experiences of sexual outsiders, such as lesbians and gays, gender crossers, and prostitutes.

In any exploration of the past, but particularly when investigating sexuality and morals, researchers must be vigilant about studying evidence within the context of the time in which it was created, rather than simply applying modern categories to behavior in the past. One of the most common examples of such risks comes from LGBTQ history. Same-sex love and desire has carried a variety of different meanings over time, from being a republican ideal to a perfectly acceptable form of devotion to a category of mental illness. Thus, a love letter between two men would have quite different implications whether written during the revolutionary period, the 1840s, or the 1950s.[17]

Sharing the History of Sexuality with Visitors

Historic house museums can introduce the history of sexuality in ways large and small. It can be as simple as adding a few sentences of explanation and historical context after previously unexamined statements such as, "His parents did not approve of his interest in marrying Sarah." It can be as substantive as revamping your standard visitor tour to better interrogate the ways that sexual assumptions and stories permeate domestic space.

Possibilities abound. Plan an adults-only evening tour with cocktails and focus on the secrets about love, sex, desire, affection, and heartbreak that historic homes likely hold. This approach is similar to the LGBTQ social hour that Historic New England hosted at its Beauport site (Glouces-ter, Massachusetts) to herald the start of interpretation related to its owner's homosexuality. Put together an exhibit of historic lingerie, as did the Fashion Institute of Technology (New York City), and feature it in place of the traditional spring wedding dress event. Take inspiration from Two Chicks Walking Tours in New Orleans and offer a "History of Burlesque" tour through your local entertainment district led by (historically trained) contemporary burlesque dancers.[18]

The Woodlands National Historic Landmark in Philadelphia offers one example of the innovative potential of incorporating sexuality into interpretation. This site, originally the eighteenth-century estate of William Hamilton, struggled to find its interpretative raison d'être. Located in a city rife with stories of the nation's founders, the Woodlands represented the life of a wealthy bachelor who was more interested in being a gentleman gardener than a revolutionary, and in fact was twice tried for treason during the American Revolution. Woodlands staff were intrigued by the various ways that William Hamilton went against the patriotic image of "founding father," and they received funding from the Pew Center for the Arts & Humanities to explore this idea. Further research confirmed what the staff had already suspected—that Hamilton's primary emotional relationships were with other men (although there is no evidence that he had sexual relations with them); that he left a sizable inheritance to select members of his household staff, some of whom had previously been enslaved by Hamilton's relatives and may have been biologically related to him; and that Hamilton (who never married) adopted his brother's children when they were orphaned, including two nieces who never married.

Furthermore—to the surprise of all—the research revealed that Hamilton had also fathered a child out of wedlock, whom he never acknowledged as his son. As a result of this new research, a vivid tapestry of eighteenth-century life emerged, one that challenged the idea that "traditional American families" involved only heterosexual marriage and nuclear family. The site is currently in the process of planning how to incorporate these new findings into interpretive programming revolving around the question of "What is normal?," which will invite visitors to confront their own assumptions about the past and present.

I have already argued that incorporating the history of sexuality into your museum can enable your visitors to better relate to the past. This topic also has potential to increase the relevance of your site by providing a unique forum in which to explore contemporary issues. Numerous au-thors have elaborated on the idea of museums as one of the last physical spaces in which people can engage in civic dialogue.[19] Sexuality provides a rich field with which to involve your commu-nity in such conversations, as sexual politics promise to capture a good deal of attention in the upcoming years. Issues surrounding access to birth control and abortion; growing awareness of human trafficking; an increase in HIV transmission connected to the opioid epidemic; debates over how to address sexual assault on college campuses; changing understanding of same-sex relationships and transgender identities; criticism of Muslim immigrant communities for their understandings of female sexuality; and the conflation of Mexican immigrants (presumably all male) with rapists—such public debates provide a wide array of contemporary topics to consider within the museum environment.

President Lincoln's Cottage, a nonprofit National Monument in Washington, DC, provides a creative example of such an effort. The site is located on the grounds of the Armed Forces

Retirement Home, known as the Old Soldiers' Home in Lincoln's time. Abraham Lincoln and his family lived on the grounds for a total of a year of his presidency, mostly during summer months. While Lincoln developed many ideas and policies while living at the cottage, it is perhaps best known as the place where he developed the Emancipation Proclamation (freeing those who were enslaved in the rebel states).

Within such an environment, it is easy to imagine a traditional approach to interpreting the cottage—describing the furnishings (though, in fact, the site has opted to sparsely furnish the home) and the significance of our sixteenth president. Instead, staff at Lincoln's Cottage have made the bold decision to build on the legacy of the Emancipation Proclamation and brand the site as a "Home of Brave Ideas." The site now actively engages with all manner of contemporary issues, and some of these concern sexual topics. For example, using Lincoln's romantic, though probably not sexual, relationship with Joshua Speed as a starting point (the two lived together and shared a bed for nearly four years before each married), the site has offered programs exploring changing standards of male intimacy. In addition, the cottage hosts an exhibit and various programs looking at contemporary issues of human bondage, including sex trafficking, and connecting it to the issues of slavery prevalent during Lincoln's lifetime. By breaking out of staid ideas of what a historic presidential site can and should be, staff at Lincoln's Cottage have distinguished themselves among a sea of DC sites related to Lincoln, raised awareness of important and provocative issues, and lived up to their promise of being a Home of Brave Ideas.

Finally, because the history of sexuality is rife with secrets, silences, and a lack of sources, it becomes a perfect terrain on which to explore the current trend in history museums of "pulling back the curtain." Originating in the 2014 National Council on Public History presidential address given by Robert Weyeneth, "pulling back the curtain" refers to a trend of historical organizations becoming more transparent with their audiences, and involving them in the process of historical analysis. Rather than telling the audience what we as historians know about the past, we can instead give them some analytical tools and some evidence, and let them draw their own historical conclusions. This approach, Weyeneth argues, promotes a fuller understanding of the work that historians do and allows visitors to see how professional historians reach conclusions about the past. I find this to be a particularly effective approach when presenting sexual history, because truthfully, the evidence is often so scanty that solid conclusions are simply not possible. The sources tantalize, but do not offer definitive answers.[20]

* * * * *

By considering the ways that sexual assumptions, desires, and mores affected the lives of previous generations, historic house museums can open up new interpretive territory. The history of sexuality provides a way of accessing power relations in the past and does so in a way that can help visitors relate to historical agents as real people who struggled with many of the same issues that we do today (albeit within a different historical context). Opening your site to discussions of sexuality can lead the way to civic dialogue about contemporary issues and help reveal the historian's craft, by welcoming visitors to think about the past in new ways, using new tools.

Notes

1. Jennifer Tyburczy, "All Museums Are Sex Museums," *Radical History Review* 113 (Spring 2012): 199–211; Jennifer Tyburczy, *Sex Museums: The Politics and Performance of Display* (Chicago: The University of Chicago Press, 2016).

2. Alison Oram, "Sexuality in Heterotopia: Time, Space, and Love between Women in the Historic House," *Women's History Review* 21, no. 4 (September 2012): 533–51, doi:10.1080/09612025.2012.658178; see also Alison Oram, "Going on an Outing: The Historic House and Queer Public History," *Rethinking History* 15, no. 2 (June 2011): 189–207; James H. Sanders III, "The Museum's Silent Sexual Performance," *Museums & Social Issues* 3, no. 1 (Spring 2008): 15–25; Joshua G. Adair, "House Museums or Walk-In Closets? The (Non)Representation of Gay Men in the Museums They Called Home," in *Gender, Sexuality, and Museums*, ed. Amy K. Levin (New York: Routledge, 2010), 264–78.
3. Sarah Forbes, *Sex in the Museum: My Unlikely Career at New York's Most Provocative Museum* (New York: St. Martin's Press, 2016), 41.
4. Elizabeth Reis, ed., *American Sexual Histories* (Malden, MA: Blackwell Publishers, 2001), 3.
5. John D'Emilio and Estelle B. Freedman, *Intimate Matters: A History of Sexuality in America, Third Edition* (Chicago: University of Chicago Press, 2012), vii; see also Kathy Peiss, ed., *Major Problems in the History of American Sexuality: Documents and Essays* (Boston: Houghton Mifflin Co, 2002), xv–xvi; Susan Ferentinos, *Interpreting LGBT History at Museums and Historic Sites* (Lanham, MD: Rowman & Littlefield, 2015), 7; Victoria Harris, "Sex on the Margins: New Directions in the Historiography of Sexuality and Gender," *Historical Journal* 53, no. 4 (December 2010): 1085–1104; Leila J. Rupp, "What's Queer Got to Do with It?," *Reviews in American History* 38, no. 2 (June 2010): 189–98; Sharon Marcus, "Queer Theory for Everyone: A Review Essay," *Signs: Journal of Women in Culture & Society* 31, no. 1 (September 2005): 191–218.
6. Christina Simmons, *Making Marriage Modern: Women's Sexuality from the Progressive Era to World War II* (New York: Oxford University Press, 2009); Stephanie Coontz, *Marriage, a History: From Obedience to Intimacy or How Love Conquered Marriage* (New York: Viking, 2005); Nancy Cott, *Public Vows: A History of Marriage and the Nation* (Cambridge, MA: Harvard University Press, 2000); George Chauncey, *Why Marriage? The History Shaping Today's Debate over Gay Equality* (New York: Basic Books, 2004); Rebecca L. Davis, "'Not Marriage at All, but Simple Harlotry': The Companionate Marriage Controversy," *Journal of American History* 94, no. 4 (March 2008): 1137–63; Kristin Celello, *Making Marriage Work: A History of Marriage and Divorce in the Twentieth-Century United States* (Chapel Hill: University of North Carolina Press, 2009); Karen M. Dunak, *As Long as We Both Shall Love: The White Wedding in Postwar America* (New York: New York University Press, 2013).
7. Beth L. Bailey, *From Front Porch to Back Seat: Courtship in Twentieth-Century America* (Baltimore: Johns Hopkins University Press, 1988); Karen Lystra, *Searching the Heart: Women, Men, and Romantic Love in Nineteenth-Century America* (New York: Oxford University Press, 1989); Ellen K. Rothman, *Hands and Hearts: A History of Courtship in America* (New York: Basic Books, 1984); Rebecca J. Fraser, *Courtship and Love among the Enslaved in North Carolina* (Jackson: University Press of Mississippi, 2007).
8. John Gilbert McCurdy, *Citizen Bachelors: Manhood and the Creation of the United States* (Ithaca, NY: Cornell University Press, 2009); Howard P. Chudacoff, *The Age of the Bachelor: Creating an American Subculture* (Princeton: Princeton University Press, 1999); Trisha Franzen, *Spinsters and Lesbians: Independent Womanhood in the United States* (New York: New York University Press, 1996); Katherine Ott, "Spinsters, Confirmed Bachelors, and LGBTQ Collecting—O Say Can You See?," blog, *National Museum of American History* (August 19, 2014), http://blog.americanhistory.si.edu/osaycanyousee/2014/08/spinsters-confirmed-bachelors-and-lgbtq-collecting.html.
9. D'Emilio and Freedman, *Intimate Matters*, 242–55; Peiss, *Major Problems in the History of American Sexuality*, 308–36; Reis, *American Sexual Histories*, 250–79; Simone M. Caron, *Who Chooses?: American Reproductive History since 1830* (Gainesville: University Press of Florida, 2008); Judith Walzer Leavitt, *Brought to Bed: Childbearing in America, 1750 to 1950* (New York: Oxford University Press, 1986); Richard W. Wertz and Dorothy C. Wertz, *Lying-in: A History of Childbirth in America, Expanded edition* (New Haven, CT: Yale University Press, 1989); Andrea Tone, *Devices and Desires: A History of Contraception in America* (New York: Hill & Wang, 2001); Susan E. Klepp, *Revolutionary Conceptions: Women, Fertility, and Family Limitation in America, 1760-1820* (Chapel Hill: University of North Carolina Press, 2009); Elaine Tyler May, *America and the Pill: A History of Promise, Peril, and Liberation* (New York: Basic Books, 2010); Jacqueline H. Wolf, *Deliver Me from Pain: Anesthesia and Birth in America* (Baltimore: Johns Hopkins University Press, 2009).

10. Helen Lefkowitz Horowitz, *Rereading Sex: Battles Over Sexual Knowledge and Suppression in Nine-teenth-Century America* (New York: Knopf, 2002), 86-122; Ronald G. Walters, *Primers for Prudery: Sexual Advice to Victorian America* (Englewood Cliffs, NJ: Prentice-Hall, 1973); Jeffrey P. Moran, *Teaching Sex: The Shaping of Adolescence in the 20th Century* (Cambridge, MA: Harvard University Press, 2000); Steven Mintz, *Huck's Raft: A History of American Childhood* (Cambridge, MA: Belknap Press of Harvard University Press, 2004); Paula S. Fass and Mary Ann Mason, eds., *Childhood in America* (New York: New York University Press, 2000); Susan Ferentinos, "An Unpredictable Age: Sex, Consumption, and the Emergence of the American Teenager, 1900-1950" (Dissertation, Indiana University, 2005).

11. Megan Springate, "A Note on Intersectionality," in *LGBTQ America: A Theme Study of Lesbian, Gay, Bisexual, Transgender, and Queer History* (Washington, DC: National Park Foundation, 2016), 1-7; Cornelia H. Dayton and Lisa Levenstein, "The Big Tent of U.S. Women's and Gender History: A State of the Field," *Journal of American History* 99, no. 3 (December 2012): 793-817; Crystal N. Feimster, "The Impact of Racial and Sexual Politics on Women's History," *Journal of American History* 99, no. 3 (December 2012): 822-26, doi:10.1093/jahist/jas466; Siobhan B. Somerville, *Queering the Color Line: Race and the Invention of Homosexuality in American Culture*, Series Q (Durham, NC: Duke University Press, 2000).

12. D'Emilio and Freedman, *Intimate Matters*, 84-108; Peiss, *Major Problems in the History of American Sexuality*, 142-86; Somerville, *Queering the Color Line*; *Sex, Love, Race: Crossing Boundaries in North American History* (New York: New York University Press, 1999); Heather Lee Miller, "Sexologists Examine Lesbians and Prostitutes in the United States, 1840-1940," *NWSA Journal* 12, no. 3 (Fall 2000): 67-91; Jennifer Terry, *An American Obsession: Science, Medicine, and Homosexuality in Modern Society* (Chicago: University of Chicago Press, 1999), 114-18; Stephen C. Kenny, "The Development of Medical Museums in the Antebellum American South: Slave Bodies in Networks of Anatomical Exchange," *Bulletin of the History of Medicine* 87, no. 1 (Spring 2013): 32-62; Tyburczy, *Sex Museums*, 65-98.

13. Ashley Whitehead Luskey and Robert M. Dunkerly, "From Women's History to Gender History: Revamping Interpretive Programming at Richmond National Battlefield Park," *Civil War History* 62, no. 2 (2016): 149-69, doi:10.1353/cwh.2016.0049, quote from 157.

14. Diane Miller Sommerville, *Rape & Race in the Nineteenth-Century South* (Chapel Hill: University of North Carolina Press, 2004); Merril D. Smith, ed., *Sex without Consent: Rape and Sexual Coercion in America* (New York: New York University Press, 2001); Mary R. Block, "Rape Law in 19th-Century America: Some Thoughts and Reflections on the State of the Field," *History Compass* 7, no. 5 (September 2009): 1391-99, doi:10.1111/j.1478-0542.2009.00623.x; Wilma King, "'Prematurely Knowing of Evil Things': The Sexual Abuse of African American Girls and Young Women in Slavery and Freedom," *Journal of African American History* 99, no. 3 (Summer 2014): 173-96; Aliyyah I. Abdur-Rahman, "'The Strangest Freaks of Despotism': Queer Sexuality in Antebellum African American Slave Narratives," *African American Review* 40, no. 2 (Summer 2006): 223-37; Thomas A. Foster, "The Sexual Abuse of Black Men under American Slavery," *Journal of the History of Sexuality* 30, no. 3 (September 2011): 445-64.

15. Horowitz, *Rereading Sex*; Helen Lefkowitz Horowitz, *Attitudes Toward Sex in Antebellum America: A Brief History with Documents* (New York: Palgrave Macmillan, 2006).

16. For more on primary source methodology, see Timothy J. Gilfoyle, "Prostitutes in the Archives: Problems and Possibilities in Documenting the History of Sexuality," *American Archivist* 57, no. 3 (Summer 1994): 514-27; John D. Wrathall, "Provenance as Text: Reading the Silences around Sexuality in Manuscript Collections," *Journal of American History* 79, no. 1 (June 1992): 165-78; Estelle B. Freedman, "'The Burning of Letters Continues': Elusive Identities and the Historical Construction of Sexuality," *Journal of Women's History* 9, no. 4 (Winter 1998): 181-200.

17. David M. Halperin, *How to Do the History of Homosexuality* (Chicago: University of Chicago Press, 2002), 1-23; Leila J. Rupp, *A Desired Past: A Short History of Same-Sex Love in America* (Chicago: University of Chicago Press, 1999), 1-11.

18. Kenneth C. Turino, "The Varied Telling of Queer History at Historic New England Sites," in Ferentinos, *Interpreting LGBT History*, 132-35; "Two Chicks Walking Tours: The History of Burlesque," webpage, http://www.twochickswalkingtours.com/french-quarter-tour-history-of-burlesque.html. On the Fashion Institute of Technology exhibit, see Colleen Hill, *Exposed: A History of Lingerie* (New Haven: Yale University Press in association with the Fashion Institute of Technology, New York, 2014). Note, however, that at least one review of the exhibit called for greater attention to historical context for the artifacts. See

Ken Johnson, "Built on Historic Foundations: Review of A History of Lingerie at the Fashion Institute Museum," *New York Times*, June 12, 2014, online edition, https://www.nytimes.com/2014/06/13/arts/design/a-history-of-lingerie-at-the-fashion-institute-museum.html.

19. Bill Adair, Benjamin Filene, and Laura Koloski, eds., *Letting Go?: Sharing Historical Authority in a User-Generated World* (Philadelphia, Walnut Creek, CA: Pew Center for Arts & Heritage; Distributed by Left Coast Press, 2011); Robert R. Archibald, *The New Town Square: Museums and Communities in Transition* (Walnut Creek, CA: Alta Mira Press, 2004); Jennifer Barrett, *Museums and the Public Sphere* (Malden, MA: Wiley-Blackwell, 2011); Teresa Bergman, *Exhibiting Patriotism: Creating and Contesting Interpretations of American Historic Sites* (Walnut Creek, CA: Left Coast Press, 2013); Graham Black, *Transforming Museums in the Twenty-First Century: Developing Museums for Visitor Involvement* (Hoboken, NJ: Taylor & Francis, 2011), 143–65; Nina Simon, *The Participatory Museum* (Santa Cruz, CA: Museum 2.0, 2010).

20. Robert R. Weyeneth, "What I've Learned Along the Way: A Public Historian's Intellectual Odyssey," *The Public Historian* 36, no. 2 (May 1, 2014): 9–25, doi:10.1525/tph.2014.36.2.9. After Weyeneth's speech was published, NCPH hosted a series of blog posts exploring its implications. See http://ncph.org/history-at-work/tag/pulling-back-the-curtain/; especially Susan Ferentinos, "Lifting Our Skirts: Sharing the Sexual Past with Visitors," digital content, May 2014 issue, *Public History Commons: The Public Historian* (July 1, 2014), http://ncph.org/history-at-work/lifting-our-skirts/.

Recommended Resources

D'Emilio, John, and Estelle B. Freedman. *Intimate Matters: A History of Sexuality in America, Third Edition.* Chicago: University of Chicago Press, 2012.

Ferentinos, Susan. *Interpreting LGBT History at Museums and Historic Sites.* Lanham, MD: Rowman & Littlefield, 2015.

Forbes, Sarah. *Sex in the Museum: My Unlikely Career at New York's Most Provocative Museum.* New York: St. Martin's Press, 2016.

Levin, Amy K., ed. *Gender, Sexuality, and Museums: A Routledge Reader.* New York: Routledge, 2010.

Tyburczy, Jennifer. *Sex Museums: The Politics and Performance of Display.* Chicago: The University of Chicago Press, 2016.

Chapter 18

*Reflecting Race and Ethnicity
in House Museums*

JANE M. ELIASOF AND CLAUDIA OCELLO

In February 2017, thirty-five men and women gathered in the Founders' Room of the Crane House and Historic YWCA in Montclair, New Jersey, for an event that featured a tour of the buildings, speakers, and a tea. Although this sounds routine for a historic house, the event marked a seismic shift in the relationship between the Montclair Historical Society (now the Montclair History Center) and the African American community in town.

Until 2014, the building, known as the Crane House, had three distinct lives. Built by prominent local businessman Israel Crane in 1796, the house served as the Crane family home for more than one hundred years. From 1920 to 1965, the home served as headquarters for a segregated YWCA for African American women and girls. In 1965, after the house was moved to save it from demolition, the Montclair Historical Society's founders transformed the house into a historic house museum that told the story of Israel Crane in the late eighteenth and early nineteenth century primarily through decorative arts. The building's past as an integral and vital part of the African American community during the de facto segregation years was omitted.

Many African American women were hurt by this omission and feared that monies that could have gone to help them build their new YWCA would be funneled to the restoration of the Crane House. Fifty years later, that hurt persisted.

In 2014, after several years of research, the Crane House closed for four months and underwent an extensive restoration. When it reopened, the Crane House and Historic YWCA told a more inclusive story of the house's history: Israel Crane, his family, the enslaved workers, domestic servants, boarders who lived at the YWCA, women and girls who attended programs there, and the early preservationists who founded the Montclair Historical Society (see Figure 18.1).

The reinterpretation of the house was part of a multifaceted effort to tell the story of the YWCA from 1920 to 1965. The process began with a community gathering designed to solicit input and a scholars' panel designed to help guide research and place the Montclair YWCA within a broader

Figure 18.1 In an immersive experience, students gather in the 1940 Club Room at the Crane House and Historic YWCA to listen to short clips in which African American women talk about the discrimination they faced in the twentieth century and look through period copies of *Jet*, *Life*, and *Ebony* magazines. Photo by Kate Albright.

historical context. After researching archives and conducting oral histories, the Montclair History Center launched public programs related to African American history, a documentary based on the oral histories, a newly reinterpreted historic house museum, and new public and school tours based on the reinterpretation.

The changes did not instantly heal the fifty-year-old wounds. The healing was (and continues to be) a slow process of building bridges by offering quality and thoughtful programs and interpretive experiences.

> Changing the public's perception of who and what your organization is takes time, quality programming, and one-on-one outreach. *Jane M. Eliasof, Executive Director, Montclair History Center*

It's almost not surprising that race and ethnicities were—and sometimes still are—glossed over at best and, at worst, ignored in historic house museums. A quick survey of the founding dates of many historic house museums across the United States show their origins lie before or during the civil rights movement. Some of the most iconic historic houses/sites—Colonial Williamsburg (1926), Mount Vernon (1853), and Monticello (1923)—all explored the country's Founding Fathers, predominantly European wealthy white males.[1] While historians knew that women, enslaved people, and immigrants have a good deal to do with the founding of our country, early historic house proponents explored "the glory of the story" and "swept the 'dust' under the rug."

Jane M. Eliasof and Claudia Ocello

This status quo of white male dominance may have sufficed for a while in historic house museums. Visitors to the museums generally reflected the same demographics as the story the museums told. When attendance dropped off and many smaller historic house museums started to struggle finding an audience, they began a cold, hard look at themselves. Changes in demographics (such as more immigrants and African Americans in their neighborhoods) prompted some museums to consider that the stories they were telling were not relevant to these audiences. Digging deeper, some historic houses—like the Montclair History Center—realized they had an untold story. It became time to reframe the narrative to better serve the community, to allow previously unheard voices to be heard, or in some cases to forge new alliances with the changing demographics in their communities and embrace new stories and new opportunities for storytelling and linking the past and present.

How can a historic house/historic site make these changes? What's the best plan of action? Should the interpretation be changed to reflect the diverse stories, or the exhibits/period rooms themselves? What else needs to be done to become more relevant to changing demographics and new audiences? Unfortunately, there's no one "right" way to go about the process. To begin, it could help to look carefully at the owners of the house for stories that are not being told such as those of enslaved people, or immigrants employed as domestic servants. Sometimes sites have gaps in their histories, which can be glossed over in interpretation because of (perceived) lack of information about that time period (hint: dig deeper with your research). Some sites decided to explore a lesser known aspect of the owner/residents' personality, employment, or background as a jumping-off point for inclusivity. Instead of going deeper into the history they already knew, some house museums viewed themselves more broadly around a theme or idea inherent in their story. It's helpful to know your local audience (or who it isn't, as the case may be) and what issues/ideas might be relevant to them. Being open and more receptive to exploring a new, hidden, or diverse perspective is often the first step in the transformation to a broader, more inclusive audience for historic house museums.

Sites around the United States that have "reconstructed" themselves around stories of race and ethnicity appear to have two things in common:

- the sites explored their history in the context of their current community to find this story;
- the story is relevant to the site itself, not layered on as an "extra."

The Montclair History Center didn't go into their project looking for a new audience demographic. They wanted to tell the complete and organic history of the house including its "three lives": the Crane family years, the YWCA years, and its early years as a historic house museum. Using these three periods of significance and the people who inhabited the house as a jumping-off point, the Montclair History Center now interprets the house and offers programs that relate to early American history, the history of Montclair, the historic preservation movement, the African American story, civil rights, and immigration. Their mission is to "share the stories of the people" who have made the community what it is today, not just the stories of the wealthy white men.

Across the country, San Francisco Heritage's Haas-Lilienthal House is undergoing a similar transformation. Founded in 1971 to ensure the continuity of the city's architectural legacy, San Francisco Heritage played a leading role in establishing preservation protections. Today, they continue to advocate for historical resources, lead education programs, and offer tours and rentals of the Haas-Lilienthal House.

For forty-five years, docents have led visitors through this Gilded Age house telling the story of William Haas, an early Jewish pioneer, his family, and his descendants. In 2015, they undertook a $4.3 million capital campaign earmarked for physical and interpretive improvements to the house.

In the same year, San Francisco Heritage convened a panel of interpretive specialists, representing an array of disciplines including decorative arts, immigration, and architecture, to explore new ways and technologies to interpret the Haas-Lilienthal House. From the scholars' essays, San Francisco Heritage agreed on the following primary interpretive strategy: "The Haas-Lilienthal House reveals how immigrants shape the continually evolving architectural and cultural identity of San Francisco, preserving ties to the past while embracing hopes for the future."[2]

Because of the extensive research that has been done on Haas as a Bavarian Jewish man, as well as the Jewish influence on the development of San Francisco, this theme will likely be elevated in the final interpretation. The key challenge, according to President and CEO Mike Buhler, has been accurately telling the story of the servants with any depth. "We know their names and ethnicities, but very little else other than anecdotal evidence without third-party evidence."[3]

> Have a good understanding of what you have and what you are lacking. Set realistic goals about what to include in the final plan. Is it enough to have a series of anecdotes? *Mike Buhler, President and CEO, San Francisco Heritage*

When the Haas-Lilienthal House reopened in 2018, it had undergone an extensive restoration, with rooms returned to their original color palette. A permanent photo exhibit and orientation video now connect the Haas-Lilienthal House with the organization's broader mission of historic preservation throughout San Francisco. Tour guides interpret the house and its inhabitants, touching on architecture, technology, urban development, immigration, entrepreneurship, and cultural identity in San Francisco and the West.

Sometimes it's an outside catalyst that encourages the reflection that can lead to change. In Charleston, South Carolina, the transformation of the Aiken-Rhett House Museum took place in 1995 when the Historic Charleston Foundation purchased the property. Prior to the acquisition, a Chicago radio DJ had visited some of the historic houses in Charleston and, in a scathing commentary, remarked on the absence of any discussion on slavery.

When the Aiken-Rhett House Museum opened to the public in 1996, they wanted to make sure slavery was a prominent piece of their story. Under the guidance of Executive Director Carter Hudgins, tours included the family home as well as the enslaved people's quarters, but even that wasn't enough to ensure consistency of their story. As Valerie Perry, manager of the Aiken-Rhett House Museum, recalls, "In the early years, our docents went rogue. Tours took anywhere from forty-five minutes to an hour and a half. Some docents weren't spending any time talking about African American history; others were really good at it." In addition, some docents couldn't finish the tour before the next group was starting. "We developed an audio tour because of the challenges we had with our staff."[4] The tour begins outside the house, then moves into the enslaved people's quarters, then finally into the family home. The objective is to level the playing field and ensure African American history is not an afterthought or omitted entirely.

Jane M. Eliasof and Claudia Ocello

Twenty years later, the audio tours, which are updated as new information becomes available, are still an effective way to ensure consistency in tours. Paid docents are stationed to respond to visitors' questions. Perry says, "We train docents to underscore how complicated and complex slavery was and to use words that engage people rather than shut the conversation down." Even with consistent training, docents may still revert to platitudes and stereotypes. Perry recalls one docent who insisted on saying "slaves were treated well," despite the lack of evidence to support it. "We know he had a truly huge investment in human cargo with a conservative estimate of 800 enslaved workers. Logically, he would want to protect that investment. But he probably didn't know his people. They were enslaved, they couldn't leave the plantation."[5]

> Educate your staff the right way and consistently. Concentrate on the use of words, which can either engage people or shut the conversation down. *Valerie Perry, Manager, Aiken-Rhett House Museum*

The Nathaniel Russell House Museum, also owned by the Historic Charleston Foundation, follows a similar approach to interpreting their house. On docent-led tours, in every room visitors hear about both family members and enslaved people. "Our Executive Director Katharine Robinson hasn't wavered," says Perry. "She feels it's imperative we consistently tell the African American story."[6]

The Royall House and Slave Quarters in Medford, Massachusetts, has the same imperative, but with a twist. In the South, visitors know slavery was a key part of the culture and economy. In the North, visitors at historic house museums are often surprised it existed. Isaac Royall, for whom the original five-hundred-acre estate was named, has the dubious distinction of heading up the largest slaveholding family in Massachusetts, with more than sixty enslaved workers.[7] Royall made his fortune growing sugar in Antigua, and trading sugar, rum, and slaves. He brought his wealth back to his estate just outside Boston.

Although the house opened as a historic house museum in 1898, it took the organization nearly one hundred years to address the issue of slavery, despite having the only extant freestanding slave quarters (albeit uninterpreted) in the North. "The Royall House was a sleepy old historic house museum that told the story of a rich, white man," Co-president and Treasurer Peter Gittleman recalls. "The trigger for me was when the Bay State Historical League celebrated its 100th year in 2005 and went out of business in its 101st. We couldn't take it for granted that we were going to be open. Something had to change."[8]

Today, the Royall House and Slave Quarters has an inclusive mission to "explore the meanings of freedom and independence before, during and since the American Revolution, in the context of a household of wealthy Loyalists and enslaved Africans."[9] To that end, they offer programs and public and school tours. They are unapologetic about the Royall family's involvement with slavery, noting on their website that their goal is to "tell their story accurately, in the context of Europe and America's legacy of chattel slavery, and in particular of the North's direct colonial-era involvement and continued complicity in slavery."[10]

At the time the transition was underway, many of the board members were aging out and, according to Gittleman, just didn't have the energy to either block or adapt to the changes. New people joined the board who enthusiastically supported the changes.

Not everyone was happy with the change. Gittleman recounts, for example, that one room had long been used by the Daughters of the American Revolution (DAR) to pay homage to the Boston Tea Party. "The 1739 inventory clearly told us that the room was where the enslaved people lived." Despite objections from DAR, they cleared out the room and put in a giant blow-up of the inventory and a piece of silk and a piece of linen to show the dichotomy between the lives of the family and enslaved workers. Since then, they have interpreted the room as it is reflected in the inventory. "The DAR has come around," says Gittleman. "It took a long time and a lot of patience on both sides."[11]

Some historic houses have led changes in their interpretation through connections between programs and exhibitions. Latimer House, located in the borough of Queens, New York, served as the home of African American inventor Lewis Latimer from 1903 to 1928. The house now stands in an area of New York City where no single racial or ethnic group holds a 50 percent or more majority.[12] Besides English, people in the community speak Korean, Chinese, and Spanish. Since opening as a museum in 1988, the site mainly served school groups and showcased Latimer's late 1880s home. To make the site more relevant, staff had to go beyond exploring how its African American owner lived. Digging into Latimer's story, they discovered not only did he work as an inventor, this "Renaissance man" contributed to other areas of science, technology, the arts, and poetry. By broadening their focus to include these aspects universal to other cultures, the leadership at the site began to plan exhibitions and programs that embraced their diverse community. In 2013, Latimer House received a grant to create an exhibition that combined science and the arts. *Light on Sound* opened in 2015—an exhibition with lamps in each room attached to headphones playing recorded poems as you turned the lights on (a mission-related take on Latimer's work on the light bulb with Thomas Edison). The exhibition was so popular with the public and brought in so many people that it is now part of the permanent installation in the house. In conjunction with the exhibition, a live poetry event was held twice (once on-site and once off-site in the community) where participants were invited to write or speak lines of a poem in any language to commemorate Latimer and bring together voices from the community.

To further welcome the community, Latimer House hired a Mandarin speaker from the neighborhood who became program director. Ran Yan started working as part of the grant-funded project and Latimer House subsequently hired her. Hiring a person from the community who can link back to the community is what Nina Simon deems an "inside-outsider" in her book *The Art of Relevance*.[13] Changing building signage to include Mandarin, Korean, and Spanish and offering tours in those languages further signaled to the community that they were welcome within. Currently, Latimer House also runs a Tinker Lab—open to all—offering "high-quality hands-on activities treating science and technology as an integral part of the humanities."[14] Choosing to focus on activities and themes that are open to many cultures and ethnicities (light, poetry, science, and technology) has expanded the house's audience. Yan explained they are moving slowly on the Tinker Lab, offering it only on weekends, with the plan of expanding to after school on weekdays. "It's important to do it well, not just to do it," she explained.[15]

One caution from Yan when reaching out to diverse ethnic and racial groups: don't generalize your audience. An early attempt to reach the Chinese-speaking audience included a partnership with a local community group that works with Chinese immigrants on a program about the "Do-it-Yourself (DIY)" movement in American culture. The event drew a large crowd, but not a local audience from Flushing neighborhoods. Attendees came from Manhattan and New Jersey. Lesson learned: think carefully about the audience as subgroups and figure out which ones you want to target for your programs and exhibitions.[16]

> In order to attract [diverse] people, you can't just stay in your place. You need to reach out.
> *Ran Yan, Program Director, Latimer House*

Sometimes, though, you may have to overcome negative attitudes in the community before you open your doors to them. In the Fruitvale district of East Oakland, California, the Peralta Hacienda Historical Park's 1870 farmhouse, once owned by the Peralta family, stands proudly on land granted by the king of Spain to the Peralta family. In an area where 51 percent of the local population is Latino, the house could have told stories of the historic Native Americans and of the Spanish colonial peoples as well as stories of contemporary Spanish and Latino communities. Until Executive Director Holly Alonso took over, the house was often closed to the public. Someone who worked there used to throw rocks at children who entered the six-acre park, and people generally felt unwelcome. Since 2001, Peralta Hacienda has evolved to be a hub for the community, expanding beyond their Spanish and Native American stories to embrace and celebrate everyone with the vision: "Every human being makes history." Beginning with the *Faces of Fruitvale* exhibition, which was composed of oral history excerpts and photos of fifty-five current Fruitvale residents, programs, exhibitions, and staffing strategies all evolve from the community itself. According to Alonso, the woman who started the park wanted it to be an "archive of community memory."[17] Peralta's mission states, "We present and interpret the untold history of the Peralta rancho and the stories of the Fruitvale community today, giving voice to the many cultures that have created—and are still transforming—California."[18]

Members of the local community are refugees from Cambodia and Laos. When approached by a local nonprofit serving the Southeast Asian community about using some of the land for farming and gardening, Alonso agreed, welcoming these Laotian women who suffered from PTSD and isolation to work the land. As Alonso got to know these women, she found their stories fascinating. She dreamt up a collaboration between community youth (mostly African American and Latino) and the Laotian women, where both groups grew plants, cooked, and ate together. As everyone learned each other's stories, community empathy blossomed, and crime in the area dropped by a factor of four.[19]

The community now views the house and grounds as open and welcoming to them, and many residents have gotten involved in Peralta Hacienda in other ways such as volunteering at festivals and other events. Alonso advocates "bringing in the community at every stage. Get input. They want to know what you have to offer."

Despite these successes in exhibitions and programming, not all on the Friends of the Peralta Hacienda board expressed pleasure with the changes. After the *Faces of Fruitvale* exhibition, one board member resigned in protest, calling the exhibit "the alien invasion." A founding board member asked Alonso, "But what does this have to do with the Peraltas?" One initiative, the Community Storytellers Corps—where people could be trained as part-time tour guides only if they lived less than a one-mile radius from the park—folded because of lack of funding. While raising money to fund the programs and for general operating support is a constant struggle, Alonso noted that "creative fund-raising" is important: some of the spaces in the large house are rented out to other nonprofits to provide additional income.[20]

> It's like a pebble in a pond—the good vibes are spreading. *Holly Alonso, Executive Director, Peralta Hacienda Historical Park*

In Chicago, the Jane Addams Hull-House Museum keeps alive Addams' work as a social reformer and political activist. Part of the University of Illinois at Chicago, the museum consists of two buildings: Hull Home, which features exhibitions about the history of the Hull-House Settlement, and the Residents' Dining Hall, which holds an event space, the museum's gift shop, and staff offices. Its goal is to be a "dynamic memorial to social reformer Jane Addams."[21]

Just as Addams worked with immigrants in her settlement house, the museum develops exhibitions and programs relevant to the immigrants in the community today. The U.S. Citizenship Test Samplers project by artist Aram Han Sifuentes, a noncitizen of Korean descent living in the United States, featured workshops where noncitizens study the questions on the naturalization test through the act of sewing an 8.5-by-11-inch sampler. As the workshop is described on the website, "In the spirit of the social settlement, the sampler workshops organically become grassroots roundtable discussions addressing immigrant rights, labor politics, and everyday concerns of intergenerational and multiethnic people. These roundtables are ephemeral snapshots of the realities of immigrant life in the United States today." The samplers are exhibited at the museum and offered for sale at $620, the cost of the U.S. naturalization test. All proceeds are given back to the noncitizen who created the sampler.

Says Curatorial Manager Ross Jordan, "As a museum, we are socially engaged. We want to be a platform for people's voices." They did just that during the 2016 election with the exhibition *Official Unofficial Voting Station: Voting for Those Who Legally Can't*, featuring artist Aram Han Sifuentes and collaborators Lise Haller Baggesen (also a noncitizen) and Sadie Woods. Working with twelve different sites throughout the United States and Mexico, they set up voting stations that invited people to vote and write down why they were voting at the unofficial voting station rather than an official election site. The ballots were in five different languages, to encourage voting from different communities. The responses were telling: "My whole family is undocumented." "I am an ex-felon." "I don't believe my vote in the real election counts."

As Jordan notes, "Jane Addams wasn't allowed to vote. Immigrants couldn't vote because of the time of day elections were held and the language barrier led to reduced power. At the voting station project enthusiasm was high and the connection to the Hull-House Settlement wasn't lost on anyone."[22]

The answer to reinventing your historic house may lie in the reflection of the current community's stories, and it doesn't mean it has to be a museum. Thinking outside the box of how to save a historic structure and adaptively reuse it for another purpose that is still relevant to the community is just what Miami Hispanic Cultural Arts Center did with the J. W. Warner House. Warner founded South Florida's first floral company with the business occupying the first floor of the home. The house remained in family hands until 1981 when Magic City Restoration Company adaptively reused it for office space, carving out separate offices into its historic architecture.[23]

The building and gardens stand at the edge of the Little Havana section of Miami. When Miami Hispanic Ballet outgrew its office and began looking for a larger space, they realized that many Hispanic arts organizations needed room to grow, and ballet director Pedro Pablo Peña thought it would be great to bring them all together under one roof. When the Warner House became available, Peña obtained grants to revitalize and restore the building to more of its original layout and details. Now the center boasts an art gallery and a ballet studio as well as office spaces, and plans for expansion include a black box theater. When it opened in 2011, though, the building and space struggled to reach their audience. Local walking tours of the Little Havana neighborhood don't stop at the building because its location ten blocks from the center of the neighborhood is deemed "too far to walk." Rentals seem to be the most effective way to spread the word about the building and its programs. "Allowing other groups and events to take place in the renovated spaces widens audience," noted Karen Couty, assistant to the director.[24] Charged with preserving the Hispanic cultural legacy, the reinvented Warner House/Miami Hispanic Cultural Arts Center is just beginning to see an uptick in the local community taking advantage of all it has to offer.

While there is no one "right" way to reinvent historic house museums based on race and ethnicity, these examples show that telling a more inclusive story opens historic house museums up to a wider audience. Inclusion can be in the form of stories, projects, programs and exhibits, events, collaborations—and better yet, all the above. They all can help you reframe your historic site into a vibrant, relevant, approachable, and responsive community asset.

Several common threads emerge from our examples. First, look to your community. Who are they? What do they need? What can they offer you? Second, find a story that is organic to your site or your community. Jane Addams' legacy of social justice is alive and well at the Jane Addams Hull-House Museum. It's a natural and appropriate fit. Third, the process cannot be rushed. It takes time to build trust and acceptance. Fourth, set realistic goals based on the size of your staff, the depth of your knowledge, and, of course, your budget. Fifth, think outside the box. It's likely you'll be blazing new territory in historic house museums. While you can get ideas from other sites, you'll need to create your own way of doing things. Finally, recognize that history related to race and ethnicity can be uncomfortable, challenging people to confront their own inherent bias and/or overcome their stereotypical perceptions of race or ethnicity.

Another common thread is the enthusiastic agreement that the change has made the organization more in touch with people and issues today. "The change at the Royall House and Slave Quarters has been completely worth it," says Co-president and Treasurer Gittleman. "We have gone from being a museum that is invisible and irrelevant to one that is sought after and current in its ability to present issues and programs that matter today." Then, perhaps in a sentiment many historic house museums can empathize with, Gittleman says, "We are not going to stay in business if we don't change."[25]

Notes

1. "The History of Colonial Williamsburg," *Colonial Williamsburg*, accessed March 18, 2017, http://www .history.org/foundation/cwhistory.cfm; "Mount Vernon Ladies' Association," *George Washington's Mount Vernon*, accessed March 18, 2017, http://www.mountvernon.org/preservation/mount-vernon-ladies-as sociation; "Monticello," *History.com*, accessed March 18, 2017, http://www.history.com/topics/monticello.
2. "Haas-Lilienthal House Interpretive Outcomes and Themes," San Francisco Heritage, May 28, 2015.
3. Michael Buhler, interview by Jane M. Eliasof, February 10, 2017.
4. Valerie Perry, interview by Jane M. Eliasof, February 7, 2017.
5. Valerie Perry, interview by Jane M. Eliasof, February 7, 2017.

6. Valerie Perry, interview by Jane M. Eliasof, February 7, 2017.
7. "Slave Life at the Royall House," *Royall House and Slave Quarters*, accessed March 30, 2017, http://www .royallhouse.org/slavery/slave-life/.
8. Peter Gittleman, interview by Jane M. Eliasof, February 13, 2017.
9. "Mission, Board and Staff," *Royall House and Slave Quarters*, accessed March 30, 2017, http://www.royal lhouse.org/about-us/mission-board-and-staff.
10. "The Royalls and the Antigua Slave Conspiracy," *Royall House and Slave Quarters*, accessed March 30, 2017, http://www.royallhouse.org/the-royalls-and-the-antigua-slave-conspiracy-of-1736/.
11. Peter Gittleman, interview by Jane M. Eliasof, February 13, 2017.
12. "Welcome to Quick Facts," *U.S. Census Bureau*, accessed March 30, 2017, https://www.census.gov/ quickfacts/table/PST045215/36081.
13. Nina Simon, *The Art of Relevance* (Santa Cruz, CA: Creative Commons, 2016), 71–73.
14. "Lewis Latimer House Museum and the Tinker Lab," information sheet, *Lewis Latimer House Museum*, no date.
15. Ran Yan, interview by Claudia Ocello. February 14, 2017.
16. Ran Yan, interview by Claudia Ocello, February 14, 2017.
17. Holly Alonso, interview by Claudia Ocello, March 7, 2017.
18. "Who We Are," *Peralta Hacienda Historic Park*, accessed March 30, 2017, http://www.peraltahacienda .org/pages/main.php?pageid=74&pagecategory=3.
19. Holly Alonso, interview by Claudia Ocello, March 7, 2017.
20. Holly Alonso, interview by Claudia Ocello, March 7, 2017.
21. "About the Museum," *Jane Addams Hull-House Museum*, accessed March 20, 2017, http://www.hull housemuseum.org/about-the-museum/.
22. Ross Jordan, interview by Jane M. Eliasof, March 2, 2017.
23. National Register of Historic Places Nomination Form, U.S. Department of the Interior, April 21, 1983, accessed March 23, 2017, from focus.nps.gov/GetAsset?assetID=1bc38b18-0b5f-4200-8724-a090 7f313ce5.
24. Karen Couty, interview by Claudia Ocello, February 8, 2017.
25. Peter Gittleman, interview by Jane M. Eliasof, February 13, 2017.

Recommended Resources

American Association for State and Local History. *Views from the Porch* (blog). http://blogs.aaslh .org/historichouse/.
Eliasof, Jane. "The Many Voices of a Historic House." *History News* 72, no. 1 (Winter 2017): 14–18.
Lau, Barbara, Scott Jennifer, and Suzanne Seriff. "Inviting Disruption and Contested Truth into Museum Exhibitions." *Exhibition* (Spring 2017): 20–31.
Simon, Nina. *The Art of Relevance*. Santa Cruz, CA: Museums 2.0, 2016.
Vagnone, Franklin D., and Deborah E. Ryan. *The Anarchist's Guide to Historic House Museums*. Walnut Creek, CA: Left Coast Press, 2016.

Chapter 19

Why Do Furnishings Matter?

The Power of Furnishings in Historic House Museums

LAURA C. KEIM

As contemporary visitors wander the rooms and spaces of historic houses, the furnishings they encounter structure their experiences. Furnishings represent a complicated past; they embody human action; they convey layers of meaning; and they symbolize both the everyday and the beautiful. Furnishings make important contributions to telling stories and creating visually compelling domestic spaces. A set of mahogany chairs, for example, can reveal the complex web of past and present. Furnishings shape and convey site narratives, provoke visitor inquiry and imagination, and reinforce the character and meaning of the house and place. In these ways, objects are essential to bringing the past alive for all visitors.

Furnishings are central to the unique nature of most historic sites. Although visitors may encounter the same objects in other museums, such as historical societies and history museums (for their stories and associations), or art museums (as examples of artistic achievement and craftsmanship), encountering furnishings in a historic house is a distinctive experience. Most importantly, furnishings have the power to connect us to people and contexts from another time and bring them into our present reality. They represent the small everyday actions that shape human lives, and in so doing remind us of our essential humanity.

Furnishings Represent a Complicated and Layered Past

The use and display of furnishings in house museums has drawn the ire of some writers who critique furnishings and the way historic sites interpret them as elitist and off-putting.[1] The founding of many historic house museums resulted from an often nostalgic and sentimental Colonial Revival impulse. Beginning in the late nineteenth century, the Colonial Revival movement preserved and collected the past, creating connections especially to America's founding era, albeit through an idealized lens. In addition to generating an object-based and inventive approach to history, however, the Colonial Revival also expressed "xenophobic sentiments" and "Anglo-white-gentrified and elite" values, which included Americanizing "immigrants, African Americans, and other people of diverse origins."[2]

In addition to the problematic origins of many historic site collections, specialized terminology may strike visitors rather like a foreign language. But the language of the decorative arts can also deepen visitors' engagement and add another layer of understanding, much as knowing how to speak a language can inform a visit to another country. Furnishings have styles, such as Queen Anne, Chippendale, Federal, or Art Deco, and come from various eras such as Victorian or early twentieth century. Moreover, such language need not burden historic house visitors unless the aesthetic details of furniture are their interest.[3] Style is a useful tool, a visual index to time. Style offers understanding, but it is not a form of interpretation or vehicle for generating deeper meaning. Understanding stylistic developments in context helps to unravel the social and cultural values of different time periods and generates some meaning from the object.

Viewing the complicated construction of the past solely through notions of social or linguistic exclusion fails to acknowledge furnishings as gateways into the complicated past that can help us understand our equally complicated present. It reduces the flexibility of the house museum as a medium for conveying many pasts, which we can explore through furnishings. To consider and wrestle with the varied messages and meanings of furnishings is a culturally powerful and potentially transformative societal endeavor. Encounters with furnishings can tell complex stories, at once conveying social inequalities while also evoking wonder at the experience of old things from the past, rather like a visit to grandmother's attic. The best historic house museums help visitors to conjure these multiple meanings, which can and should go hand in hand.

At Stenton, a historic house museum in Philadelphia, visitors confront a group of six mahogany Chippendale-style side chairs and one arm chair lining the walls of the best parlor (see Figure 19.1). Typical of their time in overall form, these lavishly carved chairs are exceptional specimens of eighteenth-century Philadelphia craftsmanship. John Dickinson (1732–1808), a lawyer and prominent leader during the American Revolution, commissioned a total of twelve of these chairs with two matching arm chairs in the early 1770s. Seated on the chairs, gathered around a tea table or at rectangular dining tables, the Dickinsons and their guests enjoyed genteel tea and dining rituals.

Visitors can engage with objects like the Dickinson chairs on multiple levels however. While contemplating the beauty of the chairs, house museum visitors also learn that such status symbols were expensive to purchase and even more costly to humanity and the environment. Very likely, enslaved laborers harvested and milled the Caribbean mahogany logs for shipment to Philadelphia. Closer to Philadelphia, Dickinson's enslaved Africans toiled on his plantations in Delaware and Maryland to support his family's comfortable and fashionable lifestyle. Free and unfree servants alike poured the tea, prepared the food, and rearranged the furniture in the Dickinson's eighteenth-century home.[4]

Colonial American furnishings resulted from Atlantic trading networks and exhibited East Asian design influences filtered through a British lens of conquest and cultural appropriation. In other words, these chairs offer the possibility of understanding a complex web of connections related to their creation and use over time, engaging with some of the best and worst of human nature simultaneously.[5] It is important to recognize that layered meanings co-existing in furnishings generate a powerful historic house museum encounter.

Laura C. Keim

Figure 19.1 Engaging with these chairs and their history simultaneously provokes an appreciation of beauty and an understanding of the origins of systemic racism in America. Such an encounter with chairs might inspire more visitors to recognize the legacies of slavery that remain ingrained in American culture. Photo by Will Brown, courtesy of Stenton.

Furnishings also bring variety and human presence to the house museum. Their mobility and everyday nature are key to the house museum's flexibility, relatability, and symbolic power to represent the people of the past. Rearranging furnishings allows us to tell various aspects of a site's story or for a change in focus. More than providing atmosphere, furnishings put the house in motion, enlivening the house museum and offering relatable connections to the past in domestic space. Because people live with objects in their homes today, interacting with historic counterparts helps visitors imagine the past. In furnished historic spaces, visitors can relate to sitting on chairs, eating, drinking, writing at tables, and sleeping in beds, regardless of era. Symbolically, furnishings embody the people who once lived and worked within the walls and help to present houses and work spaces as a series of lived-in domestic interiors. House museums enable objects and narratives to coexist in conversation, each enriching and contextualizing the other, and fostering experiential learning through a variety of senses. Exploring the past through the material objects of everyday life connects us to the core of common human experience across time.[6]

Many people also enjoy beautifully furnished spaces and visit historic houses to see, learn about, and understand how people lived and furnished houses in the past. Period interiors inspire visitors who viscerally like interiors and old things. Historic house museums are magical for the immersive environments that furnishings in period and original domestic contexts provide. The broad and powerful appeal of aesthetic experiences is a value in historic house museums that attracts visitors and is a layer of meaning that deserves attention. We can continue to enjoy historic furnishings for their period charm and attractiveness, while using their physical and historical contexts to reimagine the house museum.

Furnishing Case Study: Stenton, Philadelphia

An excellent example of a furnished historic house museum that has evolved over time is Stenton, an eighteenth-century brick gentleman's house in Philadelphia, Pennsylvania. As Pennsylvania's colonial secretary, James Logan built the house in the 1720s. After occupancy by the same family until the late nineteenth century, it became a museum managed by the National Society of the Colonial Dames of America in the Commonwealth of Pennsylvania in 1899.

Nearly 120 years of operation by this lineage-based women's preservation organization has defined Stenton as a historic house museum and continues to shape its character and operations.[7] Stenton's history as a museum explains the research that underpins the site's furnishing decisions and some of the presentational strategies that have enlivened visitors' experiences. It can serve as a model for generating meaning from furnishings in context and for rethinking presentation strategies to gently interrupt the sense of "period time" in the historic house museum to make objects more than just historic props.

Inspired by models such as the Mount Vernon Ladies Association, the Colonial Dames concluded that furnishings were a necessary and important ingredient for a proper historic house museum.[8] Because Stenton was almost empty in 1899, the Dames furnished the house with items from their own and friends' attics, with many of the objects on loan. The first interpretive focus combined some emphasis on understanding the decorative arts with a display of antique relics, gadgets, prints, and photographs.

Mary Johnson Brown Chew (1839–1927), who led the cause to restore Stenton and operate it as a public museum, participated in the colonial kitchen display at the 1876 Centennial World's Fair.[9] She cared about artifacts of everyday life in the Colonial period and intended Stenton to function as an historic "object lesson, keeping in memory the worthy lives and deeds of the founders of the Province."[10] In addition to serving its role as a history museum, Stenton functioned as the society's clubhouse until the 1920s, with many of the furnishings actively used.

While early collecting for the house tended to be generic antiques, the Dames solicited Logan family descendants to lend furnishings and convey oral histories and remembrances. By the 1920s, as the furnishings took on a decidedly domestic character, the Dames recognized the power of Logan family objects to convey Logan family stories. In 1928, the governing committee "voted to refurnish the house as far as possible with Logan things."[11] This tenet has since guided the Dames' collecting policy for Stenton, which still holds Logan family objects as its highest collecting priority.

Today, about 50 percent of the furnishings at Stenton have a family provenance, and Stenton is always on the lookout for opportunities to acquire or borrow family objects. The remaining furnishings reflect estate inventories of the 1750s and 1770s, so that the furnishings on view substitute for known family objects and help to bring the house to life. Archival research in the family papers sheds light on family furnishings and offers new stories. As a result, furnishings shift in response to the addition of new objects and new information.

Re-creating historic rooms is a worthwhile endeavor as it allows visitors to experience authenticity of materials and visual surroundings that hopefully brings them closer to the past and invites

Figure 19.2 The assemblage of archeological tea wares disrupts the sense of re-created period time in the Stenton parlor. The first disruption is the mended and incomplete state of the artifacts. The second is the decorative and unrealistic arrangement with more teapots than would have been used at once, prompting questions about who used all the pots. The tabletop exhibition is a playful injection of contemporary time furnishing the table with the Logan family's artifacts excavated on site. Photo by Laura Keim, courtesy of Stenton.

them to explore the differences between life in the past and life in the present. Furnishing an interior, however, does not necessarily need to replicate a period room setting.[12] In 2009–2010, Stenton staff and volunteers mended many pre-1760 archaeological ceramic and glass artifacts excavated from a cistern behind the house. Many of these vessels were almost completely reconstructed. The variety of teapots and other tea wares from the archaeological deposit presented as an assemblage on the parlor tea table is an evocative visual and teaching tool. The tabletop is a gallery exhibition in the midst of a parlor setting, a display of mended artifacts used by the first generation of inhabitants and discarded by the second (see Figure 19.2).

Some collections committee members wrestled with displaying a "bunch of broken ceramics" on the table and had difficulty accepting more objects exhibited than would have been used to take tea in the eighteenth century. Yet visitors find the assemblage compelling, and it generates meaning on several levels: it becomes a playful way to look at the importance of tea in the household, a comparative exercise about the types and hierarchies of teapots, and offers a venue for understanding a variety of ceramic clay bodies and their properties. The grouping presents an interesting interpretive conjunction in eighteenth-century thinking that whiteness and translucence were valued in human and ceramic bodies. Because there are an unrealistic number of teapots, their display interrupts the flow of "period time" in the historic house setting and gives visitors pause to think and ask questions.

Sometimes displays such as Stenton's parlor tea table offer welcome variety, a disruption to the historic interior, and alternative learning opportunities. Table and desk tops, beds, cupboards, and closets offer a variety of potential settings for temporary displays. These vignettes enliven the furnishings interpretation and keep it fresh and real, reminding us that we can appreciate past domestic settings without necessarily following all the rules of domestic arrangement and engagement.[13]

In 2017, Stenton completed re-creation and restoration of the best bedchamber, the Yellow Lodging Room, based on more than a decade of research and scientific investigation including analysis of paint and a Logan family textile to re-create authentic colors.[14] The decorative (upholstery, curtains, carpets, paint, wallpaper) rather than the collections management side of furnishing, can be quite costly. Typically, expensive decorative furnishing occurs rarely and is a long-term interpretive and presentational strategy that will last a generation or more. The expense and enduring nature of such installations, however, give historic house museums their reputation for static interiors. Thus, historic site managers should employ short-term strategies for change involving object movement and small exhibitions in tandem with strategies for permanence. Stenton is considering engaging a ceramic artist to create a contemporary set of garniture (vases) for the top of a maple high chest in the Yellow Lodging Room. Such an intervention might offer the possibility for an even bolder disruption of "period time" and juxtaposition of past and present.[15]

Assessing and Making Furnishing Decisions

Physical attributes of place and collections, combined with the values of the people who manage a historic house, shape the character of a museum. Therefore, strategies that work well for one museum will not necessarily work well for another. The best way to furnish a historic house museum must be explored on a case-by-case basis, as there are no universal solutions in historic site management. As museum managers and practices evolve over time, the values that formed a collection and selected furnishings can become less relevant. While some historic house museums opened complete with family furnishings, others had to collect furnishings over time and a few have no furnishings.[16]

Furnishings not associated with the inhabiting family, or not similar to those owned by the family, convey little contextual meaning. The greater the number of artifacts that belonged to the inhabitants of the house, or which have had long association with the house, the greater the resonance between the furnishings, the architectural space, and the stories the place can illustrate, question, and convey. Many visitors respond to the sense of authenticity, inquiring whether objects are "real." As Jessica Muttit notes, "the collections alone have the ability to create an air of authenticity in the space for the visitor . . . the way the visitor reacts to the stories told within the house can be affected by how authentic they view the space to be."[17]

Some historic site professionals argue that the most relevant historic house museums are those furnished with objects that invite sitting and touching.[18] Sometimes hands-on or interactive use is appropriate for a particular object, but sometimes not.[19] Special programs and events can offer up-close and hands-on encounters with furnishings to learn the ins and outs of a topic such as Queen Anne chairs or nineteenth-century sprung seating. Determining how to use objects is

Laura C. Keim

another case-by-case decision. Evaluating and selecting furnishings (or sit-able reproductions) should come from a purposeful, coherent strategy to maximize visitors' experience of the house.

Considerations for Furnishing the Historic House Museum

Despite reputations as static places, historic house museums are never complete in the way a decorator selects colors, paint, and wallpaper, places furnishings, and finishes a project. With the exception of large or built-in furnishings, house museum displays are quite easily remade without the need for customized cases and labels for every object. While there may be moments along the journey to furnish and interpret a historic house museum that celebrate the completion of particular projects, the reality is that the interior arrangements are always evolving based on new research, new finds, object changes, and the creation of vignettes and exhibits.

Once museum managers have a general understanding of the site history from the period of family habitation, the recent history of the house becoming a museum, and the overall importance of the place, as well as a general understanding of the forms, styles, and periods of the furnishings, ask a series of questions:

- If we don't have furnishings, do we want them? Why or why not?
- If we do have furnishings, do we understand the provenances and origins of the objects?
- What are they? Who owned/made them and when in time? Where were they created?
- Where were they situated in the house historically? Why are they in the historic house?
- How do they help to convey stories of the past in the present?

Answering these basic questions for every object requires an investment of time for research. The results will provide key knowledge about and context for the existing furnishings. It is imperative that collections staff and museum managers know why the objects they have inherited are in the museum. Without a full appreciation for what is there and why, deploying objects to tell stories is impossible, and arguments for deaccessioning some furnishings and seeking different objects are not well formed. Time spent on internally focused research will help the museum plan for a clarified collections policy and priorities so that furnishings can represent the past and help interpreters and guides to tell stories.[20] William Seale's *Recreating the Historic House Interior* (1979) remains a solid reference work for the many considerations involved in researching and furnishing a historic house museum.

Keep in mind that there are varying approaches to furnishing historic house museums, based on types. In his discussion of furnishings plans, Bradley C. Brooks encourages the use of Alderson and Low's three interpretive categories: documentary sites, representative sites, and aesthetic sites.[21] Representative house museums speak to a period more than to the specific or documentary history of the house and its inhabitants. The aesthetic site focuses on decorative arts and displaying the house as a series of period rooms.

The various combinations of interpretation and collection types has prompted me to place most house museums in a few representative categories:

- The **Authentic House Museum**, with furnishings that belonged to previous inhabitants, offers the best opportunity for visitors to connect to a real, place-based past, which invites wrestling with the truths of history.

- The **Family Repository** can also offer that close connection with the authentic past, but its visual complexity may challenge visitors' ability to comprehend the varied range of artifacts associated with the house over many generations.
- The **Representative House Museum** may be largely aesthetically driven as its furnishings are not specific to the house and therefore do not offer a sense of authentic connection to an actual past. However, historical research (such as locating probate or other inventories) may make it possible for the chosen furnishings to represent or approximate furnishings that were or could have been in the house.
- The **Period Room Approach** is entirely aesthetically motivated with objects chosen for their decorative style, with little consideration for provenance, historical narrative, or the actual mix of furnishing styles and types that coexisted in most homes.
- The **Unfurnished House** is driven by the importance of its architecture, landscape, or non-mission-based rental use.

Every house museum can be placed within one of these categories and the more that a house museum can engage with multiple types, the more expansive the interpretive possibilities.

Take Risks

- Do not be afraid to exhibit objects in unconventional ways. Taking presentation too seriously leads to a lack of experimentation and play, which is crucial for providing compelling non-historic intervention in the museum.
- Do not be afraid to move objects, even big ones, with proper handling and care. The flexibility of the historic house medium is one of its great strengths. Avoid stagnation in your furnishing arrangements. Enjoy exploring and placing the furnishings, and that enthusiasm will translate into meaningful exhibitions and vignettes in the museum.
- Do not be afraid to reproduce or commission objects that may be important to your larger message, developed through research, but which are not possible for your display. Do not be afraid to play with object labels or text, perhaps quotes from a letter or diary that can inject a sense of historical personality into a space.
- A secondary message of the Colonial Revival is that people do enjoy being playful with objects. Continue to play with the past so visitors can enjoy their interactions with the furnished interiors in approachable ways, even if not always as strictly "correct" historical settings.

Some would argue that the house museum field today is in crisis or conflict, with some recent authors demanding "anarchy" in operations and arguments about the centrality of object-based versus narrative-centered interpretation.[22] We are at a crossroads about whether there are too many house museums.[23] Our lens on the past changes as society shifts and evolves in the present. Many house museums came into the public realm as a means of preserving old houses without much forethought for the sustainability of that endeavor, grounded in a Colonial Revival, nostalgic mentality. Indeed, many people disconnect from a past that feels out of step with contemporary values and are seeking meaning and diversity through expanding narratives.

Museum objects and furnishings are critical to this diversification of perspective and the desire for inclusivity because they powerfully embody simultaneous narratives. Nostalgia and heavy history are two sides of the same story, worth comparing and exploring in using our past as a vehicle for understanding our present. Recontextualizing historic furnishings can help house museums tell a holistic story and speak to present-day cultural values, including objective examinations of nostalgia, and our need for social change. This evolution is not predicated on de-valuing or disposing of collections saved or acquired to suit aesthetic and nostalgic cultural values. The way forward is to layer on additional understandings of furnishings in wider, even global contexts. Through examining all of the past, we arrive at a multifaceted comprehension that acknowledges change over time and mobilizes the meanings of objects in new ways.

Historic house museums reassemble the past with objects and use them to tell stories. With skillful interpretation, they offer successful immersive experiences that bring the past into the present and invite visitors into the mysteries that remain, provoking their imaginations on multiple levels. Furnishings and narratives need not be in opposition, as they work best when mobilized together. When furnishings are well-chosen for the stories they represent, they not only set the stage of a historic house, they help to relate the stories of the house and its occupants. We articulate who we are as Americans by redefining our historic houses.

Notes

1. Franklin D. Vagnone and Deborah E. Ryan, *Anarchist's Guide to Historic House Museums: A Ground-Breaking Manifesto* (Walnut Creek, CA: Left Coast Press, Inc., 2016), 130–33, 138–41.
2. Richard Guy Wilson, "Introduction," in *Re-creating the American Past: Essays on the Colonial Revival*, ed. Richard Guy Wilson, Shaun Eyring, and Kenny Marotta (Charlottesville: University of Virginia Press, 2006), 3, 6.
3. Glenn Adamson, "Design History and the Decorative Arts," in *Cultural Histories of the Material World*, ed. Peter N. Miller (Ann Arbor: University of Michigan Press, 2013), 33–38. An excellent book for understanding the basics of furniture styles and forms is Joseph T. Butler, *Field Guide to American Furniture* (New York: Roundtable Press, 1985). Ray Skibinski's line drawing illustrations are visually accessible. The vocabulary of furnishings is a useful curatorial tool but does little to expand visitors' experiences of furnishings on a human level.
4. Milton E. Flower, *John Dickinson: Conservative Revolutionary* (Charlottesville: University Press of Virginia for the Friends of John Dickinson Mansion, 1983), 20–21.
5. Zara Anishanslin, *Portrait of a Woman in Silk: Hidden Histories of the British Atlantic World* (New Haven, CT: Yale University Press, 2016), 313–17.
6. Many scholars of vernacular architecture and material culture have eloquently made this case, including Bernard L. Herman, Henry Glassie, and Cary Carson.
7. Sandra Mackenzie Lloyd, *"An Uncommon Trust," Or How the Dames Saved Stenton* (NSCDA/PA, 1999).
8. The Mount Vernon Ladies Association, founded to purchase and preserve George Washington's home for the nation, was the first national historic preservation organization and is the oldest women's patriotic society in the United States. Beginning in the 1860s, the Ladies began collecting antique furnishings for the rooms, creating a pioneering and precedent-setting model for the presentation of historic houses. http://www.mountvernon.org/preservation/mount-vernon-ladies-association/mount-vernon -ladies-association-timeline/, accessed May 12, 2018.
9. Lloyd, *"An Uncommon Trust,"* 2.
10. Ibid.
11. "Minutes of April 30, 1928," Stenton Mansion Committee Minute Book, 1927–1937. See Stenton Collections Policy.
12. Some helpful sources on historic furnishing styles and arrangements are: Peter Thornton, *Authentic Décor* (New York: Random House, 1993, originally published 1984); Peter Thornton, *Seventeenth-Century Interior Decoration in England, France & Holland* (New Haven, CT: Yale University Press, 1978); Charles Saumarez Smith, *Eighteenth-Century Decoration: Design and the Domestic Interior in England* (New York: Harry N. Abrams, Inc., 1993); Charlotte Gere, *Nineteenth-Century Decoration: The Art of the Interior* (New York: Harry N. Abrams, Inc., 1989); Stephen Calloway, *Twentieth-Century Decoration* (New York: Rizzoli, 1988); William Seale, *The Tasteful Interlude: American Interiors through the Camera's Eye, 1860–1917* (New York: Praeger Publishers, 1975); Mario Praz, *An Illustrated History of Interior Decoration, from Pompeii to*

Art Nouveau (Milan: Longanesi & Co., 1964; New York: Thames & Hudson, 1982); Edgar de N. Mayhew and Minor Myers, Jr., *A Documentary History of American Interiors from the Colonial Era to 1915* (New York: Charles Scribner's Sons, 1980); Harold L. Peterson, *Americans at Home, from the Colonists to the Late Victorians* (New York: Charles Scribner's Sons, 1971); Elizabeth Donaghy Garrett, *At Home: The American Family, 1750–1870* (New York: Harry N. Abrams, Inc., 1990).

13. Aesthetically, the Colonial Revival took a light-hearted approach to furnishings that looked to the past for inspiration. If we become too rigid in our pursuit of historical accuracy and authenticity, we might lose the element of play that captures imaginations in the present. Herein lies the art of furnishing.

14. Laura C. Keim, "Ochre, Old Fustic, and Maple: Stenton's Yellow Lodging Room Restored," *Antiques and Fine Art Magazine* 16, no. 4 (Winter 2017): 112–17. Also https://www.stenton.org/yellowroom, accessed May 12, 2018.

15. The Morris-Jumel Mansion in New York City has mounted exhibitions in a "Contemporary Meets Colonial" series, http://www.morrisjumel.org/past/, accessed May 12, 2018; Vagnone and Ryan, *Anarchist's Guide*, 150–54.

16. For more on house museum types, see Bradley C. Brooks, "The Historic House Furnishing Plan: Process and Product," in *Interpreting Historic House Museums*, ed. Jessica Foy Donnelley (Walnut Creek, CA: AltaMira Press, 2002), 131–32, and William T. Alderson and Shirley Payne Low, *Interpretation of Historic Sites* (Nashville: American Association for State and Local History, 1976), especially chapter 2, "Setting Objectives," 7–19.

17. Jessica D. Muttitt, "Visitors and Originality in Historic House Museums: A Look at the Impact of Furnishing Plans," AASLH blog, December 6, 2016, https://aaslh.org/visitors-and-originality-in-historic-house-museums-a-look-at-the-impact-of-furnishing-plans/, accessed July 24, 2018.

18. Vagnone and Ryan, *Anarchist's Guide*, 130. See also Franklin Vagnone, "One Night Stands," Twisted Preservation (blog). By spending the night in historic house museums, sleeping in the beds and understanding the place as an inhabitant, Vagnone is attempting "to highlight more nuanced and latent understandings of these places as vessels for life, social issues, politics, and habitation—not merely as decorative arts objects and collections artifacts." https://twistedpreservation.com/one-night-stand-series/. Although readers can benefit from Vagnone's insights gleaned from his "sleeping around," his approach creates an exclusive experience that is not sustainable on a larger scale for most historic house museums. For a more moderate approach to balanced stewardship and collections access to benefit all visitors, see James M. Vaughan, "Rethinking the Rembrandt Rule," *Museum* 87 (March/April 2008): 33–34, 71.

19. Historic New England opened the Eustis Estate in 2017, which came with only two rooms of original furnishings and some hall pieces. The decision there was to furnish the rest of the house with period pieces that visitors could sit on and touch. Interactive kiosks and tablets were added for the visitor to explore on their own.

20. Stenton underwent a historic structures study and report in 1982. Stenton generated a room furnishings history in 2001 that laid out the Colonial Dames' management and furnishing of the house from 1899–2001. Building on this report, an interpretive plan identified four major themes the house presents and aligned spaces, objects, stories, and people with the themes. A 2011 room furnishings study analyzed the 1750s Logan family estate inventories in combination with known surviving family objects and the evidence provided by architecture and arrangement of space in the house to reimagine Stenton in its early decades with a series of furnishing recommendations including a re-creation of a flying tester bedstead in the Yellow Lodging Room. https://docs.wixstatic.com/ugd/29e2a6_5dda0a3cbe9c454988ece0fba124a4f2.pdf.

21. Bradley C. Brooks, "The Historic House Furnishings Plan," in *Interpreting Historic House Museums*, ed. Jessica Foy Donnelly (Walnut Creek, CA: Altamira Press, 2002), 131–32.

22. Vagnone and Ryan, *Anarchist's Guide*, 38–41.

23. Donna Ann Harris, *New Solutions for House Museums: Ensuring Long-Term Preservation of America's Historic Houses* (Lanham, MD: Altamira Press, 2007), 4; Ruth Graham, "The Great Historic House Museum Debate," *Boston Globe* (August 10, 2014), https://www.bostonglobe.com/ideas/2014/08/09/the-great-historic-house-museum-debate/jzFwE9tvJdHDCXehIWqK4O/story.html, accessed May 12, 2018.

Chapter 20

Rethinking Architecture in the Realm of House Museum Interpretation

CHERYL A. BACHAND

In many ways, the title of architectural critic Paul Goldberger's 2009 book, *Why Architecture Matters*, poses the central question faced every day by those who have devoted their careers to interpreting the architecture of America's historic houses. While those same professionals would have little trouble responding in the affirmative that, yes, architecture does matter, answering the questions of why and how it matters and for whom it matters have been less easy to articulate.

Within the historic house museum field are architectural house museums whose primary criteria for significant and outstanding merit is tied to their design. They've achieved national or regional landmark status on the basis of the exceptional and often innovative nature of their architecture or constructed features. Many of these sites have been designed by history's most well-known architects—Frank Lloyd Wright, Mies van der Rohe, Philip Johnson, Richard Morris Hunt, Julia Morgan, Alexander Jackson Davis, to name a few. Historic houses such as Hearst Castle, designed by Julia Morgan for William Randolph Hearst; The Breakers, the summer "cottage" designed by Richard Morris Hunt for Cornelius Vanderbilt II; or Lyndhurst, designed by Alexander Jackson Davis, provide visitors with a glimpse of "high-style" architecture coupled with the lifestyles of America's wealthiest and most prominent families. At Wright's Fallingwater, Mies van der Rohe's Farnsworth House, Philip Johnson's Glass House, and Greene and Greene's Gamble House, some of the nation's most iconic works of architecture are celebrated (see Figure 20.1).

For the majority of historic houses, the building, often the largest object in the collection, may not have been designed by a well-known architect. Designed by local architects or representative of the architecture of a particular geographic region or period, the architecture of historic houses is often a neglected or secondary area of interpretation at many sites.

The role of research and interpretation at architectural house museums does not differ all that much from the role it occupies for historic houses—a thorough investigation of the histories and significance of the site and the elucidation of that content to those who visit. What is different at

Figure 20.1 Brothers Charles Sumner Greene and Henry Mather Greene designed and supervised the construction of the Gamble House in Pasadena, California, in 1908-1909 as a winter home for Mary and David B. Gamble of the Procter & Gamble Company Photograph by Carol M. Highsmith, Jon B. Lovelace Collection of California Photographs, Library of Congress, LC-DIG-highsm-24438.

architectural house museums is the focus of research and interpretation. At historic houses, the residents and their lifestyles are afforded primacy in research and interpretation. At architectural house museums, the architect as creator takes precedence and the history of the site's design takes center stage. The architect's design philosophies and artistic intentions are discussed. The relationship between the architect's vision and the client's personal preferences is explored. The unique qualities of the landscape and the building's relationship to the natural site is examined. The technologies and craftsmanship employed are introduced and probed. We learn about the negotiation of the artistic, technical, practical, and personal that have produced some of the nation's most significant and evocative works of architecture.

Increasingly, interpretation of architectural house museums is moving beyond the sole consideration of the site as an aesthetic or designed space. The use of the building, its subsequent habitation, and its functionality as a place for human interaction and lived experience, is questioned and investigated. The architect's role is still primary in architectural house museum interpretation, but at many sites it is balanced by a recognition of the contributions of client, craftspeople, and construction personnel. The histories and lifestyles of residents has gained ground. Current research trends at architectural house museums focus increasingly on the individuals who inhabited the sites and the ways the architecture has framed or contributed to their habitation. The interpretation has become richer, more nuanced, complicated, messy, and more human.

It's clear that interpretive methodologies of historic houses have informed architectural house museum interpretation. But what of the reverse? How can the interpretive lens of the architectural house museum add depth and dimension to other types of historic houses? What can a focus on the architecture add to the interpretation of the historic house?

　　　　　　　　　　　　　　　　　　　　　　　　　　　　Cheryl A. Bachand

Meaning and Relevance

One could argue that there is an inherent relevance in architecture that we often fail to consider. Architecture provides us with the physical spaces where we live our lives, spend time with family and friends, work and worship, among other activities too numerous to list. As Goldberger observes, "To be engaged with architecture is to be engaged with almost everything else as well: culture, society, politics, business, history, family, religion, education. . . . The job of architecture as art is only an aspect of the experience of architecture, profound though it may be; there is also great satisfaction to understanding the built environment as a form of engagement with every other function imaginable."[1] Architecture has the potential to be relevant, to be meaningful in a broad way since it provides the spaces for social connectivity in our world. We often squander this potential to make connections with visitors when we limit ourselves to interpretation that overemphasizes the history of design or neglects to explore the manner by which architecture has impacted the ways that humans live, interact, and experience the built environment.

Architectural house museums address the question of why architecture matters. And in what ways does it matter to the visitors who have come to experience the architecture that we have taken such pains to preserve and present. At many historic house museums, the architecture occupies a secondary position in the site's interpretation. But what can the interpretation of the building—the place where the residents' lives were lived—contribute to enrich the histories we wish to tell, and to connect human lives to place and to community?

Every building has its own story to tell, whether it was designed for a particular occupant or chosen by an owner for habitation. How does the design of the building represent the character of the original owners, their desires, their attitudes, their aspirations? Were renovations made to the building to enhance the lifestyles of those who lived within it? Does the building relate to vernacular architecture in the region? Was it constructed of materials or utilizing craft traditions that were important to the economic or social history of the community?

Orienting visitors to the relationships between the built and unbuilt features of the site is an effective way to draw connections between the historic site's residents, their narratives, and the buildings, landscape, and community where those narratives unfolded. Was the building originally oriented to take advantage of landscape views that have since changed or are now absent? Is the historic house located in an urban setting where privacy concerns affected the building's design? Were relationships established between other buildings on the site? Are there connections or changes to the surrounding landscape or neighborhood that have occured over time that reveal the community's history? Considering questions such as these in historic house interpretation will incorporate additional layers of meaning and can help to integrate the history of the lives of the inhabitants with the building and the surrounding community.

Challenges

Interpreting historic house architecture requires research to understand the design and construction that contributed to the unique qualities of the building. Providing insight about the materials, building technologies, innovative techniques, and changes in design will help visitors to understand the site within the context of architectural and social history. While design research is often well-supported in the skill set of architectural house museum staff, historic house sites may require additional resources to begin to plumb questions of architectural design and building construction. This can be an opportunity for historic house sites to forge partnerships with local building trade professionals and with regional colleges and universities. Dedicated student research projects, internships, and community member contributions are valuable ways for historic house sites to augment their own research and form relationships that can blossom into special research affinity groups.

What's equally important and often lacking are opportunities for visitors to experience and engage with the architecture of historic houses for themselves. In our efforts to protect our historic sites, we have reduced the visitor's experience to passive reception of verbal information. We've favored a prescribed and controlled path of movement that limits the visitor's ability to follow their own curiosity. Guided tours often thwart visitor curiosity, limiting the ability of visitors to self-direct their own discovery and form personal connections. The experiences that visitors have at many of the nation's historic houses often negate rather than contribute to the type of meaningful interaction that visitors can have with the built environment and that they can carry with them beyond their visit.

For the most part, visitors to our sites rarely lack in interest. They display a keen and earnest desire to partake of all we have to offer. Yet for all the intentionality and effort visitors have expended to get to our sites, they are often lacking in the visual literacy skills that are key to understanding architecture without our coaching. How can we impart visual literacy skills, share the rich historical content of our sites, and facilitate experiential learning within the limits of a forty-five- to ninety-minute tour? These are the key challenges we face in sharing architectural and historic interpretation in ways that visitors find interesting, thought-provoking, meaningful, and, yes, that matters to them.

Active critique of our methods of interpretation and engagement have surfaced within the field in recent years. Museum professionals such as Nina Simon, Franklin Vagnone, and Deborah Ryan call into question a tradition of museum practice that fails to actively engage the public and encourages passive learning and experience. In her book, *The Participatory Museum*, Nina Simon explores concrete strategies in content delivery and interpretation that can provoke conversation and increase personal connection. When skillful docents are successful in "personalizing the experience" by weaving discussion and active conversation into their tours, social engagement and connection are enhanced. Simon's discussion of the merits of incorporating Visual Thinking Strategies (VTS), pioneered by Philip Yenawine and Abigail Housen, to encourage visual learning should be particularly interesting to those engaged in interpreting the architecture of their historic sites.[2] Originally developed for use in art museums and school programs, VTS encourages focused observation and active discussion by asking open-ended questions such as "What do you see?" When used in interpreting the historic house's architecture, VTS can be adapted to spark active participation and invite visitors to contribute their own observations about the building's design features.

Vagnone and Ryan's challenge for historic house museums to seek new strategies for community engagement have been much discussed. The conceptual approach and interpretive strategies Ryan and Vagnone propose in *The Anarchist's Guide to Historic House Museums* invert the emphasis on architecture as preserved place and assign primacy to human habitation and experience. Not only does their work embrace experimentation and risk-taking, their focus on exploring tactics under the thematic rubric of "Shelter, Habitation, Community, and Experience" points the way to exploring interpretive strategies that will lead to increased experience of architecture and enhanced visitor connection.[3]

Cheryl A. Bachand

The critique of museum leaders like Simon, Vagnone, and Ryan is important not only for the questions they raise. It is with the strategies and approaches they investigate that we can begin to modify and replace the ineffective practices that have become mainstays of our field. Analysis, experimentation, and assessment will be the keys to confronting the challenges that we face and to charting a new course.

What's New, What's Tried and True, What's Old and Needs New Life?

So, what are historic houses doing to plumb their research, make connections, and promote meaningful experiences with the architecture of their sites? When we look broadly at research and interpretation across the historic house museum field, accepted practices and delivery techniques are evident. At the same time, we are also witnessing an increasing emphasis on experimentation and a willingness to try new and varied approaches.

Guided tours continue to be the primary means by which historic houses provide access and deliver their interpretive content. At the Glass House site where Philip Johnson designed multiple buildings over the course of his more than fifty-year residency, the visitor can choose from as many as six different tours with corresponding price points, calibrating the degree of immersion with a willingness to pay. Led by a contemporary woodworker, the Gamble House's *Details and Joinery* tour offers visitors an in-depth look at the craftsmanship, materials, and technical complexities of the house and its furniture. With its focus on the construction of the house, the *Details and Joinery* tour provides a perspective on craftsmanship that moves beyond the notion of the architect as sole creator. In addition to its more in-depth tour options, visitors to the Gamble House can opt for a less committed way to enjoy the architectural site. One day per week, visitors are encouraged to bring their own picnic lunch to enjoy on the terrace and reserve their ticket for the twenty-minute mini-tour. Offered on a day when most other cultural attractions in the area are closed, the Gamble House's mini-tour option endeavors to attract casual visitors, an attempt to matter to different people in a different way. At Maymont in Richmond, Virginia, the narratives of the domestic staff are being presented in the restored *Belowstairs* portion of the site. Visitors are presented with a guided tour of the *Upstairs* floors of the Gilded Age mansion and a self-guided *Belowstairs* tour—a unique approach that merges guided and self-guided experience of architectural space and domestic narratives.

Springing from architecture's position within the realm of the fine arts, many historic houses have developed programs in partnership with visual and performing arts organizations. Through temporary exhibitions and musical performances within the building, a different type of architectural experience emerges as a way to explore broader themes and expand audience. Developing program and curriculum linkages to STEAM education (Science, Technology, Engineering, the Arts, and Math) is another way for historic houses to connect the architecture of their sites to K–12 learning initiatives in their communities. Chicago Architecture Foundation's online *Discover Design* platform and their award-winning *Skylines to Schoolyards* curriculum guide, provide educational resources for making connections between architecture, design thinking, and the development of twenty-first-century learning skills.

Digital Engagement and Experience

Historic house museums continue to lag behind other types of museums in the use of digital technologies and digital engagement practices. Many publish extensive histories, visual imagery, and use multimedia on their websites, providing a rich resource that can be used by students and those wishing to know more about the site prior to visiting. The Glass House website is particularly worthy of note as it combines 360-degree views of the buildings along with detailed interviews with architect Philip Johnson as he walked around the site sharing his design ideas, architectural philosophy, and reminiscences.

Many historic houses present extensive research via websites, resulting in online publishing that can be accessed pre- and post-visit but does little to contribute to a digital experience while on site. Simple touch screens and tablets located strategically throughout the historic house would provide the means to present complicated concepts such as structural systems or a way to display the changes made to the building over time through historic images or other visual media. How much better would a visitor's experience be if they were able to walk around the Glass House and listen to Johnson's interview about the landscape on a mobile app in real time?

Visitors to the Eustis Estate in Milton, Massachusetts, can explore the house and site through this type of self-guided experience with interpretation delivered using kiosk, tablet, or personal device. Interpretive topics include architecture and design, lifestyle, and family history. Making use of location maps, historic photographs, census research, collections, and restoration details, visitors can craft a personalized, inquiry-based experience.

The Chicago History Museum's augmented reality (AR) application, "The Chicago 00 Project" uses the museum's rich media archives in film and photography to connect visitors with physical locations within the city of Chicago where historical events took place. In the first episode, seventy captioned historical photographs and newsreel films can be viewed as an AR tour along Chicago's Riverwalk, a popular pedestrian walkway of the city where the 1915 nautical *Eastland* disaster occurred. Through this AR project, the Chicago History Museum is using digital engagement technologies to share the rich and often hidden reserves of their archival holdings, and to connect them to the physical places and spaces of the city beyond their museum.[4]

Using smartphone technology, the San Francisco–based company Detour is providing cultural tourists and residents alike with immersive interpretive and place-based experiences of architectural, artistic, and urban landmarks. Detour's GPS, audio-based tours provide the casual user with engaging content often delivered by cultural and architectural historians, just the sort of experience that visitors to historic houses are craving. In Chicago, much of Detour's offerings are architectural. Historic houses would benefit from study and adaptation of the delivery approaches to architecture and place-based history used by the Chicago History Museum and Detour.

National Public Housing Museum—Encouraging Social Connections

The National Public Housing Museum in Chicago embraces a more active societal role, delving into the history of its architectural site as it seeks to create connections among the building, its history, and social issues. The museum is located at the site of the Jane Addams Homes, the first public housing project in the city of Chicago. Created under the aegis of the Public Works Administration and designed by noted Chicago architect John A. Holabird, the Jane Addams Homes offered the first integrated public housing in Chicago. Named for the pioneering social reformer, the Jane Addams Homes are located close to the site of Addams' Hull-House, Chicago's first settlement house.

Cheryl A. Bachand

At the local level, a group of public housing residents led a grassroots effort to save the last extant building of the historic Jane Addams Homes from destruction in the 1990s. The National Public Housing Museum was created out of this movement that advocated for the preservation of the building as a place to tell the stories of public housing residents and the history of public housing in Chicago.[5] According to Daniel Ronan, former manager of public engagement, "the building was seen by residents as a monument to their experience in public housing."[6]

The preservation of the building follows a historically familiar path of grassroots preservation and community organization. Yet this site differs significantly. Neither a high-style building of a wealthy industrialist nor a modern architectural masterpiece, the National Public Housing Museum interprets the site through the stories of public housing resident families.

Informed by the model of the Lower East Side Tenement Museum, the National Public Housing Museum's first interpretive spaces include two apartments—one that housed a Jewish family from the 1930s and another that housed an African American family from the 1970s. The museum features galleries for thematic exhibitions, flexible spaces for public gatherings and programs, and an entrepreneurship hub to support cooperatives and small business activities of public housing residents. Its goals are not a pristine preservation of the architecture or to prioritize the history of its design. The site provides a platform for public housing residents to be the storytellers of their own stories and for the museum to engage in public dialogue and active community engagement. In contrast to the practice of documenting and presenting history, the National Public Housing Museum takes an active role in using its history to encourage dialogue and social debate.

Rudolph Schindler House—Bold Experimentation and Layering Interpretive Experience

At the Rudolph Schindler House, the visitor experiences a hybrid architectural house museum and exhibition site. The site's history began with a grassroots effort in the 1970s to preserve the house by the Friends of the Schindler House and became the MAK Center for Art and Architecture at the Schindler House in 1994. The California satellite of the MAK, Austrian Museum of Applied Arts/Contemporary Art of Vienna, the MAK Center operates three residential sites in and around Los Angeles designed by Viennese architect Rudolph Schindler including the national historic landmark Schindler House.

Architectural historians recognize the Schindler House as one of the world's first modern houses. Designed as combined residence/workspace without traditional room divisions, the original occupants were two young couples—Schindler and his wife, Pauline, and Marian and Clyde Chase. The house's design challenged notions of the traditional separation between indoor and outdoor and public and private. Schindler conceived the house as a series of flexible-use spaces that embraced communal living. It was a bold experiment that would have profound influence on residential architecture in the ensuing decades.

Rudolph and Pauline Schindler occupied the house in combination or separately throughout the remainder of their lives. Throughout the Schindlers' residency, the house was a social gathering place for independent artists, writers, and left-wing political figures. As noted by deputy director Anthony Carfello, "there is more publicness and gathering space designed into this house than any other Schindler residence."[7] This open-hosting idea is inherent in the design of the space and the way that the Schindlers used the house. It is also at the core of the MAK Center's interpretation and programming as an exhibition site layered onto an architectural house site.

Arts programming at the Schindler House is in keeping with the core lifestyle and history of the house as a site for independent artists and creatives who visited the house and drifted through in social and artistic relationships with Rudolph and Pauline Schindler. "If we kept the house as a bubble, as simply a historic house, we wouldn't be using the house to its full intention, the intention and use established by its original creators and residents Rudolph and Pauline Schindler."[8]

The Schindler House is a unique model of interpretation and experience. It is neither an architectural house museum nor a contemporary arts center, but both. Visitors experience art exhibitions installed throughout the architectural site. Activating the arts legacy of the house, the exhibition program encourages the exploration of art and architecture as another level of programming that is layered onto the historic house site. The visitor experience is self-guided. Visitors wander throughout the site for as long as they care to, exploring these two experiences as one. A historic brochure and exhibition checklist with written prompts provides visitors with a guide for context and understanding. Visitors are transformed from passive to active viewers who self-direct their own learning and experience.

Moving Forward

As we can see from the few examples explored in this chapter and countless others, the most successful interpretive programs—whether traditional or untraditional—stem directly from the research base of each particular historic house site. New partnerships and other voices are often key ingredients that can help to reveal the uniqueness of the historic house through different eyes and perspectives. A willingness to experiment, to try and fail, to pilot and assess, have yielded the avenues for change. It's through the process of experimentation that the real questions were asked and answered.

> Applying what we've learned through years of piloting and experimentation, we can begin to make our content more relevant—to matter to more people.

We need to continue to experiment with multiple modes of interpretive program delivery, including participatory and digital engagement. Digital engagement is an underutilized platform that could be tapped to deliver more of the research that already exists at historic house sites. The ability to include other histories and to integrate broader access to research archives through on-site digital-engagement platforms has yet to be fully explored. The goal is not digital for its own sake. To be successful, digital tools should enhance the delivery of research content and deepen engagement. Key questions must be asked and thoughtfully considered. Is there content that is being delivered orally that could be better delivered through digital means? Are there detailed and complicated ideas that would be better communicated through links to other information and modes of visual display? Do the site's archival and research holdings include imagery that can and should be shared? Are there ways to make use of digital tools to provide visitors with deeper levels of meaning and engagement? Historic house museums should be looking at how our colleagues at other types of museums are employing digital-engagement tools. Their example may enhance the way we think about our own research and interpretation strategies and provide us with the inspiration needed to launch our own digital initiatives.

We need to embrace interpretive strategies and delivery practices that enhance the visitor's experience of the architecture of our sites. Experiencing architecture is integral to fully appreciating and understanding it. While guided tours incorporate experience of the building, they confine the visitor's experience to a prescribed path and therefore establish limits to the type of connected learning that is our goal. By virtue of their relative lack of dialogue and discovery, guided tours minimize curiosity and engagement. Visitors on our guided tours are unable to linger longer over an architectural detail or space that intrigues them. If halfway through their tour they are intro- duced to a concept or recognize a design detail that reminds them of something they witnessed earlier in the tour, they are unable to go back to explore that relationship.

We've constructed our tours and our tour routes based on a combination of additive content delivery, sequential experience of space, and practical logistics. While we may have arrived at the most efficient solution to delivering our content and moving visitors through the site, what have we lost when visitors are not allowed to learn, explore, and discover in a way that is more self-directed and engaged? Through guided tours and stanchion-protected spaces, we've created a visitor experience that essentially invites our visitors to respectfully imagine life in an intimate domestic space but from a respectful distance behind a constructed barrier that makes them wonder if they are truly welcome. In our quest to protect material culture, we've provided an object-centered approach to architectural space and historical narrative that has created a dis- tance between our historic sites and our visitors.

Historic house museums are about presenting narratives of domestic life within domestic space. Are there better ways to share the narratives of domestic life within residential space that add value to both layers of the historical and architectural content? Is there a way to do this without sacrificing our responsibilities as effective stewards of historic sites? Is there another way to achieve the results we desire for a visitor-connected experience? For too long, our structural and operational best practices have been rooted in an object-centered tradition. Are we willing to challenge ourselves to give up some control and adopt the practice of truly facilitating learning rather than delivering content? It's time we remove the barriers—the unseen velvet ropes that are omnipresent on our guided tours—and encourage the freedom of movement that is at the core of architectural experience.

If we are going to matter to more and different people than we have in the past, we need to interact with individuals and communities that have not traditionally been our partners or constituency. As Ryan and Vagnone note, it is time for museums to look beyond our field to others who have employed community-engagement strategies successfully.[9] Engaging with new partners and new communities from outside our orbit will bring in new and different points of view. These conversations can be infinitely valuable in causing us to think differently about the multiple histories and meanings of our sites. If we are going to matter to more and different people than we have in the past, we need to step up our efforts to reach out to communities outside our doors. We need to listen to what they have to say and be open to experimenting with new ideas and nontraditional program delivery. When coupled with a willingness to con- sider other voices in the development of new interpretation and programs, enhanced commu- nity connection can be engendered.

The histories and content of our sites become relevant when visitors believe it matters to them. The goal is to provide opportunities for visitors to explore what's valuable to them and form their own connections. The historic sites that are achieving the greatest success with visitor engage- ment are offering multiple content entry points. Architecture and design can be one of those entry points. We should be facilitating a variety of ways for visitors to consider and actively ex- perience our historic sites and interpretive content. Establishing a connection is the beginning of the process. Being open to what happens next will take us to a place that may be messy but that has the capacity to unlock the door to something that our visitors find valuable and meaningful. This is the experience that we can facilitate and deliver.

Notes

1. Paul Goldberger, *Why Architecture Matters* (New Haven, CT: Yale University Press, 2009), 15.
2. Nina Simon, *The Participatory Museum* (Santa Cruz, CA: Museum 2.0, 2010).
3. Deborah Ryan and Franklin Vagnone, "Reorienting Historic House Museums: An Anarchist's Guide," *ARCC Conference Repository* (July 2014): 97–106, accessed March 4, 2017, http://www.arcc-journal.org/index.php/repository/article/view/255.
4. "Chicago 00—The Eastland Disaster," Chicago 00 Chicago History Experience, Chicago History Museum, accessed February 25, 2017, http://chicago00.org/.
5. Stephanie Lulay, "Public Housing Museum Plans to Break Ground in Former ABLA Building in 2016," *DNA Info* (August 14, 2015), accessed December 9, 2016, https://www.dnainfo.com/chicago/20150814/little-italy/public-housing-museum-plans-break-ground-former-abla-building-2016.
6. Daniel Ronan (manager of Public Engagement, National Public Housing Museum) interview by Cheryl A. Bachand, December 7, 2016.
7. Anthony Carfello (deputy director, MAK Center for Art and Architecture at the Schindler House) interview by Cheryl A. Bachand, December 9, 2016.
8. Carfello interview by Bachand, December 9, 2016.
9. Ryan and Vagnone, "Reorienting Historic House Museums," 98–99.

Recommended Resources

Chicago Architecture Foundation, "Educator Resources," http://www.architecture.org/teach-learn/educators/.

Goldberger, Paul. *Why Architecture Matters*. New Haven, CT: Yale University Press, 2009.

Simon, Nina. *The Art of Relevance*. Santa Cruz, CA: Museum 2.0, 2016.

Vagnone, Franklin D., and Deborah E. Ryan. *Anarchist's Guide to Historic House Museums*. New York: Routledge, 2016.

Chapter 21

Looking beyond the Front Door to Find Spirit of Place

LUCINDA A. BROCKWAY

The 2007–2009 economic downturn left in its wake a challenge for historic house museums: how to discover unexplored and untapped opportunities for bringing properties to life, increase donor appeal, and open doors to new audiences that would stop the downward visitation spiral. With an entire nation of historic sites seeking solutions that didn't damage their cultural reputation, house museums across the country had permission to creatively explore new possibilities. If those new ideas failed, alternate solutions could be explored without risk of criticism. The era allowed for experimentation, for outside thinking, and for open dialogue about relevancy to contemporary audiences and the potential for new creative dynamism, often engaging donors in this process of rediscovery. Most importantly, the pursuit allowed us to look beyond the front door of historic houses, to the landscapes, the gardens, the scenery, the structural ruins, and the genius of place that could be harnessed to become evocative and impactful opportunities for building membership, visitation, and enterprise.

This chapter explores the experiences at the Trustees of Reservations, a Massachusetts preservation and conservation organization with twelve individual historic houses across the Commonwealth. In 2012, a new president and CEO challenged the staff to reveal untapped opportunities for connecting people to place. Though a large organization, their pursuit reveals lessons applicable to institutions of all sizes, budgets, and staffing models. The work confirms that creativity can lead to impactful change as much as to financial security and dynamic leadership.

The Trustees (formerly known as the Trustees of Reservations) is a statewide preservation and conservation organization that was founded by landscape architect Charles Eliot in 1891. Eliot envisioned an organization separate from the politics of government that could set aside, or reserve, land for the public enjoyment. He and his cofounders structured the organization under a volunteer board of trustees, who held these lands in trust just as libraries hold books or art museums hold paintings. The mission of the organization was to "preserve, for public use and enjoyment, properties of exceptional scenic, historic, and ecological value in Massachusetts." Over the next 125 years, the focus of the organization grew and adapted, gathering properties through donation or purchase that upheld its mission.

Today, the 140,000-member organization protects more than one hundred properties and more than twenty-six thousand acres of Massachusetts' special places including working farms, prime ecological habitat, historic landscapes, historic house museums, miles of coastline, and 320 miles of hiking trails. From the Berkshires to the islands, Trustees' reservations connect people with the natural, historical, and cultural treasures that make Massachusetts home through individual property experiences. When the conservation and preservation movement took their specialized, often divergent, paths under the National Historic Preservation Act of 1966 and the National Environmental Policy Act of 1969, the Trustees became best known as one of the nation's leading land trust and conservation organizations but retained its collection of historic house museums and historic sites as a quieter, less well-known, part of the organization even though the collection of properties included several National Historic Landmarks.

A new president, Barbara Erickson, came to the organization in 2012 and recognized the potential for the organization's more balanced original mission. The changes in national economics, particularly its impact on our visitation and membership, encouraged us to refresh our strategic plan under her new leadership, looking creatively at ways in which we could inspire and infuse the organization with new opportunities for success while supporting and continuing areas of the organization that were working well. The refreshed strategic plan had four pillars:

1. Excite our audience, engaging a broader, more diverse membership.
2. Grow our finances to support this work through increases in endowment returns, property revenue, and membership support.
3. Protect more of Massachusetts' most treasured cultural, natural, and scenic properties.
4. Steward our properties by prioritizing and analyzing our capital and operating funds to improve our baseline standards.

Under these four pillars, cultural properties offered untapped opportunities for change in all four areas. The first step was to assess what the organization had, understand its current condition, and strategically analyze the potential for igniting new paths for organizational growth.

As an organization whose primary focus was on the land (historic, natural, and scenic), this reassessment was perhaps easier than it might have been had the organization been building-centric, but it took a creative and comprehensive look at *all* cultural resources as defined by the United Nations Educational, Scientific and Cultural Organization (UNESCO). Using the UNESCO terms for cultural resources, particularly cultural landscapes, a table of properties was developed that identified the size, location, specific cultural resources, significant dates, significant people, thematic associations, and any specific designations they had received over time. This was created for all 109 properties held at the time, but the process can be adapted as easily to a single site as it is to a statewide organization. The table is continuously updated as new properties are acquired.

The UNESCO terms for defining cultural landscapes are particularly useful as they identify three main categories: (1) landscapes designed or created intentionally by people, (2) landscapes that organically evolved (in the United States we refer to this category as "vernacular"), and (3) associative landscapes, which recognize the powerful religious, artistic, or cultural associations of a place. UNESCO further defines the second category (organically evolved landscapes) into two distinct types: (a) a relict or fossil landscape where the evolutionary process has ended and (b) a continuing landscape, one which retains an active role in contemporary society under an evolutionary process that is still continuing (such as farming).[1] The results of the inventory were surprising: of the 109 reservations, 95, or 87 percent, of them were relict landscapes and of these, 77 contained significant ruins. This means that the largest category of cultural resources were archaeology sites and ruins, though people most often think of historic house museums and

Lucinda A. Brockway

designed landscapes as leading the list. Only half (54) of the properties held historic structures and less than one-quarter (21) contained significant designed landscapes.

Since most properties include ruins and relict landscapes, it brought forward the power and the potential impact these resources could have on bringing history to hikers, dog-walkers, and non-historians, and blurred the silos between conservation and preservation once again. Recently, the Trustees reactivated the ruins of the former rose garden at Castle Hill (Ipswich, Massachusetts) as a test to determine the value and appeal of this approach for areas previously closed to the public. Sections of rusty nineteenth-century picket fencing were purchased from an architectural salvage company and installed to guide visitors safely through the ruins. Former garden beds were rejuvenated and planted with hardy perennials and new cultivars of shrub roses. The central fountain basin was cleaned, but not restored, and the former fountain urn, which is only partially intact, was stabilized and planted with container plants. The area became a favorite of all visitors and has recently been awarded funding to further stabilize and reinterpret the garden.

Cultural resources do not stop at the door but in fact can be found on even the remotest hiking trail. One of the Trustees' most picturesque ruins sits on a popular hillside trail at Ashintully, in Tyringham, Massachusetts. Robb and Grace de Peyster Tytus built their summer mansion in 1903 on the brow of a hill with a spectacular view down the Housatonic Valley. The house burned in a 1952 blaze, leaving only the terrace and porch columns, some foundational remains, and the view. Rather than erase the site, the Trustees continue to preserve the columns, which today rise out of the building ruins like a feature in a Bronte novel (see Figure 21.1). The columns draw hikers to pause, take in the view, and capture the ruin in evocative photographs.

Figure 21.1 The picturesque ruins of a historic house survive along a popular hiking trail at Ashintully in Tyringham, Massachusetts. Photo courtesy of the Trustees Archives and Research Center.

These resources offer powerful opportunities for interpretation and "reading" of the cultural landscape without necessarily pointing the way for shard hunters to "dig here." The Trustees, in fact, have many house and barn ruins, stone walls, former fields, and pasture oaks found beneath Massachusetts' ever successful successional tree canopy. Most of these are passed on a trail without a glance, but they offer a missed opportunity for us to take history and genius of place off the beaten track, moving the historic house museum experience outdoors to new audiences. The landscape assessment taught us important lessons about site stewardship as well. It acknowledges the inevitability of growth, maturation, and loss that affects *all* cultural resources including intact buildings and designed landscapes. It reveals the inevitable life cycle of each cultural resource, recognizing that all need careful management and, in some cases, an occasional restarting of the clock. In planning capital needs, the recognition of ruins, and their inevitability if we do not care for our buildings and grounds, brought forward discussions about what to save and what to let go. In the past, these decisions, whether made conscientiously or inevitably (and usually by those who owned the property before us), resulted in the ruins that we owned today. Yet these ruins remain a powerful and evocatively moving cultural resource within our landscapes, with just as much ability for exceptional interpretive experiences as our furnished historic houses. By recognizing the life cycle of a roof, a coat of paint, a retaining wall, a collection object, and the life cycle of plants within a historic garden, the global conversation about preservation priorities feels more comfortable. In fact, preservation became not a discussion about loss, it became a conversation about managing change, something that our cultural counterparts around the world have become more comfortable with than we have here in North America.

The Trustees continue to look for models of rediscovery and connection with ruins that offer powerful experiences with limited staffing. It has certainly put history and culture back into nature and allows us to work closely with ecology and trail teams to blur the edges of the former silos we all live within. Trustees' tours have highlighted the inevitable decline of structures and continue to reinforce the allure of ruins in the imagination of its visitors. There continues to be something very powerful about the value of ruins to even the most ardent non-historian.

The recognition of continuously evolving landscapes and relict resources was brought forward once again as the organization sought to understand the stewardship responsibilities for coastal properties. The seventy-six miles of coastline owned by the organization in Massachusetts is continuously threatened with extreme weather events and sea-level rise. Modeling the impacts of these changes with professional consultants included a graded inventory of natural and cultural resources that could potentially be impacted and has put cultural landscapes into sobering focus as the organization works to understand and document them before their loss. The study proved archaeology sites the most threatened, and limited financial resources have allowed documentation of only those sites impacted by proposed projects. The organization is, however, acutely aware of these fragile resources in planning for Massachusetts' changing coastline. The organization continues to explore the role of new technologies to understand how to capture their allure before they are gone, including virtual and augmented reality programs, aerial drone documentation, 3-D printing of models, and interactive online exploration. Just as we look to slow the decay of a stone house foundation, we must understand the destructive process of climate change and manage organizational stewardship priorities appropriately. Before the organization begins new interpretive techniques, however, we are learning to face the reality of what will be here and what will be lost over the next decades.

Not surprisingly, most funding continues to be focused on the care of National Historic Landmark properties (now seven in number), including historic structures and designed landscapes. As the

Lucinda A. Brockway

organization began to look intently at these resources, we wanted to think about them in new ways. Many of the historic houses, which had operated as museums for decades with declining visitation, were closed when the economy sank and forced the organization to prioritize its labor force. Open occasionally by appointment or for simple seasonal cleaning, mothballing these houses was considered a responsible stewardship practice until increased interest would allow for more open hours. The discovery after five years, however, was that lack of air movement and lack of weekly monitoring allowed pest problems to fester and, in fact, encouraged the decline of interiors and object collections rather than preserving them.

So how could the organization reimagine each historic house? Where were the successful models and new approaches that could connect with contemporary audiences? Staff talked and traveled and investigated emerging success stories. The organization invited noteworthy consultants and colleagues to visit for a "blink"—a quick visit to evaluate visitor experience and potential new directions based on reimagining existing resources. These visits included engagement experts, theater and outdoor concert specialists, leaders in the public garden industry, curators, appraisers, and conservators. For five years, small groups of staff visited National Trust (UK) operations in England, an organization perceived to be the most successful at engaging with a diverse public. For one season, UK National Trust experts conducted a consultancy visit "across the pond" to help rethink the Trustees' most prominent historic houses, historic farms, and designed landscapes and gardens.

The Trustees management structure was reorganized according to the UK National Trust model; property business plans were created under general managers responsible for a "triple bottom line" that established measurable annual goals in increased visitation, property revenue, and stewardship metrics. Stewardship and engagement staff work under each general manager to achieve these annual goals, and specialized teams of statewide engagement professionals, curators, farmers, horticulturists, and trail stewards focus their technical expertise where it is most effective to help realize these annual goals and statewide programmatic priorities. For small museums, this specialist teamwork could be achieved through small consultant contracts or specialized volunteer leadership. As work with the property business plan model evolves, they can be edited to revise content, goals, and the process for producing them. For the Trustees, the organization is working to include better engagement metrics, to incorporate specialty team priorities, and to build a collaborative review process that represents all voices and appropriate annual goals across the triple bottom line.

These business plans, and their programmatic or interpretive counterparts, are built on two foundational statements: a Statement of Significance and a Spirit of Place Statement. The Statement of Significance recognizes the importance of a property to the history, architecture, archaeology, engineering, or culture of a community, state, or nation during a particular era. For all who work with National Park Service standards or have prepared National Register nominations, this statement is familiar. It links the physical remains of the past, such as structures, landscapes, circulation systems, objects, and ruins, with historic themes, eras, people, events, settlement patterns, and context. It looks backward, building stewardship and interpretive decisions on historic themes and contributing physical resources.

A Spirit of Place Statement identifies the emotive responses to a place. It identifies the physical and spiritual elements that give meaning, value, emotion, and mystery to a place.[2] It links the same structures, landscapes, circulation systems, objects, and ruins to the more intangible qualities of memory, emotion, values, textures, colors, light, and sounds that make a place cherished. It links what a visitor sees, smells, or hears to how they feel, and seeks to capture that feeling repeatedly through enhanced visitor experiences that reinforce the emotional response to place. For the UK National Trust, writing the Spirit of Place Statement is a three-step process: (1) review and update the Statement of Significance, (2) identify and gather stakeholder groups that care deeply about the property, and (3) work with the stakeholder groups to define what is unique, distinctive, and cherished about the property and incorporate these into a Spirit of Place Statement.

Once complete, these two statements are the springs from which flow site-inspired, site-specific, tours and programs. For example, at one of the Trustees' flagship properties, Naumkeag (Stockbridge, Massachusetts), its Statement of Significance includes phrases such as "an outstanding example of a late nineteenth century country estate," "a major surviving early work of McKim, Mead & White," and "its landscape reflects the collaboration of 20th century landscape architect Fletcher Steele and owner Mabel Choate."[3] The working draft for its Sprit of Place Statement use phrases such as: "For Naumkeag, two Choate family ideals—love of family and love of art—will continue to drive Naumkeag's rebirth" and "Coupled with a passion for horticultural experimentation, antiques, world travel and life-long learning, Naumkeag remains alive with this spirit."

The Spirit of Place Statement sounds easy, but in practice it has been very difficult to do quickly. Even the UK National Trust admits that draft Spirit of Place Statements are tested and tried, revised, and then finalized into their property business plans. When done well, they provide the litmus test for proving if a program or proposed event is suitable and appropriate for the property; only those that can be linked in some way to these two statements are appropriate. For the Trustees, impatience has caused frustration. Often, Spirit of Place Statements read as descriptive literature rather than crowd-sourced emotive responses to a place. Rather than asking visitors what makes this place special, the staff often want to define it for them. At first, the organization built impossibly short deadlines to produce these statements in an insatiable hunger for something, instead of listening, watching, and asking visitors to produce the words. Facebook postings, travel advisor reviews, and other social media tools have helped, but the organization has grappled with this process for two years before deciding to write a simple draft to include in each business plan with the understanding that they would be revised and rewritten properly over the following two years. Some of the most memorable visits to National Trust properties in England were inspired by these statements, so the real results are transformational when done well.

The process has been easier on more notable properties where visitation is high and popular house tours, events, or programs capture the distinctive and most cherished aspects of the property. For these properties, stakeholder groups are large and diverse, making it easier to find the most common emotive responses. Spirit of Place is much harder to define on properties in transition or properties with low visitation. The best attempts have resulted in a series of bulleted lists that capture some of this spirit, which can be tested with programs or events as the real focus of the property's excitement comes alive. The Trustees will continue to experiment and define this valuable process in hopes that these two statements combined can turn the key for property visitation and memorable site experiences for all properties, spurring even the most difficult sites to life.

A primary goal for the organization is to encourage and entice place-based, meaningful experiences, including ways in which new themes can be explored within the context of regional history. In 2014, the Trustees began a new journey, linking site-inspired contemporary outdoor art installations to cultural properties. Rather than curate a series of outdoor exhibitions of an artist's work, nationally renowned artists were commissioned to create a piece inspired from the history, scenery, or natural beauty of the site. Each piece was designed to be temporary, to be installed for no more than one year, and offered free of charge for all visitors to enjoy. This effort has been one of the organization's most bold initiatives and has been executed successfully despite some significant challenges, not the least of which is the change that occurs when a contemporary art installation is erected on a historic landscape. These installations have had to consider parking for increased visitation, the site impacts on archaeological and ecological resources, local and state permitting processes, and a myriad of community concerns. Three installations have been completed as of this writing. For those who have interacted with the pieces and participated in their associated programming, they have been deeply meaningful. They do, however, require commitment and dedication on the part of many staff to fulfill their greatest potential.

Perhaps one of the most surprising finds along this path of rediscovery seems obvious in retrospect. In building a series of internal assessment reports for a cultural resources campaign, cultural sites were grouped together in common "buckets," defined by similarities in property resources. Some properties were best known for their collections or archives, or for their period of significance; some for their gardens; others as sources of inspirational scenery that spawned great literature or art. Eleven sites had significant period gardens or landscapes, some of National Landmark status, and others better known for their horticultural depth and diversity.

To better understand the potential of these properties as public gardens, a group of experts from the American Public Garden Association visited several of these properties as a "blink" exercise. The group visited six sites in two days and offered feedback on their potential as public gardens. Expanding the identify of these properties beyond their traditional roles as historic house museums was of concern, particularly since each of these sites had gardens and landscapes that were expensive to maintain. Committing to the upkeep and higher standards of these properties as public gardens that included a historic house museum, rather than a historic house set in a garden, shifted the focus and skewed the kaleidoscope in new directions.

Recently published research on domestic travel and garden tourism stated that seventy-eight million people visit a botanical garden each year.[4] Seventy-three percent of the people that visit public gardens come to appreciate their beauty; the remaining 27 percent—those representing the avid gardening audience—represent the most financially supportive and the most engaged. Worldwide, cultural sites with impressive gardens top the list of properties visited; two-thirds of those visitors will make repeat visits to the garden and only one visit to see the house. The consulting experts consistently reminded staff that success in U.S. public gardens is found where the gardens are an integral and important part of their communities—providing solace, social interaction, personal value, and meaning. With this encouragement, the Trustees began a strategic look at building recognition for these properties as public gardens first and as historic house museums as an integral, yet distinct, opportunity during a garden visit. The change linked the historic house community *and* the public garden community, but it was the potential for regular, repeat visitation and its related opportunities for increases in membership sales, gate receipts, and associated enterprise that inspired a further look. Surprisingly, even for houses that were closed in 2011, the consultants were supportive and excited about reopening these houses and offering house experiences as part of the public garden visit. Instead of the garden overtaking the historic house, it offered a means to entice audience visitation that then could take advantage of the house experience as part of an expanded site visit.

In 2015, a director of public gardens and a curator of horticulture were hired to organize site horticulturists into a specialty team. This provided statewide consistency and peer support for these experts and allowed the development of baseline standards and approaches to horticultural diversity that enhanced and did not detract from the historic integrity of each property. General site stewardship activities (plowing, lawn mowing, leaf raking, and property maintenance) became the responsibility of stewardship managers while the tasks that required the focused skills of a technical horticulture expert were separated and became the responsibility of the site horticulturist. Throughout the first two years, the stewardship manager and horticulturist have worked closely together to better define their roles and refine their responsibilities, but the change in the depth, diversity, and quality of the horticultural experience has been tangible.

As with the historic house collections, the garden's living collections are being catalogued, assessed, mapped, and interpreted. New plants are being added and historic gardens restored. Even for well-known historic properties, such as Naumkeag (Stockbridge, Massachusetts) and Castle Hill (Ipswich, Massachusetts), visitation was up by double digits during the first two years, drawn by substantial investments in the gardens, the goals of the property business plans, and creative engagement and interpretive programming. In three years (2013–2016) at Naumkeag alone, program participation increased 83 percent, revenue rose 179 percent, and membership purchases increased 416 percent. Marketing and communication efforts have highlighted the gardens and their horticultural contents, including regular features on the organization's social media. Between 2013 and 2016, 175 print, broadcast, and online press features appeared. Horticulture Friday Facebook postings saw more than one hundred thousand views. Properties once known only for their historic houses have been rediscovered for their gardens, including their more extensive trail systems through native woodlands and wildlands. Garden tours, plant sales, pick your own flower bouquets, and shop sales were added to the income from historic house tours. Multigenerational families, day-trippers, and tourists were encouraged on the grounds, and groups such as the Association for Garden Communicators (formerly the National Garden Writers Association) began writing about the gardens *and* houses to new audiences.

This effort has been a shift in focus. Rather than the historic house experience starting at the front door of the house, and the gardens serving as backdrop or scenery, the site experience begins at the property entrance. Visitors are encouraged to wander the gardens and grounds and, if desired, to take a house tour while on site. Interpretive and engagement staff was encouraged to develop garden and landscape tours, either self-guided, with a tour guide, or using a landscape app. The living collections are being catalogued and will soon be publicly accessible via an online app. The goal of these changes is to encourage a longer site experience, repeat visitation, audience diversity, and a cultural site experience that encompasses the entire property, not just its house and contents.

The Trustees' rediscovery process has been humbling, with many lessons learned. Cataloguing the landscape and its features is something that comes easily to those familiar with the National Register process and the registration of contributing and noncontributing elements. The process may seem overwhelming for those unfamiliar with cultural resources, but it can also be a teaching and engagement exercise for staff, boards, and volunteers. Reading the landscape brings rich rewards for all who chase these three-dimensional textbooks.

Recognizing the life cycle of cultural resources is an eye-opening process but shouldn't be used to justify loss or lack of strategic stewardship. All preservationists can learn more about the aging process and ways to slow decay while engaging audiences with evocative and significant site ruins. The climate change debate is fostering good scholarship in preservation techniques, strategic planning, and resource documentation, particularly in conversations with those who have seen significant loss and with those anticipating future losses. This research, however, is in its infancy as are cultural resource strategies for advocacy, proactive preservation, and determinations of what to document, what to save, and what to lose. Participating in these conversations is essential at all levels.

The use of consultants, museum colleagues, or expert volunteers in seeking new ideas is essential in the process of rediscovery. Whether invited for a "blink" or a "stare," their fresh eyes, larger world context, and impartial observations help to see things previous invisible to familiar eyes. The preparation of internal assessment reports by technical staff, volunteers, and consultants helps to build a body of scholarship that provides words for grants, donor appeals, programming, publicity, and site interpretation. These technical papers, however, should be written using familiar language so that the information is accessible and appealing to all with footnotes and links that provide more information when needed. Making National Register or Landmark nominations readily available for all staff and volunteers can serve as the first step in this information-assembly process.

Thinking outside the box comes hard to those comfortable with the past and aligning new management strategies has its hurdles along the path. New management models, specialty teams, and shifting priorities requires consistent internal education, positive reinforcement, and a listening ear, particularly through significant staff changes. Spirit of Place has opened options for appropriate site programming that blends the significant with the distinctive, special, and emotional appeal of place. It is, however, hard to define unless staff are willing to listen to a wide diversity of audience and visitor opinions, capturing these personal perspectives to find the common thread that defines what is most cherished, distinctive, and unique about each historic property.

The Trustees' journey continues to evolve, seeking new partnerships, new ways to connect people with historic houses and landscapes, and new ways to harness the full scope of each property's cultural resources in powerful and meaningful ways. Over the past eight years, the organization's cultural program has expanded from a series of twelve historic houses and their collections to a richer portfolio that includes interpreted ruins, historic landscapes, public gardens, and contemporary art. As we all continue to pursue a welcoming site experience that entices a widely diverse, multigenerational and multiethnic public, there are more creative roads ahead. The organization will continue to pursue the best format for property business plans that reach triple bottom line goals: expanded site revenues, expanded visitation, and better site stewardship, with additional goals for engagement and programming metrics and specialty team review. This work will be spurred by good Spirit of Place Statements and a rededication to exceptional property care, creating memorable site visits that encourage guests to repeatedly return. Most importantly, the organization will work with our colleagues to constantly seek new resources, new interpretive stories, and new ways of looking at our cultural resources that support our mission of protection, historic legacy, and public enjoyment. From the smallest of volunteer house museums to the largest multiproperty statewide historic organizations, there is much to learn and much to share beyond our own front door.

Notes

1. United Nations Educational, Scientific and Cultural Organization World Heritage Centre, "Annex 3: Guidelines on the Inscription of Specific Types of Properties on the World Heritage List," in *Operational Guidelines for the Implementation of the World Heritage Convention* (2008), 83–90.
2. International Council on Monuments and Sites, "Quebec Declaration on the Preservation of the Spirit of Place," 2008.

3. Trustees, "Property Business Plan for Naumkeag and Mission House" (2016), 7.
4. Richard W. Benfield, *Garden Tourism* (Boston, MA: CABI, 2013).

Recommended Resources

Benfield, Richard W. *Garden Tourism*. Boston, MA: CABI, 2013.
National Park Service. "Coastal Adaptation." https://www.nps.gov/subjects/climatechange/coastaladaptation.htm.
National Trust (UK). "Conservation Principles." https://www.nationaltrust.org.uk/documents/conservation-principles.pdf.

Lucinda A. Brockway

Part IV

Methods

Chapter 22

The Historic House Museum Tour

A Matter of Life and Death

PATRICIA WEST

In joining the chorus calling for reform of the traditional historic house museum tour, we can take inspiration from Marianne Moore's iconic poem about poetry that provocatively declares "I, too, dislike it." While Moore's poem criticizes poetry in terms we may find familiar ("there are things that are important beyond all this fiddle"), in the end it strongly reaffirms poetry's utility, proposing a path that we may follow to explore our current dilemma. Moore suggested that we'll know we "have it" when we find "imaginary gardens with real toads in them."[1] Here is our task. Like poetry, the historic house museum is a complex interplay between imagination and reality with the potential to provide a very particular kind of useful enchantment.

The historic house museum tour as a genre of cultural experience and expression is being so sharply questioned as a literal "thing of the past" that it is in danger of being discarded as irredeemably boring, irrelevant, and useless.[2] The chapters in this volume recognize this problem, while at the same time demonstrate the dedication of many thoughtful people to reimagining the house museum for the twenty-first century. For some, this is a matter of creatively employing the latest technology or refashioning the house museum absent its traditional house tour. I would propose, however, that by profoundly reframing our perspective on the house tour, we may find a place for it after all as an experience that can enrich lives, advance critical thinking, promote empathy, and enliven participatory democracy. The house museum tour is a journey that can be made meaningfully tangible, personal, and imaginative, and by reaffirming it in these terms, perhaps we can clarify why it is worth rescuing.

As we do so, our understanding is deepened by placing the house museum in historical context, recalling its colorful roots as a "social instrument."[3] House museums have often been founded as agents of enthusiastic political culture, and in this way, they have embodied the concerns of the eras in which they were established. We ignore this dimension of the original cultural function of house museums at their peril because pertinence has historically been the wellspring of their vitality. Yet we are also aware that the agendas of the house museum's early years created a problematical legacy. Arising from various anxious perspectives, house museums that were formerly plantations ignored slavery, "colonial revival" museums were xenophobic, and women's history was all but invisible.[4]

Accounting for the breadth and commonality of the special brand of Anglo-American tribalism so often promulgated by house museums is a daunting endeavor. The work of Pulitzer Prize–winning cultural anthropologist Ernest Becker provides a key. Becker proposes that culture arises from our unique capacity to be aware of the passage of time, to imagine ourselves in the past and future, and, most pointedly, that we are by this capacity aware (if subconsciously) of our own impending death. Becker argues that the human knowledge of the inevitability of death sponsors a vast range of cultural phenomena, including religion, art, and ideology, as ways of generating a palliative sense of immortality. These "immortality projects" can serve both unifying and divisive purposes because when the worldviews of others call our own into question, anxiety arises and ameliorative "cultural hero systems" are defended.[5]

Building on Becker's work, social psychologists Sheldon Solomon, Jeff Greenberg, and Tom Pyszczynki have explicated ways that the fear of death is held at bay by gestures of "symbolic immortality" and have devised a term for the way this functions: terror management theory.[6] The central tenets of terror management theory are:

> We as humans all manage the problem of knowing we are mortal by calling on two basic psychological resources. First, we need to sustain faith in our cultural worldview, which imbues our sense of reality with order, meaning, and permanence. Although we typically take our cultural worldview for granted, it is actually a fragile human construction that people spend great energy creating, maintaining, and defending. Since we're constantly on the brink of realizing that our existence is precarious, we cling to our culture's governmental, educational, and religious institutions and rituals to buttress our view of human life as uniquely significant and eternal.[7]

What better assertion of "symbolic immortality" could there be than the timeless "enshrined" home of a person long dead, preserved in perpetuity to receive generations of admiring house-guests? The docent-led tour consisting of tales false and true about "our" Anglo-American male heroes and their splendid furniture was the stock in trade of the historic house museum's early years. Visitors reveled in what we might call the romance of the house museum "shrine." Seth Bruggeman analyzes this in a detailed case study of the fabricated "birthplace" of George Washington, where even today "the reliquary impulse is alive and well."[8] However, across the first half of the twentieth century, the house museum was subject to an uneven but determined process of professionalization in which the compelling, but often quite incorrect, assertions that made up the typical house museum tour were challenged.[9]

At the same time, a newly articulated philosophy of house museum interpretation emerged, built on the transcendentalism of Ralph Waldo Emerson and disseminated by Freeman Tilden. Tilden's influential 1957 *Interpreting Our Heritage* describes the need for guided tours to foster a particular relationship between the internal life of the visitor and direct experience of "the Thing itself."[10] Tilden's perspective, based on an apparently close reading of Emerson's iconoclastic 1838 speech to the Harvard Divinity School, asserts that tours must be addressed to the "whole man" and supply not information, but "provocation."[11] Tilden was explicit that interpretive tours must be based on accurate information, but also that their periential dimensions arise more from art than science, an art that he claims to be teachable. With this, Tilden left the door open for others to provide the details about how this was to be achieved.

Unfortunately, Tilden's precept that interpretive skills needed to be taught for tours to be effective became entangled with the professionalization process cited above, which was busy policing against a plague of rambling house tours consisting of sloppy proclamations posing as facts, along with other characteristic features of the early house museum genre, such as undetermined objectives and the damaging of objects through careless handling. For example, Alderson and Low's classic 1976 *Interpretation of Historic Sites* praises the new American Association of Museums accreditation process for historic sites and advocates a tightly planned system of board-approved interpretive objectives that would give rise to "a limited list of facts, ideas, and historical concepts that will constitute the core of the interpretation." Alderson and Low warn sternly that tours should "tell the story as it was, without indulging in fantasy." Docents' flights of fancy would be purged from the new professional house tour; neither they nor visitors would have a say about content: "Developing general outlines for the interpretation of the historic site is a major responsibility of top-level staff members, working within the general objectives that have been agreed upon by the trustees. It is not a task to be delegated to the interpreters themselves."[12] In this way, modern house museum visitors could rest assured that they were receiving just the facts, vetted by "top-level" staff and trustees. Yet the ascendancy of such an authoritative, scientized professionalism contributed to the unintended consequence with which we must now grapple, increasingly sterile house tours.[13]

Fast forward to the present, and the unthinkable has happened: a diminishing sense of the power of house museums to inspire has taken hold, which we are now tasked to address. Drawing from Tilden's own muse, we can take Emerson's suggestion and "let the breath of new life be breathed into the forms already existing."[14] To reimagine the house museum tour, we should reclaim its unique strength as a romance of place and time, of connection with others, past and present. As Victor Frankl so cogently observes, the search for meaning is a boundless and essential human drive, supplying the energy that fuels all cultural endeavors, with the potential to enliven our own.[15] From this perspective, how might we make use of house museums that come to us as history-bound expressions of the wish to "enshrine" the homes of the dead, so we can facilitate deeply meaningful experiences for our time? To our emergency supplies for house tour resuscitation (storytelling, dialogue, technology, etc.) well described in this volume, we may add another: deep insight and reflection.

Going forward, it is difficult to argue that the linchpin concept of history, that it is past and manifests our shared mortality, could be anything less than extremely relevant. This is, in the language of the late David Larsen, a "universal concept," if not *the* universal concept.[16] That the subjects of our house tours are dead and we are not goes to the very core of what historic house museums mean. If it is true that house museums are a matter of life and death, then the foundation of reimagining the house tour can be this most factual of facts. But if we face this head-on and upset the soothing "cultural worldview" that underpins the traditional house tour's formulaic patter, we can expect resistance. Terror management theory research has established that outward reminders of mortality give rise to urgent anxiety that circles back to reinforce a strong need for comfort and a rejection of the unfamiliar. If we don't thoughtfully engage this subterranean dimension of historic house museums, we can "update" them all we want and we will end up where we started in the nineteenth century, with a set of institutions feverishly defining us versus them. Adding information that we find interesting or designing cell phones tours will simply not be enough.

To prepare for defensive resistance, we should look closely at the terms by which terror management theory explains that cultural constructions built on our primal fear of death are not mere folly. To the contrary, these rich expressions are the most meaningful of all, at the very heart of the human endeavor, as they provide opportunities for the development of such life-sustaining faculties as gratitude, empathy, and attachment. Solomon, Pyszczynki, and Greenberg hope that insight into the defensive nature of cultural institutions might help us halt the damaging outcomes of clinging to cultural constructions against feared others. Wisely framed, an experience that encourages us to face our mortality can "make life sublime by infusing us with courage, compassion, and concern for future generations," as well as "tolerance for uncertainty and others who harbor different beliefs."[17]

If house museum tours are revised with this keen awareness, we might prevent them from continuing to be agents of a defensive worldview. Approaching revision with a compassionate recognition of our shared human journey and with a determination to resist the impulse to amass vetted facts that supersede old versions of vetted facts, or on the other hand to indulge in self-congratulatory fictions, we may arrive at a new house museum experience. As "literalists of the imagination,"[18] we can share with our visitors the poignance of the human wish to reach imaginatively across the chasm of death itself.

Numerous scholars have explored ways that the rich potential of the house museum to host a search for meaning can be more fully realized. Cary Carson prompts us to recognize that "storytelling is the powerful medium in which modern learning takes place" and urges us to find ways for visitors to "join in the action of the story being told." Similarly, Hilary Iris Lowe emphasizes the deeply compelling nature of narrative, in particular when it allows visitors to participate with us in a "reflexive" engagement with the museum itself, thereby encouraging visitors "to stake a claim in the stories we most want to tell." Adding a rich complexity to the discussion is Christine Arato's investigation of the challenging process of navigating personal memory in a house museum context.[19] Inspired by these scholars and others engaged in rethinking house museums, at the Martin Van Buren National Historic Site in Kinderhook, New York, we have experimented with ways to include affective, narrative, and dialogic elements in the interpretation of Van Buren's home and farm, Lindenwald, to deepen connections with visitors while maintaining interpretive attention to the history of the antebellum period.

For example, a Museum Hack workshop was convened in Kinderhook in February 2017 for the explicit purpose of fostering a spirit of innovation and interpretive freedom.[20] Among other things, the process prompted a small but powerful change in the way we engage visitors in the upstairs bedroom where Martin Van Buren died in 1862. Previously, visitors were arrayed within the room in a traditional formal placement along a wall in a row, behind stanchions, to hear about the end of Van Buren's life from an interpreter standing apart from them. The revised method removes the stanchions and invites visitors to join the interpreter in a circle around Van Buren's bedside. This substantially changes the tone of the experience, which is underpinned by the following content: Van Buren was born in 1782 in the shadow of the American Revolution, and he spent his life carrying out the unfinished work of the Founding Fathers, making a nation from the hopeful but flawed raw materials of the new Constitution; he fell ill in 1862, disquieted by reports from the battlefields of the Civil War, and died not knowing whether the America the Founding Fathers envisioned would "perish from the face of the earth."

Another case in point is the interpretive use of a mid-nineteenth-century Bible given to Martin Van Buren for his seventieth birthday, inscribed by his niece Christina Cantine, an object that offers insight into a family's private experience as the nation moved toward what we know from our vantage point in time would be a civil war. That this was a family deeply immersed in politics is made apparent by the prayers transcribed inside the Bible, appealing to God to "defend our country in its hour of peril." By the time this gift was offered in December 1852, it was becoming clear even to less politically astute families that peaceful solutions to the slavery problem were failing and the country was becoming increasingly divided. The Compromise of 1850 had recently passed, the principal features of which were, for the North, that California would enter the Union as a free state and the slave trade would be criminalized in Washington, DC. The South for its part received a stringent Fugitive Slave Law denying trial by jury to northern blacks claimed as runaway slaves, aggravating tensions that would soon shear the Democratic Party, destroying both Van Buren's life work as party builder and the opportunity for a political solution to the crisis. By December 1852, several notorious cases of seizure of purportedly "fugitive" northern blacks had lit up Northern headlines. And, not inconsequentially, Harriet Beecher Stowe's *Uncle Tom's Cabin*, describing the horrors of slavery in general and the Fugitive Slave Law in particular, had become the nation's first best seller. These events were the larger context for the inscription in the Bible asking God to "preserve the goodly heritage which thou gavest to our fathers." The more personal context was that this was a subject on which Van Buren and his niece shared deep concern. This object connects to our own fraught time by offering us an image of a family at the hearthside, anguishing over a nation increasingly polarized to the point where they feared compromise might no longer be possible.

Below Christina Cantine's inscription, "To my Uncle on his 70th birthday," she adds the words of a psalm: "To teach us to number our days that we may apply our hearts unto wisdom." At its

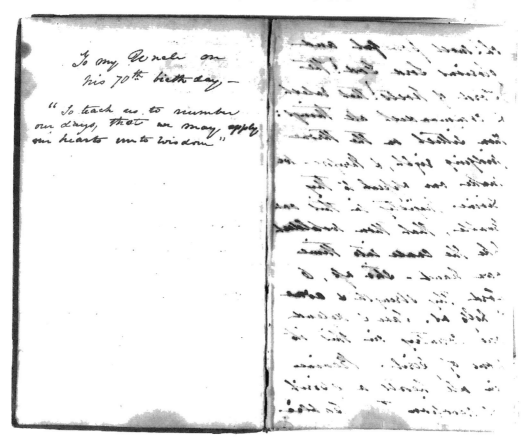

Figure 22.1 Bible inscribed in 1852 by Christina Cantine to her uncle, Martin Van Buren: "To my Uncle on his 70th birthday—'To teach us to number our days that we may apply our hearts unto wisdom.'" Courtesy of Martin Van Buren National Historic Site.

Figure 22.2 The mantle clock at Grant Cottage State Historic Site in Wilton, New York, remains as it was, stopped at 8:08 a.m. on July 23, 1885, by the son of Ulysses S. Grant, who then reached over to touch his father's forehead for the last time. Courtesy of Grant Cottage State Historic Site.

best, the house museum tour can do just that, reveal to us that days are indeed numbered and that each generation leaves its time-bound legacy: political, material, and spiritual. In reimagining the house tour for our century, we can fashion a rich journey highlighting the precious nature of time, offering opportunities to learn history's prescient lessons and apply them in pursuit of civic wisdom fostering justice, peace, and compassion. This would be a house museum tour to conjure with, artful in its exploration of the interplay between truth and personal meaning, replete with unassailable resonance.[21] These enchanting "imaginary gardens with real toads in them" can hold all the dimensions of the human body at home: childbirth, illness, joy, work, worry, love, and, yes, death—the real rhythms of human life, bound by time and place. As house museum reformer Frank Vagnone puts it, perhaps in the end "they simply are houses, built—lived in—and loved by people just like us. Ill-defined, messy, complex and not at all professionally manicured."[22] A house museum tour for our century, carried out with attention to the need for us to care for each other as we search for meaning in a trying time, may become at last "a place for the genuine."[23]

Notes

1. Marianne Moore, *Selected Poems* (New York: Macmillan, 1935), 36–37.
2. For example, see Gerald George, "The Historic House Museum Malaise: A Conference Considers What's Wrong," *History News* 57, no. 4 (2002): 4; Carol Stapp and Ken Turino, "Does America Need Another House Museum?" *History News* 59, no. 3 (2004): 7–11; Jay D. Vogt, in "The Kykuit Summit: The Sustainability of Historic Sites," *History News* 62 (Autumn 2007): 17–20; Donna Ann Harris, *New Solutions for*

Historic House Museums (Lanham, MD: Alta Mira, 2007): Linda Norris, "What Makes Historic House Tours So Boring: Upstate Thoughts," Uncataloged Museum (blog), http://uncatalogedmuseum.blogspot .com/2008/05/what-makes-historic-house-tours-so.html; and especially Franklin Vagnone and Deborah E. Ryan, Anarchist's' Guide to Historic House Museums (Walnut Creek, CA: Left Coast Press, 2016).

3. Theodore Low, The Museum as a Social Instrument (New York: Metropolitan Museum of Art, 1942).

4. Patricia West, Domesticating History: The Political Origins of America's House Museums (Washington, DC: Smithsonian Institution Press, 1999).

5. Ernest Becker, The Denial of Death (New York: Simon and Schuster, 1973).

6. Sheldon Solomon, Jeff Greenberg, and Tom Pyszczynki, The Worm at the Core: The Role of Death in Life (New York: Random House, 2015).

7. Solomon, Pyszczynki, and Greenberg, The Worm at the Core, 9.

8. Seth C. Bruggeman, Here, George Washington Was Born: Memory, Material Culture, and the Public History of a National Monument (Athens: University of Georgia Press, 2008), 18, 115-16.

9. West, Domesticating, 94-99, 121-27; James Lindgren, "'A New Departure in Historic, Patriotic Work': Personalism, Professionalism, and Conflicting Concepts of Material Culture in the Late Nineteenth and Early Twentieth Centuries," Public Historian 18 (Spring 1996): 41-60.

10. Freeman Tilden, Interpreting Our Heritage, 4th ed. (Chapel Hill: University of North Carolina Press, 2007).

11. Emerson, Divinity School Address, 1838, http://www.emersoncentral.com/divaddr.htm; Tilden, Interpreting Our Heritage, 18.

12. William T. Alderson and Shirley Paine Low, Interpretation of Historic Sites (Nashville: American Association for State and Local History, 1976), 22, 33, 44.

13. For further discussion, see Patricia West, "Of Babies and Bathwater: Birthplace 'Shrines' and the Future of the Historic House Museum," in Seth C. Bruggeman, ed., Born in the U.S.A.: Birth, Commemoration, and American Public Memory (Amherst: University of Massachusetts Press, 2012), 259-66.

14. Emerson (1838), http://www.emersoncentral.com/divaddr.htm.

15. Victor Frankl, Man's Search for Meaning, 4th ed. (1959; Boston: Beacon Press, 1992).

16. David L. Larsen, Meaningful Interpretation: How to Connect Hearts and Minds to Places, Objects, and Other Resources (Fort Washington, PA: Eastern National, 2011).

17. Solomon, Pyszczynki, and Greenberg, The Worm at the Core, 225.

18. Moore, Selected Poems, 36-37.

19. Cary Carson, "The End of History Museums: What's Plan B?," The Public Historian 30 (November 2008): 18-19; Hilary Iris Lowe, "Dwelling in Possibility: Revisiting Narrative in the Historic House Museum," The Public Historian 37 (May 2015): 60; Christine Arato, "This House Holds Many Memories: Constructions of a Presidential Birthplace at John Fitzgerald Kennedy National Historic Site," in Seth C. Bruggeman, ed., Born in the U.S.A.: Birth, Commemoration, and American Public Memory (Amherst: University of Massachusetts Press, 2012), 49-71.

20. On Museum Hack, see https://museumhack.com/audience_development/.

21. Stephen Greenblatt, "Resonance and Wonder," Bulletin of the Academy of Arts and Sciences 43 (January 1990): 11-34.

22. Franklin Vagnone, "The Narcissism of Details," https://twistedpreservation.com/2014/10/03/the-narcissism-of-details/.

23. Moore, Selected Poems, 36-37.

Recommended Resources

Becker, Ernest. The Denial of Death. New York: Simon and Schuster, 1973.

Frankl, Victor. Man's Search for Meaning. 4th ed. Boston: Beacon Press, 1992.

Larsen, David L. Meaningful Interpretation: How to Connect Hearts and Minds to Places, Objects, and Other Resources. Fort Washington, PA: Eastern National, 2011.

Solomon, Sheldon, Jeff Greenberg, and Tom Pyszczynki. The Worm at the Core: The Role of Death in Life. New York: Random House, 2015.

Tilden, Freeman. Interpreting Our Heritage. 4th ed. Chapel Hill: University of North Carolina Press, 2007.

Chapter 23

Everyone's History Matters

School Programs at Historic New England

CAROLIN COLLINS

A group of bored and fidgety ten-year-olds endure a forced march through a bunch of dusty old rooms, the tour guide droning on about the furniture, the students becoming more and more glassy-eyed and desperate with each step . . .

* * * * *

Unfortunately, this continues to be what a field trip to a historic house museum is in the popular imagination, even if not in reality. Many of us in the field are devoting our careers to changing this perception with programs that are truly engaging—even exciting.

At Historic New England, we share in the myriad challenges involved in creating, maintaining, and attempting to grow school and youth audiences, beginning with perception. We frequently have teachers remark as they are leaving the program or when they are completing our online survey, "Wow! I expected that to be so boring, but it wasn't!" We can only imagine what messages he or she was sending to the students while preparing them for the trip.

Even with enthusiastic teachers, however, there are obstacles. Securing funding from foundations and private donors has become increasingly difficult. Pricing programs to help cover institutional costs while remaining as accessible to as many students as possible is a delicate balancing act. For teachers, getting kids out of their school and onto a bus can seem, and often is, impossible. Offering programs that find the sweet spot between staying relevant and merely chasing trends can be tricky. Teachers are overloaded and overwhelmed. Instructional time devoted to social studies in general and history in particular is, in many school systems, miniscule compared to time given to English language arts and math.

Historic New England has some structural advantages that allow us to experiment with ways to overcome these challenges. We are a large organization with more than three dozen historic house museums in New England. We currently offer school and youth programs at thirteen of those sites.[1]

From 1985 (when our first school program was introduced at Otis House in Boston) through 2015, attendance at our programs grew annually, reaching a high of more than fifth-three thousand young people served. We are fortunate to have strong institutional commitment to our school and youth programs and to have professional staff develop, teach, and evaluate those programs. The thirteen sites are divided among five education program coordinators, each of whom manages a group of part-time museum teachers.

These sites include urban, suburban, and rural locations; affluent areas where schools have easy access to funds and buses and underserved districts with schools that cannot provide those things; grand mansions and humble family homes; access via public transportation and by narrow dirt road; ample bathrooms, program space, high-tech capability, and none of those things. Some sites have been offering school and youth programs for more than thirty years and some have programs that are just getting started. Some sites have programs so popular that registration is taken by lottery and others have only one or two classes sign up each year. At some sites, there are aspects of the story and collection so closely tied to learning students are doing in school that deciding the program's focus is obvious. Other sites require more creativity in order to make programs that are both attractive and useful to teachers.

"Everyone's History Matters"

Historic New England's education tagline is "Everyone's History Matters," but it is not merely a marketing tool. Rather, it is a guiding principle and the basis for everything we do. We know that there cannot be a one-size-fits-all template for programs at such varied locations and with such different needs. What is possible on a three-hundred-acre farm is different from what is possible in a seventeenth-century house on a quarter-acre lot. Reimagining the traditional historic house tour for students takes many forms; so many, in fact, that we currently offer fifty-one different programs. Underpinning all of them is the understanding that we seek to present as much breadth of human experience as possible.

There are additional commonalities between these programs. First and most important, each was developed in conjunction with local teachers. Having classroom teacher input from the earliest stages of development guarantees buy-in and relevance. We evaluate programs regularly through online teacher surveys, observation, and by tracking participation to ensure that as these programs grow they remain relevant. In 2012, we switched from handing out paper surveys to teachers at the conclusion of programs to sending them a link to an online survey shortly after the program's conclusion. This has both increased our response rate and made the feedback we receive more useful. Whereas in the past, the paper surveys tended to end up in a folder somewhere, now we carefully monitor responses and make changes accordingly. For example, when the introductory portion of a long-running program started dragging as new museum teachers added little bits and pieces of new information, teachers spoke up. We took a hard look at what needed to stay and what could go and pruned it back.

Second, all of our programs are based on the curriculum standards of the state in which they are located. When those standards are changed or updated, we make whatever adjustments are necessary in order to maintain those curricular ties. Over the past ten years, we have reviewed programs and made changes when necessary as the New England states adopted the Common

Carolin Collins

Core State Standards (www.corestandards.org); Connecticut, New Hampshire, Rhode Island, and Vermont adopted the Next Generation Science Standards (www.nextgenscience.org); and Connecticut updated its social studies standards based on the C3 (College, Career, and Citizenship) Framework (www.socialstudies.org/c3). Currently, the Massachusetts Department of Elementary and Secondary Education is revising its social studies standards, a process we will continue following closely.

Third, each program is multimodal. Information and activities throughout the program are specifically designed to engage all students, whether they are visual, audio, kinetic, or tactile learners. Our on-site school programs include at least one hands-on component that reinforces learning and provides a tangible, take-home reminder of the day.

Finally, each program is designed to be authentically tied to its location. Programs must be grounded in the stories of the people who lived or worked at the sites or they will not be successful.

These principals have been in place from the beginning. *Unknown Hands: Everyday Life of Bostonians in 1800*, our longest-running program, has brought students to the Otis House, a large Federal-era mansion at the base of Beacon Hill, since the 1980s. It remains popular because it places the Otis family in their neighborhood, which included other wealthy residents such as Nathan Appleton (grandfather of Historic New England founder William Sumner Appleton), skilled artisans, apprentices, servants, and sailors, as well as Primus Hall (who established in his home the first dedicated school for African American boys). Students prepare for their field trip by completing a pre-visit lesson provided by Historic New England to be completed in the classroom. In the lesson, students are given a sheet with information about the characters they will portray, including where they live, how much if any real and personal property they own, and a description of their job and how it fits into the life of the neighborhood. This is presented to teachers as an important preparatory step, and almost all classes come to the museum with the activity completed and the students eager to talk about who they have become. Throughout the four-hour visit, students wear a tag with their character name and job and are asked to think about how they fit into the life of the neighborhood. Museum teachers also wear name tags identifying themselves as Otis family servants while leading the activities, which include time exploring the Otis House museum, the opportunity to learn the plaster trade while crafting an ornament to take home, and a walking tour of Beacon Hill.

Commit to Students: Pierce House

At Pierce House in the Dorchester section of Boston, Historic New England has taken advantage of the opportunity to reimagine the historic house school program from the ground up.

The Pierce House was built in 1683. A few years later, Thomas and Mary Pierce purchased it with ten generations of the Pierce family living there until 1968, when the family sold the house to Historic New England. The house became a study property, opened for tours a few times a year, and attracting mostly architecture students and aficionados.

Around 2000, inspired and emboldened by the continued success of Otis House school programs, Historic New England realized the potential for Pierce House to become a center for education.[2] Over the next few years with support from a Learning Opportunities grant from the Institute of Museum and Library Services, education staff worked with a group of local teachers from six pilot schools, including the Thomas J. Kenny Elementary School (located directly across

Figure 23.1 Third-grade students participating in *Colonial Trades* at Pierce House, Dorchester, Massachusetts. Photo by Daniel Nystedt.

the street from the Pierce House), to create programs for elementary school students. With such a wealth of materials available, such as the archival records at Pierce House, our teacher group was invaluable in the program development process. It was important to find the correct focus and to make authentic connections with what educators were teaching in their classrooms. Out of this process came three programs for elementary school students, designed to seamlessly fit within existing state curriculum frameworks.

The first to be completed was a third-grade program, *Colonial Trades: Making Community Work*, during which students learn what life was like at Pierce Farm during the years leading up to the revolution. A pre-visit activity allows students to take on the roles of real Dorchester residents, including farmers, weavers, and blacksmiths. As with the pre-visit lesson plan for *Unknown Hands*, discussed above, almost all classes have completed this prior to their program. The program itself is broken into four main activities. There is an interactive slideshow introduction during which we introduce the Pierce family and farm and discuss changes in the neighborhood over time. We then discuss each of the eight trades represented and how each is connected to the others. We have a variety of reproduction artifacts that we pass around during this discussion, including a shoe, iron nails, and a length of handwoven linen cloth. Students practice weaving using a notched cardboard loom that is theirs to keep. We also do a "Now and Then" activity, in which they must pair an object from today (e.g., a flashlight) with an object from the colonial era (a glass and tin lantern). Finally, we play a bartering game in which students are given a list of items to acquire and a set of cards to trade away. They make a series of trades with their classmates, and at the conclusion of the exercise, we emphasize again the connections that were necessary within the community.

Next was *A Revolution in Dorchester* for fifth-grade students, which provides a window into the Revolutionary War era through the journal of Colonel Samuel Pierce, in which he recorded everything from the details of daily life on his farm to major events such as the Boston Massacre, the Boston Tea Party, and the fortification of Dorchester Heights. In this program, we emphasize Pierce's status as an ordinary farmer living in extraordinary times, and by reading his journal, we are able to see the war as experienced by an average person, not a famous, wealthy, or influential one. We work together to create a timeline of events leading up to and at the beginning of the Revolutionary War, starting with James Otis' quotation "No taxation without representation" and ending with the signing of the Declaration of Independence. To start with, each event is printed on a card kept visible but out of order at the front of the room and there is a clothesline to hang the cards on. We hand out excerpts of Pierce's journal for small groups of students to look at together, and we have a visual prompt on a slide for each event. As we go through the slides, students identify the event, place it chronologically on the clothesline, then read the associated journal event and add that as well. For example, we show the Paul Revere engraving of the Boston Massacre, and in addition to discussing differences between what is pictured and what actually happened and the engraving serving as a particularly effective piece of propaganda, the students look at the journal excerpts and find the one from March 6, 1770, in which he wrote: "Four men kild [*sic*] in boston by the Soldiers."

We also show a reproduction of the *Boston Gazette* with an article about the event and a large illustration of four coffins. This leads to a discussion of why both the newspaper and Pierce say four people died, when we know that it was five. Eventually, someone realizes that one person must have died later from injuries sustained during the event. For some students, this is a review of the work they have done in their classroom and a chance for them to show their knowledge. For others, it is an introduction to their Revolutionary War unit and the museum teacher must do much more scaffolding as we explore the images and journal entries. Also during the program, one student is dressed up as a minuteman. We talk about each piece of clothing and examine the contents of his or her haversack. Finally, the students write about something they have learned using a quill pen.

The third curriculum-based school program completed was *Family Ties at Pierce House*. This program was based on a model in use at several other Historic New England properties and is the most direct embodiment of "Everybody's History Matters," providing students with the tools to tell their stories. During the program, students learn how the Pierces preserved their ancestral home in Dorchester and other family treasures through ten generations. Students learn how to conduct oral history interviews; examine historical documents, objects, and photographs; and design a family crest. Afterward, they apply these techniques to make albums that chronicle their own families' pasts and record daily lives. Throughout this program, we emphasize that all families are unique. We are very careful to use inclusive language and recognize that families come in many configurations. We want all students, no matter what their background or current circumstances, to feel comfortable and to know that everyone's story is equally valid.

Although each program stands alone, they were designed to build on each other year by year, and some schools visit in third, fourth, and fifth grade. By that time, students have grown familiar with and comfortable in the house and love showing off what they remember from previous visits.

Each program is two and a half hours long and includes an introduction and several hands-on activities in the multipurpose rooms, as well as time exploring the period room. Because of the small size of the rooms at Pierce House, we can only accommodate twenty-five students at one time. After the introduction to the entire class, they are split into two groups to cycle through the activities. Although this approach is staff-intensive, necessitating two museum teachers for each program, it guarantees that all students receive individualized attention throughout the program.

The program's limit of twenty-five students is not a problem for the neighborhood schools whose students can walk to the site, but it is a large barrier for schools in other neighborhoods in Boston and for suburban schools. For Boston Public Schools outside of walking distance, we received grant funding from the Institute of Museum and Library Services to provide free buses over two separate three-year grant cycles, the second of which ended in 2010. Since then, we have allocated funds from our operating budget for buses while seeking funding from smaller foundations. Although expensive, this additional funding has enabled the growth of programs on-site at Pierce House, from 286 students in 2003 (the first year programs were offered) to a high of 2,902 students in 2014. In those years when less transportation funding has been available, on-site visitation has declined. For schools that are not able to travel to Pierce House, we developed ninety-minute outreach versions of each program. These have been particularly attractive to suburban schools and, along with preschool, afterschool, and summer programs held off-site, account for a large proportion of total program participation.

The outreach versions of the programs also offer a much-needed source of revenue. The Pierce House school programs do not make money and we rely on grant funding and individual donors to help defray the cost.

Despite the financial challenges, Historic New England remains fully committed to providing high-quality programs to schools in Dorchester and throughout Boston. As our Pierce House programs have grown, and standards have changed, we have continued to rely on teacher input so that they remain a vital part of the curriculum.

Tell the Untold Stories: Spencer-Peirce-Little Farm

Spencer-Peirce-Little Farm is in Newbury, Massachusetts. It has been a farm since 1635, when John Spencer was given a four-hundred-acre land grant that includes the present site. Currently, the fields are leased to two local farmers. In 2003, Historic New England realized the potential of the site as a family-friendly destination. Several rooms were reinstalled to include a traditional period space in one half of the room and a hands-on, interactive space in the other half; tours were reimagined; a year-round preschool program was implemented; and a partnership was established with the Massachusetts Society for the Prevention of Cruelty to Animals that allows the site to foster farm animals that had been abandoned or rescued from other sites.

School programs have been offered at Spencer-Peirce-Little Farm since it opened as a museum. *Dirt Detectives* focuses on the work of archaeologists and makes use of a test pit left at the site for educational purposes after an archaeological dig at the site. *In Search of a Story* allows students to gain historical research skills by studying authentic documents in order to inspire their own creative writing. *A Day at the Farm* is an overview of farm life geared toward young students.

Historic New England had succeeded in transforming Spencer-Peirce-Little Farm into a lively public space, a beloved and vital gathering place for the local and regional community. However, there was one story, central to the farm, which was not being told.

In 1912, Jacob Stekionis left his parents' farm in Lithuania, bound for Boston. He quickly got a job in the city but missed working outdoors and went to an agency that placed farm laborers. There he met and was hired by Edward Francis Little. He took up residence in the tenant farmhouse, first as a single man and later, after a brief trip back to Lithuania, with his new wife, Dorothy. When Little died in 1935, he left the property to his sister Eliza and their three nieces. Eliza offered Jacob the use of the farm, as long as he bought the cattle and provided the women with milk, firewood, vegetables, and eggs. Jacob and Dorothy accepted the offer and stayed on, raising their three daughters in the tenant house. The girls grew up and moved out, and Jacob died in 1984, but when Amelia Little died in 1986 and Historic New England took ownership of the property, Dorothy was still alive and in residence.

After Dorothy's death in 1993, and with the manor house already open for tours, the tenant house remained closed. Although the three Stekionis daughters—Olga, Nancy, and Mary—lived locally and were frequent visitors to the property, their family story was given only a glancing mention.

With their cooperation, that changed starting in 2010. Historic New England conducted oral histories with Olga, Nancy, and Mary; conducted additional research on the family's story and the twentieth-century immigrant experience; and undertook a restoration of the first floor of the Stekionis House that includes an entryway and stairwell, parlor, and kitchen. The rooms were interpreted to the early 1980s, when Jacob was still alive and the girls were grown up. The Stekionis House opened to the public for the first time in spring 2012.

With Stekionis House about to open to the public, we knew we wanted to make it the centerpiece of a new education program. At the same time, one of our area school partners was looking for a field trip experience to tie into their fourth-grade immigration unit. We were able to work with them to adapt the fourth-grade Pierce House program into *Family Ties at Stekionis House*.

As with *Family Ties at Pierce House*, the program is intended to help students develop skills needed to tell their own unique family histories. For *Family Ties at Stekionis House*, the program begins with a pre-visit lesson in the classroom introducing students to the Stekionis family and their story.

During the field trip, students rotate through four stations, spending thirty minutes at each. In the farmhouse, they first visit the kitchen and talk about Dorothy and Jacob's favorite foods and treasured recipes Dorothy brought with her from Lithuania. In the parlor, they interview each other about their own family traditions and favorite recipes. The next rotation is outside at Dorothy's kitchen garden and laundry yard. Here they talk more about Dorothy's life on the farm, and her chores. Students rinse and wring laundry and hang it on the clothesline. Depending on the season, they gather beans from the garden or eggs from around the henhouse.

The next station is in the barn, where students learn more about Jacob's duties as a dairy farmer and about his relationship with the Little sisters. Before leaving the barn, students try their hands at milking, using a full-size wooden replica cow. In the final station, students turn their attention back to their own family stories. As homework, they have spoken to their families about their geographic backgrounds. During the activity, we discuss that information then choose one country of origin each and add that person's journey to a map of the world already labeled with Jacob's passage from Lithuania to Newbury. Although Newbury has a predominantly western European population, students are always amazed by how many countries of origin we have labeled by the end of the day.

After the field trip, the students work with their classroom teachers for several weeks to create family albums. Throughout their work with us and with their teachers, we emphasize that each and every family is different. We never prioritize one child's experience over another. At the end of the unit, they truly understand that everyone's history matters, including their own.

Look Beneath the Surface: Quincy House

Unlike the Pierce House, with its multipurpose rooms designed especially for school groups, or Spencer-Peirce-Little Farm, with its sheer size, multiple buildings, and adorable animals offering practically endless program possibilities, Quincy House in Quincy, Massachusetts, is a traditional historic house museum. It was built for Colonel Josiah Quincy in 1770. After falling out of family ownership, it was purchased in 1937 by a consortium of family members and presented to Historic New England and the interpretation was based on records kept by Quincy's great-granddaughter, Eliza Susan Quincy. Recently, the house was given a much-needed restoration and reinterpretation that further focused on Eliza Susan's nineteenth-century period of occupancy. The house looks wonderful and public tours have been more popular than they had been in decades. For the school-age audience, the draw of the house is not the nineteenth-century interiors, but the family's fascinating and turbulent Revolutionary War history.

Colonel Quincy was sixty years old and had lived a very full life by 1770 when the house was completed and both of his sons, Samuel and Josiah Jr., were practicing attorneys. Revolutionary fervor was rising in Boston and while Josiah Jr. was a staunch Patriot, Samuel was a Loyalist. Later in 1770, after the Boston Massacre, both brothers were involved in the trial of the accused British soldiers, but each argued opposite their personal beliefs. Josiah Jr. joined John Adams in defending the soldiers, both eager to prove the fairness of the court system. Samuel prosecuted the case.

Colonel Quincy was also a Patriot. Although by the time the war began in earnest he was too elderly to join the fighting, he kept watch on the Boston Harbor from a window at the top floor of his house, taking notes that he would later send to General George Washington. At least once, he scratched a message into a pane of the window glass.

In fifth grade in Massachusetts, students study the American Revolution. In Boston, there are many different institutions offering school programs focused on the war, and area schools have a surfeit of high-quality options. However, fifth-grade teachers in the city of Quincy (which is a suburb of Boston) were interested in working with us to create a program for their students, in their town, that drew upon the story of the Quincy family.

Creating the background materials for what became *Quincy Revolution: A Family Divided* was the easy part. Thanks to Eliza Susan, we had access to family letters and writings. Samuel and Josiah Jr.'s ideological differences were well documented, but so was their familial warmth and affection. The Massachusetts Historical Society has the transcript from the Boston Massacre trial. During the program, students would examine letters between Samuel and Josiah Jr. then use a quill pen and ink to copy a quote from one of the brothers, choosing whether to be a Patriot or a Loyalist as they did. They would go into the attic, two or three at a time, to peer out the window used by Colonel Quincy, even though the view to the harbor is now obscured by the neighborhood that has built up on what was once part of the property. Later in the program, they would reenact parts of the massacre trial, donning wigs and other costume pieces, and reading from the transcript. Several students would serve as the jury, rendering their verdict before being told how the actual jury voted.

Carolin Collins

We also wanted students to spend time in the period rooms and get an understanding of what daily life was like for the Quincy family, but the period of interpretation did not match the period of the revolution. We needed to find a way to go back further. Here, once again, we became indebted to Eliza Susan. Because of her dedication to her family history, she saved as much as she could from the revolutionary period. The pieces were relics in her time, just as they are today. For example, that piece of glass from the window inscribed by her great-grandfather is framed and hanging on the wall. There are pieces of significance to the family, such as mourning jewelry, monogrammed china, and the family Bible. There are everyday items as well, including eyeglasses, an inkwell, and a tea set. In each room, students are given visual clues to find the eighteenth-century items hidden in plain sight within the nineteenth-century trappings, which leads to a discussion of how that room was used during Samuel and Josiah Jr.'s time.

We began offering the program in 2010, and it has become a centerpiece of the fifth-grade social studies curriculum in Quincy. One of the teachers who helped in its development has since retired from the classroom but returns each spring as part of the Historic New England staff to continue teaching the program.

Conclusion

In May 2017, Historic New England opened the Eustis Estate Museum and Study Center in Milton, Massachusetts. We will be identifying teacher partners from the surrounding communities and working with them to develop school programs for the site. As we do so, we will follow our own guidelines and make sure that we are working in conjunction with curriculum standards to create multimodal experiences authentically tied to the location. We will tackle the obstacles head-on, determining a fair pricing scheme, a fund-raising plan, and the right mix of topics and activities that make students, teachers, and administrators consider a visit to the Eustis Estate a necessary part of student learning, worthy of the expense and the time away from the school building.

At the same time, Historic New England will look carefully and strategically at this expansion of school programs and determine how much growth is possible, given staff capacity and budget realities. We will find the correct balance and fulfill our mission to save and share New England's past to engage and inform present and future generations.

Notes

1. Currently, school and youth programs are offered in Maine at Castle Tucker and Nickels-Sortwell House in Wiscasset and at Hamilton House and Sarah Orne Jewett House in South Berwick. In Massachusetts, Spencer-Peirce-Little Farm and Coffin House in Newbury, Otis House in Boston, Pierce House in Dorchester, Quincy House in Quincy, and the Codman Estate in Lincoln host programs. Rhode Island programs take place at Casey Farm in Saunderstown and Arnold House in Lincoln, and in Connecticut, programs are at Roseland Cottage in Woodstock.
2. The conversion of the Pierce House involved compromise, negotiation, and cooperation among the property care, collections, and visitor experience teams at Historic New England as preservation priorities were balanced with the desire for accessibility. Property care staff worked with contractors to make the site usable, work that included the removal of asbestos-cement siding. Collections staff installed one colonial-period room on the ground floor. Three additional rooms were made into multipurpose spaces for programs, crafts, and student exhibitions, and one room became office space. Compromises included the addition of floor coverings in the multipurpose spaces to protect original floors and updates to the existing twentieth-century bathroom to accommodate more students. The fact that the house

had very few collection items associated with it eased concerns somewhat. Pierce House remains unique among Historic New England properties in its focus on serving school groups.

Recommended Sources

Coquillon, Naomi. "Museums in a Common Core World." *Center for the Future of Museums* (blog), July 30, 2013. http://futureofmuseums.blogspot.com/2013/07/museums-in-common-core -world.html.

Johnson, Anna, Kimberly Huber, Melissa Bingmann, and Tim Grove. *The Museum Educator's Manual: Educators Share Successful Techniques.* Lanham, MD: Rowman and Littlefield, 2009.

Ng-He, Carol. "Common Goals, Common Core: Museums and Schools Work Together." *Journal of Museum Education* 40, no. 3 (October 2015): 220–26.

Shuh, J. H. "Teaching Yourself to Teach with Objects." *Journal of Education* 7, no. 4 (1982): 80–91.

Taba, Hilda. "The Key Role of Questioning." In *Teacher's Handbook to Elementary Social Studies: An Inductive Approach,* 104–23. Menlo Park, CA: Addison-Wesley Publishing Company, 1971.

Chapter 24

Creating Minds-on Exhibitions in Historic House Museums

ROBERT KIIHNE

Exhibitions can excite, inspire, and educate in historic houses, but their role depends upon what you want to accomplish. House museums can use them in different ways, from orientation experiences to period rooms to temporary in-depth explorations. Exhibitions in historic houses traditionally deliver the who, when, and where through a few common approaches. The family tree or early photographic introductory exhibition is a standard starting gambit for many historic properties. Period rooms with a large text panel and individual object labels present passive information soon to be forgotten. Some historic house exhibitions include tangential content related to the place, materials such as objects recovered during archaeological digs on the property or the former owner's widget collection. These often feel like a coda to the tour.

History—whether it is within a museum or historic house—must be accessible, relevant, and meaningful to the visitor. Exhibitions can help reach those goals, but they can also make you fumble. We might agree that a 250-word label full of arcane information is disrespectful of your visitors' time, a waste of your organization's resources, and represents a lost opportunity, but what about a well-produced exhibition at a major tourist attraction? Early in my career at the USS *Constitution* Museum in Boston, we finished installing a major exhibition exploring two hundred years of the ship's history. There were great objects, lots of graphics, some scenic elements, and a few interactives. The exhibition filled 3,500 square feet and contained well over 4,500 words. When we tracked visitors using the exhibition, they spent on average of eight minutes in the entire gallery. They stopped consistently at the four interactives but paid little attention to the numerous text panels that the museum staff had spent so many hours crafting. No one would have called the exhibition a failure, but was it a success? It seemed that learning was only happening in a few islands within the exhibition: the hands-on interactives. Otherwise, our great stories remained locked away in squiggly lines almost never to be read and rarely understood. The hard part was recognizing that exhibition creators do not get to decide what's successful— the audience alone makes that judgment.

As a result, my thinking about exhibitions changed, and for the next twenty-five years, I studied how exhibitions can leverage social learning at the USS *Constitution* Museum. The USS *Constitution* is best known as the oldest commissioned naval ship still afloat, but it was also the home of sixty officers and sailors. Many of the processes and methods we've used to interpret this eighteenth-century frigate can be easily adopted by historic homes on land as well.[1]

Historic houses offer distinct challenges for exhibitions. Most museums have stark cool white walls that are deliberately nondescript, while kitchens, bedrooms, and dining rooms of houses include colors, textures, and details that can evoke emotions on their own. The visitor experience is inevitably chunked in historic houses by function while at the same time rooms are connected, often creating a fixed path. These conditions make exhibitions in historic houses fundamentally different from most museums but are still full of possibility.

Like most museums, historic houses are trying to expand their audiences. Many are looking to serve an audience that resides nearby but rarely visits: families. A recent study by Wilkening Consulting for the American Alliance of Museums concluded that "parents are 50 percent more likely than those without minor children to have visited a museum in the past year."[2] In other words, families with kids seventeen and under are significantly more likely to visit museums in general than older single visitors. Yet this is clearly not the case for the vast majority of historic house audiences. Families are actively looking for social experiences that their children can participate in, and many historic house museums could fit the bill. Exhibitions can engage all visitors, but it will require reimagining traditional approaches.

Hands-on Techniques in Historic House Museums

Historic house museums have been using hands-on elements for decades. Encouraging visitors to touch a beaver pelt, lift a wooden bucket, or dip a wax candle are common tactics, but they could be part of a wider engagement strategy. Can they be presented in a thoughtful way that sparks the imagination of all users, not just children? Can they be connected to the people or events that make a historic house important or unique?

One of the first experiments with interactive activities within a historic house is at Historic New England's Spencer-Peirce-Little Farm in Massachusetts. The house includes period rooms with wall text. Rooms are divided, one side made up of a vignette using collections pieces and the other a mirror vignette that is touchable. The house offers family-friendly active experiences, such as stereo card viewing in the parlor, pumping water outside the kitchen, and farm animals in the yard. This was all done strategically to attract a family audience. Its connection to the local community has strengthened and attendance has grown tremendously. The Lefferts Historic House in Brooklyn, New York, is another example of a family-friendly place. A temporary interactive exhibition in the kitchen connected spices to their origin and the journey required to get them to New York. Developed by a group of students from Parsons School of Design including Obinna Izeogu, the interactive was aimed at four- to seven-year-old children though meant to also be relevant to adults. Kids could smell different spices and trigger animations that showed where these spices came from and how long their journeys would have been. The content was communicated by touch, smell, and animation.

Notice how these exhibitions expanded their audience. Rather than create hands-on experiences that are solely for children, they included adults as well. Many visitors love tactile elements, but more thoughtful approaches take inspiration from universal design principles, which provide solutions that serve all users no matter their age, size, or ability.[3] These principles have been successfully used to improve architecture and computer interfaces, and in museums they can inspire practical solutions for the youngest and oldest visitors, for example providing plenty of seating,

Robert Kiihne

text in larger font sizes and fewer words in labels, and developing hands-on elements that aren't awkward for little hands or those suffering from arthritis. Exhibitions that succeed with a wide range of ages and encourage interaction among visitors are particularly effective with families because they come as intergenerational groups.

Secondly, aesthetics should appeal to all users. Hands-on exhibitions can be limited to a designated room or incorporated throughout the site, but colors, materials, and design matter. Bright primary colors communicate that this place is for kids and not for adults. Typefaces quickly tell visitors if they are the intended audience. Teenagers may avoid exhibitions that are dominated by black-and-white images, illustrations, or artwork.

Shifting from Hands-on to Minds-on Exhibitions

While some may see hands-on exhibitions as a way of broadening the visitor experience by adding a tactile dimension, they can also address big ideas, turning them into minds-on activities. The historic context of your house, the family's background, emotional personal stories, and contemporary issues can be tackled in graphics, text panels, audio, visual, and other formats, but visitor engagement and impact is a more important issue. What will your audience remember a week after the visit? Will they visit again? Will they tell their friends and family?

To create a minds-on exhibition, its core ideas or message must connect to the visitor. Content that might be complex, abstract, or just plain boring as a written narrative is often much more meaningful when presented in other formats. Consider communicating with multiple techniques such as text, images, audio, tactile objects, kinesthetic experiences, or charts. By providing multiple entry points, exhibitions can engage the mind successfully. As a bonus, in order to effectively use multiple entry points, exhibition developers must truly come to terms with what they want to communicate.

Secondly, create active, user-driven experiences that that involve a response from the visitor, or even better from a group of visitors. Individuals within a group of visitors may interpret the same content differently, and those differences can leverage learning by creating situations where the group must work together to solve a challenge. Interactives that foster social learning through problem solving, collaboration, and competition provide visitors ways to learn from each other as much as from the exhibition. Within a family group or social group that know each other well, communication takes place much more efficiently than any exhibition can communicate ideas to users.

Reimagining Exhibitions in Historic Houses

Historic houses are a perfect environment for minds-on exhibitions. Historic houses are not empty white galleries; they are warm, unique places designed at human scale and full of historical content. The house itself is the primary object and scenic backdrop, therefore exhibition furniture and panels play a supporting role.

Recently, I designed an exhibition for the Durant Kendrick House in Newton, Massachusetts, which is managed by Historic Newton, a public/private partnership between the Newton Historical Society and the City of Newton. The historic house interprets the history of three families that lived and worked on this property for a period of three hundred years. The Durant family built the house in 1734, farmed the surrounding land, and were active in the American Revolution. In the 1830s, the Kendrick family owned the house and it became the center of a horticultural empire and ultimately the home of academics and early preservationists.

These families had great stories, and Historic Newton had money to restore the house and even add a classroom space, but its future financial sustainability was unclear. Historic Newton's long-term goal for the Durant Kendrick House is to keep the home open throughout the year for local families while keeping staffing obligations down. As a result, they made the strategic decision that the Durant Kendrick visit would be unguided. Visitors would be greeted by staff, but then explore the house on their own through a series of small experiences in each room. While each individual experience is related to the house, their organization is not linear. Executive Director Cindy Stone suggested dividing the rooms in two: one side set as a period room with historic furniture and the other side with an exhibition telling the stories of life within each space.

Historic Newton hired me, Elisabeth Nevins (script developer), and Fred Brink (media developer) to work with their staff to design and develop these exhibitions. The project took two years and encountered many issues common to historic houses. The Durant Kendrick House contains small rooms filled with light from large windows; wall space is limited; and the walls, floors, and ceiling were historic and couldn't be damaged. We concluded that the exhibitions could not dominate the visual space, they should be reduced in size and scale, they needed to be physically self-supporting, and, most importantly, we could only tell one story in each room well. These decisions defined how much could go in each historic room, which meant that some stories ended up in exhibitions outside of the historic rooms. The team set aside an additional room in the house for hands-on exhibitions specifically aimed at families, an approach that may be a good option for other historic sites.

The resulting exhibitions featured robust interactives in almost every room and full-size cutout illustrations of the home's occupants over time (see Figure 24.1). The content is aimed at a wide

Figure 24.1 The kitchen of the Durant Kendrick House in Massachusetts with the period room in the background and the activity area on the carpeted floor in the foreground. Photo by Robert Kiihne.

Robert Kiihne

age range, but it was important to Historic Newton that the house be accessible for young families with school-age children in the neighborhood. Topics tackled within the house included colonial land use, the American Revolution, 1830s horticulture, and colonial slavery. Even though the exhibitions deal with some darker themes, content is appropriate for even the youngest visitor.

Planning Exhibitions in Historic Houses

Exhibition planning in house museums is significantly different from a museum gallery. You're not faced with a large blank room that needs to be filled with scenic elements, large graphics, and case work to transport the visitor to another time or a place. A sense of place is preinstalled at house museums—take advantage of it. Exhibitions in historic houses can start with deeper-level content without the expense of setting the stage. Smaller exhibition elements cost less to create. Historic homes are human scale; even grand ballrooms are dwarfed by the scale of modern museum spaces and packed with emotional content deliberately absent from most empty museum galleries.

The real cost of successful exhibitions within historic houses is the time needed to plan, test, and think. Painted backdrops, platforms, cases, temporary walls, and lighting may not be as important within historic house exhibitions, but thoughtful planning and design is crucial to both. For example, a historic photograph of the family sitting down for a holiday meal can be displayed in the dining room, but if the visitor is not asked to respond, it becomes lifeless. On the other hand, an emotional media presentation or an effective interactive that allows visitors to make personal connections to your content can create a spark that lasts a lifetime.

In 1998, the Philadelphia-Camden Informal Science Collaborative (PISEC) developed a helpful set of criteria to support family learning in exhibitions.[4] Based upon their research, a family (and to some extent any group of visitors) communicates more effectively between its members than between an exhibition and a family or group member. The PISEC criteria encourages a variety of experiences, including:

- multisided: users can gather around
- multiuser: can be used by multiple people at the same time
- multioutcome: allows users to make choices with different results
- accessible: equally usable by everyone
- multimodal: conveys information in different ways and/or allow for different kinds of user interactions

While intended for science centers, I have found that these criteria can be easily adopted by house museums as well. If you place an interactive on a table whose content is easy to understand and meaningful for your audience, then you are very close to meeting many of these criteria.

Traditional Methods Used in Better Ways

Text panels are a mainstay of exhibitions and their purpose may be self-evident but using them effectively requires thoughtfulness and observation. Visitors need a reason to read a text panel. When a visitor walks into a room, they ask themselves, "What is this place and why do I care?" Since the room is already a scenic environment, your main text panel does not need a huge font or to be wrapped in neon. What it does need to do is reward the visitor for taking the time to read it. Can you describe what excites you about this space in fewer than one hundred words?

Can you include a fact, concept, or idea that visitors will remember long after their visit? Can you include information that appeals to more than a small percentage of your visitors? Is there something here that will allow visitors to see the space in a new light? Creating text panels that are visitor focused takes time and effort, but the reward is that visitors will use the resource if it is useful to them.

Video and sound within a historic house setting offer huge opportunities to connect emotionally with your visitor and is now within the grasp of small budgets more than ever before. The Marden-Abbott House and Store at Strawbery Banke in Portsmouth, New Hampshire, uses a 1940s radio to play period music and news announcements to set the stage for the 1943 interpretation of this historic house. Tucking video in unusual places is an effective technique for exhibitions within museums. One of the most successful uses of video is in "Open House: If These Walls Could Talk" at the Minnesota History Center in St. Paul, an exhibition about a historic house and its occupants. Rooms from a house in the Railroad Island neighborhood on St. Paul's East Side are presented within the gallery as a backdrop for stories of the immigrant families that lived there. From Germans to Italians to African Americans to Hmong, visitors explore the exhibition though hidden labels and media to uncover a diverse set of family stories. Today, with LED projectors getting smaller and computer tablets dropping in price, the cost and maintenance of media installations has fallen considerably. The Durant Kendrick House in Massachusetts includes a computer tablet embedded in a picture frame in one of the bedrooms. The tablet plays a short video about a teenager confronting slavery for the first time based on letters home in the 1830s.

Games, mechanical models, hands-on reproductions, and even lift-flaps fall into the category of interactives. Historic houses already know how transformative an interactive experience can be for a visitor that handles raw flax, churns butter, or touches a beaver pelt. These historic house experiences are the same as interactive exhibitions within a museum setting. Interactives require a laser focus on what is important; it's too easy to become distracted by their gee-wiz aspect. Over the course of the last thirty years, I keep learning the same lesson over and over when developing interactives: keep it simple! A simple interactive with less content often results in more learning. The Hearthstone Historic House Museum in Appleton, Wisconsin, the first hydroelectric home in the state, includes exhibitions that make the connection between water wheels and electricity. One of the simplest—and most successful—is a hand-crank generator on top of a radio.

Consider shrinking exhibitions to the size of a table. Imagine walking into a room with a tabletop exhibition that quietly communicates that it is here for the visitor. There's no large text panel introducing the space or inviting visitors to sit. Visitors young and old can sit down around the table at the same time, encouraging social learning. Grandmother and granddaughter will sit down and try your activity with little to no prompting. At the Durant Kendrick House, for example, visitors decide how they will use the land on this farm to provide everything that the family needs along with a small surplus. The activity is on a small table and includes a game board that represents the available land in the 1760s and game pieces that provide resources for the family. A wood lot for heat, grazing land for cows providing cheese and meat, and a garden plot are just some of the land uses visitors can consider. The content is appealing to children and enlightening for adults. The exhibition sits in the kitchen near artifacts that speak to the many colonial chores required to convert the products of a 1700s farm into supplies the family needs.

The game delivers a fair amount of critical content. It illustrates the idea that colonial families provided everything they needed for themselves and only then produced extra for sale. The game play also delivers specific content on land use that is interesting and new to most visitors. When we developed the exhibition, we had to decide what was the most important message to explore in the kitchen (there were many possibilities), do additional research on how the Durant's used their farm, and test a prototype version of the activity. Testing with friends and members refined the game play, instructions, and format. The result has been very successful with visitors, with family members collaborating, and even talking to each other about the content.

Inevitably, you will be confronted by someone who will advocate a computer interactive based on the idea that "it will engage a young audience." Computers in exhibitions are a means, not an end. There are many companies out there trying to sell the newest computer service: virtual reality, 3-D tours, first-person experiences, custom apps, or beacon tours. Over the last twenty-five years, I have been contacted nearly every week by a company offering new technology with amazing results with little effort. Instead, it is highly likely that the result will be expensive, ineffective, and unused. Computer interactives and other technology can be used within museums and historic houses effectively, but just like anything else, it requires focusing on what you want to do rather than how. To put it another way, you cannot compete with Nintendo on the small screen, but Nintendo can't compete with your content. Technology may be a great way to show images of the property over time or to quiz visitors on how long it took for the railway to get to this house, but ultimately it is just another tool. It is not the real thing.

* * * * *

Historic house museums can reimagine their traditional exhibitions by adopting some of the techniques and approaches I've shared. An interactive, minds-on approach for all visitors will be the most successful. While house museums are often focused on the materials, colors, media, and interactivity of exhibitions, we can get more out of them if we spend more time on planning and testing—that requires a rethinking of exhibitions as minds-on, not hands-on, encounters.

Notes

1. To explore what we've learned at the USS *Constitution* Museum, we've gathered the documentation and strategies from our exhibitions and programs since 2005 at EngageFamilies.org.
2. Susie Wilkening, "The Toughest Audience Out There: Parents, Part I," *The Data Museum* (website), September 12, 2017, http://www.wilkeningconsulting.com/datamuseum/parentbubble1.
3. For more details, visit UniversalDesign.ie.
4. Philadelphia-Camden Informal Science Education Collaborative, *Family Learning in Museums: The PISEC Perspective* (Philadelphia, PA: Franklin Institute, 1998).

Part V

Imagining New Kinds of House Museums

Chapter 25

Reinventing the Historic House Museum

Three Potential Futures

ELIZABETH MERRITT

Editors' note: In this chapter, Elizabeth Merritt explores the future of house museums, proposing three provocative alternatives that may result from today's reinventing efforts. To encourage an ongoing conversation about the reimagining of historic houses, leaders with diverse perspectives in the field share their thoughts in response.

Because I'm a museum futurist, people are always asking me, "What's the future of museums?" I take perverse pleasure in telling them that answering that question would violate my professional ethics. Somewhat counterintuitively, the job of a futurist isn't to foretell the future. Futurists help people envision *potential* futures—many different possibilities, any one of which could plausibly come to be. Futurists observe the forces acting on us in the present—trends, significant events, and the choices people make in dealing with the world—analyze how these forces interact, and, based on these vectors, plot paths forward through time.

Which is a fancy way of saying futurists tell stories—stories that, in the best tradition of fiction, tell the truth about things that haven't happened yet.

As a museum futurist, I might note the rapid adoption of mobile, internet-connected devices and the increasing sophistication of augmented reality and geo-specific technologies, and describe a future in which every visitor experiences a given museum in a unique way. What a visitor sees, what they hear, even what they smell is tailored just for them. Combining the physical world of the museum with digital content, this mixed reality might lock visitors into their own private worlds, or it might create experiences they can share with others. Either way, this story, if it comes true, could blow traditional models of exhibit design and interpretation out of the water.

Despite the fact that I framed that future around technological disruptions, what makes it plausible is the way those technologies fulfill human desires. In an increasingly flattened global world, people are turning away from mass-produced products and services and seeking bespoke, boutique, personalized experiences that speak to them as individuals, catering to their individual wants and needs. I suspect this craving for personalization is one factor contributing to the waning popularity of the traditional docent-guided tour. Other forces are working to dethrone the docent, as well, of course, include the declining value of expertise or authority; the desire for interactive experiences; even our shrinking attention spans.

Futurists call their stories scenarios, and we use them to help people reexamine their assumptions about how the world works today, think about how they want to world to behave tomorrow, and identify actions they can take to build the future they'd prefer to live in. Here's one way to create the seeds of a scenario: identify something you aren't happy with today and ask what it would take for the opposite to be true. If "visits to historic house museums are declining," what would it take to change that fact to be "visits to historic house museums are at an all-time high, and continue to climb"? Granted, telling a story about a world in which that second statement is accurate may require us to be flexible about our definitions: What constitutes a historic house? What counts as a visit? This exercise is more than mere verbal legerdemain, however, as it forces us to identify the core of what it means to be a historic house museum, and what kind of change we want to create through the interaction of person and house.

In that spirit of questioning, I'm going to spin three stories of historic house museums we may see in the future, stories that would let us make positive statements about the role these museums play in society and about their popularity. In each case, I'll touch on some of the trends that will fill a stable niche in a plausible future for this kind of museum and identify a few assumptions we might need to let go of in order to create this new institution.

Alternative Histories

First up, I present for your consideration the Museum of Alternative Histories. Alternative history, more informally alt-history, explores the imaginative fiction of "what if?" It starts by identifying a key event that shaped our current world and asks how things may have played out had that event taken a different turn. Livy pioneered the genre circa 25 BC when he explored what might have happened had Alexander the Great, marching his armies west instead of east, had gone to war with Rome. In 1836, Louis Geoffroy imagined what would have happened if Napoleon successfully invaded first Russia and then England. Given the wealth of (real) historical detail an author can draw on in crafting these scenarios, alt-history is a useful exercise in how to explore plausible futures and develop skills for imagining the various ways history might play out from this time forward.

Enter the alt-historic house. I imagine a house, perhaps in Charleston, South Carolina, which reflects three histories of the United States: the one that actually occurred; one in which the Civil War ended in a draw and the Confederacy became a sovereign nation; and one based on the premise of Terry Bisson's *Fire on the Mountain*. (Bisson's novel imagines a world in which John Brown's raid on Harper's Ferry succeeded, leading to a full-scale slave revolt and the establishment of an independent black nation called Novo Africa.)

There are a number of ways the interpretation at the Museum of Alternative Histories could play out. The "house" could in fact be three adjacent row houses. The experience starts at a kiosk outdoors where a visitor, choosing the outcome of the war, is directed to the house that exists in that timeline. The interior of each house will be a snapshot in time, as if the resident had just stepped out and might be back any minute. There might be a meal half-eaten at the table,

Elizabeth Merritt

dishes in the sink waiting to be washed, an unmade bed. By perusing the photographs on the walls, reading the correspondence lying on the desk, even peeking into the account book for the household, visitors are encouraged to deduce who lives there and how their lives were affected by the outcome of the war. The three houses will be designed to echo each other in ways that play up both the similarities and difference between the timelines.

Alternately, there could be one house, almost empty (or perhaps containing some basic furnishings). Visitors would trigger the interpretation for any of the three timelines through their smart phone, by accessing recordings, viewing augmented reality overlays for the rooms, and reading biographic notes on the residents.

Or, a la China Miéville's novel *The City & the City*, evidence of all three timelines could exist physically in one house, at one time. The visitor would be challenged to untangle the clues, deducing which artifact, which bit of evidence, belonged to which version of history. As in David Wilson's redoubtable Museum of Jurassic Technology in Los Angeles, California, the contents of this house would be a combination of the absolutely true, the slightly warped, and inspired fictions. It would take a bit of detective work for a visitor to unravel what fit into which category.

The Museum of Alternative History builds on the potential for museums to be playful, mysterious, and challenging. It is a museum that asks questions rather than giving answers. It invites people to exercise the muscles of imagination and of critical thinking. Perhaps most radically, it requires staff to step down from the pedestal of authority, admit that our understanding of history is contingent, and that any narrative of history is shaped by the facts one chooses to see.

Every House a Museum

My second model for our future historic house: the house you live in, or the house belonging to your child, grandchild, or great-great grandniece. In this scenario, we look at Your House Museum (YHM), a nonprofit organization founded by the Historic House Committee of the American Alliance of Museums in 2020. The primary target of YHM is dedicated amateur enthusiasts interested in high-grade restoration of their properties to historic standards. The organization supports the creation of accessible, linked, open datasets covering a range of topics from building permits to local history to genealogy, and the easy-to-use Your House web portal facilitates finding and using this data. Working with the National Trust for Historic Preservation, YHM helps connect homeowners with the resources they need to apply for landmark status for their home or to create historic districts in their neighborhoods.

YHM also fosters programs that transform inwardly focused explorations of personal history and personal property into shared, communal experiences. YHM maintains a registry of owners who open their houses for historical tours, provides a Yelp-like listing platform (encouraging visitors to rate their experience), and offers ticketing services that enable owners to schedule visits and control attendance. YHM also provides training and certification that validates the accuracy of their restoration and interpretation, a service particularly valued by owners who operate their houses as historic B&Bs.

A secondary target for YHM's work is a larger pool: the general public who want to explore the history of the building in which they reside. In this future, in which 3-D printers are common household appliances, YHM provides libraries of 3-D scans of domestic artifacts from various historical periods. (It's become a common history assignment for fifth graders to use this library to replace implements in their house with equivalent tools from previous centuries, often to the great annoyance of their parents.) Building on the infrastructure of on-demand manufacturing, YHM offers an affordable line of quality reproduction artifacts, furniture, and historical clothing. For do-it-yourself types, YHM's YouTube channel hosts an award-winning series of instructional videos on historical carpentry, metalworking, sewing, and other skills. People who don't want to invest in physical objects can use YHM's digital tools to create a virtual rendering of what their house might have looked like, inside and out, at a given point in time. History PenPal—YHM's own artificial intelligence (AI) program—draws on historical documents, genealogical research, machine learning, and natural language processing to correspond with any child writing in the voice of a real resident from the community's history or as a real or composite fictional resident of the child's own home.

The YHM scenario builds on a lot of technological trends—AI, linked open data, 3-D printing—but its central premise is that deep, personal engagement with history is an attractive "hook" for users, even as it fosters curiosity and learning. Even as attendance at history museums and historic sites declined in the early 2000s, YHM observed that consumption of historical content via books, films, musicals, and historical reenactments soared. YHM arrives at its core philosophy—"history begins at home"—by observing how personal insights can lead to self-directed learning. At many historical libraries and archives, hobbyists digging into their own genealogies far outnumber researchers looking at broader topics. The availably and affordability of personal DNA sequencing is prompting interest in patterns of human migration on a global historic scale. In effect, YHM is attempting to flip the model of immersive historic re-creations, equipping people to become first-person interpreters in their own homes.

YHM's approach also addresses fundamental flaws in the financial models that support, or rather fail to support, historic houses as a whole. It is widely recognized that there are more historic house museums in existence than can be maintained by existing sources of support. Philanthropic foundations, in particular, feel tapped out by the demands of myriad small house museums that hover on the brink of extinction. So many small house museums fit this description that one of the recommendations of the 2007 Kykuit II Summit on the Sustainability of Historic Sites was that many historic sites should consider transitioning to private ownership rather than trying to sustain themselves as nonprofit organizations. YHM tackles this problem from the other end by providing accessible ways for people to develop and share the historic value of their homes while keeping them in private hands.

Stone Soup

My first scenario described a single museum, the Museum of Alternative History, that takes a new approach to interpreting a historic house. My second looked at how an organization, Your House Museum, helps people explore the history embodied in their own homes. My last scenario describes a genre of historic house museums—a movement if you will—that may take hold in the future.

The 2020s saw the rise of the community house movement—an informal coalition dedicated to linking historic preservation to community service. Community houses are created in structures that were significant to a community's past for a variety of reasons. They include grand domiciles, humble homes, abandoned churches, Grange halls, fraternal lodges, and corner stores. Some were inhabited by people considered significant by mainstream historians. Others housed families who "merely" reflect the history and traditions of cultures that inhabited the neighborhood through time.

Community houses are dedicated to preserving their structures in service of their neighbors, whatever form that service might take. They typically serve as homes for myriad local groups in need of common social space including sewing circles, book clubs, natural history societies, amateur theatrical groups, and tinkering groups. Community houses are often hubs of political and cultural activity—events such as community meals and poetry slams often serve as a means of exploring contentious issues. Many devote their associated land to community gardens, some support the local food and creative economies by hosting farmers' markets and crafts fairs. Community houses are typically governed by a nonprofit board consisting of members of all these groups together with preservationists and historians.

Because community houses provide flexible, adaptable space to a variety of users, they rarely are furnished with original artifacts. More typically, interpretation of the history of these structures is provided through text, photographs, and digital content. Often the groups using the space interpret the history through their own particular lens—art, poetry, plays, book discussions. Community houses have a particularly strong tradition of opening themselves to teenagers. It's considered the norm to have teen representation on the governing board, and many houses have separate teen councils with significant authority over programming and development. A majority of community houses are dedicated to exploring so-called hidden histories of cultures and individuals underrepresented in dominant cultural narratives.

None of the practices that characterize the community house movement are new: they amplify a variety of trends shaping history houses around the turn of the twenty-first century. The movement took significant inspiration from Rick Lowe's Project Row Houses in Houston's Ninth Ward, which famously is dedicated to serving community needs, including providing local residents with much needed day care and a laundromat. It was also spurred by Frank Vagnone and Deborah Ryan's *Anarchist's Guide to Historic Houses*, a manifesto that encourages preservationists to question almost every aspect of traditional practice in order to serve the culture and interests of the neighborhood, build community trust, and create emotional experiences. What's new is the scale—community houses have become as common as public libraries (indeed, many often operate in partnership with their local library, drawing on the digital and maker-space expertise of library staff). And because they are connected via a vibrant digital community, including social media and digital forums, they are slowly building a shared set of best practices.

As with Your House Museum, the community house movement addresses the financial challenges of house museums, in this case by making themselves valued assets to a broad range of community members, and in this way building a broad base of support. The typical community house has a diverse income stream made up of fees from various groups using the space, philanthropic support from local foundations, and local government funding. Of particular note is the fact that on average about 30 percent of these organizations' operating income comes from small, individual donations. Having community members as the largest single source of operating income helps ensure that community houses remain nimble and responsive to community needs.

So those are my three stories for your consideration, my attempts to tell the truth about things that haven't happened yet. Now it's up to you to use these stories as tools in your futures thinking. They may shape how you look at what is happening in the world around you—Do you see things happening in the historic house sector and in the wider world that strengthen, or weaken, the potential success of these models? Do you see elements in these stories that can change how you think about your own practice? Even a house museum that hews more or less to traditional practices may benefit from becoming a bit more playful and open to ambiguity; to reaching out to people who may never visit its own site; and to devoting its resources to serving community needs. I encourage you to start writing your own stories as well—What kinds of history house museums can you imaging that might thrive in the future? The more plausible fictions we share with each other, the more likely we are to discover a promising truth.

＊ ＊ ＊ ＊ ＊

Responses

Carol B. Stapp, Director, Museum Education Program, George Washington University

Elizabeth Merritt's provocative vision of three potential futures for historic house museums merits a zestful rejoinder:

- Museum of Alternative Histories: Alt-history makes for great fiction and arch experiences for the culturally literate, but what happens when there's no respect for the boundary between the authentic and the artificial? In a time of "alternative facts," should historic house museums play games?
- Your House Museum: How will focusing on interpreting one's own home inspire the public to visit an actual historic house museum? Does opening up one's home for an annual house and garden tour simply flip the proposition of "saving" historic house museums through privatizing them?
- Community Houses: There are historic house museums already "preserving their structures in service of their neighbors," but is dismantling a historic house museum and essentially turning it into a community center a viable approach for sustaining historic house museums?

Entertaining these potential futures can indeed be refreshing but embracing the concept of "the period of significance is now" holds the most promise for revitalizing historic house museums as avenues into the past that generate meaningful gateways to the future.[1]

Susie Wilkening, Wilkening Consulting

Soulless. That's how I would describe most historic house museums. Perhaps beautiful, or aesthetically interesting, but soulless. It is, admittedly, hard to infuse domestic spaces with soul when no one truly lives there. Soul, to me, means idiosyncratic touches that are hard to stage. A space has to be lived in to have soul . . . and to most effectively tell a story of a family.

The third scenario does gives houses their souls back. Not the soul of a family, but the soul of a community. A soul that is just as idiosyncratic, but thrives from a community making the house a home again, infusing it with new stories and character. Bringing it to life once again through, well, life and its messiness, joy, sorrow, love, friendship, and play. And isn't that the true story of all true homes through time?

Brian Joyner, Chief of Staff, National Mall and Memorial Parks, National Park Service

What if I told you that *you* were the future of house museums? That's right! The old gray dudes and chicks don't draw like they used to, but through a mash-up of the National Historic Preservation Act, Restoration Hardware, Trading Spaces, AI, with a dash of social media narcissism, the next-level house museum—Your House Museum (YHM)—could be generated by the people and for the people. A hyper-personal approach as a way forward to combat flagging visitation.

What's intriguing about what Elizabeth Merritt suggests is that the future starts with the idea that people want to see themselves (and values) in house museums. Her idea of alternative histories uses innate curiosity and problem solving to reveal historical facts. It assumes combing through personal bias and bad history lessons to get to an empirical truth, potentially offering the sort of context and interpretation lacking at current places of cultural memory (hello Confederate statues!).

Merritt removes the preciousness from the house museum, which if museums are to become third spaces within communities, like in the community house movement, has to happen. Could that become contentious? Given the current environment, oh yeah.

Jorge A. Hernandez, Park Ranger/Interpreter, Mission San Jose y san Miguel de Aguayo

Elizabeth Merritt's futuristic scenarios inspire a unique alternative methodology for the inter-pretation of historic houses. As she suggests, modern technological innovations can create a bridge between past and present, allowing historic houses to customize visitors' experiences and provide them with the resources to find a meaningful connection with a historic house, or even their own. However, the application of Merritt's futuristic envisioning can potentially enhance the interpretation of historic sites that had been overshadowed by "mainstream" history. If tech-nology is paired with an alt-history lens, those stories, voices, and controversial events that have been omitted from history books or deserve more attention will find their relevancy in today's socioeconomic and political developments. An adobe house with a farm sitting in the Southwest can showcase the legacy of its residents, historical continuity, and shared heritage of an area that has been under control by three nations: Spain, Mexico, and United States.

Emiliano "Nano" Calderon, Site Educator, Casa Navarro State Historic Site, Texas Historical Commission

Historic house museums of the future will certainly be impacted by demographic changes in age, ethnicity, and population density at the national and local level, which brings to mind many questions. How will house museums in urban areas adapt to the increased affluence or poverty of the communities that surround them? How will rural and suburban sites be impacted by population growth and the proliferation of diverse communities? How will historic homes find relevancy in these changing communities? It will be critical that house museums anticipate and reflect these changes through interpretation and community engagement. The community house movement provides the greatest opportunity for historic house museums and communities to interact with one another moving forward; however in planning for these changes, house muse-ums could consider adopting more lenient policies toward use that will encourage visitation in nontraditional and creative ways. Likewise, opening historic house museum operations to small businesses, nonprofits, cultural groups, and community organizations could provide a pathway toward relevancy in an uncertain future.

Nathan Ritchie, Director, Golden History Museum, Colorado

To understand their existential paradox, one need look no further than their name—historic house museums. Historic houses are saved for their perceived significance (mission), not for their utility as a viable museum (business model). Yet, this is the pattern that thousands of communities across the nation have unquestioningly followed when confronted with the conundrum of how to save a beloved if deteriorating landmark—save it, turn it into a museum, mission accomplished. No market research, no feasibility study, no long-term analysis required.

Modifying interpretation strategies is an important aspect of reimagining HHMs of the future, but it is not a panacea. The existential crisis facing HHMs today is about not only their waning audiences, but an inability to earn revenue because of limitations or prohibitions intrinsic to these types of properties. Not a single new museum is built today without a significant allocation of space for catering kitchens, rental spaces, classrooms, and meeting facilities—they have become indispensable to the museum revenue model. Historic houses that try to operate a museum business while lacking the necessary infrastructure or ability to modify their space can never succeed. Those preexisting limitations, compounded by other factors like geographic isolation, directly inhibits a museum's ability to function as a business. Given these realities, at some point historic house leadership will be forced to decide between which is more important—preserving a building or operating a museum. Depending on each site's unique situation, it's possible that the two might be mutually exclusive.

Barbara Silberman, Museum Studies Program, Tufts University

One possibility for the future of some HHMs may be turning some into private homes with preservation protections in order to provide affordable housing.

Younger Americans face unheard of financial burdens. College debt, rising housing and child-care costs, and the use of permanent part-time labor ensure that millennials will find it difficult to pay off student debt and purchase a home.

Several states have curatorial programs that might be adapted to address this need. Most programs work by accepting sweat equity in lieu of rent or a mortgage. A change in a curatorial program would allow a family to restore a home, but at the end of the lease period, a family could purchase the home for its market value at the time the lease was signed. This would give a family time to drastically reduce or eliminate student debt and allow them to keep pace with rising housing costs.

Houses that were radically altered or without original collections would be candidates for this program. This scenario allows for preservation and could include an annual open house to ensure that a home remained available to the public.

Joe McGill, Founder, Slave Dwelling Project

The future of house museums cannot be considered without recognizing their difficult histories. In embracing diversity, I would wager that a large percentage of house museums honor white males who have something in their past that is unacceptable by today's standards. Forty-one signers of the Declaration of Independence, twenty-five signers of the U.S. Constitution, and twelve former presidents were slave owners. Portraying these men as slave owners has not been the norm for telling their stories at the sites that honor them, yet because chattel slavery was an institution, these men were not carrying out their actions in a vacuum. Archival, archaeological, DNA, and genealogical research are disciplines that are inserting the enslaved into their rightful place in the narrative.

Behind the Big House: Ninety-three degrees is the temperature away from the fire in the detached kitchen. The enslaved woman Ester and her two children were up since 4:00 a.m., stoking the fire and preparing a breakfast of eggs, ham, grits, and biscuits, a meal that they could not consume.

Elizabeth Merritt

The master spared no expense because the hearth was as wide as it was high and deep. It had cranes on both sides with many pots and Dutch ovens indicating that there was a big family in the big house or he liked entertaining guests.

Note

1. Erin Carlson Mast, Morris J. Vogel, and Lisa Lopez, "The Period of Significance Is Now," *Forum Journal* 28, no. 4 (Summer 2014): 43–51.

Recommended Resources

Miéville, China. *The City & the City*. New York: Del Rey, 2010.
Vagnone, Franklin D., and Deborah E. Ryan. *Anarchist's Guide to Historic House Museums*. Walnut Creek, CA: Left Coast Press, 2016.

Chapter 26

Yes, America, You Need Another House Museum (But Read This Book First)

KENNETH C. TURINO

In an article for *History News* in 2004, Carol B. Stapp and I posed the question, "Does America Need Another Historic House Museum?," and outlined the challenges facing historic houses, including financial instability, declining attendance along with aging populations, poor stewardship, and relevancy. I followed this with the more provocatively titled, "America Doesn't Need Another House Museum (And What about Collections?)," in 2009.[1] These articles came at a critical time, when the field was reevaluating the sustainability and relevance of our historic houses. Although these articles, and the influential 2007 Kykuit forum to discuss the sustainability of historic sites, are more than a decade old, sustainability and relevance are still some of the most pressing challenges facing the historic house field today. Many historic houses are still struggling. Recently, a headline in the *New York Times* proclaimed, "Edna St. Vincent Millay's Farmhouse Faces Closure," and described a litany of challenges. "The cost of operating the site, even with a small staff and an extremely tight budget, exceeds the money brought in each year from donations and visitor fees," wrote Vincent Elizabeth Barnett, president of the organization's board of trustees.[2]

Sound familiar? The good news is that while many houses are struggling, more and more sites have adapted to change so as to better engage their communities and become more sustainable. Many chapters in this book give examples. Another is the North Dakota Historical Society. When it purchased the boyhood home and farm of bandleader Lawrence Welch (the Welch Homestead near Strasburg, North Dakota) from members of the family in 2015, the house was struggling financially and attracted only approximately 650 visitors per year. Threatened with cuts in state budgets earmarked to operate the site and the fact that fewer and fewer people knew who Lawrence Welch was, the historical society needed to make the site more relevant. Since the Welch family was German-Russian and 70 to 80 percent of the tri-county area claim their ethnicity as German or German-Russian, the society decided to make ethnic heritage one focus of the site. Because the site had been a farm, and agriculture is still a major industry in the state, they also decided to make agriculture an additional focus. These changes have improved engagement with the local community and increased attendance.

Since the 2007 Kykuit forum, numerous conferences, articles, blogs, classes, workshops, and books addressing the sustainability of historic houses have assisted the field. Donna Harris' *New Solutions for House Museums* proposes solutions for sites in peril, including alternative uses, easements, long-term or short-term leases, mergers, property consolidation, and study properties, essentially mothballing a property permanently or temporarily.[3] In 2008, the American Association for State and Local History's Historic House Affinity Group Committee produced the technical leaflet, "How Sustainable Is Your Historic House Museum?" The leaflet outlines eleven points that "summarize the sign of a healthy, thriving historic house museum." It is still a useful guide.[4] More recently, Franklin D. Vagnone and Deborah E. Ryan's *Anarchist's Guide to Historic House Museums* enlivened our discussions about how historic houses do business, suggesting that much of it is "the same old business."[5] The book offers guidelines for evaluating historic properties and adopting practices "to not only survive, but thrive in a rapidly changing world." This publication was the source of much debate but it remains an important resource that questions the "standard rules" of historic house museum practice.

The Fogg-Rollins House in Exeter, New Hampshire, is an example of the options available to those who would preserve historic buildings. My 2009 article follows the house board of trustees through the process of deciding whether preservation as a historic house museum was the best use for the circa 1790s Fogg-Rollins House, barn, wheelwright shop (both dating from the first half of the nineteenth century), and landscape—and if it was sustainable. The property had remained in the family since construction and never had running water or electricity. It was furnished with household effects dating from the nineteenth century to the 1950s (when it was last used as a summer camp). The barn was full of wagons, carriages, and farm equipment, and the wheelwright shop with tools and equipment.

The intent of the last owner, Ms. Rollins, was to form a trust and the board she assembled was charged with turning the property into a historic house museum. Unfortunately, no money came with the donation. Instead, Ms. Rollins left her house in Massachusetts and her money in trust to her ten cats, who had life occupancy of that house. Only after the cats died could any money be used for the care of the house. Cats can live (and these did) a long time! Even after careful consideration, a scholar's report found that "the house had no compelling story" (relevance) and that a glut of historic sites already existed in the area. Even with no foreseeable means to make the property a viable house museum (sustainability), it still took ten years of debate to come to that conclusion. The decision to sell the property to a private owner with easements that protect the land, house, barn, and wheelwright shop in perpetuity was not easy for the board and the discussions were contentious. Finally, approximately 2 percent of the artifacts at the property were distributed to appropriate museums and the remainder were sold. The proceeds of the sale were distributed to the museums that took artifacts to assist with their care and preservation.

What we attempted to do in our previous articles was give readers an example of one alternative to a traditional house museum. We were not calling for the closure or repurposing of all historic houses, nor for a moratorium on the establishment of new historic houses museums. We wrote that in evaluating a prospective house museum, the site's viability should be tied to its sustainability and that its fate should depend on the particular context and specific circumstances of its community. In the Fogg-Rollins House case, we concluded that America didn't need another house museum!

The ultimate decision of the Fogg-Rollins House board was to preserve the buildings and landscape through an easement (also known as a covenant or restriction). This legal agreement between the property owner (easement donor) and a qualified preservation organization (easement holder), recorded with local land records, gives the easement holder rights and responsibilities associated with perpetual protection. The easement does not preclude future sales, leases, or estate planning. The current owner continues to be responsible for maintenance and taxes.

The board selected Historic New England to hold the easement because of its vigilance in administering preservation easements and its ability to pursue legal action for violations. Historic New England is the oldest and largest regional heritage organization in the nation, operating more than three dozen properties that span four centuries of architectural styles in five New England states. Most significantly, Historic New England holds more than a hundred properties in its Preservation Easement Program, which is financed through endowments deposited in a restricted fund.[6] This fund allows the program to function in a self-supporting capacity and provides the resources to pursue legal action if necessary. With easements in place, the board sold the Fogg-Rollins House to a private party and the house was restored with Historic New England guidance. Historic New England arranged to work closely with the owner, inspect the house annually, and remain on call to answer questions and make recommendations for any proposed work. This turned out to be a win-win solution for the Fogg-Rollins House and Historic New England: the building was preserved, some of the collection was placed in public repositories, and owners were secured who will maintain the property.

Another example of the use of a preservation easement is Upsala in the Germantown neighborhood of Philadelphia, a historic house owned by the National Trust for Historic Preservation and managed by Cliveden, another house museum across the street. After years of unsuccessful attempts at programmatic options and partnerships, Upsala still could not be made viable. Through a detailed process in line with current museum standards, including community input, the National Trust deaccessioned the property, placed easements on it, and then sold it in 2017 into private hands. Like the Fogg- Rollins House, it returned to its original use—a private home— and will be preserved.[7]

These cases dealt with deaccessions, but what about creating a new a historic house museum? There are resources on legal and tax obligations, missions, boards, financial management, and collections policies available from the American Association for State and Local History (AASLH) and the American Alliance of Museums, but few of the criteria assess whether creating a historic house museum is the best use of a property. A good source for anyone considering a new house museum is Donovan D. Rypkema's *Feasbility Assessment Manual for Reusing Historic Buildings*.[8] This manual contains forms, checklists, matrices, and source references that lead users through the historic rehabilitation process. Though not specifically for historic houses, the publication, particularly the Proposed Use Matrix, can be adapted for that use.

Another resource comes from Historic New England, which is committed to acquiring properties that fill gaps in its collections to remain relevant in the twenty-first century. Because Historic New England aspires to represent the full spectrum of peoples who have made New England home through the untold stories of marginalized peoples, the organization adopted a policy in 2002 for considering the "Acquisition of Real Property" (i.e., historic buildings, landscapes, and objects) (see textbox on next page). According to Benjamin Haavik, Historic New England's team leader for property care, this policy "was based on our own work from the late 1970s, looking at our collection and thinking more critically about how we take on properties."[9] The policy helps Historic New England determine if a property will be best served in the preservation sense by being owned by Historic New England. The criteria Historic New England

Summary of Historic New England's "Acquisition of Real Property" (2002)

The importance of endowments:

To address sustainability as a priority, the property must come with an endowment "sufficient to support foreseeable operating expenses." In negotiating with a donor, funds to cover initial capital expenses are included. Depending on the condition and status of the property, funds may be needed for the preparation of a historic property report, to complete an inventory of all collections, an assessment of conservations for those collections, oral histories, and record photography.

No restrictions:

- The assignment of life rights by the grantor to a designated party
- Restrictions against sale or conveyance to another party of its choosing
- Limitation on alterations or additions deemed appropriate

A formal written evaluation (with staff recommendations) that looks at:

- The architectural importance of the structures and landscapes
- Its historical standing, and the significance of the collections including archival and documentary records over a long period of time
- The physical condition of the building
- The financial viability including potential sources of income
- Local interest and support
- Exposure to physical threats (vandalism, fire, flooding, emergency vehicle access)
- Legal or regulatory restrictions on the use of the property
- Whether the historic house will attract an audience
- Wether the site is accessible to visitors (e.g., public transportation, parking)

outlines when it considers taking on a new historic site can be applied by others considering whether to preserve a property as a historic house museum.

Once completed, the evaluation/report might recommend the house be made a house museum or become part of Historic New England's easement program. This document goes to the Historic New England president and CEO for review and comment before it is brought to the properties committee, which oversees recommendations for new properties. That committee then advises the board of trustees, who must ultimately approve the decision.

As part of the evaluation, the Historic New England committee also considers whether the site has a compelling story, one that goes beyond the traditional architecture and decorative arts tours, to illuminate information meaningful to today's audiences. Stories that visitors can relate to, stories where they can in some way see themselves or their family's histories reflected, are what Historic New England seeks. These stories may also tackle difficult history or social issues. While not explicitly stated, properties acquired by Historic New England need to attract sufficient audiences to justify the cost of maintenance and management.

Historic New England's detailed procedure for acquiring a property for historic house museum use is a valuable tool in evaluating any site under consideration. As the case of Upsala demonstrated, alternative use may turn out to be the best choice. To be sustainable, a historic house museum

Kenneth C. Turino

must engage with its community. That's the bottom line—you can't have one without the other. We must continue to build our engagement with our communities. To do this, we need to understand who our communities are and then evaluate the ways we present history to them. Too often, what is presented through tours or programs is not relevant to the people we hope to attract.

Across America, our communities are changing. According to a *Time* magazine report, "In several states and dozens of cities, whites are no longer in the majority." Demographers predict that by the mid-2040s, people of color will be the nation's majority population. Millennials, who number 83.1 million now, have surpassed the 75.4 million baby boomers and are the most diverse generation in history.[10] We recognize that our field as a whole is less diverse, inclusive, accessible, and equitable than it should be, and thus many people and institutions have championed new initiatives in their recruiting and hiring practices for staff and at the board level. This effort will make the biggest contribution to incorporating different perspectives at our historic sites. These initiatives go beyond how we hire and train staff to how we interpret and work with people from different cultures and backgrounds. The Abbe Museum in Bar Harbor, Maine, is leading the charge on the urgency of museum decolonizing practices. "Decolonization," according to Cinnamon Catlin-Legutko, president and CEO of the Abbe Museum, "means, at a minimum, sharing governance structures and authority for the documentation and interpretation of Native culture."[11] This is especially relevant to historic houses on Native lands and holding Native objects in their collections.

In addition to the changes mentioned above, people expect to get their information and encounter it in different ways. The 2017 Culture Track report by LaPlace Cohen asked more than four thousand demographically diverse people from across the nation why they seek cultural experiences. They found that 81 percent were interested in having fun, 78 percent in learning content, 76 percent in experiencing new things, and 68 percent in interacting with others.[12] Historic New England had recently completed a survey to identify the needs of its audiences and found virtually the same results: people wanted experiences that were fun, social, interactive, and relevant. These studies point to the fact that we need to move beyond the velvet rope tour and stop telling the same stories in the same ways. How many sites do you know that talk about or demonstrate candle making, butter churning, or spinning wheels? Enough! In the future, tours can no longer be the only way we engage visitors; tours need to be more focused, social, and relevant and we need to find other ways to inform and engage.

There are many options. One site that takes a different, more sensory approach is the Benjamin Franklin House in London, where Franklin lived for sixteen years. This house employs costumed interpreters (actors) who use the historic spaces as a stage, blending live interpretation, sound, lighting, visual projections, and interactives "to remove the distance between visitor and history."

Another example is the Dennis Severs House, also in London, where visitors explore the home of a fictitious family of Huguenot silk weavers living from 1724 to the start of the twentieth century. As visitors move through the house, they smell food cooking in the kitchen. As they enter the dining room, they hear imaginary people exiting through another door, laughing and talking. Visitors may hear snippets of music as they move through the house, see a spilled glass of wine on the table and candles burning in another room with a roaring fire, and in the bedchamber, they see an unmade bed while a cat may brush their legs.

Other sites like Abbotsford, the home of Sir Walter Scott in Scotland, the Thomas Cole National Historic Site in Catskill, New York (home and studio of the artist), and the Eustis Estate in Milton, Massachusetts, each allow visitors a choice of a guided tour or self-guided exploration, and rely on technology to enhance the experience. Kiosks in the period rooms at Abbotsford and the Eustis Estate allow visitors to dig deeper into the family's life to learn more about the rooms and the objects in them (see Figure 26.1). Abbotsford also offers visitors optional audio guides: a tour led by Sir Walter Scott, Maida the dog, or Hinse the cat (two of Sir Walter Scott's favorite pets). At the Eustis Estate, visitors are allowed to sit on period furniture in all but two of the rooms. The Cole House in Catskill, New York, employs a multimedia experience with a film on the Hudson River School and projections in the living room as well as exhibitions of contemporary art.

Our historic houses need to tell different stories, more relevant stories, stories beyond those of dead rich white guys (and the occasional white woman) to interpret the vast range of stories of people and events traditionally excluded—because of culture, skin color, place of origin, sexual orientation, or abilities—from mainstream discussions of the past. One well-known site embracing change is Monticello in Charlottesville, Virginia. Starting with research in the 1950s, Monticello has shed light on its enslaved community, but it was not until recently that the site truly embraced inclusive interpretation, bringing stories of the enslaved to the broader public. Monticello continues to present its difficult history of enslavement. In 2018, the site reinterpreted a room to acknowledge the ties between the enslaved Sally Hemings and her owner, Thomas Jefferson.[13] James Madison's Montpelier in Montpelier Station, Virginia, like Monticello, has worked closely with descendants of enslaved people to tell the stories of slavery through award-winning interactive exhibitions in the main house and reconstructed slave quarters.[14]

In the case of La Casa Cordova in Tucson, Arizona, the preservation and restoration of the site "provides an example of how narratives of exclusion grounded in settler colonialism got imprinted on the built environment." The City of Tucson, after acquiring La Casa Cordova (the rear section is claimed to be the oldest surviving structure in Tucson), enlisted the Junior League and the Tucson Art Museum (which would operate the building) to restore the site to what has been called a "mythical Mexican history." In doing this, they essentially erased the history of the Cordovas, a Mexican American family who had lived in the house since 1896 and were evicted by the city in 1972. It is only recently that this erasure has been rectified. Starting in 2016, the museum initiated a series of repairs to the house and used this as an opportunity to tell a more inclusive history. In June 2017, the museum opened a room to tell the story of the Cordova family along with Mexican Americans, reflecting on urban renewal and downtown Tucson's history. The museum plans to open other rooms to tell a fuller story of Mexican Americans.[15]

In the future, we need both existing sites and new historic houses to tell the stories that have not been told before. Being inclusive means telling the stories of all Americans. These houses and stories are coming online, but we need more to be told. Examples include the California home of renowned labor leader César Chávez and his family and the headquarters of the United Farm Workers in Keene, California, which President Obama declared a national monument in 2012. Another is the Tenement Museum in New York City that opened a new exhibition, "Under One Roof," in the summer of 2017 to tell the stories of three post–World War II immigrant families: the Epsteins, Jewish refugees from Nazi Poland; the Saez-Valez family from Puerto Rico; and the Wongs, immigrants from China. There are still other stories to tell and sites in development including the Palmer-Warner House in East Haddam, a Connecticut Landmarks property researching the LGBTQ history of the site with the intent of focusing the interpretation of the house on this history.

So, does America need another historic house museum? Yes—if the site has a compelling and relevant story that engages with its community *and* has a well-crafted plan for sustainability.

Figure 26.1 The Eustis Estate in Milton, Massachusetts, allows visitors to choose their experience: guided tour or self-exploration. Visitors can interact with the kiosks, use computer tablets in the rooms, or use their mobile devices to learn more about the family or the room. Guests can also sit on the period furniture or view exhibitions in dedicated galleries. Photo courtesy of Historic New England.

Through this book and in the Reinventing the Historic House Museum workshops, AASLH, Max van Balgooy, and I are committed to providing a wide range of tools and techniques like these resources to address the opportunities and threats facing historic sites as well as strong examples of those who have addressed these opportunities and threats by reinventing themselves. In the future, if museums are to keep pace with societal changes, we must be open to such reinvention. We hope this book stimulates, engages, and encourages those in the field to do just that.

Notes

1. For more detailed information on this case study, see Carol B. Stapp and Kenneth C. Turino, "Does America Need Another House Museum?" *History News* 59, no. 3 (Summer 2004): 7–11, and Kenneth C. Turino, "America Doesn't Need Another House Museum (And What about Collections?)," *History News* 64, no. 2 (2009): 12–15.
2. Andrew R. Chow, "Edna St. Vincent Millay's Farmhouse Faces Closure," *New York Times,* June 16, 2018, https://www.nytimes.com/2018/04/24/arts/edna-st-vincent-millays-farmhouse-steepletop-faces -closure.html (accessed October 26, 2018).
3. Donna Ann Harris, *New Solutions for House Museums: Ensuring the Long-Term Preservation of America's Historic Houses* (Walnut Creek, CA: Altamira Press, 2007).
4. AASLH's Historic House Affinity Group Committee, "How Sustainable Is Your Historic House Museum?" *History News* 63, no. 4 (Autumn 2008): 1–12.
5. Franklin Vagnone and Deborah Ryan, *Anarchist's Guide to Historic House Museums* (Walnut Creek, CA: Left Coast Press, 2015).
6. Historic New England began its easement program by deaccessioning several historic house museums that were not sustainable. See https://www.historicnewengland.org/preservation/for-homeowners -communities/preservation-easement-program/ (accessed October 26, 2018). There are many organizations across the country that hold easements: national organizations like the National Trust for Historic Preservation; regional organizations like the Trust for Architectural Easements serving areas in New England and middle and south Atlantic states; and state organizations like the California Preservation Foundation. The District of Columbia alone has more than 1,700 historic properties, divided among five organizations, protected by private historic preservation easements.
7. Thompson Mayes, Carrie Villar, and David Young, "Giving Upsala Its Best Shot," *History News* 73, no. 3 (2018): 19–23.
8. Formerly published by the National Trust for Historic Preservation in 2007, the booklet was updated in 2015 and is now published by PlaceEconomics. For more information, visit http://www.placeeconomics .com/ (accessed October 26, 2018).
9. Telephone conversation with Benjamin Haavik, Team Leader, Property Care, on August 27, 2018.
10. Josh Sanburn, "U.S. Steps Closer to a Future Where Minorities Are the Majority," *Time,* June 25, 2015. http://time.com/3934092/us-population-diversity-census/ (accessed October 26, 2018).
11. Cinnamon Catlin-Legutko, "We Must Decolonize Our Museums," *Abbe Museum Strategic Plan* (blog), November 7, 2016, https://abbemuseum.wordpress.com/2016/11/07/we-must-decolonize-our-museums/ (accessed October 26, 2018).
12. Deborah Howes. "Handheld and Expansive, Mobile Platforms Help Museums Foster Better Visitor Experiences," *Museum* (January–February 2019): 17–21.
13. Farah Stockman, "Monticello Is Done Avoiding Jefferson's Relationship with Sally Hemings," *New York Times,* June 16, 2018. https://www.nytimes.com/2018/06/16/us/sally-hemings-exhibit-monticello .html (accessed October 26, 2018).
14. Montpelier Foundation, "The Mere Distinction of Color: Telling the Story of Slavery at Montpelier," https://www.montpelier.org/visit/mere-distinction (accessed October 26, 2018).
15. Lydia R. Otero. "New Directions for La Casa Cordova: Recentering the Latinx Past and Present in Tucson," *History News* 73, no. 3 (2018): 8–12.

Selected Bibliography

We developed this bibliography of more than two hundred books and articles published since 2000 as a gateway to the breadth of challenges and opportunities facing house museums in the United States. When combined with the resources in each chapter, it provides a sense of the lively discussion revolving around reimagining house museums. It is intended as an antidote to the common perception that house museums are dull and boring places that are unwilling or unable to change (that may be true for individual sites, but not the field as a whole). The bibliography focuses on the management and interpretation of historic residences (e.g., houses, apartments, hospitals, ships, forts, and prisons) but generally not historic sites (which is a much wider subject that includes battlefields, memorials, cemeteries, and railroad depots); historic preservation (which is also a much bigger topic ranging from window repair to real estate easements to economic development); or places that are named "house" but are not residences (such as schoolhouses or custom houses). To keep the bibliography to a manageable length, it is not comprehensive nor definitive and it excludes book and exhibition reviews, newspapers, magazines, theses, dissertations, papers presented at conferences, webinars, blog posts, guidebooks and individual site histories, and walking tour brochures.

AASLH Committee on Professional Standards and Ethics. "When a History Museum Closes: Ethics Position Paper." *History News* 62, no. 3 (Summer 2007): 24–28.

AASLH Standing Committee on Standards and Ethics. "Ethics Position Paper #3: Repurposing of a Historic House/Site." *History News* 64, no. 2 (Spring 2009): 16–19.

AASLH's Historic House Affinity Group Committee. "How Sustainable Is Your Historic House Museum?" *History News* 63, no. 4 (Autumn 2008): 1–12.

Abram, Ruth J. "Kitchen Conversations: Democracy in Action at the Lower East Side Tenement Museum." *Public Historian* 29, no. 1 (2007): 59–76.

Adair, Joshua G. "House Museums or Walk-In Closets? The (Non) Representation of Gay Men in the Museums They Called Home." In *Gender, Sexuality, and Museums: A Routledge Reader*, edited by Amy K. Levin, 264–78. New York: Routledge, 2010.

Alleyne, Shirley Brown. "Making Programs Self-Sustaining at a Small Historic House Museum." *The Journal of Museum Education* 35, no. 2 (2010): 201–5.

Anderson, Terri. "Too Much of a Good Thing: Lessons from Deaccessioning at National Trust Historic Sites." In *Museums and the Disposals Debate*, edited by Peter Davies, 230–53. Boston: Museums Etc., 2011.

Bailey, Dina A., ed. *Interpreting Immigration at Museums and Historic Sites.* Lanham, MD: Rowman & Littlefield, 2018.

Barrientos, Tanya. "Houses, Histories, and the Future." *Trust*, April 30, 2008. Accessed August 7, 2018. http://pew.org/2yl1INq.

Barthel-Bouchier, Diane. "Authenticity and Identity: Theme-Parking the Amanas." *International Sociology* 16, no. 2 (June 2001): 221–39.

Baumann, Timothy, Andrew Hurley, Valerie Altizer, and Victoria Lowe. "Interpreting Uncomfortable History at the Scott Joplin House State Historic Site in St. Louis, Missouri." *Public Historian* 33, no. 2 (May 2011): 37–66.

Beaulieu, Rebekah. *Financial Fundamentals for Historic House Museums.* Lanham, MD: Rowman & Littlefield, 2017.

Bench, Raney. *Interpreting Native American History and Culture at Museums and Historic Sites.* Lanham, MD: Rowman & Littlefield, 2014.

Bergman, Teresa. *Exhibiting Patriotism: Creating and Contesting Interpretations of American Historic Sites.* Walnut Creek, CA: Left Coast Press, 2013.

Best, Katie. "Making Museum Tours Better: Understanding What a Guided Tour Really Is and What a Tour Guide Really Does." *Museum Management and Curatorship* 27, no. 1 (2012): 35–52.

Black, Graham. "Remember the 70%: Sustaining 'Core' Museum Audiences." *Museum Management and Curatorship* 31, no. 4 (2016): 386–401.

Bones, Marta E. "Ask, Don't Guess: How a Visitor-Centered Business Model led to Record-Breaking Attendance for a Historic House in Oregon." *Museum* (May/June 2017): 22–27.

Boudreau, Deborah, Lauren Kaushansky, and Carla Keirns. "Is There a Doctor in the House? Students Explore Home, History, and the Evolution of Medicine." *Journal of Museum Education* 41, no. 1 (2016): 52–58.

Braden, Donna. "Not Just a Bunch of Facts: Crafting Dynamic Interpretive Manuals." *History News* 66, no. 3 (Summer 2014) (AASLH Technical Leaflet 267): 1–8.

Bright, Deborah, and Erica Rand. "Queer Plymouth." *GLQ: A Journal of Lesbian & Gay Studies* 12, no. 2 (April 2006): 259–77.

Bruggeman, Seth C., ed. *Born in the U.S.A.: Birth, Commemoration, and American Public Memory.* Boston: University of Massachusetts Press, 2012.

———. "Reforming the Carceral Past: Eastern State Penitentiary and the Challenge of the Twenty-First-Century Prison Museum." *Radical History News* 113 (Spring 2012): 171–86.

Buggeln, Gretchen, and Barbara Franco, eds. *Interpreting Religion at Museums and Historic Sites.* Lanham, MD: Rowman & Littlefield, 2018.

Butler, David, Perry Carter, and Owen Dwyer. "Imagining Plantations: Slavery, Dominant Narratives, and the Foreign Born." *Southeastern Geographer* 48, no. 3 (November 2008): 288–302.

Byrne, Karen. "The Power of Place: Using Historic Structures to Teach Children about Slavery." *CRM* 23, no. 3 (2000): 9–10.

———. "We Have a Claim on This Estate: Remembering Slavery at Arlington House." *CRM* 25, no. 4 (2002): 27–29.

Cabral, Magaly. "Exhibiting and Communicating History and Society in Historic House Museums." *Museum International* 53, no. 2 (April 2001): 41–46.

Camarero, Carmen, and María-José Garrido. "Fostering Innovation in Cultural Contexts: Market Orientation, Service Orientation, and Innovations in Museums." *Journal of Service Research* 15, no. 1 (2012): 39–58.

———. "Improving Museums' Performance Through Custodial, Sales, and Customer Orientations." *Nonprofit and Voluntary Sector Quarterly* 38, no. 5 (October 2009): 846–68.

Cameron, Catherine M., and John B. Gatewood. "Excursions into the Un-Remembered Past: What People Want from Visits to Historical Sites." *Public Historian* 22, no. 3 (Summer 2000): 107–27.

Campbell, Colin G. "Sustainability: The Ongoing Challenge for Historic Sites." *Forum Journal* 20, no. 3 (2006): 18–20.

Carson, Cary. "The End of History Museums: What's Plan B?" *Public Historian* 30, no. 4 (Fall 2008): 9–27.

Chew, Elizabeth. "Institutional Evolution: How Monticello Faced and Interpreted a Legacy of Slavery." *Museum* 92, no. 5 (September/October 2013): 33–41.

Chhabra, Deepak, Robert Healy, and Erin Sills. "Staged Authenticity and Cultural Tourism." *Annals of Tourism Research* 30, no. 3 (2003): 702–19.

Chmelik, Samantha. *Museum and Historic Site Management: A Case Study Approach.* Lanham, MD: Rowman & Littlefield, 2015.

Christensen, Kim. "Ideas versus Things: The Balancing Act of Interpreting Historic House Museums." *International Journal of Heritage Studies* 17, no. 2 (March 2011): 153–68.

Clark, Carol, Pat Stephen Williams, Michael Legg, and Ray Darville. "Visitor Responses to Interpretation at Historic Kingsley Plantation." *Journal of Interpretation Research* 16, no. 2 (July 2011): 23–33.

Clement, Jason Lloyd. "Introduction: The Power of Light." *Forum Journal* 30, no. 3 (Spring 2016): 3–6.

Corn, Wanda. "Artists' Homes and Studios: A Special Kind of Archive." *American Art* 19, no. 1 (2005): 2–11.

Davis, Lisa Selin. "Common Space." *Preservation* 70, no. 1 (Winter 2018): 26–33.

DeBenigno, Mariaelena. "The Timeshare Ghost Hunt: Interpretive Techniques at a Historical House Museum." *Response: The Digital Journal of Popular Culture Scholarship* 2, no. 1 (June 2017). Accessed August 7, 2018. https://bit.ly/2BfjNYa.

Decter, Avi Y. *Interpreting American Jewish History and Culture at Museums and Historic Sites.* Lanham, MD: Rowman & Littlefield, 2016.

DeLyser, Dydia. "Ramona Memories: Fiction, Tourist Practices, and Placing the Past in Southern California." *Annals of the Association of American Geographers* 93, no. 4 (December 2003): 886–908.

Donath, David. "Funding the Fundamentals." *Forum Journal* 22, no. 3 (Spring 2008): 25–28.

Donnelly, Jessica Foy, ed. *Interpreting Historic House Museums.* Walnut Creek, CA: Altamira Press, 2002.

Doyle, Debbie Ann. "The Future of Local Historical Societies." *Perspectives on History: The Newspaper of the American Historical Association*, December 2012. Accessed on August 7, 2018. https://bit.ly/2vOZnQy.

Dubrow, Gail Lee, and Jennifer B. Goodman, eds. *Restoring Women's History Through Historic Preservation.* Baltimore, MD: Johns Hopkins University Press, 2003.

Dupuis, William O. "The Hillside Solution: Readapting an Historic House for the Community." *History News* 60, no. 3 (2005): 12–16.

Durel, John, and Anita Nowery Durel. "A Golden Age for Historic Properties." *History News* 62, no. 3 (Summer 2007): 7–16.

Dwyer, Owen. "Interpreting the Civil Rights Movement: Place, Memory, and Conflict." *Professional Geographer* 52, no. 4 (2000): 660–71.

Dwyer, Owen, David Butler, and Perry Carter. "Commemorative Surrogation and the American South's Changing Heritage Landscape." *Tourism Geographies* 15, no. 3 (August 2013): 424–43.

Eichstedt, Jennifer, and Stephen Small. *Representations of Slavery, Race and Ideology in Southern Plantation Museums.* Washington, DC: Smithsonian Institution Press, 2002.

Elias, Megan. "Summoning the Food Ghosts: Food History as Public History." *Public Historian* 34, no. 2 (Spring 2012): 13–29.

Eliasof, Jane Mitchell. "The Many Voices of a Historic House." *History News* 17, no. 1 (Winter 2017): 14–18.

Emmons-Andarawis, Deborah. "Embodying Value in Harrowing Times." *History News* 67, no. 3 (2012): 22–25.

Ermenc, Christine, Christina Vida, and Scott Wands. "A Please Touch Historic House Tour." *History News* 72, no. 1 (Winter 2017): 30–31.

Facca, Amy, and J. Winthrop Aldrich. "Putting the Past to Work for the Future." *Public Historian* 33, no.3 (Summer 2011): 38–57.

Ferentinos, Susan. *Interpreting LGBT History at Museums and Historic Sites*. Lanham, MD: Rowman & Littlefield, 2015.

Ferentinos, Susan, and Kenneth Turino. "Entering the Mainstream." *History News* 67, no. 4 (Autumn 2012): 21–25.

Filene, Benjamin. "Passionate Histories: 'Outsider' History-Makers and What They Teach Us." *Public Historian* 34, no. 1 (Winter 2012): 11–33.

Forbes, Robert T. "Connecticut Connections: African American Sites in Connecticut: A Laboratory for the History of Slavery and Human Rights." *Connecticut History* 44, no. 2 (Fall 2005): 316–20.

Gable, Eric, and Richard Handler. "Persons of Stature and the Passing Parade: Egalitarian Dilemmas at Monticello and Colonial Williamsburg." *Museum Anthropology* 29, no. 1 (2006): 5–19.

Gallas, Kristin L., and James DeWolf Perry. "Developing Comprehensive and Conscientious Interpretation of Slavery at Historic Sites and Museums." *History News* 69, no. 2 (Spring 2014): 1–8.

———. *Interpreting Slavery at Museums and Historic Sites*. Lanham, MD: Rowman & Littlefield, 2015.

George, Gerald. "Historic House Museum Malaise: A Conference Considers What's Wrong." *History News* 57, no. 4 (Autumn 2002): 21–25.

Glines, Timothy, and David Grabitske. "Telling the Story: Better Interpretation at Small Historical Organizations." *History News* 58, no. 2 (April 2003): 1–8.

Godfrey, Marian A. "Historic House Museums: An Embarrassment of Riches?" *Forum Journal* 22, no. 3 (Spring 2008): 9–16.

Godfrey, Marian, and Barbara Silberman. "A Model for Historic House Museums." *Trust*, January 29, 2008. Accessed August 7, 2018. https://bit.ly/2w3n72A.

Grim, Linnea, Allison Wickens, Jackie Jecha, Linda Powell, Callie Hawkins, and Candra Flanagan. "Taking the Next Step: Confronting the Legacies of Slavery at Historic Sites." *Journal of Museum Education* 42, no. 1 (2017): 54–68.

Halifax, Shawn. "McLeod Plantation Historic Site: Sowing Truth and Change." *Public Historian* 40, no. 3 (August 2018): 252–77.

Harris, Donna Ann. "New Uses for Existing House Museums." *Forum Journal* 21, no. 4 (Summer 2007): 39–46.

———. *New Solutions for House Museums: Ensuring the Long-Term Preservation of America's Historic Houses*. Walnut Creek, CA: Altamira Press, 2007.

Hawkins, Callie. "'The Discourse We All Need So Seriously': An Evening of Reflection at President Lincoln's Cottage." *Public Historian* 40, no. 1 (2018): 97–104.

Hayashi, Robert. "Transfigured Patterns: Contesting Memories at the Manzanar National Historic Site." *Public Historian* 25, no. 4 (November 2003): 51–71.

Hays, Frank. "The National Park Service: Groveling Sychophant or Social Conscience: Telling the Story of Mountains, Valleys, and Barbed Wire at Manzanar National Historic Site." *Public Historian* 25, no. 4 (November 2003): 73–80.

Hendrix, Harald, ed. *Writers' Houses and the Making of Memory*. New York: Routledge, 2012.

Hindley, Anna F., and Esther J. Washington. "Race Isn't Just a 'Black Thing': The Role that Museum Professionals Can Play in Inclusive Planning and Programing." *Journal of Museum Education* 42, no. 1 (2017): 2–7.

Hodge, Christina J., and Christa M. Beranek. "Dwelling: Transforming Narratives at Historic House Museums. *International Journal of Heritage Studies* 17, no. 2 (2011): 97–101.

Huh, Jin, and Muzaffer Uysal. "Satisfaction with Cultural/Heritage Sites." *Journal of Quality Assurance in Hospitality & Tourism* 4, no. 3 (2004): 177–94.

Jackson, Antoinette T. "Shattering Slave Life Portrayals: Uncovering Subjugated Knowledge in U.S. Plantation Sites in South Carolina and Florida." *American Anthropologist* 113, no. 3 (2011): 448–62.

———. *Speaking for the Enslaved: Heritage Interpretation at Antebellum Plantation Sites.* Walnut Creek, CA: Left Coast Press, 2012.

Janssen, David, Bill Hosley, and Ron M. Potvin. "The Power and Predicament of Historic Places." *History News* 65, no. 2 (Spring 2010): 7–11.

Johnson, Joan Marie. "'Ye Gave Them a Stone': African American Women's Clubs, the Frederick Douglass Home, and the Black Mammy Monument." *Journal of Women's History* 17, no. 1 (Spring 2005): 62–86.

Kammen, Carol. "On Doing Local History: The Future Survival of Historical Societies." *History News* 59, no. 1 (Winter 2004): 3-4.

Kane, Katherine. "The Impact of Standards on the Sustainability of Historic Sites." *Forum Journal* 22, no. 3 (Spring 2008): 36–42.

Kaufman, Polly, and Katharine T. Corbett. *Her Past Around Us: Interpreting Sites for Women's History.* Malabar, FL: Krieger Publishing Company, 2003.

Kenney, Kimberly A. *Interpreting Anniversaries and Milestones at Museums and Historic Sites.* Lanham, MD: Rowman & Littlefield, 2016.

Kern, James F. "Brucemore: A Cultural Center for Cedar Rapids." *Forum Journal* 22, no. 3 (Spring 2008): 56-60.

Klugh, Elgin L. "Reclaiming Segregation-Era, African American Schoolhouses: Building on Symbols of Past Cooperation." *Journal of Negro Education* 74, no. 3 (Summer 2005): 246–59.

Kolk, Heidi Aronson. "The Many-Layered Cultural Lives of Things." *Winterthur Portfolio* 47, no. 2/3 (2013): 161-95.

Kudick, Catherine. "The Local History Museum, So Near and Yet So Far." *Public Historian* 27, no. 2 (Spring 2005): 75–81.

Laporte, Suzanne B., with National Trust Staff and Compass Volunteers. "Finding Our Compass: Lessons in Planning from National Trust Historic Sites." *Forum Journal* 28, no. 4 (Summer 2014): 32–42.

Lau, Barbara, Jennifer Scott, and Suzanne Seriff. "Designing for Outrage: Inviting Disruption and Contest Truth into Museum Exhibitions." *Exhibition* (Spring 2017): 20–31.

Lee, Lisa Yun. "Peering into the Bedroom: Restorative Justice at the Jane Addams Hull-House Museum." In *Routledge Companion to Museum Ethics: Redefining Ethics for the Twenty-first Century Museum*, edited by Janet Marstine, 174–88. New York: Routledge, 2011.

Lee, Lisa, and Lisa Junkin Lopez. "Participating in History: The Museum as a Site for Radical Empathy, Hull-House." In *Jane Addams in the Classroom*, edited by David Schaafsma, 162–78. Urbana: University of Illinois Press, 2014.

Leggs, Brent. "Growth of Historic Sites: Teaching Public Historians to Advance Preservation Practice." *Public Historian* 40, no. 3 (August 2018): 90–106.

Levin, Amy K. *Defining Memory: Local Museums and the Construction of History in America's Changing Communities.* Lanham, MD: AltaMira Press, 2007.

Levin, Jed. "Activism Leads to Excavation: The Power of Place and the Power of the People at the President's House in Philadelphia." *Archaeologies: Journal of the World Archaeological Congress* 7, no. 3 (December 2011): 596–618.

Levin, Kevin M., ed. *Interpreting the Civil War at Museums and Historic Sites.* Lanham, MD: Rowman & Littlefield, 2017.

Levy, Barbara, Sandra Lloyd, and Susan Schreiber. *Great Tours!: Thematic Tours and Guide Training for Historic Sites.* Walnut Creek, CA: AltaMira Press, 2002.

Lopez, Lisa Junkin. "Open House: Reimagining the Historic House Museum." *Public Historian* 37, no. 2 (May 2015): 10–13.

Lowe, Hilary Iris. "Dwelling in Possibility: Revisiting Narrative in the Historic House Museum." *Public Historian* 37, no. 2 (May 2015): 42–60.

Lowe, Tukiya L. "Commemorating African American History Through National Historic Landmarks." *OAH Newsletter* 36, no. 1 and 2 (May 2008): 11.

Malinick, Cindi. "Innovation at National Trust Historic Sites." *Forum Journal* 28, no. 4 (Summer 2014): 25–31.

Mårdh, Hedvig. "Re-entering the House: Scenographic and Artistic Interventions and Interactions in the Historic House Museum." *Nordisk Museologi* 1 (2015): 25–39.

Marino, Michael P. "Urban Space as a Primary Source: Local History and Historical Thinking in New York City." *Social Studies* 103, no. 3 (May 2012): 107–16.

Mast, Erin Carlson, Morris J. Vogel, and Lisa Lopez. "The Period of Significance Is Now." *Forum Journal* 28, no. 4 (2014): 43–51.

Mayes, Thom, and Katherine Malone-France. "When Buildings and Landscapes Are the Collection." *Forum Journal* 28, no. 4 (Summer 2014): 19–24.

Mayes, Thompson, Carrie Villar, and David Young. "Giving Upsala Its Best Shot" *History News* 73, no. 3 (2018): 19–23.

Meeks, Stephanie. "Stepping into the Future at Historic Sites." *Forum Journal* 28, no. 4 (2014): 3–5.

Miles, Tiya. "'Showplace of the Cherokee Nation': Race and the Making of a Southern House Museum." *Public Historian* 33, no. 4 (November 2011): 11–34.

Mills, Elizabeth Shown. "Demythicizing History: Marie Thérèse Coincoin, Tourism, and the National Historical Landmarks Program." *Louisiana History* 53, no. 4 (Fall 2012): 402–37.

Modlin, E. Arnold, Jr. "Tales Told on the Tour: Mythic Representations of Slavery by Docents at North Carolina Plantation Museums." *Southeastern Geographer* 48, no. 3 (November 2008): 265–87.

Modlin, E. Arnold, Jr., Derek H. Alderman, and Glenn W. Gentry. ""Tour Guides as Creators of Empathy: The Role of Affective Inequality in Marginalizing the Enslaved at Plantation House Museums." *Tourist Studies* 11, no. 1 (2011): 3–19.

Moe, Richard. "Are There Too Many House Museums?" *Forum Journal* 16, no. 3 (Fall 2002): 4–11.

Moon, Michelle. *Interpreting Food at Museums and Historic Sites.* Lanham, MD: Rowman &Littlefield, 2016.

Moore, Porchia. "Our Stories, Our Places: Centering the Community as Narrative Voice in the Reinterpretation of an African American Historic Site." In *Positioning Your Museum as a Critical Community Asset*, edited by Robert Connolly and Elizabeth Bollwerk, 79–85. Lanham, MD: Rowman & Littlefield, 2017.

Moore, William. "Interpreting the Shakers: Opening the Villages to the Public, 1955–1965." *CRM: The Journal of Heritage Stewardship* 3, no. 1 (Winter 2006): 49–69.

National Park Service. "Teaching with Historic Places." Last updated June 16, 2016. https://bit.ly/2Mo8Hob.

O'Connell, K. "New Directions for the Old Retreat—With Its President Lincoln's Cottage Project, the National Trust Puts Environmental Principles to Work." *Preservation* 60, no. 1 (January/February 2008): 27–31.

Oram, Alison. "Going on an Outing: The Historic House and Queer Public History." *Rethinking History* 15, no. 2 (June 2011): 189–207.

Otero, Lydia R. "New Directions for La Casa Cordova: Recentering the Latinx Past and Present in Tucson." *History News* 73, no. 3 (2018): 8–12.

Pavoni, Rosanna. "Towards a Definition and Typology of Historic House Museums." *Museum International* 53, no. 2 (2001): 16-21.

Petersen, Anne. "Community Partnerships Activate Santa Barbara's Presidio Neighborhood." *Forum Journal* 30, no. 3 (Spring 2016): 46-55.

Pharoan, Sarah, Sally Roesch Wagner, Barbara Lau, and María José Bolaña Caballero. "Safe Containers for Dangerous Memories." *Public Historian* 37, no. 2 (May 2015): 61-72.

Pinna, Giovanni. "Introduction to Historic House Museums." *Museum International* 53, no. 2 (2001): 4-9.

Pitcaithley, Dwight. T. "Lincoln's Birthplace Cabin: The Making of an American Icon." In *Myth, Memory and the Making of the American Landscape*, edited by Paul Shackel, 240-54. Gainesville: University Press of Florida, 2001.

Pogue, Dennis J. "Interpreting Slavery at Mount Vernon." *American History* 38, no. 6 (2004): 58-59.

Poria, Yaniv, Arie Reichel, and Avital Biran. "Heritage Site Perceptions and Motivations to Visit." *Journal of Travel Research* 44, no. 3 (February 1, 2006): 318-26.

Potvin, Ron M. "Washington Slept Here? Reinterpreting the Stephen Hopkins House." *History News* 66, no. 2 (2011): 17-20.

Price, Rebecca. "Working with a Private Collector to Strengthen Women's History: Sewall-Belmont House and Museum." In *Positioning Your Museum as a Critical Community Asset*, edited by Robert Connolly and Elizabeth Bollwerk, 65-70. Lanham, MD: Rowman & Littlefield, 2017.

Pustz, Jennifer. *Voices from the Back Stairs: Interpreting Servants' Lives at Historic House Museums.* De Kalb: Northern Illinois University Press, 2010.

Rabinowitz, Richard. "History in Every Sense: Public and Academic History." In *The Future of History*, edited by Conrad Wright and Katheryn Viens, 20-30. Boston: Massachusetts Historical Society, 2017.

———. *Curating America: Journeys Through Storyscapes of the American Past.* Chapel Hill: University of North Carolina Press, 2016.

Racine, Laurel A., Gregory R. Weidman, Lenora M. Henson, and Patricia West McKay. "The Curator's Role in Crowd-Pleasing Events." *Collections* 10, no. 1 (Winter 2014): 47-66.

Rael-Gálvez, Estevan, and Cindi Malinick. "Reflections on the Senses of Place." *Forum Journal* 28, no. 4 (Summer 2014): 6-18.

Reid, Debra A. *Interpreting Agriculture and Culture at Museums and Historic Sites.* Lanham, MD: Rowman & Littlefield, 2017.

Reigle, Brenda. "But Is It Really History? Interpreting the Colonial Revival at Your Historic House Museum." *History News* (Spring 2006): 14-17.

Risnicoff de Gorgas, Mónica. "Reality as Illusion: The Historic Houses that Become Museums." *Museum International* 53, no. 2 (2001): 10-15.

Rogers, Ashley. "Incorporating Descendant Community Voices: The Whitney Plantation." In *Positioning Your Museum as a Critical Community Asset*, edited by Robert Connolly and Elizabeth Bollwerk, 137-42. Lanham, MD: Rowman & Littlefield, 2017.

Rose, Julia. "Interpreting Difficult Knowledge." *History News* 66, no. 3 (July 2011): 1-8.

———. "Melancholia to Mourning: Commemorative Representations of Slave Dwellings at South Louisiana Historical Plantations." *Journal of Curriculum Theorizing* 31, no. 3 (2005): 61-78.

———. "Preserving Southern Feminism: The Veiled Nexus of Race, Class and Gender at Louisiana Historical Plantation Home Sites." *Taboo: The Journal of Culture and Education* 8, no. 1 (2004): 57-75.

———. *Interpreting Difficult History at Museums and Historic Sites.* Lanham, MD: Rowman & Littlefield, 2016.

Ruffins, Fath D. "Revisiting the Old Plantation: Reparations, Reconciliation, and Museumizing American Slavery." In *Museum Frictions: Public Cultures/Global Transformations,* edited by Ivan Karp and Corrine Kratz, 395–434. Durham, NC: Duke University Press, 2006.

Rutherford, Janice Williams, and Shay, Steven E. "Peopling the Age of Elegance: Reinterpreting Spokane's Campbell House—A Collaboration." *Public Historian* 26, no. 3 (Summer 2004): 27–48.

Ryan, Debora, and Emily Stokes-Rees. "A Tale of Two Missions: Common Past/Divergent Futures at Transnational Historic Sites." *Public Historian* 39, no. 3 (August 2017): 10–39.

Rypkema, Donovan D. *Feasibility Assessment Manual for Reusing Historic Buildings.* Washington, DC: National Trust for Historic Preservation, 2007.

Saperstein, Pat. "House as Museum Piece." *Variety* 331, no. 4 (February 23, 2016): 42.

Schreiber, Susan P. "Interpreting Slavery at National Trust Sites: A Case Study in Addressing Difficult Topics." *CRM* 23, no. 5 (2000): 49–52.

Scott, Jennifer. "Reimagining Freedom in the Twenty-first Century at a Post-Emancipation Site." *Public Historian* 37, no. 2 (May 2015): 73–88.

Scott, Magelssen. "'This Is a Drama. You Are Characters': The Tourist as Fugitive Slave in Conner Prairie's 'Follow the North Star.'" *Theatre Topics* 16, no. 1 (March 2006): 19–34.

Ševčenko, Liz. "The Power of Place: How Historic Sites Can Engage Citizens in Human Rights Issues." Liam Mahoney, ed. *The Center for Victims of Torture, Tactical Notebook Series* (2004). Accessed August 8, 2017. https://bit.ly/2vLrY9i.

Small, Stephen. "Still Back of the Big House: Slave Cabins and Slavery in Southern Heritage Tourism." *Tourism Geographies* 15, no. 3 (2013): 405–23.

Smith, Bonnie Hurd. "Women's Voices: Reinterpreting Historic House Museums." In *Her Past Around Us: Interpreting Sites for Women's History,* edited by Polly Welts Kaufman and Katherine T. Corbett, 87–101. Malabar, FL: Krieger Publishing Company, 2003.

Smith, Charlotte. "Civic Consciousness and House Museums: The Instructional Role of Interpretive Narratives." *Australasian Journal of American Studies* 21, no. 1 (2002): 74–88.

Smith, Gary N. "House Museum Partnerships with Local Governments: A Broken Model?" *History News* 66, no. 2 (2011): 21–25.

Springate, Megan E., ed. *LBGTQ America: A Theme Study of Lesbian, Gay, Bisexual, Transgender, and Queer History.* Washington, DC: National Park Foundation, 2016. Accessed August 7, 2018. https://bit.ly/2MqY4AW.

Stapp, Carol B., and Kenneth C. Turino. "Does America Need Another House Museum?" *History News* 59, no. 3 (Summer 2004): 7–11.

Stone, Lisa. "Playing House/Museum." *Public Historian* 37, no. 2 (May 2015): 27–41.

Strange, Carolyn, and Michael Kempa. "Shades of Dark Tourism: Alcatraz and Robben Island." *Annals of Tourism Research* 30, no. 2 (2005): 386–405.

Strobel, Margaret. "Hull-House and Women's Studies: Parallel Approaches for First- and Second-Wave Feminists." *Women's Studies Quarterly* 30, no. 3/4 (Fall 2002): 52–59.

Sugawara, Bethany Watkins. "But They're Not Real! Rethinking the Use of Props in Historic House Museum Displays." *History News* 58, no. 4 (2003): 20–23.

Swanson, Drew A. "Wormsloe's Belly: The History of a Southern Plantation Through Food." *Southern Cultures* 15, no. 4 (Winter 2009): 50–66.

Tucker, John. "Interpreting Slavery and Civil Rights at Fort Sumter National Monument." *George Wright Forum* 19, no. 4 (2002): 15–31.

Turino, Kenneth C. "America Doesn't Need Another House Museum (and What about Collections?)." *History News* 64, no. 2 (2009): 12–15.

Tyson, Amy. "'Ask a Slave' and Interpreting Race on Public History's Front Line." *Public Historian* 36, no. 1 (February 2014): 36–60.

Ulrich, Laurel Thatcher. "A Harvard Seminar Looks at the Wards." *Proceedings of the American Antiquarian Society* (2005): 53–57.

Vagnone, Franklin, and Deborah Ryan. *Anarchist's Guide to Historic House Museums*. Walnut Creek, CA: Left Coast Press, 2015.

van Balgooy, Max A. "Creating a 21st Century House Museum." In *The Museum Blog Book*, 578–87. Cambridge, MA: Museums Etc., 2017.

———. "Crisis or Transition? Diagnosing Success at Historic Sites." *Forum Journal* 22, no. 3 (Spring 2008): 17–24.

———. "Turning Points: Ordinary People, Extraordinary Change." *History News* 68, no. 2 (Spring 2013): 7–13.

———, ed. *Interpreting African American History and Culture at Museums and Historic Sites*. Lanham, MD: Rowman & Littlefield, 2015.

Vaughan, James. "Introduction: A Call for a National Conversation." *Forum Journal* 22, no. 3 (Spring 2008): 5–9.

Vogt, Jay D. "The Kykuit II Summit: The Sustainability of Historic Sites." *History News* 62, no. 4 (Autumn 2007): 17–20.

Wands, Scott, Erica Donnis, and Susie Wilkening. "Do Guided Tours and Technology Drive Visitors Away?" *History News* (Spring 2010): 21–25.

Webb, Amy, and Carolyn Brackett. "Cultural Heritage Tourism Trends Affecting Historical Sites." *Forum Journal* 22, no. 3 (Spring 2008): 29–35.

Weinberg, Carl R. "The Discomfort Zone: Reenacting Slavery at Conner Prairie." *Magazine of History* 23, no. 2 (April 2009): 62–64.

West, Patricia. "Uncovering and Interpreting Women's History at Historic House Museums." In *Restoring Women's History Through Historic Preservation*, edited by Gail Dubrow and Jennifer Goodman, 83–95. Baltimore, MD: Johns Hopkins University Press, 2003.

Wood, Elizabeth, Rainey Tisdale, and Trevor Jones. *Active Collections*. New York: Routledge, 2018.

Young, David W. "The Next Cliveden: A New Approach to the Historic Site in Philadelphia." *Forum Journal* 22, no. 3 (Spring 2008): 51–55.

Young, David W., Stephen Hague, George W. McDaniel, and Sandra Smith. "Not Dead Yet: Historic Sites and Community Leadership." *History News* 64, no. 3 (Summer 2009): 15–20.

Young, Linda. "Is There a Museum in the House? Historic Houses as a Species of Museum." *Museum Management and Curatorship* 22, no. 1 (2007): 59–77.

———. "Villages That Never Were: The Museum Village as a Heritage Genre." *International Journal of Heritage Studies* 12, no. 4 (July 2006): 321–38.

———. *Historic House Museums in the United States and United Kingdom*. Lanham, MD: Rowman & Littlefield, 2017.

Zar, Howard. "Liberating Lyndhurst from the Tyranny of the Period of Significance." *Forum Journal* 30, no. 3 (Spring 2016): 27–36.

National and Regional Organizations

Many of these organizations offer information, resources, and affinity groups for house museums.

American Alliance of Museums (AAM). aam-us.org
American Association for State and Local History (AASLH). aaslh.org
American Historical Association (AHA). historians.org
Association for Living History, Farms, and Agricultural Museums. alhfam.org
Association of African American Museums. blackmuseums.org
Association of Children's Museums. childrensmuseums.org
Association of Midwest Museums. midwestmuseums.org
Classical American Homes Preservation Trust. classicalamericanhomes.org
DEMHIST (Demeures historiques-musées): International Committee for Historic House Museums. demhist.icom.museum
Historic House Museums professional interest committee of AAM. housemuseums.us
International Council of Museums (ICOM). icom.museum/en/
Mid-Atlantic Association of Museums. midatlanticmuseums.org
Mountain-Plains Museums Association. mpma.net
National Association of Interpretation. interpnet.com
National Council on Public History. ncph.org
National Park Service (NPS). nps.gov
National Trust for Historic Preservation. savingplaces.org
New England Museum Association (NEMA). nemanet.org
Small Museum Association. smallmuseum.org
Southeastern Museums Conference. SEMCdirect.net
Western Museums Association. westmuse.org

Index

About the Editors and the Contributors

Cheryl A. Bachand is a consultant and lecturer with twenty-five years of experience working in the fields of architecture, museums, community arts, and cultural heritage. Throughout her career, she has developed innovative programs and strategic initiatives that leverage resources for new impacts and challenge cultural institutions to engage with the public in creative and meaningful ways. Cheryl is a visiting professional lecturer at DePaul University, Chicago. She earned her MA in art and architectural history from the University of Massachusetts, Amherst, EdM from Northeastern University, Boston, and BA in geography/urban planning from Clark University, Worcester, Massachusetts. She may be contacted at cheryl.bachand@gmail.com.

Lucinda A. Brockway is program director for Cultural Resources at The Trustees, a 125-year-old Massachusetts preservation and conservation organization that protects more than twenty-six thousand acres of cultural, natural, and scenic landscape. Brockway leads a team of cultural resource specialists seeking innovative solutions for historic sites. Prior to joining The Trustees, she ran her own landscape preservation consulting firm for twenty-five years. She is the author of *A Favorite Place of Resort for Strangers* (2001) and *Gardens of the New Republic* (2004), and has work featured in *Old House Journal*, *Victoria Magazine*, *Colonial Homes*, *Nineteenth Century*, and other publications. Reach her at cbrockway@thetrustees.org.

Carolin Collins has been the education program manager at Historic New England since 2010, overseeing school and youth programs at thirteen sites in four states that reach fifty thousand people each year. She earned her MS in education with a concentration in museum education from the Bank Street College of Education in New York City. Before coming to Historic New England, she served as the director of education at the Maine Historical Society in Portland, Maine.

Monta Lee Dakin with Friesen/Dakin Museum Consulting (friesendakin@aol.com) has worked in the museum field for more than forty years. Dakin worked at Gadsby's Tavern, Strawberry Banke, Mount Vernon, and the Smithsonian. Dakin also was the executive director of Colorado Preservation, Inc., and Mountain-Plains Museums Association, from which she retired in 2017 after sixteen years.

Dawn DiPrince is the director of El Pueblo History Museum and director of Community Museums for History Colorado. She served as co-chair of the Governor's Ludlow Centennial Commemoration Commission, which remembered the Ludlow Massacre. She was lead developer of the *Children of Ludlow* exhibit—recognized by the American Alliance of Museums for Excellence in Writing. Her work at El Pueblo History Museum was acknowledged as a national model for engaged humanities by the National Humanities Alliance. DiPrince was selected as a Creative Community Fellow for National Arts Strategies for her program that uses memory writing to create defensible neighborhoods.

Jane M. Eliasof is the executive director of the Montclair History Center and a freelance writer. In her eight years as director, she has revitalized the organization and expanded the "stories" the Montclair History Center tells to reflect the rich diversity of the community. Prior to her work at the Montclair History Center (formerly the Montclair Historical Society), Jane spent more than twenty-five years designing and writing marketing, educational, and training programs for the health care industry. In 2010, she opted to use her expertise to further a cause she has always been passionate about: history and historic preservation. Contact: jane.eliasof@gmail.com.

Susan Ferentinos is a public history researcher, writer, and consultant dedicated to bringing underrepresented histories into museums and historic preservation efforts. She is the author of *Interpreting LGBT History at Museums and Historic Sites* (Rowman & Littlefield), which received the 2016 Book Award from the National Council on Public History. You can find her online at www.susanferentinos.com and through her Twitter handle, @HistorySue.

Steve Friesen with Friesen/Dakin Museum Consulting (friesendakin@aol.com) has worked in the museum field for more than forty years. Friesen has been director of the 1719 Hans Herr House, the Molly Brown House, and the City of Greeley Museums. In 2017, he retired after twenty-two years as director of the Buffalo Bill Museum and Grave in Colorado.

Conny C. Graft is a consultant in interpretive planning and evaluation for museums. Conny has served as a consultant for museums including the International Coalition of Sites of Conscience, Smithsonian Institution, Pew Center for Arts and Heritage, American Association of State and Local History, Thomas Jefferson's Monticello, and National Trust for Historic Preservation. She is a faculty member of the History Leadership Institute (formerly known as the Seminar for Historical Administration). Her prime interest is in helping museums articulate and evaluate their impact and learn how to apply those insights to provide more intentional and meaningful visitor experiences.

Donna Ann Harris is the principal of Heritage Consulting Inc., a Philadelphia-based Women's Business Enterprise (WBE) consulting firm that aids nonprofit organizations and government agencies nationwide in the following practice areas: downtown and commercial district revitalization, historic preservation, tourism product development, and nonprofit organizational development. AltaMira Press published her book *New Solutions for House Museums: Ensuring the Long-Term Preservation of America's Historic Houses* in 2007. For fourteen years, Ms. Harris has been speaking about and consulting with historic house museums around the country about alternative uses and stewardship responsibilities. Please see http://www.heritageconsultinginc.com.

Callie Hawkins is the director of programming at President Lincoln's Cottage in Washington, DC. A staff member since 2009, Callie develops public programs, exhibits, and strategic partnerships and has spearheaded projects that won national and international recognition, including awards from the American Association for State and Local History, American Alliance of Museums, and the 2016 Presidential Award for Extraordinary Efforts to Combat Trafficking in Persons for Students Opposing Slavery, a youth education program at President Lincoln's Cottage dedicated to raising awareness of modern slavery among high school students.

Katherine Kane is Harriet Beecher Stowe Center Executive Director Emerita. Under Kane's leadership, the center in Hartford, Connecticut, transformed into a publicly oriented museum with a diverse audience. Consisting of three historic buildings and extensive collections, the museum is a program center and tourist attraction whose innovative programs include the award-winning Salons at Stowe (bringing the public into the parlor for conversations around contemporary issues) and the Harriet Beecher Stowe Prize (for writing and promoting social justice). A major interior renovation of the National Historic Landmark Stowe House was completed in 2017 with an inventive new tour experience. Ms. Kane was director of the collections services and access division at History Colorado and director of special projects at the Denver Art Museum. She is chair of the American Association for State and Local History, serves on the Connecticut Historic Preservation Council, and was as a member of the American Association of Museums Accreditation Commission.

Laura C. Keim is curator of Stenton, the circa 1730 seat of the Logan family in Philadelphia. She is a lecturer in the graduate program in historic preservation at the University of Pennsylvania and holds an MS from that program, an MA in early American culture from the University of Delaware's Winterthur Program, and an AB in art history from Smith College. She has published a Stenton guidebook, *Logania: Stenton Collections Reassembled*, and articles in *Magazine Antiques, Antiques and Fine Art,* and *Ceramics in America*. She is currently working on a study of Hornor's *Blue Book, Philadelphia Furniture* (1935).

Robert Kiihne began his museum career as a historic house docent in 1985. Since 2004, he has studied how families interact with unfacilitated history exhibits at the USS *Constitution* Museum and beyond. See engagefamilies.org for more information. Since 2011, Robert has worked on a number of historic house museum projects including the development of exhibitions for the Durant Kendrick House in Newton, Massachusetts, which opened in 2014. Robert believes that small museums can save the world—really!

Erin Carlson Mast is the CEO and executive director of President Lincoln's Cottage, where she has led the organization through a phase of steady growth, groundbreaking initiatives, and transition to an independent 501(c)3 organization. Under her leadership, the organization has received numerous awards and recognition including a Presidential Medal in 2016 and being named one of the 50 Best Places to Work in the Washington, DC, area. She holds degrees from George Washington University and Ohio University.

Elizabeth Merritt is vice president for strategic foresight and founding director of the Center for the Future of Museums at the American Alliance of Museums. She is the author of the Alliance's annual *TrendsWatch* report and writes and speaks prolifically on forces shaping the future of nonprofit organizations. She holds an MA from Duke University and a BS from Yale University, Museum Management Institute.

Claudia Ocello is president and CEO of Museum Partners Consulting LLC with more than twenty-five years experience in exhibition development, education, evaluation, and accessibility. Previously, she worked full-time at Save Ellis Island, Inc; the New Jersey Historical Society; and the Barnum Museum, Bridgeport, Connecticut. A former classroom teacher, Claudia earned an MS in museum education from Bank Street College of Education and has won awards from AASLH, AAM, and the New Jersey Association of Museums for excellence in exhibitions, programs, and practice. Ever grateful, she "pays it forward" by teaching in Seton Hall University's Museum

Professions Program and volunteering on the board of the Education Committee of AAM. Learn more at www.museumpartnersconsulting.com and @museumptnrs.

Ron M. Potvin is a public humanities practitioner, researcher, and instructor with a background of working in and with museums and other humanities-based organizations. As the assistant director and curator at the John Nicholas Brown Center for Public Humanities and Cultural Heritage at Brown University, he oversees preservation and interpretation of the National Historic Landmark Nightingale-Brown House (1792) and its historic collections for the benefit of students in the public humanities program. He teaches courses on historic house museums, museum collections and collecting, and material culture. His current research focuses on the intersection of material culture and ecology.

Jennifer Pustz has worked in public history for two decades, with a focus on interpreting the lives of enslaved and free domestic workers and laborers in general. She has worked as a historian for the Brucemore National Trust Historic Site and Historic New England. Jennifer received her PhD in American studies from the University of Iowa and is the author of *Voices from the Back Stairs: Interpreting Domestic Servants at Historic House Museums*. She currently serves on the board of the Royall House and Slave Quarters and as an independent public historian while pursuing degrees in public health and nutrition at Tufts University.

Alexandra Rasic is the director of public programs at the Homestead Museum, which was her local museum growing up! She started as a volunteer in 1989, biding her time as a student and preparing to get as far away from home as possible until she joined the paid staff in 1995. Her passion for the historic site and collection, Los Angeles, and the Homestead's paid and volunteer staff have sealed her fate (for now, at least). Over the years, she has volunteered at a number of organizations and worked as a freelance archivist for corporate collections in greater L.A. Volunteering for AASLH since she graduated from the Seminar for Historical Administration in 2004, she also co-teaches the organization's annual workshop on visitor engagement and exhibits in history museums. She holds a BA and MA in history from California State University, Los Angeles, and is completing a certificate in Innovation and Entrepreneurship from Stanford's Center for Professional Development.

Kenneth C. Turino is manager of community partnerships and resource development at Historic New England. He oversees community engagement projects throughout New England an is responsible for exhibition partnerships at the Eustis Estate, Langdon House Museum, and the Sarah Orne Jewett Museum and Visitor Center. Prior to this, he was executive director of the Lynn Museum in Lynn, Massachusetts for fourteen years. Ken frequently consults on interpretive planning and community engagement projects at historic sites including Madam John's Legacy, New Orleans, Louisiana, on best practices of community engagement, James Madison's Montpellier, Orange, Virginia, where he was part of a charrette to rethink the visitor experience for the Interpretive Plan, and recently with Connecticut Landmark's Palmer Warner House on interpreting LGBTQ history. Ken holds a MA in teaching, museum education, from the George Washington University and is an adjunct professor in the Tufts University Museum Studies Program where he teaches courses on the future of historic houses. He is also Vice President of the Board of Trustees of the House of Seven Gables in Salem, Massachusetts. Along with Max van Balgooy he is an instructor of AASLH's Reinventing the Historic House workshop.

Mary A. van Balgooy is an award-winning museum professional who has worked in a variety of institutions, including archives, botanic gardens, historic houses, historical societies, museums, preservation organizations, universities, and governmental agencies at city, county, and federal levels with major responsibilities for administration, collections, education and interpretation, fund-raising, governance, preservation, and public relations. She currently lives in the Washington, DC, area and is executive director of the Society of Woman Geographers and vice president of Engaging Places LLC. Mary may be reached at mary.vanbalgooy@gmail.com.

Max A. van Balgooy is president of Engaging Places, a design and strategy firm that connects people and historic places. He has worked with a wide range of historic sites on interpretive planning and business strategy, including Cliveden, Haas-Lilienthal House, James Madison's Montpelier, and Andrew Jackson's Hermitage. He is an assistant professor in the Museum Studies Program at George Washington University, directs the History Leadership Institute (formerly known as the Seminar for Historical Administration), and regularly leads workshops for the American Association for State and Local History. He is a frequent contributor to professional journals and books, including *Interpreting African American History and Culture at Museums and Historic Sites* (2015). These experiences provide a rich source of ideas for EngagingPlaces.net, where he blogs regularly about the opportunities and challenges facing historic sites and house museums.

Amy Jordan Webb is a heritage tourism specialist with thirty-two years of hands-on experience in heritage tourism marketing and development including work at the national, regional, state, and local level. She joined the National Trust for Historic Preservation in 1993 and directed the National Trust's heritage tourism program for sixteen years. In that capacity, she worked with individual historic sites as well as regional heritage tourism efforts. Amy holds a master's in architectural history and historic preservation from the University of Virginia. She currently serves as the senior field director for the National Trust's Denver field office.

Patricia West is curator at the Martin Van Buren National Historic Site (NPS) in Kinderhook, New York, and co-director of the Center for Applied Historical Research at the University at Albany, where she teaches in the public history graduate program. She is the author of numerous articles on historic house museums and *Domesticating History: The Political Origins of America's House Museums.*

Thomas A. Woods, PhD, University of Minnesota, served as the first site manager of the Minnesota Historical Society's Oliver H. Kelley Living History Farm, director of MHS's Historic Sites Department, director of Old World Wisconsin, and executive director of Hawaiian Mission Houses Historic Site and Archives. He spent years as a frontline interpreter, developed scores of historic site interpretive plans throughout America, taught AASLH's Interpretation Workshop in the early 1990s, originated the "perspectivistic interpretation" concept in the late 1980s, published widely on interpretive and strategic planning, authored *Knights of the Plow*, and is working on two books on Hawai'i's missionaries.

Lawrence J. Yerdon is president of Strawbery Banke Museum—a living history museum telling the three-hundred-plus-year history of Portsmouth, New Hampshire. Yerdon earned undergraduate and graduate degrees in history and an MBA from Rensselaer Polytechnic Institute. He served as president of the New England Museum Association, was on the Council of the American Association for State and Local History, and was a grant reviewer and panelist for the Institute for Museum and Library Services and the National Endowment for Humanities. Previously, Yerdon served as the president of Hancock Shaker Village and as the director/curator of the Quincy Historical Society. He may be contacted at Lawrence J. Yerdon, President & CEO, P.O. Box 300, Portsmouth, NH 03802, lyerdon@strawberybanke.org.

Nina Zannieri is the executive director of the Paul Revere Memorial Association/Paul Revere House. Previously, she was curator at the Rhode Island Historical Society. Ms. Zannieri has served on the boards of AAM and NEMA, and the AASLH Council; including a term as vice chair of AAM and two terms as president of NEMA. She is currently chair of the AASLH Ethics and Professional Standards Committee. Ms. Zannieri sits on the Harvard Museum Studies Advisory Board. In 2015, she received a NEMA Lifetime Achievement Award. She has a BA in history from Boston College and an MA in anthropology/museum studies from Brown University. She may be contacted at nina@paulreverehouse.org.